Assuring the Confidentiality

of Social Research Data

Assuring the

Confidentiality of

Social Research

Data □ □ □ □ □ □ □

Robert F. Boruch □ Joe S. Cecil

University of Pennsylvania Press 1979

To our parents and to our Nancys

Library of Congress Cataloging in Publication Data

Boruch, Robert F
  Assuring the confidentiality of social research data.

  Bibliography: p. 281
  Includes index.
  1. Social science research. 2. Confidential information.
3. Privacy, Right of. I. Cecil, Joe S.,
joint author. II. Title.
H62.B6173   300'.7'2   78–65113
ISBN 0–8122–7761–9

Contents

☐   v

Preface

This monograph is a descendant of earlier books on applied social research to which we have contributed, notably *Social Experimentation* and *Experimental Testing of Public Policy,* and of a number of papers on privacy problems in social research. In one of the latter, written in 1968, one of us baldly announced that if researchers made no decisions in the privacy arena, took no major initiative in research on the topic, decisions would be made for them. Since then, decisions have been made, and judging by recent privacy legislation, many have not been made by social scientists. Most contemporary law ignores the researcher's interests in information used solely for research purposes. As a consequence, the design and execution of research, the secondary analysis of data, and other research activities can be impeded. On the other hand, a few decisions outside the legislative arena facilitated the conduct of legitimate research and will doubtless continue to do so for the next decade. Here, we focus on results of these—the invention of methods for balancing public interests in social information with parallel interests in individual privacy.

Our intended audience comprises students of privacy generally and applied social scientists, statisticians, and lawyers, in particular. The definition of social science used here is catholic, meant to encompass educational research, sociology, psychology, economics, political science, and history. We consolidate a large variety of pertinent research and development in each field and adopt illustrations from each, but lay no claim to completeness. Contemporary theoretical research on privacy in psychology, sociology, and constitutional law, in mathematics of encryption and of record linkage, is substantial enough to demand several volumes. This volume covers the major strategies for assuring the privacy of the individual and the confidentiality of response and some variations on them. More advanced work in theory, engineering, and empirical research can be based on these, and indeed, if the book helps to stimulate such work, one of its purposes will be met.

We have entered a variety of territories here, capitalizing on the experience of scholars and research managers in most Western countries, and on the productivity of a dozen academic disciplines. This intellectual poaching will violate the sensibilities of some specialists, but we believe the topic must be treated with generality, at least at times. We take pains to acknowledge intensive research along narrower lines, and to examine it attentively. For this reason, the chapters are long but self-contained, and posted with numerous titles and subtitles, and studded with references. Because the topic covers several disciplines, we have tried to reduce disciplinary vernacular to a minimum.

The National Institute of Education furnished major support for research on the monograph, as part of a multipurpose project on improving the quality, accessibility, and utility of research information. We are especially grateful to NIE staff, Virginia Koehler and Garry McDaniels (now at the Bureau for Handicapped Children), for their benign attitude toward work which falls outside the orthodox bounds of educational research and which, in the future, is likely to be a small but fundamental topic in social research methods. We could not have initiated the work without the early assistance of the National Science Foundation, nor could we have completed the book without the later support of NSF's Directorate of Applied Science and Research Applications. We are grateful to James Cowling, Frank Scioli, and Ernest Powers of NSF for their encouragement. It is also a pleasure to acknowledge the Rockefeller Foundation's provision of accomodations for final editing at the Bellagio Study and Conference Center.

Several people have been helpful because of their collegial and thoughtful efforts in related research; extending our thanks to Henry W. Riecken, Donald T. Campbell, David Flaherty, and Tore Dalenius is a pleasure. Ida Harper Simpson deserves special acknowledgment for courtesy and sympathetic encouragement on an earlier draft of this book. None of these individuals have read the manuscript, however, so they shall be blameless for its sins. Our staff, Lucina Gallagher and Jane Ingram, have displayed extraordinary fortitude, spirit, and industry in producing the manuscript. One of us, Boruch, would like to thank his spouse for her production of diverting malapropisms and her benign understanding.

Assuring the Confidentiality

of Social Research Data

□ 1 □

Introduction and Background

No weather will be found in this book. This is an attempt to pull a book through without weather.

MARK TWAIN

Sharing one's thoughts, attitudes, and experiences with a social researcher can be regarded, in principle, as a depreciation of privacy. And especially if the researcher's questions concern sensitive topics, material risks may be attached to providing information. The confidentiality of an individual's response may be threatened, for example, by governmental appropriation of the researcher's records. It may be destroyed by inadvertent disclosure of a record, or by its casual interrogation, or by theft. Even where risks to the respondent are absent, as they usually are, the principle still obtains. For example, the researcher who provides records to another analyst or to an auditor for reappraisal may breach a promise of confidentiality in doing so. Law or social custom can be violated if the archivist furnishes identified records to a researcher conducting the worthiest of studies.

In this monograph, our purpose is to clarify such problems and, more importantly, to lay out strategies for their solution. The techniques presented here are designed to eliminate or minimize the confidentiality-related problems engendered by research, without abridging severely the researcher's freedom to investigate social problems. We examine three broad classes of techniques—procedural, statistical, and law-based—developed in a score of countries and in as many disciplines. Within each class, the methods vary according to the type of problem that they are designed to solve. Some, for example, directly accommodate the individual's demand for intellective privacy even in interviews. Others are designed to assure that once identifiable information is collected, it remains confidential with respect to any outside interrogator. Still others are tailored to permit linkage of different sources of data without violating laws or social customs governing disclosure of records.

The spirit that drives invention of these techniques is an ethical one. For at their best, the techniques help sustain the personal integrity of both the research participant and the researcher. Since there is a clear need to develop concrete solutions to privacy problems, that spirit is also pragmatic. The existential pleasures of engineering solutions to live problems in this sector are no less satisfying than they are in our more deterministic sister disciplines.[1]

Organization of the Monograph: Some Issues in Brief

Like most social problems, the matter of recognizing the respondents' right to privacy in social research and making sure that the information they provide remains confidential is complicated. It is an intractable problem without some analysis of its character, and that is the first task undertaken in this chapter. The remarks that follow divide the problem into manageable packets, isolate the more tractable issues from less tractable ones, and discriminate between the legitimate issue and the red herring. A second task, undertaken later in this chapter, is to review the origin and context of the problem, and to provide an orientation.

CHAPTER 2

Two issues emerge almost invariably in discussions about privacy and confidentiality in social research. The first and more fundamental one bears on the researcher's need to identify respondents at all. For the statistician or social researcher, the justification for obtaining the respondent's identification may be obvious. But we need only look to the temperate critic of social research to see that the justification is neither obvious nor taken for granted by other principals with an interest in the privacy implications of research. Scientists, social scientists included, cannot afford the hubris that prevents justifying one's existence from time to time. So, in chapter 2, we marshal some evidence on the need to identify respondents. The focus is on longitudinal research and on research requiring record linkage, two areas that often cause argument on privacy grounds in the United States and abroad. The evidence is illustrative rather than definitive, and emphasizes the findings of these studies rather than theory. It cuts across disciplines, national borders, and standards of evidence.

CHAPTER 3

The second issue, no less important and no less frequently encountered than the first, concerns the need to assure an individual of the confidentiality of his or her response to the social scientist's inquiry. Many social scientists regard the assurance as a matter of professional ethic or principle. But the ethic may have neither legal nor social standing with others involved in debates about privacy. The pragmatic researcher generally maintains that such an assurance is essential for obtaining the respondent's cooperation. But the evidence on this, the empirical grounds for the researcher's position, is fragmented, is often inaccessible, and varies considerably in quality. In chapter 3, evidence bearing on the question is consolidated. We examine episodes in which research has been disrupted on confidentiality-related grounds, field experiments that help one understand how the cooperation rate varies with the level of confidentiality assurance, and surveys designed to establish respondent preferences and attitudes toward various methods of eliciting information.

One of the main reasons for our review of this topic stems from the pious pronouncements and poor evidence that have often been used in defending research records against appropriation by the courts or by other governmental agencies. Evidentiary support for a defense, though not always of stellar quality, is available but underutilized. A second reason is tied to scientific and social ethics: we know too little about public reaction to the social research process and about how to make the relation between researcher and respondent a more equitable one. It is doubtful that by ignoring the evidence at hand we will be in any better position to design good research, much less to accommodate legitimate ethical issues that blossom in the field.

CHAPTERS 4–9

The remaining chapters present concrete mechanisms for assuring the privacy of individual participants in survey research and the confidentiality of information they provide. This overriding theme is tied to a variety of specific problems that have emerged in research, and the detail is provided later. For the moment, it is convenient to block the problems in two categories, the first concerning privacy, and the second confidentiality. Both involve differences in the importance attached to standards of behavior that are shared in some degree by all the principals concerned with such issues.

The first problem involves the researcher's standard, shared often if not always by government and the public it represents, that the information collected on identifiable individuals should have some social and scientific value. Against this professional standard is set another: that individuals' privacy ought not to be severely degraded by the research process. As a practical matter, the latter ethic is sometimes shared informally by the public and demonstrated formally in both law and judicial decisions: for example, those preventing survey researchers from making certain kinds of inquiry. In some instances, too, this standard is paramount in a public's refusal to respond to inquiry, in an archivist's refusal to disclose records on identifiable individuals to a researcher despite the merit of the research, and in the institutional curtailment of research on privacy grounds.

The second problem stems from the idea that if the researcher tenders a promise of confidentiality to a cooperative respondent, then that promise ought to be maintained. This is clearly a matter of personal and professional ethics: most codes of ethics in social science recognize the idea in a formal way. Not only is the idea shared by an informed public, but in some instances there is a clear expectation that the promise will be supported by considerably more than the researcher's testimony to his or her own virtue. At its most formal, the ethic has been translated into statute, which, for example, forbids Census Bureau employees from disclosing information on identifiable respondents. Set against this standard is an ethic that encourages, even demands, disclosure of information where it is in the public interest to do so. At its most formal, this includes the discretionary power of the court to require that a social researcher produce information that is relevant to a case, including information on identified individuals who are incidentally participants in the research. There are less visible and equally legitimate demands of the same sort, notably those made by an auditor or a secondary analyst of a research project.

The need to reconcile differences between standards of these kinds has been identified often enough to make repetition tiresome, however basic the idea is. We take a relatively new posture here by putting reconciliation into rather concrete form. Our goal is to minimize identifiability of response, under the constraint that research itself must not be degraded intolerably by the process. This sets one value, individual privacy, as paramount, but under the constraint, research standards are only a bit less important. The modes of protection examined here are multiple—procedural, statistical, and law-based—to accommodate variety in research design and in the standards that one might choose to evaluate the costs of employing them. The costs generally concern limits on sampling validity, response validity, and latitude in research.

CHAPTER 4

This chapter covers procedural tactics that, in the simplest cases, require little or no technical expertise to apply and are devised to reduce confidentiality problems for various types of research design.[2] Here, as in succeeding chapters, issues are examined in the context of cross-sectional research design, longitudinal investigations, social experiments, and research involving multiple sources of information. The methods range from very simple ones—the use of anonymous questionnaires, anonymous telephone reporting, and the like—to very elaborate systems for linking records from different archives without breaching the law or social custom that governs the disclosure of identifiable records from each archive. More complicated tactics are designed to satisfy the requirement that even the researcher must not have access to respondent identification, while record linkage and longitudinal research must still be possible. Each method can influence the quality of information obtained: making sure that sampling is valid and responses are reasonably accurate under some of these methods is at times difficult, for example. But in many cases it is possible to solve the problem by refining the basic tactic or by coupling it to others. Similarly, many tactics are vulnerable to corruption. The contents of chapter 4 cover refinements to reduce the vulnerability and costs of these tactics.

CHAPTER 5

With some exceptions, the procedural tactics are best suited for research settings in which the mode of inquiry is impersonal. To alleviate the problem of degraded privacy in interview settings, a variety of statistical methods have been developed. Described in chapter 5, they yield information about a group without permitting even the interviewer to determine the state of an individual within the group. As a consequence, these methods also protect individual privacy at later stages of the research process. One of the best-known of these approaches falls under the rubric of randomized response models, the earliest versions of which were suggested in 1965 by Stanley Warner and, until mid-1970, virtually ignored by social scientists. In a simple variant of that approach, the researcher presents each member of a sample with two questions, one innocuous and one sensitive, each answerable with a Yes or No response. The respondent is asked to roll a die and to answer the first question if (say) a one turns up on the die, and the second if two, three, etc., show up. Given the proper sampling scheme and the odds on answering each question, it takes only a little algebra to estimate the proportions in the population who answered Yes to each question. The paradigm provides no information about the true state of any individual, but does permit computation of statistics bearing on the entire group. The techniques are being field tested in several countries, and the results of both empirical tests and analytic work are reported in chapters 3 and 5. Other methods, based on aggregation of response or aggregation of samples, have also been developed to reduce degradation of privacy, or to preserve the confidentiality of an individual's response, without needlessly undercutting research design. Though generally less vulnerable to corruption than the procedural devices, the statistical methods are costly in some respects, and the discussion covers some of their disadvantages.

CHAPTER 6

The need for competing analyses of social research data, especially where the data bear on social programs and their effectiveness, is clear, but reanalysis can be difficult. Routine audit of research records, for example, is sometimes sensible, but the practice may conflict with the researcher's equally sensible objective of maintaining a promise of confidentiality made to research participants. Secondary analysis of a data set by an analyst who is not involved in the original research is usually warranted on scientific grounds and often desirable on political and economic grounds, but here, too, assurances of confidentiality made to research participants, survey respondents, and so forth will have to be accommodated. The reconciliation of both objectives— competent reanalysis and sustaining an assurance of confidentiality— is the subject of chapter 6. The techniques covered there include combinations of methods discussed earlier and some new strategies developed from live cases, including U.S. General Accounting Office efforts to execute credible audits of social experiments.

CHAPTER 7

Publication of statistical data—counts, cross tabulations, and so forth —based on data generated by research has presented few, if any, serious threats to individual privacy in the past. That is, information specific to an identified individual is not disclosed; only statistics based on an aggregate are normally produced. Under certain conditions, however, it is possible for an outsider to deduce new information about an individual from published aggregate statistics based on a sample in which the individual happens to be included. This process of deductive disclosure can be complicated, but it is no different in principle from problems generated by the publication of literal statements of reliable sources, police informants, and so on in less formal settings. The possibility of deductive disclosure has increased with the more frequent use of survey methods by community groups, institutions, or anyone who conducts a small survey and publishes the resultant data. Chapter 7 describes some prophylactic approaches to the problem. They stem from the efforts of census staff in the United States, Canada, Sweden, Norway, and elsewhere to reconcile a public demand for detailed statistical tables with the need to prevent accidental or deliberate deductive disclosure.

CHAPTER 8

This chapter is concerned with law-related mechanisms that can be used to guarantee the confidentiality of data. The mechanisms include the discretionary power that can be exercised by a government executive at the state or federal level to facilitate research. They also include the judiciary's power to supervise the evidence admitted into a case, a power delimited in part by statute and precedent, in part by the court's own judgment about how potentially conflicting standards of public need for research on the one hand and judicial evidence on the other hand can be reconciled. The final class of mechanisms considered includes formal statutory privilege, designed to protect respondents from legal harassment, embarrassment, or more serious consequences of their incidental participation in research. Benefits as well as costs of these mechanisms for the social researcher and for the public are explored. This chapter also makes explicit some of the law-related implications of the procedural and statistical methods described earlier. For example, the use of some procedures prevents or at least attenuates discordance between the researcher's need to assure the privacy of his respondents and judicial demands for evidence in criminal or civil cases. The procedures may, however, be misused or misunderstood by the courts; some may be rendered obsolete or irrelevant by future court decisions. The chapter includes discussions of how misuse can affect the scope of a statutory testimonial privilege for social scientists, of the definitions of research and researcher under such a privilege, and of the problem of counterfeit researchers.

CHAPTER 9

The topics covered in each chapter have implications for research policy and for the laws and regulations that affect social research. We do not regard ourselves as policy makers. Nonetheless, we would be remiss if we did not attempt to make the implications more explicit. Increased governmental regulation of research, both in the United States and abroad, makes this more duty than privilege. The responsibility is met in chapter 9. Since policy also implies theory, the chapter provides an opportunity to summarize the principles, themes, and crude theory underlying earlier material.

Episodic Origins: Historical and Contemporary

Despite contemporary rhetoric, the privacy questions that emerge in social research efforts are not new. We can trace public concern about census surveys to 1500 B.C., when in Exodus (30:11–17) and Samuel (2 Sam. 24:1–5), we find both God and man opposing military demography. Popular objections are rooted at least as much in a wish for intellective privacy as in a desire for physical self-preservation, and they are no less evident in the early history of social research in the United States. An interest in sustaining at least some anonymity with respect to the government reveals itself in colonial New England's restricting the collection of data for "public arithmetic" to publicly accessible information (see Cassedy 1969 and Flaherty 1972). The privacy theme is implicit in Madison's arguments with Congress over what data should be collected in national censuses for the sake of managing the republic. It is explicit in Lemuel Shattuck's reports to the Massachusetts Sanitary Commission in 1879, which refer to public concern about the propriety of the then-novel epidemiological survey and about the government's use of the resulting data. Shattuck's work foreshadowed controversy over routine surveys of public health and the creation of archives containing information on mortality and health during the late 1800s (Duffy 1968, 1974). That controversy is no less apparent today in some developing countries, where, for example, deaths may go unreported on account of privacy custom, memory lapse, or inheritance taxes. The collection of economic data has run a similarly difficult course, with public demonstration against the Social Security Administration's record keeping during the 1930s reflecting a concern not only about personal privacy but, from commercial quarters, also about institutional privacy.

That data obtained for statistical research ought to be maintained as confidential is probably at least as old an idea. But aside from the fine work of Flaherty (1972) and Davis (1971, 1972), there is scant historical documentation on the matter. In America at least, the idea is explicit in guidelines issued in 1840 by the Census Bureau, requiring that census enumerators regard as confidential information obtained from their respondents (Eckler 1972). Indeed, the history of attempts to make certain that the respondent's fear of disclosure would not inhibit cooperation in social research can be traced throughout much of the U.S. Census Bureau's existence. As the amount of information elicited grew from the simple enumeration of 1790 to the economic and social censuses of the early 1900s, and as the quality of surveys shifted from the astonishingly inept efforts before 1840 to the remarkably high-caliber work of the present day, so too did the laws governing disclosure—from rules demanding public posting of information elicited in a census to explicit statutory requirements that information on individuals remain completely confidential in the interest of preserving the quality of data available to the nation. The same theme is evident in the early development of economic welfare statistics, notably under the Social Security Administration. The problem of deductive disclosure is not a new one either. Ross Eckler's (1972) history suggests that the risks of accidental disclosure based on published statistical tables, most evident in the census of manufacturers, were officially recognized as early as 1910.

Legislative protection has, in the case of the census, been helpful in resisting pressures brought to bear on this public interest by other public interests. The U.S. Census Bureau has successfully staved off demands for information on identified respondents that range from the trivial to the ignominious. The latter include attempts to appropriate census records during World War II in an effort to speed up Japanese internment. There have been requests that were superficially worthy, including location of lost relatives, and others that were not so worthy. But the same level of protection in one quarter may serve as a barrier in another. Under current rules, one may not access census records that are under seventy-two years old for sociomedical or psychological research, or any other type of social research. The absence of such rules evidently facilitated Alexander Graham Bell's original genealogical research on deafness, based on records available from the 1790 census onwards (Bruce 1975).

What is new, then, is not the occurrence of privacy concerns in social research, but rather their incidence and character. Social scientists, including those who have been traditionally uninterested in field research, have become more involved in identifying social problems and testing possible solutions through field studies. This increase in the policy relevance of research generates conflict with some policy makers simply because a new standard—higher-quality empirical data—is being offered as a substitute for a more traditional emphasis on anecdote and expert opinion. The increased contact between social scientists and individuals who are unfamiliar with their methods, objectives, and standards is almost certainly a cause of increased discord, including argument about privacy. Finally, the larger research efforts typically involve a variety of interest groups and commentators. The interaction of research sponsors, auditors, journalists, and groups of research participants with opposing views on the value and implications of the research complicates matters. In this setting, privacy arguments may distract attention from far more important issues; they may be entirely specious simply because reporting is inaccurate; or they may be legitimate but intractable because the standards of interest groups differ remarkably.

Of the recent conflicts that provoked our interest in the problem, those emerging from economic research come quickly to mind.[3] In the Negative Income Tax Experiment, records on identified research subjects were demanded by a grand jury and a congressional investigating committee. Though the example is complicated by political controversy, it does reflect the tension between the researcher's principle of maintaining a promise of confidentiality and the integrity of the research, and a second set of principles held by governmental investigators with an interest in administering justice. Interagency arguments, with researchers on both sides, have been characterized by cumbersome negotiations over what social research records can be or should be disclosed for audit. During both the Negative Income Tax Experiment and the Housing Allowance Experiment, such an argument stemmed from the comptroller general's mandate to ensure the quality of research by appraising the quality of respondents' reports to survey researchers, and the social researcher's need to protect the privacy of the respondent.

Educational research is no less susceptible to privacy-related controversy. Longitudinal research on career development, such as Project Talent in the United States and Project Metropolitan in the Scandinavian countries, has been attacked on the grounds that any such inquiry infringes on the privacy of children and that the confidentiality of research records is not preserved. The creation of new programs in school settings, designed to ameliorate what appear to be serious problems, has at times produced even more nettlesome problems, especially when the program is set up without adequate prior research. In *Merriken* v. *Cressman* [364 F. Supp. 913 (E.D. Pa. 1973)], for example, the court ordered that a drug abuse prevention program be terminated partly because the confidentiality of records on individuals who were thought to be potential drug abusers could not be guaranteed. Other conflicts are generated by new regulations and laws created to protect the privacy of student records, notably the Family Educational Rights and Privacy Act (Pub. L. 93-380) and the Privacy Act of 1974 (Pub. L. 93-579). These affect the outside researcher's ability to evaluate the impact of special educational programs and assay the effectiveness of teachers, curricula, screening and tracking systems, and the like. Restrictions on access to school records and to students have prevented projects ranging from mundane but critical research, such as verifying the record contents, to elaborate investigations, such as estimating the effects of a complex curriculum.

In research on mental health, concerns about individual privacy and the confidentiality of clinical records have been influential in our failure to consolidate adequately information on the impact of some mental health programs. It is partly for this reason, for example, that the United States has mounted no studies that parallel in quality the recent Danish research on biological and environmental origins of schizophrenia. Such developmental studies require the linkage of hospital and treatment records across families and generations for both adopted and natural families, a linkage that has not been feasible on privacy and bureaucratic grounds. Where limited attempts to consolidate records for the sake of estimating treatment effects have been mounted, they have not always fared well. In *Roe* v. *Ingraham* [357 F. Supp. 1217 (S.D.N.Y.)], for example, a judicial decision to have individual records removed from an archive used for both research and administration was based on testimony that even having one's record in such an archive produced anxieties among patients. Researchers who conduct follow-up studies of mental patients have, of course, always had to cope with the individual's reluctance to respond, a matter related at least as much to the wish to be let alone as to the fear that records so obtained will not or cannot be maintained as confidential.

Most research on controversial social problems involves confidentiality issues of one sort or another. School surveys designed to assay the effectiveness of integration programs on schoolchildren and their parents have been disrupted in New York City and elsewhere. The grounds for disruption include privacy, for, in the view of some publics, merely asking a question bearing on the topic is an unwarranted intrusion, and even well-meaning researchers should not be permitted to maintain information of extraordinary sensitivity. Longitudinal studies of campus protests during the late 1960s have been affected similarly, though here the threats to confidentiality are registered in more concrete fashion by governmental interest in research records. Efforts undertaken by sociologists to understand the genesis and development of draft resistance movements during the 1960s and early 1970s, and of political activist movements in the 1960s, have run into similar threats of interrogation by governmental agencies.

In legitimate research on juvenile delinquency and criminal behavior, legal threats of appropriation of records on identified research subjects have been persistent (Brymer and Farris 1967). That conflict between research standards and legal standards has been cast into more dramatic form in Germany, where the postwar constitution's explicit recognition of a right to do research has been used by criminologists to defend their participant-observer and interview approaches to understanding criminal behavior (Glaeser 1976). There are less visible but no less damaging threats to the use of archival information in this context also. Both poorly framed legislation that restricts access to criminal records, and the inclination of archive custodians, especially the Federal Bureau of Investigation, to refuse to disclose information even in anonymous form, constrain any longer-term studies of criminal behavior.

The sketch just drawn is crude, but it does illustrate some of the events that have provoked our interest in the topic. The details on each case are provided in succeeding chapters. This description is misleading, though, in two respects, and we hasten to add qualifiers. In the first place, such conflict in research, if it occurs at all, is rarely dramatic. For the most part, the questions put to individuals by social researchers are not especially intrusive or sensitive. Partly as a consequence, most research efforts are characterized by no serious public reaction or legal imbroglio, by nothing in the way of formal or informal threats to the confidentiality of an individual's report, and by negligible risks to the respondent even if his response is indeed disclosed to individuals outside the research setting. The low incidence of problems does not vitiate the principle that information once disclosed may constitute a depreciation of privacy, nor should it obscure the fact that episodic threats of disclosure can be important even in otherwise innocuous research.

The second reason this brief description is misleading is that episodes typically involve far more than a simple conflict over privacy or confidentiality. Further, confusion of issues is ubiquitous. That confusion may stem, for example, from erroneous assumptions about the functions of the research data: individuals and agencies have refused to cooperate in research under the supposition that the data will be used to make personal judgments about individuals, when in fact no legitimate social research has this aim. Confusion may also stem from competing issues, as in attacks on computer-assisted instruction: objections have been made on privacy grounds (e.g., Miller 1971) without recognizing that computer-maintained grades are not essential to the process. Issues of intellective privacy are chronically confused with those of physical privacy. *Tearoom Trade,* for example, is often talked about as if the problems posed there—the ethics of covert observation in public places—were inseparable from those occurring in direct interview field research. Yet here, too, problems must be separated to understand them if not to resolve them.

Government, Privacy Law, and Social Research

Until recently, the role of government in privacy-related problems has been a reactive one, confined primarily to the judicial sector. Legislative interest in privacy has enlarged that role considerably since 1970, and it behooves the social researcher to understand its relevance to research. Bureaucratic interests in the topic have also enlarged the government role. The interest has been a direct result of some laws, such as the Privacy Act of 1974, and an indirect result of earlier efforts by agency managers to establish policy and rules governing the propriety of research. Both legislative and bureaucratic action have enhanced the likelihood of court involvement. The pertinent laws are considered here briefly; the detail is provided in chapter 8.

Over three hundred bills on privacy have been introduced by members of Congress since 1974, and nearly as many have been drawn up by state legislators. Most, of course, are not enacted; and that is reasonable, since most are conceived thoughtlessly. Most of the laws that *are* enacted concern the social scientist as citizen rather than researcher, bearing as they do on military and civilian intelligence, credit reporting, and so on. Two themes underlie the few laws that have special implications for research.

The first is a clarification of a right to privacy, a right whose formal origins lie less obviously in constitutional law than in its judicial interpretation, notably by Brandeis and Warren and later experts. Incompetence in record keeping, for example, is a breeding ground for the violation of the rights of individuals on whom records are maintained. And though legislation in this sector cannot affect competence directly, it can make incompetence more costly. The laws that typify activity here include the Privacy Act of 1974 and the Family Educational Rights and Privacy Act of 1974. Their origins lie *not* in the abuses of records by social researchers, but rather in the administrative abuse of administrative records. The laws' impact on social research, and the impact of similar laws at the state level, are often incidental.

The Privacy Act, for example, governs records on individuals that are maintained by the federal government and its contractors, and sets up rules for record collection, maintenance, correction, and dispersal. The law was enacted partly to assure the quality of records and integrity in their use. It also had the remarkable feature of creating a vehicle for revising the law itself, the Privacy Protection Study Commission. Within government, the law is of some concern to social researchers because it may result in unnecessary constraints on the research process *despite* the exemptions stipulated for statistical research. For example, some forms of record linkage, though they involve no degradation of privacy, may be prevented. The collection of information may also be curtailed, for example, in evaluative research on social programs, without any justification traceable to congressional intent. Similarly, the Family Educational Rights and Privacy Act was designed to resolve problems of improper collection, maintenance, and dissemination of information about students. It too may have incidental but negative effects on research. Though there are special exemptions for evaluative research under the law, the general prohibition against disclosure of information has been used to stall research. Further, the requirement of informed consent to access administrative records is said to have unnecessarily truncated the research uses of those records.

A second theme underlying contemporary privacy law concerns governmental interest in generating information necessary for the governance of a changing society. A part of that interest has been translated into law protecting information collected on participants in social research. Title 13 of the U.S. Code, for example, restricts the access that any agency may have to individually identified records collected in U.S. Census Bureau surveys, and until recently that collection of law and judicial opinion served as a model for such protection.

Other, more recent statutes have been designed to help assure that the researcher who must collect sensitive information from individuals will not be legally forced to disclose it in a way that jeopardizes the respondent and the research. The earliest special laws providing testimonial privilege include the Comprehensive Alcohol Abuse and Alcoholism Prevention, Treatment, and Rehabilitation Act of 1970 (Pub. L. 91-616) and the Comprehensive Drug Abuse Prevention and Control Act of 1970 (Pub. L. 91-513). These represent a dramatic departure from conditions prior to 1970, when researchers had no formal protection against subpoena of records. With new laws such as the Crime Control Act of 1973 (Pub. L. 93-83), with court interpretations of those laws such as *People* v. *Newman* [32 N.Y. 2d 379 (1973)], and with new agency regulations, the quality of protection has improved. Many researchers and university legal counsel, however, are still unaware of the protection these afford. Partly as a consequence, research projects have failed to meet the requirements of institutional review boards and other groups responsible for protecting the rights of research participants.

The execution of these laws is no less important than their creation, and that responsibility lies partly with the bureaucrat. It is not unreasonable to argue that staff in some federal agencies have made distinctive efforts to translate law into rule effectively and have been at least as innovative in that respect as their academic counterparts. Their contributions are formal, through rule making, and informal, through conferences and working groups analogous to those created outside government. For some agencies, this is not at all a novel enterprise: the Social Security Administration and the Census Bureau in the United States are wedded to a persistent need to anticipate and resolve privacy problems. The relevant contributions to resolving problems of record linkage, internal file management, and publication of statistics are described in chapters 3, 5, 6, and 7. They stem from the efforts of an early generation of U.S. Census statisticians that includes Joseph Steinberg, Morris Hansen, Walt Simmons, Edwin Goldfield, and David Kaplan.

For other agencies, the topic is more novel, though there has been a low-level interest over the past fifteen years. The National Institute of Mental Health and the U.S. Office of Education, for example, have had periodic conferences on these matters, especially when a controversial topic, such as research on campus protests, virtually demanded face-to-face discussion among civil liberties groups, agency staff, researchers, and advisors. The early guidelines of the Department of Health, Education and Welfare governing research on human subjects have been a more uniform source of interest, sparking efforts to enumerate their benefits and shortcomings by Lorraine Torres, Matthew Huxley, and others at the National Institute of Mental Health, Ralph Chalkley at the National Institute of Health, Thomas Jabine, Lois Alexander, and others. The recent efforts by, for example, Thomas Madden, Carol Kaplan, Helen Lessin and others at the Law Enforcement Assistance Administration and others display not only a willingness to investigate conflicts arising from internal guidelines, but an inventiveness that produces some interesting mechanisms for accommodating privacy problems.

More recent bureaucratic entries to the field include the Office of Management and Budget and the U.S. General Accounting Office. Since the mid-1960s, OMB has had some responsibility for reviewing the propriety of questionnaires used by research contractors. This oversight role has been enlarged under the Privacy Act, though with no noticeable enlargement of resources. OMB, for example, was responsible for consolidating information about the privacy rules of the various federal agencies during 1974–77. Efforts have been made by staff such as Joseph Duncan to deparochialize their own views and to furnish both argument and evidence for changes in faulty law. The GAO's involvement is a consequence of its mandate, under the Congressional Budget and Impoundment Control Act of 1974 (Pub. L. 93-344), to oversee the conduct and evaluation of new social programs. In the Program Analysis Division especially, the need to balance requirements for information about the quality of program evaluation against interests in the privacy of program participants has produced another group of well-informed managers (e.g., Keith Marvin, Harry Havens).

The development of a cadre of individuals with pertinent skills is also evident in two other areas: staff assigned to national commissions whose work concerns privacy, and staff who assist in constructing privacy law. The Privacy Protection Study Commission (1977), set up by the Privacy Act, has had advisory responsibility for improving the law, and the staff assigned to that commission constitute a remarkable resource. Some members of the group, Carol Parsons for one, are veterans of earlier efforts, such as the President's Commission on Federal Statistics (1971) and the Ware Commission (Secretary's Advisory Committee on Automated Personal Data Systems 1973). Among legislative staff, Grasty Crewes has had a notable influence on the quality of law and regulations governing confidentiality in research on drug abuse (see chapter 8).

Finally, the episodic influence of the courts ought to be recognized. Judicial involvement in privacy issues stems most often from administrative action rather than research, action that one way or another impinges on the individual's exercise of control over information about himself. The range of the court's interest is broad and blandly defies simple definitions of privacy: it spans rulings on the legality of abortion and deviant sexual behavior, civilian and military surveillance, intelligence, and record systems, and journalistic inquiry and publication of private facts. The judicial activity that typically affects the social scientist is divisible into two classes: forcible disclosure of social research records, and preventing the collection or maintenance of research information. A court's demand that a researcher's records on identifiable respondents be disclosed, or that the respondent's identity be disclosed, is generally cause for grave concern, though the incidence of this is rather low. Governmental appropriation of records by a court or grand jury may affect a research project drastically in the short term and may undermine the caliber and vigor of future research on the same topic. Both legal rules and extra legal considerations (e.g., the negative impact of a subpoena on research) legitimately influence the court's decision to compel disclosure. And at least in the social research arena, the theory and factors underlying extra legal issues are only beginning to emerge (see chapter 3).

This first class of rulings constitutes an indirect constraint on research. To the extent that a subpoena of identifiable records has no effect on the research process, the constraint is negligible. More direct influence is evident in court rulings against a particular data collection and maintenance effort. Some pertain to behavior modification experiments and covert observation and do not concern us here. They are important, especially in curbing abuses in the practice of psychology, but are not clearly relevant to the social surveys that are the focus of this monograph. Other rulings, however, do concern record maintenance. For example, efforts to consolidate administrative records on the mentally ill have been prohibited by at least one court. The initial purposes of record consolidation—to facilitate record management first, and statistical research second—were viewed by the court as not justifying the allegedly negative consequences of consolidation—the risk of accidental dissemination, and patient anxiety produced by centralized "data banks." The court's opinion affects research to the extent that correlational and longitudinal studies of the development of mental illness are truncated unless some vehicle can be found that satisfies both research needs and the privacy needs of the patient. These cases occur much less frequently than those in the first class, but their effects may be more severe. Within either class, the strategies presented in the following chapters have helped on occasion to reduce or eliminate the need for a ruling or the need for the court to consider the matter at all.

The Research Community and Its Response in the United States and Abroad

This brief discussion attends mainly to professional groups and to organized professional efforts to clarify privacy problems. The contributions of individuals are more important and lie at the core of this monograph.

The formal reactions of professional groups commonly range from vigorous expressions of concern about codes of ethics to the creation of better administrative or professional vehicles for understanding privacy problems.[4] Less frequently, they involve research and development of solutions to those problems. Codes of ethics, for example, are almost invariably a touchstone in this matter. The idea that individuals who respond to a researcher's inquiry should be assured of confidentiality and that the information obtained ought not be disclosed promiscuously is endorsed by many of the major professional organizations whose members contribute to applied social research. The codes offer a perspective constructed by thoughtful people about the nature of privacy dilemmas and how they might be resolved with integrity. More importantly, codes can be tied well, though sometimes belatedly, to contemporary issues. The American Psychological Association (1973), for example, has issued four revisions of its code of ethics over the past thirty years, together with casebooks that lock the abstractions into some realities. In each instance, revisions have been based on reasonably conscientious research rather than speculation. The APA's renewed interest in privacy issues, reflected in its 1975 Task Force on Confidentiality and Privacy, is at least as much a function of its historical interest in the problem as in more recent events.

A similarly persistent concern, spiked occasionally with more intensive activity, is evident in the American Association of Public

Opinion Researchers, the American Sociological Association, and the American Statistical Association. Groups with much less interest in research have usually responded more directly to law that threatens to restrict their conventional practices. Some health insurance plans, for example, require that individuals who receive therapeutic assistance must be identifiable for the sake of assuring therapist accountability. This requirement and the demands for privacy that it engenders have been an explicit stimulus for action by the American Psychiatric Association (1968, 1970, 1972, 1973), the American Association of Orthopsychiatry, and others concerned about the propriety of maintaining detailed records on clients for third-party reimbursement. Few of the statements of ethics issued by these groups, however, discriminate between the administrative function and the research use of such files. In that respect, they fall short of the level of discrimination attained in the cruder framework of law.

A few professional organizations have no general ethical codes at all. As of 1979, those groups include the American Economic Association, the Association of Computing Machinery, the American Educational Research Association, and the American Statistical Association. The absence of codes at least in the last case is surprising. The American Statistical Association has since the 1860s often been emphatic in advocating candor in statistical reporting by the government and high standards for data, sometimes in the face of considerable political hostility. Moreover, the ASA has recently endorsed the view that confidentiality assurance in research is warranted. Their argument is based on members' implicit standards of equity in researcher-respondent relations, as well as on their belief in the importance of the assurance in sustaining respondents' cooperation (American Statistical Association 1977). The absence of codes is less surprising if one regards ethics as a personal collection of standards. And indeed, some members of each organization have made their own codes very explicit (e.g., Deming 1972). Whether the absence of a code matters much at present is not clear. Even groups with little traditional concern about privacy have become more vigorous in searching for reasonable standards. Their interest is often parochial but nonetheless promising. Economists, for example, have attended by and large to the crises produced by economic field experiments and evidently look only to medical ethics as a model (Rivlin and Timpane 1975). More catholic efforts, geared toward resolving problems as well as clarifying them, are not hard to find either.

The West German Conference on Conflicts between Social Research Ethics and Law, for instance, set a nice precedent for efforts to identify differences between the standards of social scientists and those of legal scholars, to frame issues well, and to outline their solution. The conference focused on individual and institutional privacy (Eser and Schumann 1976); a more recent conference (Müller 1978) focused on privacy law. Swedish interests have been well demonstrated in the Conference on Personal Integrity and Data Protection Research, supported by the Swedish Council on Social Science Research in 1976 (Dalenius and Klevmarken 1976). The meeting was a remarkable effort to educate parliamentarians about efforts designed to protect privacy in research and to educate the social scientist and statistician about the nature of legal constraints on that research. In Canada, David Flaherty's (1977) research on census bureaus has led to a major conference designed to facilitate the independent researcher's use of census bureau data and to make it plain that controlled access to statistical data poses no notable threat to individual privacy. The U.S. General Accounting Office Conference on Social Experimentation included a variety of academic and bureaucratic specialties, and focused on the conflict between need to audit records on respondents and the need to preserve the assurances made to respondents that the information they provide will remain confidential (USGAO 1976). The National Academy of Sciences Committee on Federal Statistics (Martin 1976) has undertaken a variety of related missions. The most pertinent include advising the U.S. Census Bureau on several field experiments to assess the role of privacy in censuses and government surveys. The Social Science Research Council (1978) has undertaken interdisciplinary efforts to better understand how governmental policy on privacy affects the quality of research.

Developing ethical codes and organizing interdisciplinary discussions on privacy are no substitute for administrative action, of course. In fact, the ideas generated in these undertakings often materialize in the policy or decisions of research institutions. This includes, for example, efforts by Cobb and others (1971) at Michigan's Institute for Social Research to examine various organizational standards, identify the conflicts among them, and recommend coherent policy on privacy. It includes management decisions to open discussion of confidentiality problems in research on campus disorders by Astin and others at the American Council on Education and the decision to try out procedural strategies for solving the problems (Walsh 1969a; Westin et al. 1972). And it includes decisions not to engage in competitive bidding on government contracts that require the researcher to violate conventional research standards that confidentiality promises be met, and decisions to object formally to the development of such contracts (Bradburn, personal communication, 1978). On the other hand, many of the smaller research units in the commercial sector have done nothing along these lines. Our little telephone survey of the for-profit units in Chicago suggests that less than 15 percent have written policy on the matter.

This monograph is concerned chiefly with still another important category of researcher response to privacy problems—concrete research and the development of solutions. At its best, that research offers the social scientist a range of options that permit closer adherence to a code of ethics. It enhances one's ability to anticipate ethical dilemmas and to lay groundwork for their resolution. Certainly the research has been stimulated by professional worries about episodic conflicts between law and research ethic, including the disruptions in field research described in chapter 4. Foundation support for Carroll and Knerr's (1975, 1976) survey of such conflicts, for example, was unavailable five years earlier to other researchers who outlined similar studies, simply because the issue was insufficiently important to foundation staff to justify research. It is equally clear, despite the absence of long-term directed funding, that the research has been persistent, and stimulated by the social scientist's interest in equity in researcher-respondent relations, and in the integrity of the research process, as well as by the conflicts that have occurred. The research has been fragmented, however, and our interest in a more unified examination serves as one justification for this monograph.

One final note on the researcher's response is warranted. Many surveys are mounted by private individuals, institutions, and the media, by hospitals, unions, community groups, and by other organizations. These efforts are often not very visible, and they almost always fall outside the purview of orthodox professional groups. Consequently, little is known about the privacy-related conflicts they engender or about their policies on privacy. Given the informality of most such efforts, it is not surprising to find that this sector has made no original contribution to clarifying or solving privacy-related problems. The lack of systematic information available on this sector is disturbing. Professionalization, including the creation of codes, is no guarantor of virtue. It ordinarily does, however, involve a level of publicity that makes some problems more visible and therefore more tractable than they might otherwise be.

Orientations, Fundamental and Otherwise

The following remarks concern definitions of privacy, confidentiality, and other ideas that are generally necessary for understanding the topic at hand. They are consistent with contemporary law, but we make no attempt to tie the definitions to specific legislation. We make our orientation explicit only to avoid infecting the reader with more confusion than we ourselves can tolerate.

PRIVACY WITH RESPECT TO WHOM?

Privacy refers here to the state of an individual: whether the individual's attitudes or experiences are known to another. The right of privacy concerns the individual's control over whether and to what extent information about himself or herself will be shared with anyone else. Our position is that in social research, as in any activity of everyday life, that right ought to be recognized explicitly. Further, responses to a researcher's inquiry ought to be voluntary, though in particular instances the need to understand a critical social problem may warrant compulsory response. Even when response is clearly voluntary, however, we believe that as a matter of principle, privacy is degraded with respect to the inquirer. And if the inquirer makes the response known to others, privacy will be degraded with respect to them as well. The latter problem, disclosure, is treated in the next section as a confidentiality issue.

As a consequence of espousing this principle, we take as an essential objective reducing the degradation of privacy to a minimum, and when possible eliminating it. This view is endorsed despite the fact that identifiers in research serve merely as an accounting device and are not ordinarily used by the researcher to make personal judgments about the respondent. Support for the same principle is implicit in some codes of ethics in the social and behavioral sciences. Accepting it implies that the social scientist has a responsibility to develop mechanisms that will help to minimize his own need for access to information on identifiable respondents but will not impede research.

An argument for this approach can be made on the basis of research practice, rather than on the basis of principle. In the past, most privacy depreciation with respect to the scientist has been innocuous, in part because social research has been innocuous and unobtrusive. As the application of social research methods to resolving controversial problems increases, public scrutiny of research is likely to increase, as will the importance attached even to innocuous questions. To the extent that reducing the depreciation of privacy also reduces the likelihood of disruption of research, then the social scientist ought to develop mechanisms to meet that objective. Similarly, the researcher's trustworthiness has, as a matter of practice, been a key ingredient of the social science endeavor, especially in regard to privacy. Nothing said in this monograph should be taken to demean that trust. We contend, however, that if it is possible to avoid simplistic reliance on trust, the researcher ought to do so. And to accommodate that view, it is essential to have available a variety of mechanisms that eliminate the need for conventional appeals to faith in the researcher's integrity.

Also germane to the matter of trust is the infrequent threat to an individual's privacy made by a counterfeit researcher. The deception may be motivated by financial gain: for example, in the case of salesmen posing as pollsters (Hofstette 1971, Baxter 1969). Or the motives may be more dangerous: the talented psychopath can pose as a survey interviewer, just as he can pose as a detective, politician, or physician. In the interest of preserving public trust in social research, the social scientist must take some responsibility for protecting would-be respondents from these less frequent hazards. The tactics described in the following chapters represent a narrow resolution of the problem. The more general attack on the problem involves licensing researchers and creating legal sanctions against imposters.

The idea that privacy degradation ought to be minimized can be made tangible in a variety of ways. The simplest, of course, involves not asking any questions at all, and indeed an elaborate technology has developed to achieve that goal with respect to at least one frame of reference. Orthodox survey sample design is dedicated in large measure to minimizing the number of individuals from whom information must be elicited and the number of questions that must be answered. That technology has been developed primarily to minimize the cost of survey research for a given level of data quality, but it also results in reduction of personal cost to members of the target population, and in this sense it can be regarded as a legitimate privacy-conserving device. Survey sample design, minimization of sample size, and so forth have been described by Kish (1967) and others. The specific techniques are not discussed here except as a common vehicle for minimizing the demands on respondents in social research.

The idea can also be made concrete by defining degradation of privacy in terms of the sensitivity of questions. This endeavor too has received attention, primarily from psychologists, but it has not been nearly so well formulated a technology as minimization of survey sample size. One might reduce sensitivity, for example, by replacing pejorative, provocative, or otherwise offensive questions by innocuous ones. And indeed, work along this line has produced a useful but fragmented technology on measuring the sensitivity of questions and of responses, a technology that can be applied to most kinds of social research. That research has been linked directly to individuals' perceptions about the intrusiveness of certain questions, and the findings have been used to modify some standardized personality inventories (see chapter 3). Under the assumption that time influences the stigma attached to a response, one might also substitute retrospective reporting for reports about contemporary activity. Where a direct question provokes anxiety, questions about surrogate behaviors, imperfectly related to the sensitive trait but considerably more innocuous in tone, can sometimes be helpful.

These approaches generally permit a coarse approximation to reality at the individual level. They must usually be coupled with other, more direct methods of eliciting information to assure the quality of inferences based on the data. At their best, they help to obtain reliable information while keeping individual privacy at its highest possible level. Again, since this topic is well documented, it will not be discussed here. Reviews appear in good texts on response bias and questionnaire design, and in reports of research on the social desirability of response (e.g., Sudman and Bradburn 1974).

In this book, the idea that degradations in privacy ought to be minimized with respect to the social researcher is made concrete by pursuing a single goal under a single constraint: identifiability of a respondent in social research must be minimized whenever possible and so long as the data will not be intolerably degraded by the operation. Though the constraint may appear to the social science critic to be a large trap door, and the goal may not appeal to some social scientists, we believe it *is* possible to achieve the goal with integrity.

CONFIDENTIALITY IN WHAT RESPECT?

Confidentiality here refers to the state of information. An individual's response to a social researcher's inquiry is regarded as confidential with respect to others if the information coupled with identifiers will not or cannot be disclosed by the researcher to anyone else. Information or a physical record containing information is said to be identifiable if it includes names or addresses, or other forms of unique identification. The only ethical aspect of confidentiality that concerns us here is that the researcher who promises confidentiality to the respondent should be able to fulfill that promise despite pressures to renege. The procedural, statistical, and law-based strategies described later help one to keep such a promise if it is made, and help to assure that records are confidential even if a formal promise is not made.

The processes that lead to disclosure of identifiable information may be accidental or deliberate. Accidental disclosure of individual records is of little interest to us, in part because the problem can be accommodated easily by employing decent record management and control systems. The more subtle forms of accidental disclosure, notably deductive disclosure based on published statistical tables or release of virtually anonymous raw records, are of interest and are discussed in chapter 7.

Most forced disclosures are based on the differences in standards already discussed. Where law is at issue, the problem is that the researcher may find it impossible to abide by both the promise of confidentiality made to a respondent and the demand of a court, legislative committee, or executive agency for information about identified respondents. Threats from governmental agencies are infrequent, primarily because the data typically collected in a research effort are often irrelevant for administrative judgment or too difficult to use, relative to information routinely available from administrative archives. The researcher deals in samples rather than populations, of course, and consequently, research records are less relevant to administrative interests. Finally, the content and form of records maintained by the researcher usually differ from those maintained by administrative agencies. Nonetheless, appropriation can and does occur. The consequences for the respondent can be serious: personal discomfort, social embarrassment, or legal sanction. The consequences for the conduct of research, examined in chapter 3, may be no less serious. For example, the social scientist must often rely on foundation or commercial support for research. Such resources may, at times, be insensitive to the matter of ensuring confidentiality, and may influence the researcher's own sensitivity. To the extent that the respondent is powerless, it becomes more important to examine the idea that confidentiality of records with respect to the research sponsor should be assured. We recognize that in the United States, at least, appropriation of identifiable research records by a governmental or private institution is a rare event. The pressures to disclose records to a sponsor are greater in the commercial sector, where, in consumer surveys, for example, market-research organizations may indeed disclose identified records to their clients.

The theft of research records constitutes the last threat to confidentiality of concern here. It too is a rare event, but it is not unimaginable, particularly if the records contain identification, are very detailed, and have some monetary value. Most social scientists normally take responsibility for protection of records against this threat. The tactics described here simply expand the range of available protection devices.

Risks such as these are real in principle, if remote in practice, and so they deserve some attention. In particular, it is reasonable for the social scientist to develop and use legal mechanisms to protect the respondent from legal appropriation of research records. This is especially true for those cases in which the potential benefits of the research clearly offset the social benefits of legal appropriation of records. The approaches described in the following chapters help to accomplish that goal.

SOCIAL RESEARCH

For our purposes, the distinction between a social research system and other kinds of data collection and storage depends on the function and form of the records maintained, and on the structure of the information system itself.

Research records here are defined as records used to create and interpret a description of a group of persons. That description will often be statistical, and this report confines attention to the statistical setting alone. The researcher, therefore, neither needs nor seeks to make a direct personal judgment about an identified individual whose record happens to be on file. In contrast, the primary function of *administrative* or *clinical records* is to sustain evaluative judgments about an individual, and decisions made on the basis of that information will normally have a direct and personal implication for the individual's status.

The secondary purpose of many administrative records is to provide statistical data for planning and evaluation. Archival files maintained at the institutional level may require linkage at higher levels of organization for the same purpose. When the research functions and administrative functions are separable, as they often are, the orientation here is that the distinction ought to be recognized and different rules and practices set up to deal with each setting.[5]

In research systems, the researcher may require identification of respondents, but the purpose of identifiers is confined to assuring the integrity of the research process and of the resultant data. Identifiers normally facilitate adequate sampling of a defined population, periodic follow-up of individuals in long-term studies, and side research on validity of response. Any identifying information obtained serves only an accounting function.

The complete research system is taken to include each stage in the research process:

- Research design, including specification of the sample, of the questions that may be put to individuals, and of information that might be drawn from administrative archives and so on

- Execution of the design, including sampling, conduct of interviews, mail surveys, or the like, employment of quality-control checks on reporting, and so forth

- Document and data processing, including the creation of a formal record system, production of statistics, and the quality-control checks at this stage

- Publication of statistics

- Linkage operations, including updating research records and linkage with other archives to expand the quality of available data.

The techniques described in this report pertain directly to at least one level of the process. The most general methods enhance the respondent's privacy at each level.

MULTIPLE METHODS OF ASSURING CONFIDENTIALITY OF DATA

Some readers may find a singular approach to confidentiality problems more attractive than the multi-method approach proposed here. But the latter is much easier to justify.

The problems themselves, for example, vary with the research design, the method of inquiry, and other characteristics of the research setting. The techniques used to assure confidentiality in one instance may be quite unsuitable in another. For example, specialized approaches have been worked out to accommodate the need for outside audit of the conduct of research. Those methods differ in character from the methods that resolve privacy problems generated by secondary analysis of research data by principals outside the original research team.

The second reason for emphasizing options rather than a single solution concerns the weakness of particular techniques. Some engender moderate financial costs, in which case an alternative technique or a combination of techniques might be used to assure the economy of the research as well as the protection of records. Any given technique may also be vulnerable to corruption. In the commercial sector, for example, pressure to satisfy criteria other than scientific ones has occassionally led to the abuse of one common device—anonymous questionnaires. The opportunity for corruption can be reduced, even eliminated, by combining some of the tactics described later.

Finally, the problem of assuring confidentiality traverses both discipline and culture. To the extent that style of research, including design and mode of inquiry, differs with discipline, it is sensible to examine a range of methods. The statistical techniques for protecting confidentiality are more pertinent to sample surveys than to anthropological research, for example. More importantly, the impressions of members of the target population, the respondents, can count heavily in this matter. Some of the techniques that they regard as secure will in fact be weak. Others, less familiar and perhaps therefore less attractive to a respondent, may offer far more privacy protection. This problem may demand the simultaneous use of several devices.

Our emphasis on diversity of solutions differs little in spirit from the views we took earlier (e.g., Boruch 1971b) or from those registered in other quarters. Ervin (1974), Greenawalt (1975), and other legal scholars have argued against a simplistic reliance on law (e.g., testimonial privilege) as a vehicle for solving privacy-related problems. In the computing sciences, Weissman (1967), Hoffman (1973), and others have argued vigorously for multi-mode approaches, involving hardware, software, staff, etc., for improving the security of information processing. This monograph treats no single approach—procedural, statistical, or legal—as a panacea. Rather, each form has its attractive features and its disadvantages. It is the social scientist's responsibility to evaluate their appropriateness for the setting at hand. This monograph is dedicated to facilitating that process.

Notes

1. The principle that privacy is decreased in any social survey is adapted from Shils (1949). The several motives for this effort are nicely discussed by Florman (1976).

2. The designation "procedural" here is consistent with language adopted by the Privacy Protection Study Commission (1977) from earlier academic research on the topic (see chapter 4).

3. These and other cases are reviewed in chapters 3 and 6.

4. See Bowers and DeGasparis (1978) for a review of ethical codes in the social sciences and Kelman (1968), Frankel (1976), Hilmar (1968), and Tybout and Zaltman (1974) more generally.

5. This functional distinction between administrative records and social research records is consistent with recommendations of the Privacy Protection Study Commission (1977) and stems from earlier research on the topic (see Boruch 1971b).

On Record Linkage and the Need

for Identifiers in Research

There is nothing more necessary to the man of science than its history and the logic of discovery . . . the way error is detected, the use of hypothesis, of imagination, the mode of testing.

LORD ACTON

One of the questions that emerges almost invariably in discussions about privacy in social research concerns the need to identify respondents at all. To the statistician or social scientist, the justification may be obvious, even taken for granted. But to those less familiar with the form of scientific inquiry and with the history of research methods, and to those attracted less by quantitative enterprise than by qualitative, the justification will often not be obvious.[1] The evidence offered here was drawn up, in part, to satisfy the legitimate demands of the literary contingent of our two cultures for an explanation of how identifiers are tied to the conduct of research.

In social research, the respondent's identification ordinarily serves solely as an accounting device. Both identification and associated data are maintained under the proviso that they will be used only for research purposes and, in particular, will not be used to make personal judgments about individuals. Despite this proviso, the need for identifiers in certain classes of research may bring the research into sharp conflict with law or custom. Here, we consider only two broad research methods for which identifiers are normally deemed essential. The first of the two major sections that follow covers longitudinal studies; the second covers correlational research. Experimental tests of public programs are subsumed under each category.

There is a special emphasis on the practical consequences, including loss or distortion of information, engendered by thoughtlessly abridging one's ability to identify individuals in research. Because the question of whether the social benefits of research offset privacy considerations is often important, there is a special emphasis on the research product. The illustrations are taken from studies in medicine, economics, education, psychology, and sociology.[2]

Longitudinal Inquiry: Its Definition, Justification, and Relevance to Record Linkage

Longitudinal research refers here to the process of tracking a group of individuals over time to establish how the state of that group varies and, more importantly, to establish the average relation between an individual's state at one time and his state at another. For example, one may conduct a study of adults to learn not only how the health status of the group changes with age, but also to understand how the individual's health at one age is correlated with health at a later age. Obtaining an accurate characterization of this sort is necessary for describing and predicting health status, and for the more demanding task of explaining the biosocial mechanisms that underlie health status.

Usually this methodology requires that an observation on a person at a particular time be linked with observations made on that person at subsequent times, for each person in a sample. The vehicle for linkage is typically, though not always, the individual's identification. The linkage implies some degradation of privacy, and so it behooves us to ask why such research is justified: to ask what we can learn or have learned from such research.

The first section below covers some of the logical traps in which we can easily be ensnared if we choose *not* to do longitudinal research. The next sections deal with examples of longitudinal research and their products.

TRAPS, ARTIFACTS, AND CIRCULARITY

One of the simplest ways to illustrate why longitudinal data may be essential for even primitive understanding is to compare it with an ostensibly equivalent but less demanding mode of data collection. It has occasionally been suggested, for example, that cross-sectional studies provide as much useful information about human behavior as longitudinal investigations. And because they involve observation of a large sample at only one point in time, they are said to degrade privacy less than the longitudinal approach.

Consider, for example, the problem of understanding how intelligence, or a measure of intellectual achievement, varies with age. One might conduct a survey of a sample of children of age three, and then continue to survey those individuals annually until they reach an advanced age. Or, in the interest of saving time and perhaps on privacy grounds, we might choose to conduct a single survey of a representative sample of (anonymous) three-year-olds, a sample of four-year-olds, and so forth at only one point in time, under the assumption that this single cross-sectional survey would yield roughly the same results as the longitudinal survey. This last assumption, that a growth curve based on longitudinal data will be roughly equivalent to a growth curve based on cross-sectional data, is critical.

The assumption also happens to be wrong with alarming frequency. In particular, its espousal by some human-development experts has led to some erroneous, not to say embarrassing, folklore about the development of human intelligence. The same assumption has been a trap in some economic welfare research, in some epidemiological work, and in other areas.

To understand one of the logical traps, consider figure 1: graph A, a chart similar to those commonly used during the 1940s and 1950s to illustrate the gradual increase in IQ from childhood to early adulthood, and the gradual decrease thereafter. The implication of the graph, which is based on actual cross-sectional data, is that at age thirty one's IQ is at its peak, and things go downhill soon after that. What makes the chart much more persuasive is that similar inverted-U patterns show up in other investigations of human ability based on cross-sectional data. This includes the quality of treatises written by eminent philosophers (rated by eminent philosophers) plotted against the age at which the author wrote the document, the level of innovativeness of theory and invention of chemists plotted against the chemist's age at the theory's production, and similar data (see, for example, Birren 1964).

Suppose now that instead of the cross-sectional data there existed longitudinal data on exactly the same individuals. The dotted lines in graph B illustrate how *actual* IQ may increase consistently with age without a notable decline, and how the *rate* of increase can depend on year of birth, that is, on cohort. The points connected by the solid line correspond exactly to what appears in the plot of cross-sectional data. The chart suggests that individuals born in 1910 increase in intelligence as they grow older. But their rate of increase is lower than the corresponding rate for a younger cohort, for example, individuals born in 1930. The reasons for differences in development rate, or "cohort effects," are a matter of speculation. They may involve any number of biosocial factors; the differences may even be an artifact of the increasing reliability or culture-relatedness of such tests. Regardless of the reasons, the point is that the longitudinal data can offer us

Figure 1. Confounding of age and cohort differences in cross-sectional research.

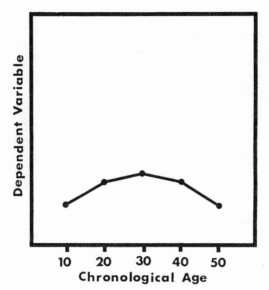

Graph A

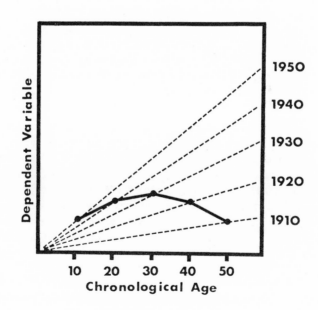

Graph B

Source: Nesselroade and Baltes 1974, p. 4.

a less misleading picture of human development than the cross-sectional data. Moreover, the theory generated by the former will differ markedly from the theory generated by the latter. It is clear that relying solely on the cross-sectional data can lead one to a conclusion that is quite contrary to the way nature behaves. In fact, there is evidence from studies by Barton et al. (1975), Schaie (1963), and others that graph B is a less misleading portrayal of nature than graph A, though neither is completely accurate, and most certainly, neither is adequate.[3]

Exactly the same inferential problems occur for a variety of physical and social measures of individual characteristics. Plots of height, for example, when plotted against age, often show an inverted-U pattern if based on cross-sectional data, simply because rates of growth and upper limits on growth are quite high for children recently born, relative to the growth rate and upper limits for those born eighty years ago. Plots of cross-sectional data on level of extroversion and age of adolescents in certain areas of the United States make it appear that extroversion declines through adolescence when it actually increases on the average and increases most quickly for recently born cohorts. Longitudinal data on adolescent tough mindedness (autonomy, assertiveness) suggest a fair degree of stability over ages twelve to fifteen; more recently born cohorts generally exhibit higher levels of the trait. But cross-sectional data show a declining trend.

Some readers may regard "soft" social data, like psychological measures, as particularly susceptible to the inferential trap just described. The fact is that data on hard social variables, such as income, are no less immune to the problem. Consider, for example, estimates of lifetime income for individuals. These predictions are important in the commercial arena, for example, in some credit and loan research in the insurance business. And they are no less important in the government sector, for example, in planning social security benefits and the like. Often there is a choice between using cross-sectional data or using longitudinal research, and if both provide equally accurate estimates, then one might choose the cross-sectional approach for managerial reasons or on the grounds that a cross-sectional survey involves less degradation of privacy because one can presumably elicit anonymous responses. Miller and Hornseth's (1970) attempt to estimate lifetime income for certain segments of the population is interesting in this respect.

That estimates of lifetime income based on the two kinds of data will not be the same is clear from tables 1 and 2. Table 1, based entirely on cross-sectional survey, suggests that annual income increases up until age 35, stabilizes during the 35–54 year age interval, then declines. The pattern is similar whether one considers data collected in

1947, or 1948, or 1949. Table 2, on the other hand, is based on longitudinal data and illustrates a much less drastic pattern, notably that increases in income persist over a wider age range, and rates of increase are substantial. The longitudinal data are, of course, affected by inflation and other factors uniquely associated with a given cohort, but similar patterns occur after adjustment for inflation. They are more accurate than the cross-sectional data in the crude sense that they better describe the way observable income behaves as a function of age.

Though the example is recent, the problem of estimating lifetime earnings from cross-sectional data is not a new one for economists.

Table 1

Estimates of mean annual income in dollars for men aged 25–64. Data is based on independent samples taken in 1947, 1948, and 1949.

Year	Age 25–34	35–44	45–54	55–64
1947	2,704	3,344	3,329	2,795
1948	2,898	3,508	3,378	2,946
1949	2,842	3,281	3,331	2,777

Source: Adapted from data presented by Miller and Hornseth (1970).

Table 2

Estimates of mean annual income in dollars over ten-year intervals for six cohorts

Year	Ages 25–34	35–44	45–54
1. 1947	2,704 (1947)	5,300 (1957)	8,342 (1967)
2. 1948	2,898 (1948)	5,433 (1958)	8,967 (1968)
3. 1949	2,842 (1949)	5,926 (1959)	9,873 (1969)

Year	35–44	Ages 45–54	55–64
4. 1947	3,344 (1947)	5,227 (1957)	7,004 (1967)
5. 1948	3,508 (1948)	5,345 (1958)	7,828 (1968)
6. 1949	3,281 (1949)	5,587 (1959)	8,405 (1969)

Note: Each cohort was surveyed every ten years. The first cohort, for example, contains individuals who were 25–34 years of age in 1947 and had an average income of $2704; in 1967, when they were 45–54 years of age, their mean income was $8342.

Source: Adapted from Miller and Hornseth (1970).

Klevmarken (1972) summarized some of the history of the problem and enumerated practical needs for better estimates in labor negotiations, actuarial sciences, and elsewhere. More importantly, he managed to show, using both longitudinal and cross-sectional data, how one could develop less misleading models of lifetime income curves if one had available only the cross-sectional data. He makes the same point as we do, however, in observing that there is no *generally* reliable way to establish longitudinal trends from cross-sectional data alone. Any attempt to do so must be based on assumptions that, for the social scientist, may be untenable.[4]

A different but no less important trap is the failure to recognize that longitudinal rather than cross-sectional data may be essential for detecting subtle influences on human behavior. The problem of designing precise investigations is particularly important in estimating the impact of social programs, whose effects, we know, are often weak but may nonetheless be politically important. Achieving that objective often depends on the availability of longitudinal data. There is a large array of analytic techniques, for example, that employ the correlation between behaviors at different points in time to expunge irrelevant variation from the data. The use of longitudinal research techniques, especially in conjunction with randomized experiments, usually makes it easier to detect influences that might otherwise be obscured by the normally high variation in human behavior.

Consider, for example, the Cali, Colombia, experiments on the impact of nutritional supplements on children's physical growth. Special nutritional supplements were assigned randomly to a sample of malnourished children; supplements, which were in short supply, were unavailable to an otherwise equivalent sample of comparison group children. The impact of the supplements was *not* evident from scrutiny of early mean changes in treated and untreated groups; the simple natural variations in heights of even malnourished children is sufficiently large to obscure real differences. More sophisticated analyses, using correlations between repeated measures of height of the children, did yield estimates of program effect that differed notably from chance level. As a consequence of the positive finding, the supplements are being put into local production and tested on a much larger scale in other less well developed countries. (Bejar 1975; McKay et al. 1978)

The same use of a longitudinal approach for sensitive analysis of program effects is evident in other areas. Heber et al. (1972), for example, have conducted six-year studies to determine the relative impact of special programs for reducing the risk of functional retardation among infants and young children. Based on these Wisconsin pilot tests, similar tests of the program are being mounted in North Carolina and elsewhere. Beyond the midpoint in Kaiser Permanente's ten-year experiments, Ramcharan et al. (1973) find some evidence for the effectiveness of multiphasic screening on prevention of disease, an impact that is bound to be negligible during the first few years of the program. In these cases and in innumerable others (see Riecken et al. 1974), the effects may be undetectable in the short run, and difficult to detect in the long run, especially if the groups involved are small. There is simply no adequate substitute for longitudinal follow-up in these instances.

Despite this kind of evidence, privacy issues have been used to argue for cross-sectional rather than longitudinal designs. In 1976, for example, the National Academy of Sciences Committee on Community Reaction to the Concorde was asked to advise the Federal Aviation Administration on FAA attitude surveys of people in the vicinity of Concorde landings. The data would be used in making judgments about perceived noise level and the desirability of increased landings. Because the effects of the airplane were expected to be weak, a committee member suggested that longitudinal rather than cross-sectional surveys be done to improve the likelihood of detecting them. A representative of the FAA announced that the design was not feasible, because it would have to be reviewed by the Privacy Protection Study Commission. The Commission, of course, was never empowered to pass on the legitimacy of surveys—but he could not be persuaded that the Commission was in fact irrelevant.

The final logical trap of interest bears on both longitudinal and correlational research. It involves analysis of data based on aggregates of individuals in an attempt to form an opinion about individuals within the aggregates. To establish the average relation between literacy and race in the United States, for example, one might obtain published census statistics on the proportion of literate persons and the proportion of blacks in each state and then compute the correlation between the two variables. Aggregated data might be used on the grounds that the relevant information is easily accessible from published tables. Or, we might justify our action on the grounds that using published data does not present the privacy-related problems that would be engendered by a special survey.

There are two weaknesses implicit in the argument that aggregate data can be used in lieu of individual data. The obvious one is that inferences made about groups are not necessarily appropriate to the individual and in fact may be quite inaccurate. The second weakness, a matter of precision rather than of accuracy, is that analyses based on grouped data are often less likely to reflect the nature of change in individuals than analyses based on data at the individual level.

To be more specific, consider the literacy-race example. At a particular point in time, the correlation between literacy rate (percent literate) and color (percent black) computed on the basis of the nine census regions of the United States is .95. When individuals are grouped by state rather than region, the correlation is .77. Finally, when individuals are not grouped at all, but the entire disaggregated population is considered, the correlation is .20. The example is from Robinson's paper (1950) on census data prior to 1950. A similar problem with a different resolution appears if we try to determine the relation between color (white versus nonwhite) and occupation (domestic service versus other) for female employees in Chicago in 1940. Though a correlation based on percentage data for each of the nine areas is .34, the actual correlation based on individuals is .29, not too different from the area-based estimate (see Duncan and Davis 1953; Goodman 1959).

In the literacy-race example, the high correlation obtained from the regional data might be interpreted as suggesting that illiteracy is pervasive among blacks and, furthermore, that a massive program of education must be put into effect to counteract the problem. In fact, if we look at data on individuals, rather than at data based on opportunistic groups into which individuals may fall, we reach a considerably less pessimistic and more accurate conclusion: that the relation between race and literacy prior to 1950 was small but notable. Any attempt to resolve the problem of illiteracy by making a massive investment in rehabilitating the reading skills of each individual based on the .95 regional correlation is bound to be a wasteful allocation of scarce resources.

An obvious problem in these matters is that aggregates of individuals are used as surrogates for individuals. Since the aggregates are usually constructed for political or administrative purposes (e.g., census regions, health-care service regions), it is unlikely that these "natural" aggregates will constitute valid replicas of real persons. We have only a little theory to guide us in the selection of "proper" aggregates. And it is impossible to verify that an aggregate will be proper without some data at the individual level.

The problem is a chronic one in the social and administrative sciences that must rely heavily on aggregated data—sociology, epidemiology, economics, statistical geography. It is a particularly crucial problem in attempts to evaluate the impact of national social programs on individuals. Many evaluations in education, for example, rely on data aggregated at the school district level to estimate the impact of a nationally supported compensatory reading program on disadvantaged youth. The inferences made about individuals (based on analysis of aggregates rather than of individuals) are generally biased in an unknown fashion (the individual data not having been analyzed), and are imprecise because the aggregate data are insensitive to changes, even some marked changes, in individuals (see Burstein 1975 for examples). This is not to say that the aggregation data will always yield biased estimates. It is to say that the problems are crucial and cannot be resolved unequivocally without some evidence based on individual rather than aggregated data.

MEDICAL RESEARCH

There is a fine tradition of longitudinal studies in medical research, dating at least from Hippocrates' efforts to characterize the progressive stages of disease among his own and his colleagues' patients (King 1971). The systematic tracking of both the healthy and the ill remains a basic weapon in the medical research armamentarium. Not only does the approach help to identify the existence and incidence of a disease, to determine symptom development and disease consequence, but it is essential in laying out the array of possible origins of the disease. Longitudinal methods in this sector have become considerably more efficient over the last forty years with the development of survey sampling technology. And when coupled to other methods, such as randomized experiments, the approach can be dramatically effective in identifying whether and how well particular treatment programs work.

Examples of the process are not hard to find. For the sake of detail, we examine a research area that, thanks to gifted science writers (such as Gilmore 1973) and researchers (such as Kannel et al. 1961), is among the best documented. Modern work on coronary heart disease appears to have reached a turning point during the 1940s and 1950s with autopsy studies. Those investigations, because of their small size and cross-sectional nature, provided only weak support for the relationships among arteriosclerosis, heart disease, and biophysical conditions such as blood pressure. More importantly, they provided the evidence necessary to justify longer-term, longitudinal study of the problem. The Framingham Study (Kannel et al. 1961), among the largest of subsequent efforts, was designed to better understand the relationship between prior physical condition and death due to heart attack. Spanning twenty-five years in the lives of nine thousand men, the effort was of sufficient size and duration to permit computation of risk factors operating in the population. Actuarial tables were developed to illustrate the likelihood of heart attack as a function of earlier serum cholesterol level, blood pressure, EKG abnormalities, and so forth. Other studies—animal experiments and comparative investigations of populations with natural differences in these factors —yielded evidence that added to speculation about the role of serum cholesterol level and other factors in heart disease.

Because the ability to describe and predict based on longitudinal studies does not necessarily yield unequivocal information on the causes of heart disease, long-term experimental tests of different treatment programs have been mounted. The best of those tests generally involve large samples tracked over long periods of time and, moreover, randomized assignment of individuals to one of the competing treatments. As a consequence, they raise logistical problems more serious than those engendered by longitudinal research alone. Nonetheless, pilot efforts, such as the Diet-Heart Feasibility Study, have furnished data on the practical difficulty of field tests and somewhat less equivocal small-scale data on the impact of diet control on heart disease. Such short-term studies have paved the way for longer-term studies that focus on the more plausible causal mechanisms, notably reduction of heart disease through diet or drugs that reduce serum-cholesterol levels. The largest of current clinical trials will run about five years and involves over fifty institutions and eight thousand patients; it is designed to evaluate the effectiveness of different drugs and drug-dosage levels for reducing cholesterol level in the bloodstream (Coronary Drug Project Research Group 1973). Although the primary response variables are mortality rates due to heart disease and related illness, a variety of social, biological, and physiological measures are being obtained. The social measures—smoking habits, life style, race, job characteristics, and so on—are expected to add precision to the results and help identify variables that, though influential, are less amenable to direct control.

The products of longitudinal studies coupled to experimental tests are described by Riecken et al. (1974), and references cited therein. Short-term study of released prisoners who have had cosmetic surgery to remedy facial disfigurement provides evidence of lower recidivism rates among them. Longitudinal experiments on the effectiveness of physician surrogates—nurse-practitioners, physician-extenders— have yielded information essential for reducing costs of medical service, planning innovative programs in health-care utilization, and the like. A new generation of pharmaceutical research focuses on short- and long-term drug use in order to determine how patients comply with medication regimens, how special packaging of medication influences compliance, and so on. In preventive medicine, tests of the impact of multiphasic screening are being run by Kaiser Permanente for a ten-year period to assure that the long-term effects of annual screening on the detection and amelioration of disease are well documented.

These examples and others like them teach us that there is no way to understand the etiology of disease or to evaluate the effectiveness of prevention and treatment programs without longitudinal study.[5] Not that longitudinal survey is sufficient. Its natural limitations must usually be offset by coupling this approach to others, notably experiments that are designed to establish cause-effect relations. But the idea is central to medical research, and it is generalizable to other areas in principle and in practice.

PSYCHOLOGY AND PSYCHIATRY: GENETIC AND EXPERIENTIAL INFLUENCES ON SCHIZOPHRENIA

For the past hundred years, the scientific and lay arguments over the causes of schizophrenia have been supported largely by ambiguous data. The information at its worst has been unreliable and no more than anecdotal in form. At its best it has been based on longitudinal study of very small numbers of individuals and on retrospective reports of unknowable reliability. The debate's focus has changed markedly over the years, however, because of longitudinal research on adopted children and their natural and adopted parents. The research depends heavily on linkage of records from different sources, including interviews.

One of the basic problems in discovering the origins of schizophrenia is how to disentangle the genetic influences from the environmental ones. To resolve the problem, Fini Schulsinger and other researchers at Denmark's New School for Social Research, at the Psykologist Institute and the Kommune Hospitalet (Copenhagen), and at the U.S. National Institute of Mental Health, have conducted studies of over four thousand adopted children to discover how the incidence of schizophrenia among them varies with the occurrence of schizophrenia in their natural parents and in their adopted parents. If, for example, the rate of schizophrenia among children born of schizophrenic parents but raised by adopted nonschizophrenic parents is high, then one has more reason to believe that the malady's origin has a genetic component.

Schulsinger and Welner of Denmark, in collaboration with Rosenthal, Wender, and Kety of the United States (Wender et al. 1974), obtained data that show that the incidence of schizophrenia among children born of schizophrenic parents and adopted by normal parents is notably higher than the incidence among children born of and adopted by normal parents. The implication is that a genetic component of schizophrenia is indeed plausible, though genetics may not be the only influence. They also found that the incidence of schizophrenia among children born of normal parents and reared by schizophrenic parents is no higher than the incidence of schizophrenia among children born of and adopted by normal parents. The authors infer that the data do not support the idea of intrafamilial influences on schizophrenia, but they do not discount the possibility that family influences were measured incompletely. Furthermore, their longitudinal data (Mednick, Schulsinger, and Garfinkel 1975) suggest that the factors that differentiate schizophrenic from nonschizophrenic adults include severe perinatal complications, early maternal separation, and childhood deviation in autonomic nervous system functioning.

This information is an elementary but important step in establishing the credibility of the idea that the origins of schizophrenia are at least partly genetic, and in directing attention to fertile areas of research. The latter include careful studies of the possible genetic mechanisms and of the role played by certain enzymes (for example) that may produce a predisposition toward schizophrenic behavior.

It is important for our purposes here to recognize that the findings could not have been obtained without longitudinal data on adopted children *and* their natural and adopted parents, obtained by linking records from the Danish State Archives of Adoption, the Institute of Human Genetics, the Central Population Register, and follow-up interviews. The ability to link records was vital.

LONGITUDINAL STUDY IN MANPOWER ECONOMICS

In human resources research, good evidence for the usefulness of longitudinal data has been scanty, in part because the relevant data have been in short supply. The recent build-up of longitudinal files has helped greatly to understand the data's benefits and limitations, however. Of particular interest are the National Longitudinal Surveys (NLS) of the U.S. labor market, begun in 1966 by Herbert S. Parnes (1975). The data are based on repeated surveys of a national probability sample of twenty thousand individuals in four labor-market strata: middle-aged men (45–59 years old at the beginning of the survey), women (30–44 in 1966), and young men and young women (14–24 in 1966). Resultant data are being updated periodically and, stripped of identifiers, are being made available to the community of manpower researchers. Aside from their obvious benefits for temporal description of the labor market, the data can be very informative on account of their longitudinal feature. Parnes maintains that:

Perhaps the single most important contribution of longitudinal data is that they facilitate the identification of causal relationships that cannot confidently be identified in any other way. Take, for example, the relationship between attitudes and behavior. In cross-sectional data, such relationships are ambiguous, since one cannot be certain whether the attitude produces or reflects the behavior. Does job dissatisfaction lead to turnover, or does an association between variables simply mean that individuals who quit jobs are likely to rationalize their behavior by reporting (retrospectively) that they were unhappy? When attitudes measured at one point in time can be related to *subsequent* behavior, such ambiguity disappears. The NLS data for middle-aged men have clearly demonstrated that the degree of job satisfaction *predicts* the likelihood of a voluntary job separation and that a commitment to work in general, as well as satisfaction with one's particular job, decreases the likelihood of early retirement.

The usefulness of longitudinal data in clarifying causal relationships is, of course, not confined to instances in which one of the variables is attitudinal. For example, finding that the receipt of training by middle-aged men between 1966 and 1971 was associated with a net earnings advantage in 1971 (controlling for such other factors as education, health, and region of residence) Avril Adams went on to demonstrate that the trainees-to-be had already enjoyed higher earnings in 1966 (again controlling for the same variables). Thus training was found to be a selective process, presumably attracting the more highly motivated or otherwise more productive individuals. To put the matter differently, some part of what would doubtless have been identified by a cross-sectional analysis as training's contribution to earnings was found to have reflected an incompletely specified model—i.e., the failure to control adequately for factors associated both with earning and the probability of receiving training. (Parnes 1975, pp. 246–47).

Professor Parnes is optimistic about the fruits of research based on his data files. We do not share that optimism, since longitudinal data alone are often insufficient for unequivocal judgments about the impact of manpower training programs. We do agree that such data are essential for better understanding and prediction of gross labor-market behavior, and for establishing the tenability of hypotheses that can later be verified using more controlled studies, and for prediction.

LONGITUDINAL STUDY OF CHILD DEVELOPMENT

Without the option of longitudinal study, pioneers in research on child development—Piaget, Bettelheim, Kagan, and others—would doubtless be in some other business. And we would know considerably less about the broad character of children's growth, the stages in development of motor and intellective skills, problem-solving ability, and the like. Not that the broad-brush picture is adequate: in fact, the desirable features of the small array of high-quality longitudinal studies at hand are being copied in newer ones, and improved, to answer more direct questions about growth.

One of the fundamental issues, for example, is whether the pattern of intellectual growth established during childhood is alterable and, if so, to what extent. The layman and some experts are often quite willing to provide an answer, based on experience with their own children and on assorted anecdotal evidence. But more verifiable data on the topic have been scarce. The question itself is important for humanistic and scientific reasons, and for developing adequate governmental programs for groups that have been deprived of early nutrition, education, and normal stimulation.

Very early studies and some contemporary ones fail to meet the need. Some physicians, for example, argue on the basis of short-term case studies, and on the basis of cross-sectional data, that the effects of early nutritional deprivation are inalterable, and that its impact on intelligence, for instance, is negative and permanent. Some psychologists and anthropologists argue on the basis of similar data for the conventional wisdom that the effects of early mother-child interaction and family state during the first three years of a child's life are, with a few exceptions, virtually inalterable. The more recent evidence bearing on the issue relies on careful case study of larger samples of individuals for the sake of detailed and more generalizable information on development, on longer-term longitudinal study for the sake of a more credible description of natural growth, and on deliberate attempts to eliminate deprivation through planned intervention and to establish the value of the intervention over the longer term.

Among the recent efforts along these lines, the Cali, Colombia, experiments are perhaps the most dramatic (McKay et al. 1978). In that study, needy children are randomly assigned to nutritional supplement programs, cultural enrichment programs, or both, in order to determine the nature and size of the effects of these programs. That is, the experiment helps us to understand whether and how well the programs work to alter, among three-, four-, and five-year-old children, what are often thought to be virtually unchangeable intellective characteristics. Their data suggest, contrary to some popular views, that nutritional supplements produce no major direct effects on children's cognitive performance or IQ, but they nonetheless affect growth and other physical characteristics. The results from five-year studies of the impact of cultural enrichment programs suggest not only that the effects of early deprivation can be reduced by intensive remedial action, but that the initial gap between the children in the program and better-fed, better-educated middle-class children can be reduced drastically if not eliminated. Similarly encouraging results have been obtained in longitudinal experiments on programs for infants and preschoolers in the United States (see Heber et al. 1972).

For the developmental researcher, the longitudinal study is a fundamental building block. The studies reviewed by Wall and Williams (1970) cover not only the types of growth discussed here, but also topics ranging from the formation of ideas about contracts, equity, charity, and so on, to the less abstract development of skills and habits essential for adult life. Empirical data, theory, and policy implications are summarized by Schaie (1963), Wohlwill (1969, 1970), Magnusson, Dunér, and Zetterblom (1975), and others. Coupled to efforts to remedy early deprivation and to evaluations of the impact of those remedial actions, the longitudinal approach becomes a vehicle for understanding better the adaptiveness of children, and their intellectual and physical elasticity, even when severely deprived at a very early age.

EDUCATION AND ITS IMPACT

For the sake of better allocation of scarce resources to education, it is reasonable to study how education affects achievement and subsequent earnings. We need to know what the most effective elements of the educational process are, how they work, and how they affect intellectual and economic development. The impact question is especially relevant to novel programs designed to overcome the disadvantages under which some social groups labor, that is, programs designed to introduce more equity into the social system through education.

Most research designed to get at these issues begins with cross-sectional surveys, and even a brief review of history shows that these have been useful despite the limitations of the cross-sectional approach. Abraham Flexner's 1910 report of his studies of medical schools in the United States relied solely on this approach and on Flexner's standards of performance to produce a major reformation in medical training. The Thorndike and Ayres studies of school record systems were similarly useful in moving schools toward better (though still imperfect) record-keeping practices (Goslin and Bordier 1969). The cross-sectional studies have been, and still are, enormously useful in this context, especially in clarifying the scope of educational problems, and especially where standards are fairly clear.

But the difficulty of making inferences, based on cross-sectional data, about the impact of education and about individual growth is no less severe in this sector than in the medical arena. It is difficult, often impossible, to disentangle the relative influence of background variables and of the school. It is not generally possible to describe growth and assay impact without at least some longitudinal data. The scientific and political traps here are exemplified by the current controversy in the United States over bussing students from the school district in which they live to another in the interest of fostering equitable, quality education. The policy analyst's position on bussing five years ago, based heavily on cross-sectional data, differs from the current position, based on new, longitudinal data and demonstration projects.

Better interpretation, inference, and prediction are conditional on better theories of social behavior and on the supporting data. As a consequence of the shortcomings of earlier data and theories, a number of longitudinal studies have been mounted to better understand the influence of education. We cannot summarize those here—there are far too many to do so adequately. So we content ourselves with examining a nice study by Fägerlind (1975).

This analysis of longitudinal data was designed to clarify polar views of the results of public investment in education. The first view, that the duration of educational experience has a major impact on earnings, has been taken by Paul Samuelson, the Nobel laureate. The second view, held by Christopher Jencks and others, is that the impact on earnings of education beyond the postsecondary level is marginal. The Fägerlind research managed to avoid the traps of relying on cross-sectional data and of short-term longitudinal study by considering individual growth over a thirty-year period. It is an efficient study of a well-defined social group insofar as it builds on survey data initially collected in 1930 on a subpopulation of children in Malmö. Economy and completeness of sampling were made possible by existing population registries. Accuracy and temporal relevance of data were enhanced by relying on archival records—military-selection test scores for men, tax registries on earnings of the respondent and the respondent's parents, and census records on demography, geographic and occupational mobility, etc. Fägerlind supplemented archival records with survey data collected during the 1940s, 1950s, 1960s, and early 1970s.

The product of this research is useful in shedding light on polar views: Fägerlind's data, of higher quality than those available to Jencks, support Samuelson's theory. It, like studies undertaken by Sewell, Hauser, and others (1975) in the United States, helps to specify the mechanism underlying education's impact on earnings and to unravel the competing influences on earnings, such as home and family. Finally, it has helped to establish the shortcomings of competing data and models. Quality of education, for example, has been ignored in many analyses. Fägerlind uncovers strong, plausible linkages between quality and earnings from age thirty onward.

Still, the longitudinal approach used here is only an interim step. It is naturally limited in the extent to which it can be applied in specific settings, particularly novel ones. More recent research, for example, stresses small longitudinal experiments, mounted alone or in conjunction with larger observational studies, to obtain better appraisals of local, innovative educational practices. Some, like the Heber et al. (1972) work, is dedicated to rectifying intellectual deprivation in early childhood. Others, like Middlestart (Yinger, Ikeda, and Laycock 1977), involve randomized tests of programs designed to improve the academic performance of adolescents who are economically deprived but show intellectual promise. Still other experiments, designed to improve medical school education, police and manpower training, and the like, follow participants over a two- or three-year period in the interest of obtaining less ambiguous information about the impact of expensive social programs (see Riecken et al. 1974).

Correlational Research: Definition, Justification, and Relevance to Record Linkage

Correlational research refers here to the process of establishing how two characteristics of an individual are related to one another. The average relation, for a large sample of individuals, may be represented in statistical form by a simple correlation coefficient, by a probability in an actuarial table, and so on. For example, to identify the relation between level of health status and level of physical activity during work, one might obtain measures of both variables from each member of a suitable sample of individuals, link the two elements of information on each individual, and then compute an index of the relation based on that linkage. The correlation may be of descriptive interest alone, in that it reflects the existence and strength of a relation between two variables. It may be more important to an individual, in that the correlation helps to predict future health status from current physical-exertion levels. Finally, such data make it possible to form tentative ideas about the biochemical mechanism by which exertion influences health status (or vice versa), that is, to build the theory necessary for the development of better control of health status. In principle, correlational investigation is a general activity of which longitudinal research is an important subclass. Both types of research usually require some form of record linkage to sustain statistical analysis. They are discussed separately here on account of traditional differences in the emphasis of each type of research.

Correlational research often requires that the contents of records maintained by independent archives be linked. The special functions of linkage vary considerably, but most can be grouped into one of the following categories adapted from Steinberg and Pritzker (1969) and others:

- to assess and improve the quality of available data from any source

- to reduce costs, duplication of effort, and respondent burden in surveys

- to clarify and enrich the data base for applied social research and policy analysis.

The illustrations of the benefits and limitations of linkage are presented below using this taxonomy.

ASSESSING THE QUALITY OF DATA AND IMPROVING THE QUALITY OF DATA ANALYSIS

Response validity refers to the association between an individual's response to inquiry under one set of conditions and his response to inquiry under a second set of conditions that are thought to facilitate near-perfect reporting. Most such studies involve some form of record linkage. Census data on income of a sample of identifiable respondents may be linked to Internal Revenue Service reports, for example, to assay the adequacy of the census interview process. Similarly, data from interviews made on one occasion under normal conditions may be linked to later, more intensive, interviews to gauge the adequacy of the "normal" interview conditions. Some mechanism for linkage is critical for computing quantitative indices of average agreement between the two types of reports.

Without some empirical basis for judging the credibility of the data, it is impossible to lend any meaning to statistical analysis, unless, of course, one is willing to cover the whole matter with a secular act of faith. The absence of validity statistics is crippling in attempts to interpret descriptive statistics and to use them to monitor and evaluate social programs. Errors in reporting will usually make it more difficult to detect changes in human status, and in situations where data imperfections go unrecognized, data analysis may result in wildly inaccurate conclusions.

Examples from statistical policy research. Many of the validity studies in the United States have been designed to furnish sufficient evidence to support an administrative decision about whether or not to continue a particular type of inquiry.

In health survey research, illustrations of the use of record linkage are easy to find (Reeder et al. 1976). The deficiencies in physicians' records, for example, have been examined by matching record content with data from interviews with patients. Distortions in reports made by physicians to their own medical societies have been investigated by linking those reports with intensive interviews subsequently conducted with the physicians themselves. Methods of interview designed to minimize embarrassment in health-related surveys have been tested and evaluated using individuals' hospital records as the standard for accuracy. Surveys of health-services utilization, necessary for planning such services at the national level, have been validated using side studies that link individual responses to records maintained by providers and third-party payers.

Analogous examples appear in manpower research. For example, to appraise the validity of self-reported "occupation five years ago," a question that has appeared in many cross-sectional manpower surveys, the U.S. Census Bureau in 1968 conducted tests on 2,800 households for which 1963 data on actual occupation were available. Despite the use of a variety of methods to elicit the retrospective report, the differences between retrospective report and actual status were in the range 23–28 percent (Jabine and Rothwell 1970). The linkage here, between 1963 archival records and the 1968 survey, was essential in establishing the validity rate and the pattern of invalidity. And the statistics themselves influenced the Census Bureau's decision to reduce drastically the use of the retrospective question in its own surveys, and to routinize the correction of other survey researchers' occupational-mobility statistics.

Housing statistics are no more immune to biasing influences, and in some cases, intensive reinterviews are necessary to determine the validity of the initial interviews. For example, it is not unreasonable to expect that interviewers will vary notably in their ability to rate quality of housing. In testing various methods for increasing the accuracy of the rating, the U.S. Department of Housing and Urban Development and the Census Bureau found, using reinterviews as a standard, that no particular method of interview classification yielded ratings at a reasonable validity level. As a consequence, the rating scheme was dropped entirely in the 1960 census. Instead, crude indicators of quality (cooking facility, indoor toilet, etc.) were included in the enumerator's protocol. Again, neither the collection of validity statistics nor the subsequent administrative actions would have been possible without a mechanism for linking initial enumerator reports with more expert reinterviews (Young, Selove, & Koons, 1966).

In estimating undercounts in the census of 1960, Marks and Waksberg (1966) report both notable benefits and negligible benefits in using archival records. The use of 1950 census records, hospital records of birth in 1950–60, records from intermediate census research, and records from the U.S. Immigration Service for special subsamples yield useful and credible evidence for underenumeration of 2.6 to 4.7 percent in the 1960 census. Similarly, for special subgroups, undercount estimates were computed. Lists of college students were obtained from colleges to estimate undercounts in the enumerated count of 2.5 to 2.7 percent; social security addresses were used in estimating a 5.1 to 5.7 percent undercount in beneficiaries in the 1960 census. On the other hand, matching of census rolls against lists of relatively inaccessible individuals—lists of welfare recipients, postal service listings—"provide no special encouragement for use of matching special lists as a coverage improvement program." Horvitz (1966) conducted similar studies in rural areas, which suggested that 20 to 25 percent underreports in death rates and 15 to 20 percent underreports of birth rates are not unusual when hospital and state medical records are used as a standard.

These examples illustrate how validity statistics, generated through record linkage, can help to delimit the credibility of social survey statistics and can serve as a basis for making decisions about the conduct of a survey effort. The practice of conducting side studies based on limited record linkage is practically nonexistent in commercial survey efforts. It is, however, typical in other sectors and is increasing, judging from the bibliographies on the topic (notably Scheuren and Colvey 1975), new reporting systems such as *Studies from Interagency Data Linkage* that describe the products of the work, and other evidence.

Examples from program evaluations. Imperfections in either social survey data or administrative records are difficult to characterize without a planned investigation. In the worst cases, the imperfections will help produce statistical artifacts that falsely make programs appear harmful. Estimates of validity, whether based on record linkage or not, are often crucial for eliminating the problems.

More specifically, one of the chronic problems encountered in the United States has been the production of biased estimates of program effects under some special but common conditions. Conventional statistical techniques, such as regression analysis, covariance analysis, and matching, when applied to the fallible data obtained in some observational evaluations, can yield biased estimates of program effects, in part because imperfect measurement goes unrecognized. Consider, for example, the Westinghouse-Ohio evaluations of "Headstart," a preschool program for the economically deprived. The initial evaluation relied on a textbook application of covariance analysis of survey data to explain how children's verbal ability varies as a function of demographic characteristics of the children and their families, and other variables. The estimates of the impact of Headstart summer programs were negative, implying that the program had a harmful effect. Secondary analysis of the same data suggests that if one adjusts the conventional analysis so as to take into account imperfect measurement, the program's effect is negligible and perhaps even slightly positive (Magidson 1977). Similar problems have been uncovered in evaluating manpower training programs (Director 1974), in estimating the impact of special medical regimens (James 1973), and elsewhere (Campbell and Erlebacher 1970).

To summarize, measures of social, psychological, medical, or economic behavior are usually imperfect and if the imperfections go unrecognized, statistical analysis of the impact of ameliorative programs will be insensitive at best, misleading at worst. Statistics bearing on the validity and reliability of response are necessary for rational adjustment of conventional statistical analyses so as to reduce bias in estimates of program effect. Record linkage is often, though not always, necessary to produce the necessary information on the validity of the observations.

The view that administrative records ought to serve as the standard against which survey records are judged is, at times, plainly unjustified. Administrative records are tied to administrative action, and for that reason are normally susceptible to a variety of biases and sources of error that do not affect survey data. One of several ways to appraise the credibility of statistics based on those records is through specially designed surveys.

Prior to 1910, for example, studies by the noted educational researcher E. L. Thorndike on the adequacy of school records led to major reforms in school record-keeping practices. Those studies relied partly on record linkage to furnish evidence concerning deficiencies in existing record systems (Goslin and Bordier 1969). Later studies, conducted by economists, contributed to what we now know about needs for record accuracy, accessibility, and adequacy in understanding the power of public utilities. More recently, Campbell (1975) and others have tried to describe more fully the reasons for corruption of administrative records and to develop some crude theory to account for the phenomenon. Most of the theory building depends in one way or another on the conduct of surveys to appraise the quality of an archive's contents. The U.S. Army reporting system on drug abuse, for example, was assessed during the early 1970s, using an experimental interview method that generally yields less distorted information on actual abuse by identified individuals (see chapter 6). The debatable quality of the criminal records maintained by the police has led to victimization surveys in Britain and in the United States to determine the nature and incidence of unreported crime, the elasticity in police definitions of crime, and so on. These more recent examples do not depend on record linkage to make their point. But whether a scientific survey can be executed to verify the quality of an archive record system depends heavily on administrative endorsement of the idea that multiple indicators of a social trait or process are desirable. As the practice of conducting this kind of study increases, the need for more depth of inquiry and, subsequently, for linkages between archive record and survey record will undoubtedly increase. It is often possible to eliminate confidentiality-related problems in this context by using the insulated data bank strategy described in chapter 4.

REDUCING COSTS, DUPLICATION OF EFFORT, AND RESPONDENT BURDEN

Partial duplication of a data-collection effort by independent agencies can be justified on several grounds. Independent archives that maintain some overlapping information, for example, may be warranted by legislation that requires independent collection and maintenance of the data. They may be better justified as a device for periodic cross validation of the contents of files. Nonetheless, exact or nearly exact duplication may be costly to the data-collection agencies, and will be burdensome to the respondents who invest their time in supplying the information to each agency.

Although existing archival records have not often been used as a basis for evaluating the impact of experimental social programs, they do have some promise in this regard. The argument that archive records can be used to mount more economical and more informative evaluations of social programs has been advanced by the Committee on Federal Program Evaluation of the National Academy of Sciences. We quote verbatim from their report.

Once the major administrative archives of government, insurance companies, hospitals, etc., are organized and staffed for such research, the amount of interpretable outcome data on ameliorative programs can be increased ten-fold. For example, Fischer (1972) reports on the use of income tax data in a followup on the effectiveness of manpower training programs. While these data are not perfect or complete for the evaluation of such a training program, they are highly relevant. Claims on unemployment compensation and welfare payments would also be relevant. Cost is an important advantage. Using a different approach, Heller (1972) reports retrieval costs of $1 per person for a study of several thousand trainees. Even if $10 were more realistic, these costs are to be compared with costs of $100 or more per interview in individual followup interviews with ex-trainees. Rate of retrieval is another potential advantage. Followup interviews in urban manpower training programs have failed to locate as many as 50% of the population, and 30% loss rates would be common. Differential loss rates for experimental and control groups are also common, with the control groups less motivated to continue. In the New Jersey Negative Income Tax Experiment, over three years, 25.3% of the controls were lost, compared with a loss of only 6.5% of those in the most remunerative experimental condition. While retrieval rates overall might be no higher for withholding tax records, the differential bias in cooperation would probably be avoided, and the absence of data could be interpreted, with caution, as the absence of such earnings. (Campbell et al. 1975, p. 12)

It does not take much imagination to see how relying on existing archives can reduce the expense of a program evaluation. It is quite another matter to employ such records creatively in difficult research settings. One of the more clever applications of archival data stems from an effort by Robertson and others (1972) to evaluate the impact of television messages that encourage drivers to wear their seat belts. In some recent tests, four types of television messages were broadcast over four television cables, each cable serving a unique set of households within a large region. The research objective was to determine which broadcast fostered the highest rate of seat belt use. To evaluate use, the researchers first observed whether or not drivers in the region wore seat belts as they stopped for lights at randomly selected intersections. To link actual use with area of residence, that is, with television message type, some mechanism for identifying each driver's residence was necessary. Rather than question each driver, the researchers merely recorded automobile license numbers and employed State Motor Vehicle archives to identify the driver's area of residence. Once each driver's residence and seat belt use were linked, it was an easy matter to compare the crude effects of alternative television messages on use.

Some examples of the savings engendered by temporary and limited linkage of governmental records have been documented by Hansen and Hargis (1966). In these cases, a sample of records maintained independently by the U.S. Census Bureau, the Internal Revenue Service, and the Social Security Administration was linked to determine how costs of surveys might be reduced.

Prior to 1954, for example, the Economic Census of manufacturing, retail, and other industries was conducted by field interview survey with some larger firms canvassed by mail. In the interest of reducing costs markedly, mail survey was considered as an alternative to expensive field interview surveys. At that time, the Census had no mechanism for construction and maintenance of up-to-date mailing lists, however. Such mailing lists, based on payroll tax records, were maintained by Internal Revenue Service and Social Security Administration files and with some modification, the basic lists were checked for validity and then adopted by the Census Bureau as a basis for the mail survey in the Economic Census. To obtain data on the retail industry, conventional Internal Revenue Service forms were modified slightly, making it possible to eliminate any additional mail or interview surveys of this industry by the Census Bureau. More than $6 million was saved by employing this last strategy. Similar savings were said to have been realized in the 1967 Economic Census, where, for example, modifications to Internal Revenue Service schedules permitted the use of these forms to elicit necessary information, and small direct-interview samples were adjoined to this effort to obtain necessary data on products, merchandise lines, and so forth. Finally, "administrative records from the Social Security Administration and from the Census have been used to construct mailing and sampling lists economically for Bureau data-collection programs and to avoid duplicating the collection of information."

CLARIFYING AND ENRICHING STATISTICAL DATA FOR POLICY ANALYSIS AND APPLIED SOCIAL RESEARCH

By *clarifying data,* we mean obtaining a better understanding of the meaning, nature, and limitations of a particular social statistic.[6] "Employment rate," for example, is a deceptively simple label for a complex phenomenon. Clarification often implies an additional objective, that of enriching the data resource with respect to the number and kind of data archived, for the sake of higher-quality analysis. Improving the interpretability of a data set can be accomplished in a variety of ways, such as linking multiple data sources. Note, however, that linkage of *all* individual records may not be essential; linking a (random) sample of records is often sufficient for the analyst's purposes.

To be concrete, consider that in the United States, the Internal Revenue Service, the Social Security Administration, and the Census Bureau each independently collect data from citizens on annual income. The separation of effort is related to differences in each agency's functions. Two of the Social Security Administration's primary missions, for example, are understanding income redistribution in the present and estimating the impact of redistribution policy in the future. Most U.S. citizens are required to pay a social security tax based in part on gross income, but federal employees often do not choose to enroll in the national social security plan, and so their incomes are not on file in SSA record systems. The Internal Revenue Service directs its attention to a different but overlapping universe, the tax-paying public; it has a different function, taxation; and it defines income differently, notably in terms of "taxable income." The U.S. Census Bureau's definition of income differs from the other agencies' because its function is unique—statistical description of the state of the population—and because there are severe limitations on the way in which census data can be collected—through self-reports in a brief interview or a brief questionnaire.

The result of these differences in definition of income, target population, and data function is that the relationships among the various sets of data on "income" have not been well understood. The economist using one source of data to predict the impact of a new health insurance policy might well develop projections that differ remarkably from projections made by an economist using another source of very similar information. The discrepancy among sources is marked in particular cases, and it is reasonable to use record linkage to bring some order out of this confusion.

A major federal effort to reconcile conceptual differences among record contents has been mounted jointly by the U.S. Census Bureau, the Social Security Administration, and the Internal Revenue Service. The relevant data base includes the Census Bureau's 1973 Current

Population Survey and administrative records from IRS and SSA files. The reconciliation has three immediate purposes: to understand the relationships among ostensibly identical categories of information maintained by each agency, to input resultant data into the SSA simulation models of the tax transfer system, and to assess relative biases in Census Bureau statistics. The reconciliation involves linking a strategic sample of records on individuals from the various sources, not linkage of the entire data bases. Preliminary results of the study reported by Herriott and Spiers (1975) suggest that Census Bureau statistics on income are quite accurate for salaried employees and regular wage earners; the overlap between Census reports contents is about 96 percent. Income reports of the self-employed show somewhat less accuracy (90 percent agreement between the Census Bureau and IRS); reports of interest and dividends made to the Bureau are considerably less reliable (less than 80 percent agreement) for most respondent groups, using IRS as a standard.

As a result of such research, the models of economic systems employed by the U.S. Census Bureau and by the Social Security Administration can be improved when differences in reporting rates based on IRS data are recognized. The differential predictability of male and female incomes becomes more interpretable with evidence on differential accuracy in reporting such income to Census Bureau interviewers. The estimates of the impact of training on income become more reliable when corrected for base-rate errors in reporting that income. And so on.

Similar benefits accrue from investigations of the differences in count data as a function of institutional source. A study by Cobleigh and Alvey (1974), for example, shows that differences in legally defined coverage of the population by the Census Bureau and by SSA produce a universe that is about 94 percent of the SSA taxable earner's listings. Given a comparable universe, reports of average annual earnings from the two sources are in remarkable agreement except for very low and very high income groups. In the very low categories, SSA data show about 20 percent more wage earners than do the Census Bureau data; in the high-income categories, however, the Census Bureau counts are 10–20 percent higher than Social Security reports. These latter differences are attributed by the authors to definitional differences and reporting irregularities, including self-employment earnings not reportable to SSA, rounding error in self-reports to the Census Bureau, late reporting to SSA, and other factors. The Cobleigh-Alvey paper also abstracts a sizable number of reports on record-linkage studies. See the *Proceedings of the American Statistical Association: Social Statistics Section* (1975) for more recent examples of linkages of sample data for scientific purposes.

Another type of enrichment involves the use of archive records for specialized research in which the record, though not disclosable by law or custom to the social scientist, is necessary for attaining research goals. Surrogates for the record may be sought, of course, but in the absence of any suitable substitute, it is often possible to capitalize on restricted-access records without claiming special privileges. For example, one of the peculiar diversions of our society involves the zealous efforts of the Internal Revenue Service to extract more taxes from citizens and the citizens' spirited efforts to pay less. In an effort to clarify the conditions under which taxpayers will fulfill their responsibility with more accuracy, and perhaps less dissatisfaction, Schwartz and Orleans (1967) mounted some experimental tests of those conditions to compare relative rates of tax payment for a particular category of income. Taxpayers were assigned randomly to one of three advertising strategies, the strategies differing in respect to their emphasis in justifying payment of taxes. The first condition relied heavily on appeals to moral conscience, the second on threats of punitive legal action, and the third on threats of social embarrassment (tax evasion being a matter for public legal action). The objective of the experiments was to determine which type of appeal yields a higher rate of reporting income. To do so credibly required that condition or form of appeal be linked with the individual's subsequent reports of income to the Internal Revenue Service. In order to link the two kinds of records (the researcher's record of condition and the IRS record of income) *without* breaching IRS rules on disclosure of records (which are confidential by law) and the researchers' rules concerning disclosure of their own records, a mutually insulated file approach (described in chapter 4) was used. (The results of the experiment are interesting. Middle-income respondents react most to the threats of legal action; low-income groups respond most to appeals to moral conscience; high-income groups were most affected by threats of social embarrassment.)

The case for merging separate data sets into a permanent consolidated pool of data is based on the assumption that the pooled data will be a more informative basis for social research than separate files. Examples of these integrated archives are few, however, because the difficulty of matching records, differences in terminology, and differences in sample design and data collection procedures have inhibited many researchers from consolidating files. Moreover, it is difficult to anticipate the usefulness of linked files without actually trying out the idea on a small sample of records. Among the large-scale examples, however, the Wisconsin Assets and Income Studies Archive (Bauman, David, and Miller 1970) illustrates what can be accomplished. Researchers appraise the effects of tax-averaging proposals, changing income after retirement, capital gains income, and so on by simulating changes in tax laws, using the linked records as the raw material for analysis. To permit this research, records from the Internal Revenue Service, the Wisconsin tax department, and the Social Security Administration are combined in a file, without jeopardizing the privacy of the individuals on whom records are kept. The products of the research are predictions about the importance of changes in tax laws on individual income, attenuating the need to rely solely on anecdotal case study, intuition, and fragmented data as a basis for legislation in the tax area.

The more elaborate and more sensitive merged systems are found in the medical arena. Most involve both administrative and research information, and because they are recent systems, the benefits of pooling both kinds of data are not yet clear. Nonetheless, good reviews of the early products of such work are available for social medicine, community health services systems, and the like (e.g., Acheson 1967). Laska and Bank's (1975) description of the Rockland Institute's psychiatric information system is one of the best-documented of its kind. There is a strong emphasis on legislative and technical safeguards for assuring the confidentiality of the records. There is a conscientious product orientation: aside from providing common demographic information, the system facilitates quality control over treatment, time series analyses of treatment effects, and projective studies of the incidence and development of mental illness, and permits some controlled studies of the effectiveness of treatment. Perhaps most importantly, the system can be coupled neatly to experimental tests of alternative treatments to better understand whether and how well the treatments work (Endicott and Spitzer 1975).

Concluding Observations

This has been an idiosyncratic effort to illustrate how some research projects depend on the availability of a mechanism for tracking individuals. The reasons for presenting the evidence are pragmatic. There is some need, judging by the demands of the nonscientist, to better justify the conduct of research that normally requires respondent identification. That the ability to track members of a sample over time or to link relevant information from different sources can yield a useful statistical product ought to be clear. The illustrations span a variety of disciplines, and although the products may seem easier to evaluate in the medical sciences, they are no less important for the more youthful social sciences. The average statistical relation, developed in a longitudinal research effort, is, as we have said, useful for description at least. And it is often essential for understanding change in human behavior, for planning and evaluating social programs, for building theory and models of social processes. Similarly, efforts to link samples of records across archives can be justified on the grounds of economy and the need to appraise and improve the quality of administrative or scientific data.

None of this should be taken to imply that the approaches engender no cost to the individual. To the extent that the identified respondent discloses information about himself or herself, the disclosure may be regarded, at least in principle, as a depreciation of the individual's privacy. That depreciation may be quite trivial in the sense that the information disclosed is innocuous; or it may be notable, as in longitudinal studies of mental health. Similarly, if in linking records from different archives, the linkage is based on clear identification in each record, privacy may be degraded here also.

For some studies, perhaps the majority, the costs to respondents will be negligible by their own standards, and the research product will have some obvious social and scientific merit. For these, mechanisms that reduce an already low depreciation of privacy may not be particularly useful. But other devices, designed to assure that the data remain confidential once they are given to the researcher, can be employed profitably. The studies of more controversial or more sensitive topics demand much more attention to balancing the costs to the individual and the benefits of research. It is for these cases that the procedural, statistical, and other devices described in later chapters may be particularly appropriate.

None of our remarks should be taken to mean that longitudinal research or the deliberate study of the union of data sets will always be productive. It is clear, for example, that longitudinal data alone will sometimes be insufficient for science, social policy, or social programs. The longitudinal approach must often be complemented by experiments to obtain more than a very tentative explanation of whether a program works. And certainly, even some very expensive longitudinal work will result in no more than a small increment to social theory, just as such contributions will often be small in the natural sciences and medicine.

Similar qualifiers must be adjoined to efforts to link records from different archives. Though the benefits of some record linkages may be obvious, they are more often subtle and at times undetectable. We know that archival records are sometimes quite unexpectedly subject to distortion and error, and documentation of that error is often difficult to obtain or understand (see Committee on Government Operations 1966, Lauren 1970, and Grubert 1971). Nonetheless, with a conscientious accounting of our experience in conducting such research, we can begin to delimit the endeavors with higher potential payoffs. At the very least we can, by conducting limited-scale studies of the kind described here, enlarge the pool of social data—in nature, quality, and relevance—so that their benefits can be appraised without intolerable compromises of individual privacy.

The material just presented ignores controversial topics of research. We have put these aside temporarily in the interest of reviewing some research products stripped of unnecessary argument. More controversial projects are, in fact, considered in each of the following chapters, along with mechanisms that can help to eliminate the privacy-related problems they engender. The actual use of the products of the research has also been treated lightly, and here we are deferential. Determining the extent of utilization of social statistics or of the products of social research is a difficult undertaking. We are content to recommend other reports, notably the Caplan et al. (1975) innovative work on the use of social research products in government, and Hauser's (1975) documentary on the use of social statistics.

Notes

1. The astute politician finds it tempting to offer advice under these circumstances, especially if innocence can be sustained by not reading about statistics. Kerstin Anér, a Swedish parliamentarian, advised a group of statisticians and social scientists to emulate Carlos Castenada in order to learn about human behavior. A Swedish colleague, less awed by the politician than by the advice, immediately set about sending her recipes for making magic mushrooms more palatable. In the United States, a former Secretary of Health, Education and Welfare, Forrest D. Matthews publicly advised researchers on one occasion to write more poetry instead of doing research. Matthews was perhaps much affected by the demands of his job.

2. We are indebted to the Swedish Council on Social Science Research for the opportunity to discuss earlier versions of this material at the conferences on Personal Integrity and Data Protection Research. The meetings were held at Hasselby Slott, Stockholm, in March 1976. The proceedings have been edited by Tore Dalenius and Anders Klevmarken (1976).

3. The heated arguments over the theoretical implications of such data are taken up by Horn and Donaldson (1976) and in a rejoinder by Baltes and Schaie (1976).

4. Cohort effects have been recognized formally by commercial market researchers as an important variable in predicting and explaining the demand for certain consumer goods. Systematic cohort variation in what is regarded as a luxury item, for example, has some important implications for planning the allocation of an industry's manufacturing resources (see *Business Week,* 12 January 1976, pp. 74–78).

5. Some comprehensive reviews of the products of specialized longitudinal research in medicine are available. They include DeBakey and Beebe's (1962) description of the long-term Medical Follow-up Studies on U.S. Military Veterans, and an updated report on that research by the National Research Council's Medical Follow-up Agency (1976), the Oxford Medical Record Linkage Projects (Acheson 1967), and others.

6. The linkage of data for the sake of improving statistical quality is not a new enterprise, of course. Davis (1971) reminds us that in the 1890 census, for example, interviewers were told to verify the causes of deaths reported by citizens in response to mortality questions by interviewing the attending physician.

On the Need to Assure

Confidentiality and on Privacy

Get your facts first and then you can distort 'em as much as you please.

MARK TWAIN

Is a promise of confidentiality necessary? Sufficient? The questions may strike some readers as a bit rhetorical, even specious. Nonetheless, we regard hard answers to them as important for several reasons. The first is pragmatic and tied to a contemporary research issue: evidence on the need for a promise of confidentiality must be uncovered to argue effectively for statutory testimonial privilege for social scientists.[1] Without an evidentiary answer to the questions, it is difficult to show the need for the privilege, much less to make a case for its constitutionality. Similarly, evidence bearing on the need must be developed to resist, legally and effectively, the sporadic attempts by governmental agencies, including the courts, to appropriate research records on identifiable individuals. Unless there is some evidence to show why information elicited under a promise of confidentiality should not be subpoenaed, it can be, and occasionally will be, subpoenaed. Finally, it is no less important that we understand how various publics regard the social scientist's assurance of confidentiality. This has implications for improving research design and for accommodating both legitimate and irrelevant criticism of the conduct of research.

Only one frame of reference is used here in attempting to answer the questions. It is an empirical one, based on evidence about the

*This chapter is based on background material prepared by the first author for the National Academy of Sciences Panel on Privacy and Confidentiality, a subcommittee of the NAS Committee on Federal Statistics, and for the American Psychological Association's Task Force on Privacy.

contention that a promise of confidentiality is often essential to foster cooperation in social research. By *cooperation* we mean that individuals in a target sample not only respond to inquiry but also respond truthfully. The validity of sampling, that is, the match between target sample and actual sample, and the validity of response are fundamental for quality in research. The relevant evidence is taken from case studies, from experimental tests of methods for assuring respondents of confidentiality, and from comparative surveys. They are discussed in the next three sections of this chapter. The red herrings fetched up from these waters are discussed in the last section.

Episodic Disruption: Its Character and Consequences

The first four cases described below illustrate how social research can be disrupted when an assurance of confidentiality, though offered, is neither persuasive nor salient enough to satisfy some influential members of a target population. The cases include the American Council on Education (ACE) Study of Campus Unrest, research on the development of children in Project Talent and Project Scope, research on aggression in children conducted by the Rip Van Winkle Foundation, and finally, Project Metropolitan undertaken in Sweden, Norway, and Denmark. The justification for assurance should also be evident when a promise of confidentiality is made, then breached or thought to be breached by the individuals to whom the promise was made. Several such incidents are also described briefly below: the Negative Income Tax Experiment, the Woodlawn Project, and the "Springdale Case." Two additional cases are examined because they differ notably from these but make roughly the same point. They include the *Merriken* v. *Cressman* case and an incident involving the *National Observer* newspaper.

It is important to recognize that these illustrations, like any other case-study material, are complicated by matters unrelated to the need for individual privacy, for example, some group's antipathy toward social research in general. Competing influences make it difficult to determine exactly how much importance a respondent may attach to a promise of confidentiality, and these make it difficult to interpret each case. One's ability to generalize is also limited, as in all such cases, by the unique circumstances of the illustration.

Consider first the American Council on Education's study of student protests during the 1960s. The study was designed to examine the incidence and severity of student protests, to identify typical characteristics of opposing groups, and to establish how campus disruptions evolve. Students and faculty were concerned that their responses to inquiries about their protest behavior remain confidential and not be used in reprisals against individual protestors. On some campuses, including Northwestern University's, the failure to make clear the promise of confidentiality and other problems led to the dissolution of efforts to collect data (Boruch 1971a; Westin et al. 1972). Demands for more persuasive assurance of confidentiality for respondents were made by the National Student Association, the American Civil Liberties Union, staff of the U.S. Office of Education, and others interested in the conduct of the research. Formal conferences among these groups and the research staff were convened to reiterate assurances that data would remain confidential, to show how that assurance would be met in practice (see Astin and Boruch 1970; Walsh 1969b), and to discuss unrelated but debatable issues. The latter concerned the idea that the National Institute of Mental Health's sponsoring the study put student activism in a bad light by implying that student activists have something wrong with their mental health. There were also claims that the privacy of a group, student activists, was being abridged by the study, and that there was no justification for the study as designed. Errors of fact were common in the arguments of opponents as well as advocates of the study; for example, there were allegations that there was no assurance of confidentiality (there was), that the American Council on Education was a government organization (it is not), that data collected permitted near-perfect prediction of who would or would not engage in campus protests in the future (outlandish).

Similar disruption of educational research has occurred in less controversial studies. For example, in Project Scope's four-state research on career development of high school students, a small but notable number of school districts did not participate, despite assurances that research records on individual students would remain confidential. The effects of this partial degradation of the target sample are not clear. Nor was the level of belief in the assurance, or the level of influence exerted by the assurance, clear. In this study, as well as other large-scale studies, the demands for confidentiality are tangled with related issues, such as the privacy of students and informed consent, and with unrelated issues, such as the validity of standardized achievement tests for minority-group members. Errors were made by program critics—for example, they alleged erroneously that sex-related questions were being asked. Those errors were magnified by press coverage and they were compounded by poorly informed researchers who attempted to counter the false allegations. Finally, this case illustrates that a small cluster of individuals of almost any political persuasion can disrupt research on confidentiality-related grounds. In this instance, "whereas some groups may have believed that Scope computers were connected to the CIA, others seemed convinced that they were connected with the Kremlin" (Tillery 1967, p. 14).

Project Talent, a national effort to document and predict the intellectual development of youth, was afflicted by similar problems during the early 1960s. In Houston, Texas, for example, a small but vocal group found some research questions objectionable and made their objections known to school trustees who knew little about the conduct of the study in their own school districts. Again, a promise of confidentiality, though apparently sufficient for most of the target population, failed to satisfy some groups. There were also other, more important matters at issue, notably parental consent for students' responding to a set of sociopsychological tests grafted by local psychologists onto the regular Talent questionnaires. The episode resulted in the destruction of the answer sheets to the offensive tests (Nettler 1959). Similar incidents have occurred elsewhere (Berdie 1965).

In a Rip Van Winkle Foundation study of the development of aggression in children, "the matters of confidentiality, invasion of privacy, lack of parental permission, etc. were all brought up" (Eron and Walder 1961, p. 237). There were vague and erroneous charges that questions about sexual behavior were being asked, when in fact such questions were neither asked nor included in the research plan; the charges were dramatically repeated in the press. Apparently the disruption of the study did not result in any great loss of data or of rapport with parents and children in the target population. Eron and Walder attributed the low level of disruption to the fact that objections were made during the terminal stages of the research and strong efforts were made by the researchers to assure that parents understood the project.

Oyen's examination of the controversy over the Metropolitan study in Oslo in 1964 is one of the best of its kind and illustrates some remarkable parallels with similar episodes in the United States (Oyen 1965, 1966, 1976). In a cooperative longitudinal study involving Norway, Denmark, and Sweden, a large sample of children was to be tracked from age eleven onwards to discover how their views of social class developed and changed, how their views influenced their vocational choice and their occupational mobility, and how their developing views were linked to their achievement. Despite the approval of the Oslo school board and assurances that the data would be used only for research purposes, protests against the study were aired by the editors of *Aftenposten* and other conservative newspapers, over the radio, and in the Norwegian parliament. About 10 percent of the children's parents put their complaints into writing. The project was directed by sociologists, and that discipline drew fire not only for their label—sociologist, evidently, being easily confused with socialist—but for their survey methods as well. "While several critics made claims about the evils of sociology, some felt that the proposed research reminded them too much of psychology and thus fired their charges at the psychologists." Here, as in other incidents, media coverage magnified errors: references were made to Kinsey's studies, when the Metropolitan Project involved no questions about sexual behavior; provocative references were made to "human experimentation," when in fact the goal was merely to survey students. The more direct claims that privacy was being invaded, that the research itself harmed the target population, and that the research data would be misused by corrupt politicians or sociologists were, in Oyen's judgment, part of a general public concern about the legitimacy of sociological research. The study was aborted in Norway, but continues in Denmark and Sweden with over twenty thousand participants (Magnusson et al. 1975, Janson 1975).

In none of the cases just described was there any documented breach of a promise of confidentiality to respondents. And it is doubtful that a major breach—a researcher's disclosure of identifiable records—could have occurred without considerable publicity. But, though rare, breaches do occur, and the disruptive consequences of a real or imagined breach serve as additional evidence for the contention that a promise of confidentiality is warranted. The important problems have stemmed from conflicts among government agencies and conflicts between government agencies and social researchers. Here, as in the earlier cases, simultaneous arguments over related and unrelated issues complicate the evidence.

The New Jersey Negative Income Tax Experiment (Kershaw and Small 1972) is a case in point. Individual records, containing identification and limited information, were released on fewer than thirty-five research respondents in Mercer County, and this led to subsequent subpoena of the complete records, which contained research-related material elicited under a promise of confidentiality. Disclosures at the first site, made of fourteen records during a grand jury investigation of alleged fraud and during congressional hearings on the experiment, apparently were of little consequence. According to David Kershaw, director of the field operations, there were no cases of respondent loss directly traceable to the investigation. The release of the identities of eighteen families participating in the experiment by a welfare officer in a second site, Passaic County, however, did "upset a number of respondents," who then refused to continue to participate. Kershaw points out a rather important aspect of this case: losses were minimized, in part, because participants simply ignored or did not care about the publicity given to these episodes, perhaps because they regularly ignore news reports of any kind. Another aspect of this case was the exploitation of the grand jury investigation by congressional opponents of income subsidy programs to derogate the quality of the research and so undermine the credibility of research findings (see Kershaw and Small 1972; Boeckman 1976).

The second pertinent case of interest involved the Woodlawn Project, a government-supported community action program. Youth gang structure was used as a base for creating a community service organization, and gang members were offered the opportunity to participate in a related manpower training program. No explicit promise was made initially to gang members from whom information was elicited, and no formal demands were articulated initially by respondents. The first threat of disclosure was induced by congressional subcommittees' subpoena of all records pertaining to the project. The "administrative and fiscal documents" were shown to an investigatory agent and copied. A second subpoena demanded researcher records of attendance at manpower training sessions and related observational records. According to Dr. Irving Spergel, director of the study, "the records taken were statistical observation forms containing data on attendance and comments about general program activity," *not* records of particular identified individuals. Though individually identified records were not at issue, the first subpoena was followed by increased difficulty in eliciting further information from respondents. The second subpoena made it impossible to continue the research, for both trainees and employers of trainees expressed concern over public access to research data on identified individuals. Consequently, the principal investigator laid plans for terminating his research on the program. The training program itself, including the evaluation, was terminated before completion, however, by the federal agency that had supported it. This case, like others, is complicated by factors other than privacy or confidentiality, concerns that also helped to produce disruption of research. Those factors included errors made by journalists and by Congressmen in reporting details about the conduct of the project, and the program's status as a political football (Spergel 1969; Walsh 1969b).

A third case of disclosure, which deviates a bit from the pattern suggested by the two preceding ones, is described by Katz, Capron, and Glass (1972). The incident involved a suburban community, the target of anthropological research on town government processes, whose members were promised anonymity by the original researchers. One researcher, evidently not directly associated with the original research team or with the assurance of confidentiality, published material in which the identities of individuals was disguised but could easily be deduced by some townspeople. The reactions to this *de facto* identification ranged from frustration and suspicion to anger, the threat of legal action, "and the feeling that [citizens] were not treated fairly and that the research was sneaky" (*Ithaca Journal,* 13 June 1958). Although journalistic coverage of the episode was substantial, and although the issues were argued vigorously at meetings of the American Anthropological Association, those issues remain unresolved. There is no way to verify what impact, if any, the incident had on communities outside the one involved in the research, but we suspect that it was negligible.

Still other instances in which assuring or failing to assure respondents of confidentiality played a notable role in the research are not hard to identify. The better-documented ones are used as a vehicle for examples in this chapter and Chapter 4. A review of episodes that involve direct conflict between the law and the social scientist's claim of a need for confidentiality is given by Carroll and Knerr (1975, 1976) and by Rosteck (1976). Their reports are discussed in the section on field surveys in this chapter.

TESTIMONY

Other incidents have been cited in testimony before legislative committees and the courts. But the incidents are difficult to verify, partly because individuals providing testimony often supply little or no documentation on them.

For instance, the examples cited by expert witnesses testifying before the U.S. Senate Committee on Labor and Public Welfare (1969, 1970) in hearings on drug research legislation are pertinent, dramatic in tone, but unremarkable in detail. Senator Howard Hughes, for example, reported that an experimental drug-withdrawal program in Des Moines was "blown clear out of the water" when local police infiltrated the program in order to circumvent staff wishes to assure the privacy of (volunteer) methadone recipients. Dr. Jonathan Cole has testified that a "confidential reporting system for addicts in the city of Chicago . . . after 2 years was turned over to the police so that the file suddenly stopped being confidential," and the reporting system, at least as far as drug research was concerned, was aborted. Another drug researcher, Dr. Helen Nowlis, reviewed the disruption of a California survey that failed to obtain reliable statistics on marijuana and LSD use in part because many respondents, recognizing the absence of any legal methods for preserving the secrecy of their response, refused to cooperate. The testimony offered by Bernard Glueck, director of the Institute for Living at Hartford, emphasized that at least some major research and treatment institutions have deliberately avoided seeking federal funds for research on sensitive topics (e.g., rehabilitation of drug addicts) partly because they anticipate disruption of research and dangers to the institution, its investigators, and research participants if patient records are forcibly disclosed to a law enforcement agency.

Testimonials that rely almost entirely on the prestige of the academician issuing the statement are easy to find. Those submitted on behalf of the social scientist involved in *Richards of Rockford* v. *Pacific Gas and Electric* are, with a few exceptions, a bit embarrassing for that reason. Nonetheless, the court cited these unsubstantiated opinions in ruling on this case (see chapter 8).

SPECIAL CASES

Two additional incidents provide unique evidence, which is also consistent with the cases already presented. They are segregated, since (1) the projects involved did not have as their main objective the production of scientific knowledge, unlike the ones just discussed, and (2) the assurance of confidentiality in each case was specious. The first involves a civil suit, *Merriken* v. *Cressman,* stemming from a private consulting group's efforts to mount a drug prevention program in a local high school. The project was enjoined by the court to halt, partly on the grounds that records on students' propensity to use drugs would not remain confidential. The project's assurance was empty in that record dissemination was virtually uncontrollable. We label the promise as well intentioned but gratuitous, and discuss resolution of the problem later (see chapter 4). The second incident involved a contractor engaged in market research, using mailed questionnaires, for the *National Observer.* Though anonymity was implied in the survey questionnaire, the documents were covertly identified (invisible ink was used). Once the discovery was made, substantial publicity was given to the deception; no information on level of disruption is available. The episode could have been avoided by using the approaches described in chapter 4.

SOME LESSONS

The cases described here offer a few lessons about the need to assure confidentiality of response, and about coincidental sources of resistance to social research. In particular:

1. The case studies suggest that in research on sensitive topics, when an assurance of confidentiality is obscure, weak, breached, or thought to be breached, some potential respondents will refuse to cooperate. The likelihood of disruption is greater when media and special interest groups play a role.

2. The cases are equivocal to the extent that in controversial re-

search, public attitudes toward researchers and the research topic influence the likelihood of disruption. In particular, even adequate assurance of confidentiality will not satisfy some individuals' objections to the research. The issues are usually tangled during a conflict over the research, and when they cannot be separated from one another, their resolution is difficult.

3. The competing influences may be unrelated to the confidentiality of individual records—for example, claims that "group privacy" is being violated, the idea that the consequences of research may be damaging to the group studied rather than to the individual. Or they may be related to the issue—for example, the question of informed consent. Any or all of these influences may override the issue of whether confidentiality of individual records is assured.

4. Errors in reporting the conduct of research, made by research opponents or advocates and magnified by press coverage, are chronic. They cannot be corrected or minimized without considerable effort.

5. A vigorous subgroup of the target sample, for which a promise of confidentiality may be necessary but insufficient, usually takes major responsibility for critical examination of the conduct of the research. That subgroup can induce noncooperation among most, if not all, members of the target sample. Where the target sample is a traditionally powerless group, disruption of research is likely to be minimal, but it is here that some more serious ethical questions emerge.

6. The tangle of issues, the errors in perception and reporting, the involvement of several interest groups, and so on should not be unexpected. They are also evident in the earliest of census surveys, and are characteristic of both ill-informed and well-informed target samples. To the extent that issues remain unresolved, disruption of research can and probably should occur.

Though all of the incidents described here were serious, they were localized, and the research projects were generally not destroyed by the disruption. The Woodlawn episode is a clear exception. No major research questions were altered by disruption, and two of the projects still conduct longitudinal surveys of the same target populations. However, we have no information on how the validity of sampling and the validity of response were affected by the disruption or by the controversy.

It is often possible to obtain a less complicated and more informative picture of the need for confidentiality assurance than one obtains from discrete case studies. The evidence stems from the field experiments and surveys that we examine next.

Experiments in the Field

A potentially useful source of information here is a study that compares the cooperation rate of research participants who have been assured of confidentiality against the cooperation rate of an otherwise equivalent group to whom no assurance has been made. Reality is usually not quite so simple, since cooperation rate may vary not only with the act of promising confidentiality, but also with the character of the physical or legal devices used to actualize the promise, with the sensitivity of the information elicited, and with other factors.

The earliest studies we have been able to locate were mounted during the 1930s and were designed to determine how requiring identification of respondents in narrow research settings affects the cooperation rate. Some of these efforts focused on sensitive topics—sexual relations, level of social and personal adjustment, physical health—and found that despite promises of confidentiality, anonymous respondents yielded more candid information than identified ones (e.g., Ellis 1947; Fischer 1946; Olsen 1936; Benson 1941). On the other hand, studies involving innocuous, even trivial, topics of inquiry suggest that the absence of concrete assurances of confidentiality has no discernible effect, especially if the inquirer is quite trustworthy, as, for example, professors seem to have been considered then. In particular, Gerberich and Mason (1948), Hamel and Reif (1952), Corey (1937), and Ash and Abramson (1952) found that the effects of anonymity were negligible under such conditions.

More recent work, stemming from the personality-test controversy of the 1960s, enlarges the early work. A variety of small studies, for example, suggest that under diverse conditions, the degree to which a personality inventory "invades privacy" can be gauged by using well-known measures of the "social desirability" of response (Walsh, Layton, and Klieger 1966), that the offensiveness of an item depends in part on the use of the data and the authority of the user (Simmons 1968), that whether the data are used for research or for supervision affects notably individuals' willingness to cooperate (see Barna 1974 and the references therein). Hartnett and Seligsohn's (1967) comparison of levels of anonymity and sensitivity of inquiry suggests that assurances of confidentiality in an academic setting do little to change students' reports of innocuous demographic characteristics. But for more sensitive topics—emotional stability and the like—various levels of assurance have some influence on even a trusting participant group.

Recent evidence stems from research designed to evaluate alternative methods of assuring confidentiality. These investigations have usually been conducted on a larger scale and in more realistic settings than the earlier experiments. The idea in many is that a simple promise of confidentiality to the respondent is an insufficient assurance and that additional mechanisms can be used to further satisfy the respondent's need for privacy. That is, individuals not only expect a promise of confidentiality in exchange for their cooperation, but also seek concrete and visible assurance that the promise can be sustained.

For example, new statistical methods for preserving privacy notably the randomized response approach, have been developed primarily to reduce the sensitivity of direct inquiry and so can be expected to enhance cooperation rates. The methods permit one to elicit information from an identified respondent (even during an interview) in a way that prevents any deduction about the true condition of any individual in a survey sample. This magic depends on a couple of simple laws of probability and involves the respondent's injecting random error into his response in a way that permits accurate statistical analysis of group data but guarantees that the respondent's state does indeed remain a private matter vis-à-vis the interviewer. In Canada (Krotki and Fox 1974), in Formosa (Chi, Chow, and Rider 1972; Liu, Chow, and Mosley 1975), and in the United States, for example, comparisons have been made of the results of using direct questions about fertility control, coupled with a promise of confidentiality, and the results of using statistical devices for assuring confidentiality. About half of these studies suggest that the new devices elicit more candid responses about potentially embarrassing topics such as birth control practices than conventional interview methods. That *all* respondents were not persuaded by the method is also clear, judging from opinions elicited from them after the main questions were asked. That is, some respondents believe that there was a "trick" involved in the novel approach (Greenberg, Abernathy, and Horvitz 1970). Evidence on the effectiveness of physical assurances has also been obtained in the Canadian studies of abortion, birth of illegitimate children, and the use of contraceptives. Results of using the statistical devices with identified respondents during interviews worked as well in eliciting responses as did anonymous mail-back questionnaires. Differences in rates of affirming potentially stigmatizing characteristics were small, but they generally favored the use of the statistical mechanisms rather than the anonymous questionnaire (see chapter 5).

A recent study of responses to questions about child abuse yielded results that further support the idea that at least some people are more candid in reporting when the mechanism for preserving confidentiality is clear. The randomized response method and the use of a self-administered questionnaire that was returned sealed either to the interviewer and or to the research firm were compared in a large experiment. Zdep and Rhodes (1977) found respondents about five times more likely to admit copororal punishment of their children under the randomized response method than under the sealed envelope one. Refusal rate was considerably lower with the statistical technique, and that alone could account for the difference. A good deal of prior field testing was necessary to troubleshoot problems in using the method.

Similar results have been obtained in studies sponsored by the U.S. Army. One large experiment in the series involved a mail-back questionnaire survey of over three thousand servicemen, who were asked about their use of illicit drugs, their racial attitudes and racist behavior, and their military attitudes. Comparing a program of anonymous response plus statistical protection against a program of anonymous response, Reaser, Hartsock, and Hoehn (1975) found that the respondents were more than twice as likely to admit undesirable behavior when the statistical devices were used. The largest differences between the results of using each method were found for race-related items in the questionnaire. A separate study on a smaller sample failed to provide similar evidence for the contention that respondents appreciate additional guarantees of confidentiality, possibly because of small sample size and the inclusion of questions in the anonymous questionnaire that could have permitted deductive disclosure of the identities of respondents (Brown and Harding 1973).

One peculiarity of the last two studies is notable. Contrary to expectations, the use of the additional statistical guarantees failed to increase the response rate and in fact appeared to undermine it a bit. The problem here seems to be tied to the novelty of the statistical methods: somewhat fewer people may respond, but those who do respond evidently provide franker opinions and admissions.

It is also evident that weak devices for assuring confidentiality will be recognized by some respondents, and they will react accordingly. For example, Zdep and Rhodes (1977) found that questions about child abuse yielded roughly the same results under two transparently weak conditions: responses were made on a form that was then sealed in an envelope and given to the interviewer, or they were made on a form that was then sealed and sent directly to the Opinion Research Corporation headquarters. The results suggest less candor under these two conditions than under one of the statistical methods to protect confidentiality also tried out in the experiment. Similarly, a weak physical guarantee and a promise of confidentiality yielded roughly the same cooperation rate as a promise of confidentiality alone in large sample surveys by Thorndike, Hagen, and Kemper (1952) on health-related topics, in small experiments by Hartnett and Seligsohn (1967) on sensitive personality characteristics, and others. Drug studies by Wilson and Rosen (1975) are more persuasive in that they show that even questionnaires to which servicemen are asked to respond anonymously are accurately viewed by servicemen as having some potential danger: the identity of a respondent can sometimes be deduced from the demographic information that a respondent may provide on an unsigned document. There are also some cases that demonstrate that the thoughtful respondent or research participant can easily detect impotent or inept promises of confidentiality and can take fairly drastic action to establish the impotency—*Merriken* v. *Cressman,* for example.

Some very concrete mechanisms to assure confidentiality of response will not always be persuasive and will not always be a consideration to respondents. For example, in the Brown-Harding (1973) Army studies on drug abuse, the results of using completely anonymous questionnaires were compared with the results of using both anonymity and specialized physical devices to assure confidentiality of response. The very small differences between rates of affirming drug use under the two conditions suggest that the use of additional mechanisms is of minor or negligible import for surveys of officers. Similarly, in King's (1970) studies of marijuana use among college students, the use of anonymous questionnaires produced results that differed little from those obtained using inquiry modes that required identification. Folsom's (1974) experiments on different modes of inquiry about drinking and driving yielded results that suggest that a simple promise of confidentiality was slightly more acceptable than the promise supported by complex statistical methods for actualizing the promise. It is impossible to tell from these reports why additional assurances failed to increase candor or cooperation rate notably. The novelty of the confidentiality-preserving mechanism may induce suspicion rather than cooperation, especially if pilot tests are not used to troubleshoot the method. Innocuousness of inquiry may produce candid responses to a social researcher, regardless of the mechanism for assuring respondents of confidentiality, so long as *some* assurance is given; and topics regarded as sensitive by the researcher may not be regarded as sensitive by the respondent.

MORE RECENT RESEARCH

Two large field experiments have been mounted to better understand how cooperation rates in social research vary with some of the parameters identified already. The benefits of each derive from their size and the confidence in findings that scale engenders, and their specific ties to policy.

In 1974 the Subcommittee on Census and Population of the U.S. House of Representatives (1975a, 1975b) conducted hearings on new legislation that would permit (1) the transfer of decennial census records to the National Archives fifty years after the census date, and (2) access to the records by researchers seventy-five years after their acquisition. One of the problems engendered by the proposed legislation, as well as earlier discussions of the topic, is that very little is known about the effect of changing disclosure rules on the public's willingness to cooperate in censuses and surveys. The Census Bureau's position was that empirical data on the topic ought to be collected beforehand to facilitate the development of law and better prediction of the law's positive and negative effects on the quality of census data. In their field experiments, members of a national probability sample of respondents have been randomly assigned to one of five assurance levels: permanent confidentiality of records; confidentiality for seventy-five years; confidentiality for twenty-five years; no confidentiality statement at all; and an explicit statement that records will not be maintained as confidential with respect to other federal agencies. The results suggest that refusal rates do indeed increase as the level of protection decreases, but the trend is weak (National Academy of Sciences, Committee on Federal Statistics 1979). One of the probable reasons for the weakness of the trend has already been mentioned: the data typically elicited in this and similar Census Bureau surveys is innocuous and the cooperation rate is typically very high—96 percent or better. A second and perhaps more important reason is that many respondents *expect* to be assured of confidentiality, especially in census interviews. Postinterview questions suggest that over 40 percent of those not given any assurance of confidentiality recalled erroneously that such an assurance had been given. At most, 76 percent of any group had a perfectly accurate recollection of the characteristics of the assurance, the sponsor of the survey, and so on.

A second randomized field test, designed by Eleanor Singer, James Murray, and Martin Frankel (Singer 1978a), directs attention to leisure activities, including sensitive ones such as intercourse, masturbation, and marijuana use. One facet of the study involved randomly assigning members of a national probability sample to one of three confidentiality-assurance conditions: an unqualified assurance that confidentiality would be maintained; an assurance qualified by the phrase "confidential except as required by law"; and a condition in which no confidentiality statement at all was provided. The overall interview-completion rate was 77 percent, with 16 percent directly of the sample refusing to be interviewed; most of the refusals occurred before any confidentiality statement was read by interviewers. For those to whom the statement was read, no significant difference in refusal rate appeared among the three confidentiality conditions. However, absolute assurance clearly increased the likelihood of response to sensitive, rather than innocuous, questions, relative to groups receiving qualified assurance or no assurance. Validity of response, indexed by higher affirmation rates, was evident only for sensitive questions under the assurance of absolute confidentiality.

REMARKS

Neither the recent field experiments nor the general methodological research cited here attends to conditions that are likely to provoke a disruption of a research effort. That is, no field tests have been undertaken to discover how resistant a research design is to journalistic or political exploitation, public misunderstanding, or public mistrust of the social research process. The field experiments are helpful, however, in that they identify the less dramatic, but important, factors that affect respondent cooperation level. Insofar as these factors also influence public reactions to the research, the work helps to avoid disruption.

Field Surveys

A variety of surveys have been designed to help determine the effect of and need for a confidentiality assurance. Most of this work can be grouped into one of three categories. The first concerns respondents' sensitivity to the privacy issue and their candor in reporting. This includes studies undertaken to compare reports made to a social scientist under a confidentiality assurance with reports submitted by the same respondents to an administrative system. The second category includes research on refusal rate in large national surveys, where refusals *may* be attributable to the respondent's concerns about the privacy issue. Surveys undertaken to understand respondent attitudes toward privacy in research make up the third category.

Consider first the comparison of research data and administrative records on the same topic. One can argue that under some conditions research records are susceptible to fewer pressures toward corruption than are records used for making administrative judgments about individuals. That is, the research records are used primarily to build statistical summaries on a group of individuals. Consequently, the respondent may regard them as more innocuous and will be less inclined to distort the information he or she provides. To help assure that social research records remain relatively free of the biases affecting administrative records, they must remain confidential.

The argument is tenable insofar as it can be shown that individuals are more likely to respond truthfully to a social researcher's inquiry, under an assurance of confidentiality, than to respond truthfully to an administrative query. In fact, there is good evidence from some surveys to support the argument for some, but not all, topics and conditions.

• One effort to get at relative biases in administrative and social research reporting systems has been made for the U.S. Army by Reaser, Richards, and Hartstock (1975) on drug abuse. The data are derived from questionnaires completed anonymously by over a thousand servicemen in group settings with both explicit assurance of response confidentiality and concrete procedures to assure anonymity. The servicemen were members of representative samples selected on site. The administrative data in this case were generated by routine urinalysis of (supposedly) random samples of men selected from army post personnel; the principle purposes of the system were the detection and deterrence of drug abuse. In fact, a notable proportion of servicemen appear to have avoided the urinalysis system without extraordinary cleverness. And so estimates of drug abuse rates from survey research were about three times higher than those from the administrative system.

• In a Canadian study on the incidence of illegal abortions, therapeutic abortions, and induced abortions of any kind, Krotki and McDaniel (1975) found that using special statistical methods to preserve privacy in field surveys yielded higher rates of affirmation than were obtained from official records collected by Statistics Canada, using a more conventional but less persuasive promise of confidentiality. According to the authors, the "traditional methods could not obtain admissions of even all legal abortions."

• At times, the researcher's interest in reliable evaluation of social ameliorative programs results in better documentation of the shortcomings of administrative records. For example, in attempting to estimate the effects of alcohol abuse treatment programs in Phoenix, social scientists discovered that over 12 percent of the DWI (Driving While Intoxicated) convictions by the municipal courts were absent from the records of the Arizona Motor Vehicle Division. About 20 percent of the motor vehicle records contained inaccurate information about dates of conviction and of birth, name, race, citation, etc. of arrestee (Crabb, Gettys, Malfetti, and Stewart 1971). The lower quality of administrative records in this instance is probably due to poor record management, as well as to the arrestee's inclination to mislead a policeman writing up a citation.

Other examples are not hard to find, especially where evidence on validity is collected as part of the systematic evaluation of major social programs. But this does not imply that research data will be perfect, or that administrative records systems will generally be less accurate than research systems. Social research data are fallible, at times considerably more fallible than administrative records on the same topic. The accuracy obtained by a researcher is a matter of degree and depends on a variety of factors, many of which are independent of the confidentiality issue. Campbell's (1975) little theory of degradation of social statistics, for example, leads us to expect that research data will become less valid to the extent that respondents recognize that they are used to make political decisions about certain target populations, if not about specific individuals within the population. Nonetheless, the comparative validity of research records is notable in some instances, and this is attributable partly to the assurance that research records will not be disclosed for use in making administrative decisions about an individual.

A different form of evidence stems from research on public cooperation in routine national surveys. During 1974–75, some experts argued that the nonresponse rate in large-scale surveys has increased over the past ten years and that the increase is attributable to respondents' fears about invasion of privacy. The actual evidence for a decline is ambiguous, however. Because even weak evidence may foreshadow real problems, it behooves us to examine it.

One of the few reports to rely on data from large samples stems from research by Love and Turner (1975). They examine response rates over time for five national surveys conducted by the U.S. Census Bureau. Summarizing the results, we learn that:

- For the Current Population Surveys, conducted monthly on samples of over forty thousand households since 1965, refusal rates have increased slightly (from 1.5 percent to 2.2 percent) with considerable inter-year variation (e.g., 1.8 percent in 1969, 1.6 percent in 1971 and 1972). Part of the increase may be due to better tracking of previously "unavailable" interviewees, since there was a drop in this category—from 2.4 percent to 1.6 percent—during 1965–75. The overall nonresponse rate (the unavailable plus refusal categories) shows a slight decline.

- The Health Interview Surveys, conducted since 1957 on over forty thousand households annually, have had a slight overall decline in nonresponse rate (4.7 percent to 3.5 percent), a slight increase in refusal rate (1.5 percent to 1.8 percent), and a decline in unavailables, an experience similar to that of the CPS.

- The National Crime Survey is conducted monthly on about ten thousand households. Annual data since 1972 suggest a fairly stable nonresponse rate (4.7 percent to 4.0 percent). Data on refusal rates for only two years, 1973 and 1974, have been compiled, and these showed a slight increase (1.5 percent to 1.8 percent) in nonresponse and a decrease in unavailable households.

- In the National Annual Housing Survey of over fifty thousand households, data are available for only 1973 and 1974, and these suggest a slight increase in nonresponse (2.8 percent to 3.3 percent), and a slight increase in refusal rate (1.9 percent to 2.5 percent).

- The Annual Housing Surveys for Standard Metropolitan Statistical Areas, based on approximately twenty thousand households, have had a fairly stable nonresponse rate, with monthly refusal rates for 1974 and 1975 in the 2.2 percent to 2.9 percent range and no obvious trend.

Considering only the longer time series from the Current Population Surveys and the Health Interview Surveys, there does appear to be a weak and unstable trend toward higher refusal rate. But it is also clear that these surveys are increasing in quality: the percentage of household heads "unavailable for interview" has declined. A plausible interpretation here is that difficult-to-find individuals are being reached for interview more frequently, but they are more inclined to refuse than more accessible people. If we consider only nonresponse rate, then, the picture is fairly stable: low nonresponse for all surveys with no strong trend. If we gauge cooperation by direct refusal rate, then cooperation may be said to have declined.

Even if we admit that the trend is notable, there are good reasons for not attributing the changes in response rate in these surveys to specific concerns about privacy. Consider, for example, Bauman and Sage's (1976) study of parents who did not respond to a letter requesting their consent to have their children participate in a school survey. Only 35 percent responded, with most extending permission. In a follow-up telephone study of nonrespondents, only about 22 percent of that group explicitly refused their consent. The most common reason given by parents for not responding earlier was that the study had, for them, a "low priority." Remaining responses ranged from the expression of parental anxiety about the effects of a questionnaire, some of whose items concerned drug use, on the child, to the fear that the data would not remain confidential. In other surveys, refusals to cooperate may have more primitive political origins, including an increase in bald distrust of government, as in the 1967 Philadelphia Census surveys of ghetto neighborhoods (Gerson 1969). Such refusals might also be attributable to changing level of education of interviewers, to the attitudes and verbal behavior of interviewers, to race, sex, and other interviewer-related factors whose import has been demonstrated in experimental tests (Cannel and Henson 1974; Marquis 1970; National Center for Health Statistics 1968). Some experts have even suggested that there is a stage of intellectual and social growth in which people prefer complete anonymity, and if that stage is linked to increasing educational level or political frustration, then there will be increases in refusals to cooperate in surveys regardless of the quality of a survey research effort (see, for example, Parsons 1972). More complicated explanations, based on surveys and case studies of nonresponse and of outright refusals to participate in social research, involve ethnic and cultural factors. A small body of evidence suggests that foreign-born respondents are less likely to countenance a visit by any pollster, much less a visit by one who asks sensitive questions (Dohrenwend and Dohrenwend 1968; Oyen 1966; and Robins 1963). Special surveys of both Sweden's National Central Bureau of Statistics (1977) and the U.S. Census Bureau are also pertinent. Their analyses of refusal rates in conventional interview surveys suggest that a habituated isolation, based on fear, indifference, and other factors, accounts for a higher refusal rate among women and the elderly, especially those living in large cities. The point is that refusals in each of these cases originate not in a distinct concern about individual privacy, but in a complex of beliefs, accurate and otherwise, which influence a good deal of normal human behavior. To label those as solely related to intellective privacy in the absence of an examination of the competing explanations is not warranted.

Consider the final category of survey evidence—studies of respondent preferences and attitudes. At its best, the information can be used to anticipate problems, for even when the correlation between attitude and actual cooperation rate is weak, the sheer size of the target sample may justify attention to the small predictive correlation. Furthermore, the accumulation of evidence helps to adjudicate arguments about whether a public is indeed sensitive to privacy, and how that sensitivity is exhibited. The special attitude surveys undertaken by the U.S. Census Bureau (National Academy of Sciences, Committee on Federal Statistics 1979) and the National Central Bureau of Statistics (SCB) of Sweden are the largest of their kind. The U.S. study concerned respondents' perception of influences on their willingness to respond; their perception of the importance of confidentiality assurances; and their knowledge and perceptions about confidentiality rules in Census Bureau surveys. The fact that 75 percent of respondents reported that the interviewer's "manner" was a major influence on their willingness to respond is a bit alarming but apparently typical. Civic responsibility is reported as influential by about the same number of people. Curiosity about being interviewed was cited least often. It is more pertinent that about half said that concern about disclosure did not affect their willingness to respond, though that concern is likely to be entrained in their generalized trust of the interviewers. The analogous Swedish surveys suggest that less than half (41 percent) of their respondents were hesitant in responding. Half of this sample hesitated on privacy grounds, rather than because of indifference, lack of time for interviewers, and so on. The topic of the survey and the sponsorship were as important as disclosure to the same number of individuals, suggesting that respondents did not treat sponsorship, topic, and disclosure factors independently.

The respondents' opinions about whether confidentiality assurance is essential were captured largely in questions about income reporting and the trustworthiness of institutions. Their views on whether guarantees of confidentiality affect the accuracy of reporting are remarkably spread out, and a minority believe assurance has a major impact. These opinions are consistent with the results of a recent survey of researchers who have strong legal guarantees that their data will remain confidential. About 20 percent believe the guarantees are essential for assuring respondent cooperation; far more believe the guarantees are important in eliciting institutional cooperation and in preserving equity of the researcher-respondent relation (Hedrick, Nelson, and Cecil 1979). The respondents in the Census experiments support their opinion with privacy-related reasons—for example, by saying that the information is private under any circumstances. But it is likely that the salience of the topic (the experiment was dedicated exclusively to exploring attitudes about privacy) and the open-ended response affected their view. One of the major *known* influences on accuracy in reporting—memory—was mentioned by fewer than 1 percent of the respondents. Most respondents in U.S. and Swedish surveys, however, put greater trust in government than in commercial organizations to keep data confidential.

Regardless of their trust, about 20 percent hold the erroneous belief that identifiable records in U.S. Census files are generally open to the public. About half admitted that they do not know whether the records are open to the public or shared with other federal agencies. Furthermore, only half even recalled whether the interviewers worked for the national government, and fewer still remembered the interviewer's statement that the Census Bureau was sponsoring the survey. About 40 percent recalled an explicit promise of confidentiality. The analogous Swedish surveys yielded results consistent with these. A majority of respondents did not know that Swedish Census records are maintained as confidential for twenty years, and that there is specific legislation (covered widely by the press) governing the collection of information that is stored in computers. Most Swedes interviewed did not recall having participated in a survey run by the Central Bureau of Statistics, despite the fact that most had participated in the census of population taken by the SCB five years earlier.

In another recent preference study, a large sample of servicemen was asked to indicate their willingness to answer a social scientist's questions about drug use, attitudes toward the army, alcohol abuse, and racial prejudice (Wilson and Rosen 1975). They were asked to predict their willingness to respond as if the sensitive information was elicited anonymously, as if it was elicited along with complete identification, and as if it was elicited under some statistical devices for assuring confidentiality of response. The willingness ratings suggest, among other things, that officers react favorably to the statistical methods of preserving confidentiality, partly on the grounds that the information on anonymous questionnaires can often be used to deduce the identity of the respondent. Respondents are also more willing to respond if they have other cues that confidentiality will be assured (e.g., civilian rather than military survey administrators) and if the information is innocuous rather than sensitive (e.g., if it concerns attitudes toward the army rather than drug abuse). Naturally, a respondent's opinion about his own willingness to respond does not necessarily reflect what he will actually do. Brown's (1974) work, for example, conflicts with the Wilson-Rosen results in some respects.

Some analogous research, conducted on a much smaller scale and on related attitudes, began after the personality-testing controversy of the 1960s. The problem, then as now, was to discover some simple ways to characterize intrusiveness of inquiry so as to eliminate or alter questions that might offend an interviewee or research participant. In one relevant study, Walsh, Layton, and Klieger (1966) requested that people rate "how socially desirable it would be to ask a person the questions" that were listed, and "how much of an invasion of privacy" it was to ask those questions. High correlations between the rated invasion of privacy and the rated social desirability of the question were obtained, and more importantly, these ratings correlated well with independently obtained ratings of the social desirability of response to each question. The point here is that one may use an old technology based simply on a theory of "social desirability of response" to anticipate respondents' attitudes toward a question. A small extension of the study by Simmons (1968) suggests, as one might expect, that "ratings of level of invasion of privacy depend on particular aspects of the situation, e.g., whether the respondent thinks there is some benefit to his response, whether he thinks the question is relevant in context." At least one result of these studies is concrete —the elimination of particularly intrusive items from a standardized personality inventory (Edwards 1967). There seems to have been little or no basic research done to extend this early work, despite the fact that it anticipated some important issues in the national data-bank controversy of the 1960s and later controversies over government-sponsored surveys during the 1970s. The exceptions include Sweden's studies of the sensitivity of items of personal information (Langlet 1975): personal finances, political ideology, and contacts with official authorities were, as expected, rated most often as being most sensitive. The Norwegian Census Bureau is apparently developing studies of roughly the same type.

MORE RECENT RESEARCH

One of the most ambitious efforts to survey conflicts between social research standards and the law has been undertaken by Carroll and Knerr (1975) under the auspices of over a dozen social science professional organizations. The effort includes a snowball sample of over two hundred incidents in which research was interrupted on privacy or confidentiality grounds, a survey of about four hundred fifty social scientists, and legal analyses of incidents. Their as yet incomplete analysis confirms the importance of factors identified earlier (see Boruch 1971b) as determinants of conflict: research methodology, topical coverage of questions and of the research, stage of the research, and others. Some new factors are identified as well, notably the researcher's prior experience, the magnitude of the research effort, and the disciplinary area. Because of the sampling method, it is difficult to judge the representativeness of the findings and the validity of the data. The study constitutes a major first step in documenting the nature of such incidents and in understanding the problems that must be overcome in future research along the same lines. It is discussed in chapter 8, on legal methods of maintaining the confidentiality of records on research participants.

Persistent Issues: Corruption, Witchcraft, Competence, and Competition

This chapter's emphasis has been on evidence for the need to assure confidentiality of individual responses in research. We conclude by examining problems that concern individual privacy less directly. They are persistent and can exercise a dramatic influence.

CORRUPTION OF THE PRINCIPLE

It does not take much imagination to expect that, at times, a confidentiality principle will be used honorifically. In the best of these instances, the appeal to principle is pious but irrelevant—that is, there is no real threat to individual privacy or to confidentiality of records. At worst, the appeal is corruptive, dedicated not to preserving individual privacy but to assuring secrecy that runs counter to the public interest.

In either case, social research and especially the evaluation of social reforms are likely to be impeded. Lobenthal (1974), for example, reports that in designing evaluative research on correctional facilities:

Even many [correctional] program personnel from whom we sought information rather than advice withheld their cooperation. There was, for example, a sudden solicitude about clients' rights to privacy and ostensible concern with the confidentiality of records. When an elaborate protocol was worked out to safeguard confidentiality, the data we requested were still not forthcoming. (p. 32)

Similarly, the privacy issue has been used to prevent legitimate evaluations of some drug treatment programs in Pennsylvania, where records were destroyed *despite* immunity of record identifiers from subpoena under the 1970 Drug Abuse Act. It has been used to prevent evaluation of manpower training programs in Pittsburgh and evaluation of mental health services programs in southern California. It has been used to argue against the System Development Corporation's studies of integration programs in the New York City school system, despite the fact that children who responded to inquiries would be anonymous. These episodes do not represent the norm, of course. They do represent a persistent minority event.

Little vignettes at the national level are no less noteworthy, though the reasons for impertinent appeals to privacy differ a bit from the ones just described. For example, according to Boeckmann (1976), Senate subcommittee members used the privacy issue as a vehicle for discrediting researchers during hearings on the Negative Income Tax Experiment. She suggests that the action was part of a drive to bury the idea of a graduated income subsidy program. More generally, the privacy issue has been a convenient vehicle for assaulting national research that could threaten political interests, and for getting votes. Mueller (1976), for example, argues that former President Nixon's support of the Domestic Council on Privacy, the Privacy Act, and theories of executive privilege did what it was supposed to do—focus public attention on matters other than war. That both uses are persistent but low-frequency events is evident from similar experience in Norway (Oyen 1965), Sweden (Dalenius and Klermarken 1976), and Denmark, as well as in the United States.

The most predictable adulteration of principle occurs before each U.S. population census, when ritualistic assault competes with thoughtful criticism for public attention. To Charles W. Wilson, a former chairman of the House Subcommittee on Census and Statistics, for example, much of the controversy over the 1970 Census was deliberately fomented by colleagues interested less in privacy than in votes, and by journalists moved less by the need for balanced reporting than by the need to generate provocative stories. Further, the evidence used in attacks on the census was often misleading.

Reference was continually made to a total of 117 [Census] questions, despite the fact that this total could be obtained only by adding all the different inquiries on the forms designed for 80% of the population, those for 15%, and those for 5%. A number of the questions appeared on one form only, and the maximum number of questions for any individual was actually less than 90. The question on whether the bathroom was shared continued to be distorted into the much more interesting version "With whom do you share your shower?" (Eckler 1972, p. 202)

Similarly, in House Subcommittee Hearings, "One witness who had been scheduled to appear in support of the legislation, proposed by Congressman Betts to restrict the 1970 Census, admitted that he had learned from earlier witnesses that his prepared statement was incorrect" (Eckler 1972, p. 204).

An agency's refusal to disclose data on even anonymous individuals, under false colors of privacy, is of course not a new problem, nor is it confined to the social science arena. Its origins, in the United States at least, date from the reluctance of the Massachusetts Bay Colony to disclose either statistical information on mortality rates or records on the death of identified individuals, for fear of jeopardizing their project (Cassedy 1969). The data, if disclosed, would presumably have made the colony much less attractive a prospect for volunteer colonists and for its conscientious sponsors. A similar reluctance appears to underlie the distortion of fatality and accident rates published by commercial contractors for the Alaska pipeline (see the *New York Times,* 7 August 1975). Institutional self-protection of the same type has hampered the efforts of biomedical researchers to understand the causes of the Thalidomide tragedy: the pharmaceutical company has refused to disclose its data on test subjects in statistical summary form or otherwise. The idea is implicit in the refusal of the Philadelphia public school system, during 1975–76, to disclose data on minority groups to the U.S. Office of Civil Rights on the grounds of student privacy, though OCR required only statistical summary data. It is transparent in at least one court case involving a school's efforts to resist, on Privacy Act grounds, the sampling of *anonymous* students by researchers who were interested in the racial biases that may underlie diagnosis of maladjusted and emotionally disturbed youths [*Privacy Journal,* 1977; *Lora* v. *Board of Education of City of New York* (74 F.R.D. 565)].

There are, at times, good administrative and political reasons for an agency's refusal to disclose statistical records to a researcher or to permit researcher access to individuals. Though we may be unable to subscribe to those reasons, it is not in our interest to confuse the reasons for refusing disclosure with the issue of individual privacy. It is reasonable to anticipate that controversy will be instigated for purposes other than those advertised, even if we can offer no general advice here on preventing dispute. And we can offer partial solutions to one problem.

Those solutions, covered in succeeding chapters, help to assure that social programs and problems can be examined without seriously depreciating the privacy of program recipients. In this sense, they limit the extent to which an honorific appeal to privacy can be used as a device for restricting access to information.

ON WITCHCRAFT AND ITS PACKAGING

Now and then, a privacy debate turns around the social scientist's prediction or imputation of individual behavior. The ingenuous critic, for example, believes that the scientist can generally impute private facts confidently by using otherwise innocuous information collected in surveys, tests, and the like. That critic may also believe, perhaps with simulated skepticism, that the scientist can accurately predict individual behavior from current data. The implication of these beliefs is that collection of data or a prediction based on the data constitutes an invasion of privacy. Because the beliefs are often far from true in the particular instance, this stream of action does no more than confuse an already complicated matter. Illustrations of the problem are not hard to find.

Sale (1974), for example, maintains that during the years of campus disruptions, 1966–1970, the "protest-prone" student could be identified with "81 percent accuracy—thanks to an elaborate study undertaken by the university-financed American Council on Education" (p. 548). This kind of inference suggests that even otherwise-astute critics of social systems can easily exhibit the neural activity of a brick. It in no way reflects reality. With that level of accuracy, few social scientists would be poor, since the principles underlying prediction can, of course, be applied in more lucrative settings. The actual prediction rates as reported in the original research suggest that about 15 percent of the total variation in students' protest behavior is predictable, but even this is a probabilistic prediction and not a deterministic one. The prediction of protest behavior is more accurate than flipping a coin, to be sure, but it is a far cry from the Orwellian claim. Moreover, it distracts attention from the more fundamental questions of whether the purposes of prediction are legitimate, how the negative effects of poor prediction and naive reliance on poor prediction will be controlled, and how individual records can be protected against forced disclosure.

Public officials are no less susceptible to this kind of error, but the better ones manage to examine the issue in a reasonable way. Barabba and Kaplan (1975), for example, report that in 1974 the U.S. Census Bureau came under fire for supplying census tract data, such as mean level of income and mean education level within tract, to marketing organizations. Critics said the organizations could use tract data to accurately predict an *individual's* characteristics and so invade privacy. The congressional committee reviewing the issue recognized that predictions were made only at the tract level, something that congressmen themselves do, often on the basis of commercial data, to determine which areas are likely to be supportive in the next election. They found that generalizing from the tract level down to the individual within the tract is generally imprecise because individuals do not behave like census tracts (see the section in chapter 2 on traps, artifacts, and circularity). Finally, the committee found that belief in a witchcraft of prediction is fostered by market researchers who, in plying their trade, feel compelled to package prediction that is slightly better than chance as a great deal more.

The prevention programs mounted during the 1960s and 1970s represent a related but distinct problem in packaging a promising approach as fact. At their worst, these programs have been set up to identify *potential* troublemakers (e.g., future delinquents or drug abusers) without recognizing that (1) the ability to predict is a research problem and cannot be taken for granted, and (2) even if research demonstrates that prediction is possible, the predictions are probabilistic and demand more than simple labeling to guarantee that both individual and social interests are met. Perhaps the best illustration here is the *Merriken* v. *Cressman* case mentioned earlier. A personality inventory completed by students was to be used as a basis for predicting potential drug abusers. These students would then be referred to supportive services. The potential negative effects of the prediction process, such as scapegoating and labeling, were unanticipated. And to exacerbate the problem, the evidence for validity of the inventory for that particular high school population was weak. The lack of evidence was virtually ignored by the agency developing the prevention program and by most parents and school officials. Their faith in the quality of prediction was not shared by the parent who took the matter to the courts.

In each of these cases, the assumption of near-perfect prediction was offered to justify an attack on the collection of data. In each case, the assumption burlesques reality. To this extent, the attack and the concern are misplaced. Lay beliefs on the matter are dictated in part by a few commercial contractors whose claims are exaggerated if not untrue. They are doubtless influenced by a few academic researchers who are caught between the need to sustain their prestige and the need to disabuse the public of its faith in their ability to predict behavior accurately. They are fostered by politicians whose expertness in the quantitative social sciences is easily surpassed by their need to scramble onto the right bandwagon.

The more fundamental problems concern whether a prediction should be made at all, given the accuracy of the prediction or imputation, and how that prediction will be used. Whether the prediction ought to be made is always arguable. We contend, however, that the *absence* of information on the accuracy of the prediction is considerably more dangerous than its presence. The consequences of poor data are obvious in situations where discrimination against individuals is based on informal impression and anecdote. The consequences are obvious where the success of expensive social programs is in dispute. They are obvious where novel social problems are not only disruptive but obscure in their origins and character. Making the statistical data available to all interest groups, not just to the empowered one, is essential in understanding those problems and in resolving them.

Finally, and most importantly, we believe that evidence for accuracy in prediction can be collected in ways that eliminate risk to *current* respondents in the research. The strategies for doing so are covered in succeeding chapters.

PROFESSIONAL COMPETENCE AND ETHICAL CONFLICT

A small percentage (10 to 15 percent in our judgment) of the serious conflicts between research and ethics or law are due to the researcher's incompetence. That is, the research design is so poorly thought out, the research question so poorly framed, that the research invites an accidental conflict with ethical or legal standards. Incompetence in research design is defined here as a failure to exploit the state of the art in research design. Our initial judgment about relative frequency is based on cases considered by the American Psychological Association's Ethics Committee.

To illustrate the issue, consider that in the controversy over psychological testing of the 1960s, the premature use of tests for selection and screening was inconsistent with high professional standards for gauging the quality of tests. It posed at least as much of a problem as the respondent's often involuntary participation in the testing enterprise. The problem was compounded by the chronic mislabeling of tests, biographic inventories, and the like as administrative tools rather than as devices that must be validated before they are used. Professional standards, in written form, also provide guidance on the propriety of asking particular questions of individuals who may be upset by them. Yet even the advice to avoid heavy-handed inquiry is at times ignored. The preparation of clear mechanisms for assuring the confidentiality of data is no less crucial. The virtue of the professional researcher no longer appears to be an acceptable substitute.

The problems here are, of course, not all new. They appear in the early history of survey research in the United States and in what would now be regarded as an ethical controversy. In the 1840 census, for example, the census director, William A. Weaver, a cashiered naval officer, sometime poet, and pamphleteer, managed to bring the enterprise to near disaster (Davis 1972). The data were poorly collected, especially on minority groups: the majority of Negroes in some cities, for example, were found by interviewers to be insane. And in their adulterated form, the data served as evidence for statesmen such as John C. Calhoun to justify slavery. It was not until the 1850 census that improvements were made by a new Census Board of competent overseers. Here, the standards of expertise were well ahead of practice in the field, a phenomenon attributable at least in part to the selection of field interviewers on the basis of political rather than professional criteria.

Nor are such problems confined to the social research sector. Physicians have adopted medical regimens on the basis of poor research evidence, and doubtless will continue to do so. Recall Brodie's claims, based on tests with fewer than a dozen monkeys, that his polio vaccine was effective. The claim was followed by the vaccine's application to children, and the death and paralysis of some of them. Krebiozen, Laetrile, and Thalidomide were advertised as successful on the basis of inadequate evidence. Just as some psychologists continue to gauge the quality of clinical therapy using weak standards, some physicians rely on poor standards of practice to produce tonsillectomies, hysterectomies, and adenoidectomies.

None of the procedures discussed in this monograph guarantee good research design in the social sciences. Their purpose is only to help maintain respondent privacy. In other respects, it is the competence of the researcher that must be assured so that this small class of extreme conflicts can be avoided.

THE JOURNALIST AND OTHER SPOKESMEN

One of the inevitable consequences of a doctrine of free speech is that some reporting will be accurate and fair, and some reporting will not. We accept the mixture because the alternative—a more controlled and therefore purer form of enterprise—is almost always invidious.

But that does not make errors in reporting any more palatable. It is the errors bred by incompetence that concern us here, for they seem to be the most unnecessary ones. In particular, misreporting as a consequence of failure to verify informants' leads appears to be no less frequent a problem in reporting on privacy matters than it does in reporting on other topics. And because privacy controversy can very quickly envelop a social research project, accuracy in reporting is critical here.

To get some idea of the nature of misreporting, recall the case studies described earlier—for example, the 1970 census controversy, in which nonexistent questions and distorted variations on real questions were discussed repeatedly in the popular media (Eckler 1972). Further, recall journalists' reports that Eron and Walder's (1961) research involved asking children unnecessary questions about their parents' attitudes toward them. In fact, such questions were not asked at all. The same problem appears in accounts of the controversy over Project Scope, where attempts to put matters right were complicated by the researchers' own imperfect recollection of question content (Tillery 1967). Oyen's (1965) analyses suggest that the Norwegian press's treatment of Project Metropolitan reflects no more than a promiscuous attitude toward accuracy in reporting.

Examples such as this are easy to find though they are in the minority: most social research is not especially exciting to anyone but the researcher or the policy maker who uses the information. Their predictable occurrence in controversial studies puts responsibility on the social scientist to develop research designs that are secure against incompetent reporting, to develop information materials that are robust against naive or hurried interpretation, and to develop a better understanding of institutional and individual prophylactics for inaccurate reporting or its effects.

The difficulty of encouraging good science reporting, especially social science reporting, is also relevant. Despite the efforts of some journalists to educate their colleagues about statistical research (e.g., Meyer 1973), and despite the successful efforts of a few journalists to educate themselves (e.g., C. Jencks and C. P. Gilmore) in the logic, if not the technical niceties, of statistics and social research, the field is underdeveloped. That poor research is applauded and good research often goes unrecognized is a reasonable consequence of technical innocence. The fact that every person must be an amateur social scientist makes the problem more difficult, because that skill is often insufficient for understanding solutions to problems in this arena. It is reflected, for example, in the *National Observer*'s willingness to report a privacy problem that embarrassed its own staff and its market-research contractor, and in the *Observer*'s inability to report the technical solutions to the problem (Gemmill 1975; Gemmill, personal communication).

In any argument over the propriety of a research effort, various groups aside from the journalists may claim to represent or interpret the public's interest. The ACE Studies of Campus Unrest, for example, were scrutinized by the National Student Association, the American Civil Liberties Union, and local chapters of Students for a Democratic Society. Community groups in Roxbury, Massachusetts, the Woodlawn Section of Chicago, and Denver, Colorado, rule on the acceptability of community surveys mounted by academic researchers, and attend to the privacy implications of the research.

These competing influences are a natural part of politically important social research. But their occurrence often comes as a bit of a shock to researchers without experience in social survey and social experimentation. As a consequence, they may fail to respond adequately to claims bearing on the privacy of respondents. Some of the techniques presented in succeeding chapters of this monograph have been used to accommodate demands from such groups that privacy be assured. Most of the techniques have been tested sufficiently to provide evidence that, regardless of an interest group's contentions, the respondent is protected.

But merely having a protection device available implies nothing about the broader issues identified by such groups, and other mechanisms must be developed to accommodate them. To be more specific, it is clear that the information-exchange process in most applied research is one-sided. The community is asked to participate in research, but tangible rewards for its participation are few, and the respondent often receives little or no feedback on exactly how research can or should be used. The problem of justifying research through such feedback mechanisms extends to the national level and at times bears directly on privacy. Side studies of the 1974 Census of Agriculture, for example, suggest that nearly half the farmers responding to agricultural surveys cannot remember which government agency actually collected the data. Further, over 40 percent believe erroneously that the Census Bureau discloses *individual* records collected under the agricultural census to other governmental and nongovernmental agencies. Most have only the vaguest idea of how the statistical data are used; about 25 percent reported that any use hurt rather than helped most farmers (U.S. Department of Commerce 1975). Ignorance about privacy regulations on census data is surprising, given the Census Bureau's explicit emphasis on the topic in field interviews. Ignorance about data uses is not: there is little formal feedback here or in most other social research projects. Related problems with more serious consequences for research were documented by Brim (1965) Brim et al. (1969) during the testing controversies of the 1960s. Although the idea of providing feedback to respondents is sometimes pursued with remarkable vigor (e.g., Caplan, Morrison, and Stambaugh 1975), it is not yet routine.[2] It is hardly surprising, then, that target populations refuse and resist research: why should they participate if the consequences are unknown?

As in any other sphere of activity, the democracy implied by competing advocates—journalists, community groups, and so on—also carries the opportunity for incompetence and corruption. Informal groups may be accountable to no one except their sponsors. They may serve themselves better than they serve the public or the interest they claim to represent. There is usually no way to guarantee either technical competence or a candid statement of interests. These problems underlie some controversies in biomedical and genetic research, and applied research on atomic power sources, as well as social research. Nothing in this monograph will resolve these ancillary problems, but they should be recognized.

Confusing them with privacy-related issues is unlikely to yield any decent solutions to either type of problem.

Summary

There have been a notable but small number of empirical studies on the problem of eliciting sensitive information from people, using various modes of assuring confidentiality. These include case studies of privacy-related problems in single research projects, experimental tests of different methods for assuring confidentiality, and surveys relevant to privacy-related attitudes and the privacy-preserving behavior of respondents. By and large, the data support the idea that an explicit promise of confidentiality is typically influential for a *minority* of respondents in social research, that a promise will at times be an insufficient condition for obtaining respondents' cooperation, and that if an assurance is breached and the fact becomes well known, the quality of the research data will be degraded. Assurance of confidentiality is more likely to be necessary when the information elicited is sensitive, when information may be appropriated for use in threatening and nonresearch activities, and when special interest groups put a high value on the principle that personal information ought to remain confidential.

The case studies of particular incidents point out that privacy-related objections to research often derive from one or more active groups that, with access to the media, can be dramatically effective in halting research regardless of its quality or purpose. At least some group objections are typically irrelevant, inaccurate, or both, and inaccuracies are usually magnified by press coverage. Finally, episodic and, especially, inaccurate objections by an interest group can be accommodated by well-informed research advocates on site. The case studies are complicated by the fact that a great many factors unrelated to the confidentiality issue may result in the cancellation of the research and the degradation of the research data. In the particular instance, these other factors may be of greater import than individual privacy.

The field experiments examined earlier have generally been designed to determine if one method of assuring respondents of confidentiality in surveys is any better than another. The main criteria for judging methods include refusal rate and candor in reporting, candor being estimated from the rate at which sensitive traits are admitted. Until recently, such experiments have been conducted on a small scale. Results suggest that some but not all respondents will understand and appreciate the use of concrete assurances beyond a promise of confidentiality, and they will react accordingly through increased candor of response, increased willingness to respond, or both. If an assurance is transparently weak or vulnerable, a minority of respondents will recognize the weakness and react accordingly. In still other instances, even concrete strategies for preserving confidentiality fail to encourage cooperation, perhaps because the mode of assurance is unfamiliar to respondents (and therefore not completely trustworthy), or the assurance is made in a very hostile context.

The surveys and experiments show that levels of "sensitivity of questions" and level of "invasion of privacy" are difficult to measure but are nonetheless measurable aspects of a research endeavor, and that the results of such measurement can be used to verify the need for assurances of confidentiality. Some survey evidence suggests that respondents are aware of the possibility of deductive disclosure in anonymous questionnaires and react accordingly. Comparative surveys of the relative accuracy of administrative records and of social research records on the same populations are clear in their implication: where research records are acquired under a promise of confidentiality they can (but do not always) provide a more accurate picture of a social problem than administrative records alone. The administrative records are distorted at least at times because respondents recognize them as a vehicle for potentially negative administrative action. The research records, on the other hand, are often viewed as confidential with respect to administrative agencies.

Other persistent influences on public controversy over privacy need to be recognized. They include honorific appeals to privacy, made by an administrator or politician, in the interest of achieving institutional or political goals. They include public misconceptions about the quality of data and the use of data in predicting behavior, and researcher incompetence in data collection. They include misreporting and exploitation by journalists and interest groups with less interest in verifying claims than in taking action on an allegation. The main source of information on these issues is case-study material. No systematic survey data is available.

This chapter's focus, on evidence for the need to assure individuals of the confidentiality of their responses, is narrow. There are other, no less important ways to examine the question of whether an assurance is warranted. For some researchers, the answer lies not in these data but in a professional ethic. For other researchers, the answer lies in a theory of social equity and law. The alternative frames of reference are considered in chapter 8, on statutory approaches to assuring confidentiality.

Notes

1. The need for systematic documentation has been recognized persistently in law journals—e.g., Boness and Cordes (1973), Nejelski and Lerman (1971), and Ruebhausen and Brim (1965)—and in governmental deliberation on assuring confidentiality in social research (U.S. General Accounting Office 1976). See also the discussion of the *Branzburg* decision in chapter 8.

2. The same problem, of course, afflicts social scientists in other countries. See the remarks by Dalenius in Dalenius and Klevmarken (1976, p. 75).

□ 4 □

Procedural Methods

"What is the use of a book," thought Alice, *"without pictures or conversations?"*

LEWIS CARROLL
Alice's Adventures in Wonderland

Procedural methods are designed to eliminate or minimize the need to maintain a direct linkage between a respondent's identification and other information that he provides to a researcher about himself. Some of these methods are quite simple; for example, the researcher can elicit anonymous responses to the inquiry. Others, such as link file systems for longitudinal research, are more complicated. All the methods enhance the confidentiality of research records, and they are useful to the extent that they do not seriously restrict research objectives.

The first section below presents a functional classification scheme for the various methods. Succeeding sections enumerate and illustrate methods falling within each class. The enumeration process is a bit tedious, but it is essential for identifying the benefits, disadvantages, and vulnerability of the methods.

A Simple Classification Scheme

Procedural strategies for assuring the confidentiality of the researcher's records on research participants vary considerably in character, function, logistical requirements, and feasibility. A previous effort to impose some structure on this variability was based on logical models for the procedures (Boruch 1972b). Although this early scheme was useful in deriving variants on the strategies and in describing complex strategies in terms of their elementary components, it was not especially helpful in showing how the strategies could be used in typical research designs.

Consequently, we will adhere to a simpler scheme based on elementary features of the research designs in which procedural methods have been used. The first three classes of methods concern, respectively, cross-sectional studies, longitudinal research, and experimental studies. Each uses the research participant as the sole source of information about himself. A fourth class bears on research that relies for information not only on the respondent, but also on archive records that contain data about the individual.

Specifically, a *cross-sectional study* involves eliciting information from members of a sample at one or more points in time, but no attempt to link individual records from one time to the next. The United States Census Bureau, for example, elicits data about the number of children in a household in each decennial census, but there is no attempt to correlate the number of children within particular households over time for every family in the population. In *longitudinal studies,* information is elicited periodically from the same individuals over time. For example, correlational studies on the emotional development of disadvantaged children are based on a statistical summary of linkages between the children's prior behavior and their current behavior. *Experimental study* refers to research in which individuals are allocated to one or another treatment program (in the field or laboratory) and the objective is to assess the impact of the treatment on them. To obtain interpretable estimates of the relative effects of a new alcoholism detoxification program, for example, candidates for the program may be randomly allocated to the novel program or to existing programs, and then monitored to determine each group's response to treatment. Any of these designs may also require that information from existing archive records be used to enrich, verify, or clarify the data collected directly from the research subject.

Cross-sectional Studies

For many social scientists, a cross-sectional survey is often a convenient way to better characterize a potentially critical social problem. So, for example, a regional survey may be undertaken to determine, with more accuracy and precision than regular information systems provide, the characteristics of child abusers, settings in which abuse occurs, attitudes and behavior of abused children, and so forth. A sequence of such cross-sectional surveys may be conducted to track gross changes in the severity or nature of the problem.

A variety of tactics have been used to preserve the confidentiality of data on respondents in this type of research. Some of the procedures, their benefits, and their application are described next, followed by an assessment of their shortcomings.

ALTERNATIVE PROCEDURES AND THEIR BENEFITS

The four procedures described here cover completely anonymous responses, temporarily identified responses, and the use of brokers to provide anonymity in response. Though not especially complicated, the procedures are also represented schematically in figure 2 to establish conventions for illustrating more elaborate approaches.

Model A.. One obvious tactic for preserving confidentiality in cross-sectional studies is to ask that research participants furnish information anonymously. Schematically, the researcher furnishes an inquiry to a prospective respondent, who then supplies information about himself without identification in response to the inquiry (figure 2: A). Despite its simplicity, the anonymous response tactic is quite common and often effective. It is more interesting for its flexibility, in that one

Figure 2. Schematic representation of procedural methods for assuring confidentiality in cross-sectional research: Models A to D.

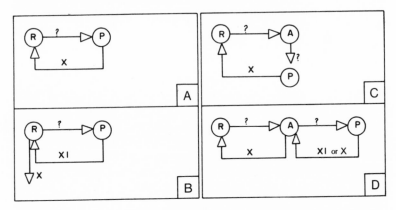

2. In each model, *R* represents the researcher, *P* represents the research participant or respondent to an inquiry, and *A* represents an agency that routinely maintains records on the participant. *X* and *Z* represent different kinds of information and *I* represents the identification of the respondent. Information or identifiers that are encoded are represented as *X'*, *Z'*, *I'*, etc. The interrogative symbol, *?*, is used to represent an inquiry.

can elicit both identified information and anonymous information simultaneously from the same respondents when differential sensitivity of the inquiries justifies this course of action. Eckler (1972, p. 195), for example, suggested this dual survey approach to accommodate congressional objections to census questions on household income. Income information would be provided through an anonymous questionnaire mailed directly to the Census Bureau, while other, more innocuous information would be provided directly to interviewers. Hauser (1975) reports incidentally that although the Census Bureau printed about twenty million forms so that respondents could furnish income information by mail, rather than directly to an interviewer, only about one hundred thousand forms were actually used. The relatively low usage rate is consistent with other research on the topic: despite political and journalistic attention, privacy issues are not a paramount and sophisticated concern to respondents in census surveys (see chapter 3). The strategy is also flexible in that it has been used in direct-mail surveys (questionnaires returned anonymously), some interviews (questionnaires, provided to individuals during an interview, returned anonymously after initial contact), and in other situations (e.g., delayed telephone response).

Model B.. In some cases, it is essential that responses to each inquiry be answered completely and that there be a good match between target sample membership and actual sample membership. One might then elicit information on each identified respondent (XI in figure 2:B), check for completeness of response and validity of sampling, and then destroy identifiers *(I),* leaving only anonymous information *(X),* in each individual's record. This strategy is also a common one, used, for example, by the American Council on Education in some of its surveys of college faculty, student, and administrator participation in campus protest activities (Astin 1968), by Michigan's Institute for Social Research in studies of juvenile delinquency (Gold and Reimer 1974), and others.

Model C.. Occasionally, even the fact that certain individuals are members of a target population constitutes sensitive information. For example, a researcher may be interested in obtaining base-line data on recent clients of a mental hospital for the purpose of planning better hospital evaluation. Hospital policy, local law, or professional custom may prohibit the hospital's disclosure of client identification. At this writing, the New York State Mental Hygiene Law, for example, prohibits the Mental Health Department from disclosing the fact of hospitalization to an outside inquirer except under extraordinary circumstances. Even if identifications were made available, the clients might be unwilling to cooperate in answering an outside researcher's questions. Under either circumstance, the researcher might then supply the hospital with questionnaires, say, and with sufficient financial support (and other incentives) for the hospital to forward the inquiries to its previous clients. The process is illustrated symbolically in figure 2:C, where A represents the hospital or any other similar institution with an archival responsibility and the willingness to serve as a broker. Using a broker in this situation is almost essential for assuring validity of response to some questions, since asking respondents directly about their membership in a controversial or socially stigmatized group can yield very unreliable data. The reliability problems are illustrated by Meyer and Borgatta's (1959) attempts to document the health status of former mental patients.

The procedure is also common, though institutional regulations may prevent its use in particular cases. The Social Security Administration, for instance, cannot permit researchers to access SSA records directly for selecting a sample. More importantly, the agency cannot even act as a broker in such cases: for example, in selecting a sample of records and forwarding the researcher's inquiry to members of the sample (Steinberg and Cooper 1967). SSA cooperation in such an arrangement is prohibited on the grounds of the procedure's susceptibility to corruption, the costs of reducing risks of unauthorized disclosure, and the costs of operating such a system. A major exception, the interagency linkage study described in chapter 2, is a limited one.

Model D.. If there is some risk that identification can be deduced from even anonymous responses, or if there is some other reason why respondents should not forward information directly to the researcher, then the archival agency may serve as an intermediary in the transmission of responses. In the example given above, hospital staff may receive responses directly from patients, excise identifying material *(I)*, and extract the information they require before sending the documents on to the researchers (figure 2:D). The feasibility of this procedure has been demonstrated in a variety of forms and settings. One illustrative effort by Knudsen, Pope, and Irish (1967) required that physicians supply their patients—new mothers—with questionnaires designed to elicit information about patterns of premarital pregnancy. Anonymous responses were returned to the physician in a sealed envelope to sustain at least a minimum level of confidentiality with respect to physicians. The physician then transmitted the anonymous documents to the researcher, preserving individual privacy with respect to the outside researcher. The U.S. Census Bureau often serves in this brokerage role for other federal agencies. For example, the Bureau periodically elicits information on employment in its Current Population Survey, at the request of the Bureau of Labor Statistics. Resulting sample data are stripped of clear identifiers and provided to BLS; identified records maintained by the Census Bureau are protected against disclosure by Title 13 of the U.S. Code (Yates 1975).

Strategies A through D are by no means clever, but they are simple to use and generally feasible, and they can be very effective. Their usefulness is most obvious for situations in which respondents can furnish information in an impersonal way: for example, through questionnaires mailed to respondents or furnished during an interview, through delayed-response telephone surveys, and so on. If responses to inquiry are in fact anonymous, the researcher removes himself from possible conflict with legal efforts to appropriate research records for nonresearch purposes. That is, the anonymity of the record and the researcher's ignorance protect the respondent from legal prosecution, social embarrassment, or other nonresearch uses on the basis of the record's contents. Furthermore, anonymous records are less likely to provoke the interest of a corrupt penetrator of a researcher's data files. This last benefit is likely to become more important as social and behavioral scientists investigate more controversial topics.

DISADVANTAGES

Although these procedures have served researchers well, they have some serious shortcomings. Their use can make it more difficult, for example, to assay the quality of data, thereby decreasing the social and scientific usefulness of research. And the procedures are considerably more vulnerable to corruption than one might suppose. The implications for data quality are discussed below. Vulnerability is discussed in the next section.

The simplest criteria for evaluating the quality of the data in this or any other type of research include sampling validity, response validity, and opportunities for further research based on data collected under the procedures. Assuring the validity of sampling—that is, the match between target sample and actual sample—is a bit more cumbersome for models B through D than in most survey research work. The temporary or indirect availability of the identities of respondents in each of these procedures makes follow-up survey of nonrespondents and subsequent validity checks possible. But it is difficult to accomplish such validity studies in the short time usually available for cross-sectional research. Checking the sampling validity when completely anonymous questionnaires are used (model A) is usually more difficult but not impossible. As a partial resolution of the problem in one project—a questionnaire survey for the National Academy of Sciences' Project on Computer Data Banks—Boruch directed that each member of the target sample be sent a blank questionnaire and a postcard containing his numeric identification. The respondent was instructed to return the completed questionnaire anonymously and to return the postcard under separate cover, preferably at a later date. The return of the postcard served to inform us that a response had in fact been made by the particular identified individual (Westin et al. 1972). Irving Crespi (1976) suggested a similar method for surveys of corporation directors.

Checking the validity of responses obtained under any of these models can also be difficult. If every member of the target sample furnishes completely anonymous information to the researcher, there is simply no easy way to estimate the validity of response: for example, to estimate an average relation between what a respondent says about himself and what his condition actually is. Internal consistency of response can be established by building checks into a questionnaire or interview protocol. But the often-necessary ability to link a response with an external criterion of high validity is absent. The questionnaire survey results from the NAS Project on Computer Data Banks, for example, could have been strengthened considerably had we been able to obtain persuasive evidence on the validity of reports by executives of insurance companies that their organizations had written policies regarding access to data files, received few complaints about their data files, and so forth. Similarly, we know that responses to many social questions are susceptible to temporal instability and other sources of variation that are irrelevant to what we really want to measure. The consequences of failing to assess this random measurement error include biases in statistical analyses and a reduction in one's ability to detect subtle relationships. For understanding weak or rare social phenomena, the problem is not trivial.

If the opportunity presents itself, conducting intensive, personal interviews with members of a random subsample of the main target sample will normally provide evidence bearing on the reliability of response. This usually requires at least temporary identifiability of some respondents, however, and it may be difficult to meet that requirement. The broker in models B, C, and D, for example, will not always be willing or able to give the researcher an opportunity to conduct such a study. Moreover, it will not always be clear that reinterview data should be the standard of comparison in judging the accuracy of questionnaire responses. Other sources of information—administrative records, for example—may be more relevant, but the strategies outlined above prevent one from linking responses to other information sources. The coincidence of the need for confidentiality of records and the absence of any need for clear identifiers in cross-sectional research, then, is a bit misleading. Identifiability in some form for a subsample of respondents is often crucial for controlling sample validity and response validity.

Finally, having only anonymous records at hand truncates the researcher's opportunity to do more informative data analyses. For example, longitudinal studies that tie current behavior to prior behavior are impossible under the models. Retrospective reporting may be one way around this problem, but the unreliability of such reports is often intolerable, and the difficulty of appraising the reliability of retrospective reports by anonymous respondents exacerbates the problem. Similarly, one cannot link the anonymous record with any other existing records on the same respondents. Yet such a linkage is often essential for enriching the data base for research, assessing the validity of reporting, and improving the precision of estimates of population parameters.

For instance, to understand how organizations are changing their practices regarding data files, a follow-up survey of the 2,500 institutions sampled in the 1970 NAS Project on Computer Data Banks might be thought appropriate. The 1970 results, however, are useless except in providing crude base rates, since mechanisms for longitudinal follow-up were not created. No average relation between the 1970 policy and the current policy of the institutions surveyed can be established; no ties among policy style, practice, and court action can be systematically documented over the period; no empirical data on conditions for policy change within institutions can be obtained. To establish such linkages is often important for understanding the social problem. To establish such linkages without violating confidentiality standards is difficult but not impossible. Some approaches to the problem are examined in the section below on research using multiple data sources.

VULNERABILITY: COVERT IDENTIFIERS AND DEDUCTIVE DISCLOSURE

These models for assuring confidentiality of response are deceptively tidy in the abstract. In practice, they can be vulnerable to corruption.

Recall that the purpose of each tactic is to eliminate or reduce the legitimate researcher's need to maintain identifiable records on respondents. Where that is not the actual purpose, the tactics can be undermined easily. A legitimate researcher may deceive respondents into believing that responses are anonymous for quite innocuous reasons tied to the goal of the research. A researcher may mislead respondents in order to capitalize on the commercial benefits of identifiable information. A fraudulent researcher may be deceptive for reasons that are criminally sanctionable. Even where the procedures are applied in accordance with the models, they are still vulnerable in the sense that data anonymously supplied can, under certain conditions, still yield unique information about a respondent.

The form of corruption need not be very imaginative. Before privacy matters were regarded as a serious concern, at least one researcher employed pin holes to permit identification of ostensibly anonymous responses to a personality inventory. Afterwards, he obtained information of exactly the same kind in a situation where respondents were asked to supply clear identification, and then established the correlation between the two kinds of responses. The goal here, establishing how individuals in clinical settings alter their responses, is not especially unreasonable. The method employed, though fairly innocuous, is not necessary. Another method requiring no deception might have been tried out: administering the inventory and requesting identification; collecting and then returning to the respondent the identified documents along with a blank inventory, which the respondent is asked to complete anonymously; having respondents delete identification from the first document, couple the two completed and anonymous documents, and resubmit them. The coupling is all that is essential for determining the correlation between responses yielded under fully identified and fully anonymous conditions. That coupling can be achieved without deception.

Deliberate deception of respondents is more likely to occur for reasons that are unrelated to social research goals, but there is little documentation on even the more flagrant examples. Thanks to Henry Gemmill, editor of the *National Observer*, we have a nice illustration of what may be a minor classic in market research. In this instance, the *Observer* commissioned a survey of its subscribers to obtain a statistical description of their demographic characteristics. The purposes of such a survey include using the statistical data to persuade potential advertisers to buy advertising space and to identify the kind of reporting, advertising, and so forth that is most likely to interest readers. In the mailed questionnaire survey, the survey contractor announced that responses would be confidential and provided information that would lead most readers to conclude that responses were anonymous. No identifying information was requested; no numerical or other identification appeared on the document. The responses were regarded as anonymous even by Gemmill until a skeptical recipient of a questionnaire discovered, on exposing the document to ultraviolet light, that an identification number did in fact appear on the document. The survey firm, Erdos and Morgan, acknowledged the invisible print but claimed that such information was necessary to follow up on nonrespondents. Of course, there are a half dozen ways of accomplishing that end—assuring the validity of sampling—without deception. The postcard device described earlier for the National Academy of Sciences survey is feasible and likely to be appropriate even in market surveys. But the firm seems to have been unaware of any of the less misleading devices. What makes the whole matter more worrisome is the *Observer*'s report that this type of deception had often been used in surveys undertaken by *Time, Scientific Ameri-*

can, and other publications, and that the surveys often contain very sensitive information (on income, travel, investments), which can easily be employed for nonscientific purposes (see Gemmill 1975; *National Observer,* 11 November 1975; and Dougherty 1975).

More sophisticated ways of corrupting these tactics are easy to identify. There is an enormous variety of photographic, microphotographic, optical, and electrochemical devices that one might use to attach covert identifiers to physical documents. Equally sophisticated electronic devices are readily available for identification of the sources of ostensibly anonymous oral reports, of electrically transmitted reports, of magnetically stored information, and the like. But even the crudest devices are impossible for the ordinary respondent to detect, unless he decides to purchase devices marketed as a prophylactic against the original trace device (Sherrill and Field 1974).

In point of fact, it is not always necessary to employ either the crude or the sophisticated trace devices discussed here. For even if clear identifiers are not obtained and the original documents are destroyed, records of anonymous response may still yield identifiable information. Suppose, for example, that an interrogator of a researcher's records knows that individual i is a member of the sample on which records are maintained and furthermore that i has characteristics $A_1, A_2, \ldots, A_p$. He can merely search the records for that individual if those characteristics are unique to i, that is, if the intruder's collateral information constitutes a *de facto* identification. The remaining information in the "anonymous" record, properties $A_{p+1}, A_{p+2}, \ldots, A_q$, is then available to the interrogator; he has accumulated new information about i. For example, in the NAS Project on Computer Data Banks (Westin et al. 1972), respondents returned their anonymous questionnaires to us by mail. The use of the postcard device mentioned earlier permitted us to verify that particular institutions had in fact responded. Type, size, and other organizational characteristics were determinable from responses to items in the questionnaire, and city of origin was determinable from the mailing envelope's postage stamp. By matching these characteristics with the information about the sample organizations that was available in published directories, journals, and the like, it would have been an easy matter to couple about 20 percent of the respondents to the proper anonymous questionnaire.

Even if the characteristics of the anonymous respondent are not unique, disclosure might be possible. One need only search the records for all individuals possessing properties $A_1, A_2, \ldots, A_p$, and then sequentially add a new property, $A_1, A_2, \ldots, A_{p+1}$, to ascertain if the number of individuals possessing characteristics A_1 through A_{p+1} remains the same. If the number remains the same, one can infer that respondent i possesses property A_{p+1}. To be specific, suppose one knew that a particular sample bank i was a respondent to the survey. From published sources we might also know that the number of employees of the organization was in the 500 to 1,000 range, and that the number of customers was in the range 10,000 to 100,000. The same information was elicited in the anonymous questionnaire, but by itself it does not uniquely identify a respondent. However, suppose that one totaled all such respondents, found, say, 45 out of 300 banks in the sample with the same characteristics, and then proceeded to search the questionnaires further to find that all 45 have had frequent complaints from civic groups about their record-keeping practices. We then have some hitherto unknown information about bank i: that is, that bank i has been subject to frequent complaints about its record-keeping practices. Hoffman and Miller (1970) appear to have been among the first to make these disclosure strategies explicit. Their work has helped to stimulate more advanced treatments of the topic: Schlörer's (1974, 1975) research in medical record systems is especially interesting. See chapter 6 for related references.

Though the process of deductive disclosure can get complicated, it is not so subtle that respondents will fail to recognize it in anonymous surveys. Some of the military officers who responded anonymously to Wilson and Rosen's (1975) drug use surveys apparently did register suspicion about the possibility of such disclosure, since the questionnaire contained a number of demographic items. The context of the research in this instance—a military installation—is likely to have made respondents a bit more skeptical than they might ordinarily be about the inquiry process. Analogous problems emerged in reviews of the Client Oriented Data Acquisition Process (CODAP) by the U.S. Senate Subcommittee on Constitutional Rights (1974). This statistical data archive maintained anonymous records generated by local drug abuse agencies, for research. However, the system employed an identification number system that included sex, race, the initials of one's mother's name, and zip code, and such information could in principle be used to identify individuals. Indeed, law enforcement agencies made unsubstantiated claims that they were able to learn the identities of persons on whom records were kept by cross-checking the anonymous records against data from the "U.S. Census Bureau, the Social Security Administration, and Educational Testing Service." Senate staff could not establish the legitimacy of claims (Bureau records are clearly not accessible to law enforcement agencies, for example), and no concrete abuse of the statistical research system was uncovered.

Actual examples of deductive disclosure based on anonymous individual records and of detection of disclosure are scarce for a variety of reasons. Deducing the identity of a respondent is difficult or impossible if the sample size is large, the amount of information available on each respondent is small, and the sample is very homogeneous.

These conditions prevail for many survey research efforts. Furthermore, the effort required to deduce respondent identification may not be worthwhile. Legitimate researchers have no interest in doing so simply because their professional rewards stem from competent analysis of data rather than creative disruption of mechanisms built to preserve confidentiality. The last possible reason for the absence of examples is a bit more disturbing. Disclosure, if it occurs, will usually be evident only to the inquirer, since outsiders do not have access to anonymous individual records, and the inquirer is unlikely to advertise his or her ability to deduce identification.

REDUCING VULNERABILITY

The respondent's trust in the behavioral scientist has always been a key ingredient in the research process. That trust is probably warranted by the scientist's use of procedural tactics such as these to conduct research without needless depreciation of respondent privacy. Now, recognizing the vulnerability of these procedures, it behooves us to justify that trust by developing strategies that reduce the possibility of corruption. This section contains a very tentative discussion of security-inducing mechanisms. It is tentative because any such list must accommodate the needs not only of the social science community and the respondent population, but also of research sponsors (e.g., the federal government) and other interest groups, and those interests are not altogether stable.

One obvious approach to reducing the vulnerability of any of the models is to channel the individual's response to a research inquiry through a trustworthy brokerage agency capable of reducing physical documents or oral testimony to anonymous, numerical form. This use of a broker, for example, would obviate the researcher's ability to employ a physical trace device, as was done in the *National Observer* episode and in the clinical research project described earlier. The broker may be a commercial organization—for example, an audit agency—with sufficient integrity or fear of public reaction or legal sanction to prevent collusion with the actual researcher. It may be a quasi-governmental agency, such as the National Academy of Sciences, with sufficient institutional integrity and prestige to justify a brokerage role. It may consist of an existing survey organization whose performance has also been marked by expertise in developing solutions to ethical problems of social research. It may consist of a network of organizations, existing or planned, which could take on the necessary filtering role.

The brokerage approach is notably cumbersome and in some situations likely to be entirely unrealistic. Instead, licensing of survey organizations (or individuals) may be a reasonable vehicle for reducing the risks of impropriety in research practice. This formalization of public trust is crude, but it can be effective nonetheless if criteria for licensing are sufficiently stringent and if it can be coupled to a strong mechanism for taking punitive action against an individual or agency breaching that trust. It is not clear whether licensing in this context can avoid the negative effects of licensing in other professions, nor is it clear that it can prevent all the problems we have described here. We dedicate more attention to the topic in the context of legal safeguards for assuring confidentiality of data (chapter 8).

Monitoring panels or review groups are often suggested for problems of this type. And apparently they have been effective in some quarters. Review panels that evaluate academic research on human subjects do in fact prevent naive abuses, although their performance has not been well documented enough to accept them without reservation. Review groups or independent monitors would probably be unacceptable to commercial agencies, and would be wildly unrealistic for application to grass-roots surveys by parent-teacher associations, congressmen, and the like.

Strategies other than the ones described here are more promising for resolving some of these problems. Notable among them are the statistical methods for maintaining privacy described in chapter 5, and the statutory devices described in chapter 8, used in combination with the procedural models.

So far, the discussion has concerned the problem of abuse of confidentiality-preserving tactics by the individual actually using the procedure. Penetration of the legitimate researcher's file of records by an outside interrogator may also occur, of course. This is a more tractable problem, partly because all the procedures described have been designed to reduce the likelihood that anyone, researcher included, will have access to identifiable records. For those tactics requiring temporary identifiability of response (models B, C, and D), some reasonable level of physical security is justified. Early separation of identifiers from response, separate storage of identifiers and response, and so forth are simple but effective. More elaborate physical security is generally justified for the more complex models.

Longitudinal Studies: Intrasystem Linkage

Recall that one of the main scientific costs of relying on anonymous respondents is that longitudinal research cannot be conducted. Using methods A through D, we could not track development and consistency of behavior over time for the average individual in the sample at hand. Yet for research on many sensitive topics—drug and alcohol use, child abuse, sexual behavior, political attitudes—the ability to do so is crucial for understanding social processes. The procedures described below have been designed to accommodate both the need for longitudinal data and the need to assure the confidentiality of records stemming from the research. Their use is restricted by the design to situations in which answers to the researcher's questions are furnished directly by the respondent. Procedures for accommodating privacy-related problems in using archive records on the respondent are considered later.

ALTERNATIVE STRATEGIES AND THEIR BENEFITS

These procedures can be useful in direct periodic surveys of a sample of individuals where the repeated measures must be linked for statistical analysis. All rely on the use of arbitrary identifiers as a basis for linking observations made over time and for preserving the confidentiality of individual responses. The procedures differ primarily with respect to the way the arbitrary identifier is treated: in procedures E through H (Figure 3), the respondent creates his or her own alias; in procedures I, J, and K, the researcher or an intermediary is responsible for the creation of alias, alias dictionaries, or code linkage systems (Figures 3–5).

Model E. The social researcher can sometimes assure confidentiality of response in longitudinal studies by having his or her respondents use nominal or numeric aliases instead of clear identifiers. For example, Peter Rossi, Eugene Groves, and D. Grafstein (1971) of Johns Hopkins University have required that students create a numeric alias in responding to surveys on drug use and other topics. Each respondent used a simple algorithm, supplied by the researchers, to compute an alias based on his or her parents' birth dates, and was instructed to recompute the alias in each periodic survey. In principle, at least, the alias was unique and easily retrievable by the respondent alone. In fact, the numbers generated on the algorithm were not all unique —a large sample relying, even in part, on multiple birth dates, for example, will result in many individuals having the same alias. Also, the alias was less retrievable than one might think—college students are evidently not consistent in recollecting and reporting their parents' birth dates, and in using the numbers in computation. Recollection of momma's birth month appears also to have been a problem for 8 percent of the women in Shimizu and Bonham's (1978) study of an unrelated method of assuring confidentiality (see chapter 5). In other research, Boruch and Creager (1969) have asked respondents to create and use a unique nominal alias, making an emphatic appeal for uniqueness, in responding to inquiry. This tactic has been successful

Figure 3. Schematic representation of procedural methods for assuring confidentiality in longitudinal research: Models E to I.

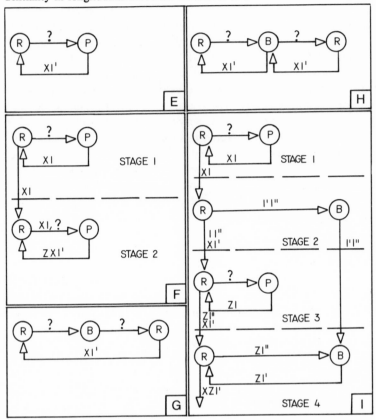

NOTE: The symbols are identical to those used in figure 2. Here, *B* represents a brokerage agency; *I′* and *I″* represent encoded identifiers or aliases, where two different encoding schemes are used.

in small field tests, where, for example, over two hundred fifty students on three college campuses created and used aliases consistently over two- to four-week intervals in our studies of the reliability of reports of political activities. The alias approach is often feasible in short-term longitudinal research, and one can sometimes assay and control the validity of sampling through the post-card mechanism suggested earlier for model A.

Model F.. The use of aliases does not, of course, preclude the concomitant use of clear identifiers. One can, for example, elicit relatively innocuous and identifiable information in a preliminary survey, and then collect and analyze the information. In a subsequent effort, one may return the questionnaires completed previously to the appropriate respondents, and request that they provide additional, perhaps more sensitive, information on an attached blank questionnaire, and that they then delete identifiers and return the two completed documents under an alias to the researcher. This tactic has some utility in studying, among other things, the validity of biographic inventories, personality tests, and the like, where the objective is to gauge the average respondent's tendency to distort a fully identified response. Simple extensions of the tactic involve the use of aliases on one set of inquiries, complete anonymity on a second set, and complete identifiability on a third and presumably very innocuous set of inquiries, when all sets of inquiries are directed toward the same individual and responses to each set are made independently. This variation can be built into many survey designs, and some special analytic techniques can be used to obtain maximum precision from the consolidated data. In any event, the survey may involve cross-sectional and longitudinal components running in parallel for the sake of reduced costs.

Model G. Where lists of potential respondents are unavailable to the researcher, as lists of a psychiatrist's patients would be, or where the researcher prefers not to have direct access to such lists, then the list custodian may be incorporated into an alias-based system for linkage. Under model G, the custodian—or, more generally, a brokerage agent —takes responsibility for transmitting inquiries and instruction from the researcher to the respondent; responses are supplied under an alias from one time to the next. The use of an intermediary here may be justified on the grounds that cooperation is more likely if the inquiry is channeled through an agency with which the respondent is familiar. Model G may also be justified in the sense that it insulates the researcher from the respondent and so prevents certain forms of corruption of the system, notably the use of covert identifiers. A variation has been independently invented and used, for example, in pilot evaluations of programs supported by the Emergency School Assistance Act, to accommodate school district interest in maintaining control over identification of students and in serving as an active intermediary in the research process (Bryant and Hansen 1976).

Model H. Channeling both the researcher's inquiry and respondent's reply through the list custodian has the same advantages as those outlined for model G. In addition, the custodian may serve a screening function, depressing the likelihood of deductive disclosure, eliminating unnecessary or inappropriate respondent types, and so forth. Some applications may demand that clearly identifiable information be supplied to the intermediary; such information may be extracted, verified, or even added by the custodian. In this case, the alias is used only in transmission from the custodian to the researcher; confidentiality is maintained with respect to researcher but not with respect to the intermediary. Some variations on the model require that both clear identification and respondent-created alias be given over to the list custodian to assure consistency in the use of the alias. Here, too, confidentiality is maintained with respect to the researcher and any outside penetrator of research records, but not with respect to the intermediary unless information is transmitted directly to the researcher by a respondent under the alias.

Model I. The alias approach is likely to be unsatisfactory in many surveys even with refinements. Furthermore, the strategy represented in Model F permits measurement at only two points in time if there is some need to destroy identifiers upon collection of sensitive data. One might alleviate these problems by applying a variation of the link file system represented by model I. One of the earliest of such systems was developed by A. W. Astin and used by the American Council on Education's Office of Research (Astin and Boruch 1970; Boruch 1971a). Earlier variations on the link file system idea have been independently invented by Manniche and Hayes (1957) and by Steinberg (1970).

The ACE system was developed in direct response to public and professional apprehension about maintaining identifiable records on respondents in longitudinal research on political activism among American college students. Under the model, identifiable data are collected by the researcher at stage 1 and then transformed into three files. One file consists of records that contain only statistical data (i.e., no identifiers), each record being coupled to an arbitrary account number (XI' in the diagram). A second file is created, containing true identifiers, each of which is coupled to a second arbitrary accounting number *(II")*. The third file is a code linkage, a file that matches the two sets of accounting numbers and therefore would permit total identifications of records if the three files were merged, shown as I' I'' at stage 2 in figure 3:I. This last file is maintained by a broker who is independent of the agency actually eliciting and maintaining the data. The broker is under contract not to disclose the code linkage system to anyone, including a government agency, for any reason. The ACE Office of Research code linkage, for example, was maintained by a social researcher in a foreign country in order to assure that research data concerning political activists on college campuses could not be appropriated for nonresearch use. Ideally, the broker is an agency that can legally resist both government interrogation and illegal attempts to acquire the file.

New identifiable data *(ZI)*, collected from the same sample at stage 3, are also transformed. True identifiers are replaced by the second set of arbitrary accounting numbers, yielding a file designated ZI''. This file of statistical records, each coupled to an accounting number, is shipped to the broker, who then substitutes the first accounting number set for the second set: each record ZI'' is changed to ZI'. Finally, the file is returned to ACE, where data from stage 1 and stage 3 can be linked using the accounting numbers common to both files (i.e., XI' is linked to ZI') as a basis for matching. The same pattern of operations is repeated for subsequent follow-up surveys of respondents.

Under ideal conditions, this link file approach gives the researcher access to only one wave of identifiable data at a time, and that access is limited to a short time interval.

Model J. Simple variations on the link file model are easy to create (figure 4). To streamline the system, the researcher can provide the respondent with an numeric identifier, instructing him to use it consistently. The researcher's own dictionary of clear identifiers and numeric alias is destroyed. The approach eliminates the brokerage system entirely but places responsibility for the maintenance of the alias on the respondent. Brokers may still be used to transmit inquiry, to receive responses, or both, and to otherwise facilitate the operation of the system.

Model K. Another variation on the basic scheme requires that the broker generate and maintain the link file. Model K (figure 5) illustrates a pattern in which the broker meets this requirement *without* obtaining identifiable records at any stage in the sequence. If the respondent can be relied on to use the alias consistently, then the broker's role may be eliminated from the scheme after the broker's initial contact with the respondent. In principle, nothing prevents the use of two or more brokers under this model. Each supplies the respondent with part of an arbitrary identifier to be used in subsequent researcher-respondent contacts. This last variant seems not to have been field tested, and though the dispersal of responsibility for alias creation may be desirable, it may not be a practical strategy.

Model L. It is sometimes *not* desirable for a research agency to take sole responsibility for setting up the code linkage system. In the ACE case, for example, to prevent even the possibility of the system's corruption by research staff, some arrangement with a distrustful agency or interest group might have helped to decrease the system's vulnerability, and to decentralize the system's elements so as to make it more secure. One device for building such a model is to have the two independent agencies (say, research staff and a national student group) each independently generate part of a numerical identifier for each individual. The complete identifier would be known only to the respondent. Such a system might work in the following way.

For a sample of 500 individuals, the researcher assigns a random two-digit number (00–99) to each individual. Any single number will

Figure 4. Schematic representation of Model J, a procedural method for assuring confidentiality in longitudinal research.

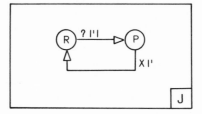

NOTE: The symbols are identical to those used in figure 2.

Figure 5. Schematic representation of procedural methods, using brokerage agencies, for assuring confidentiality in longitudinal research: Models K and L.

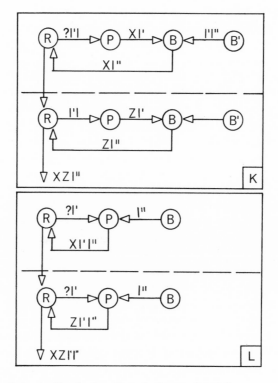

NOTE: Symbols are identical to those in figures 2 and 3.

then refer to about five individuals, and constitutes the first two digits of a unique numerical identifier, as yet incomplete. The number is printed on the questionnaire and sealed in an envelope on which all relevant individual names are printed; each packet of (about) five is then sent to an outside agency or broker. The code linkage dictionary of nonunique numerical aliases *(I'I)* is maintained by the researcher. The broker, which is administratively insulated from the research agency, then imprints a different random digit on each envelope containing the five names. So, for example, if five envelopes contain the names E. Thompson, A. D. Sakarov, K. Vonnegut, L. Deighton, and M. West, then one of the envelopes would be assigned a random number of (say) 8 and sent to Thompson, a second would receive 6 and be sent to Sakarov, and so on. The code linkage generated by the broker contains nonunique aliases and clear identifiers. The would-be respondent completes the questionnaire and then adds the third digit to identifying numbers already on the document. The strategy protects the identity of the respondent, since the broker and researcher are supposed to maintain their respective code dictionaries separately. The same pattern is used in follow-up surveys of respondents. The three-digit number is used as a basis for linking anonymous longitudinal records.

The system can be used as described to minimize the likelihood of illegal penetration of records. Decentralization of responsibility will inhibit if not eliminate even legal appropriation of identifiable records. And if one of the agencies creating a segment of the numeric identifier is entitled to immunity from subpoena under the law, the system serves as a less vulnerable device for assuring that records are not abused by insiders. An obvious extension of the basic scheme is to adjoin it to the link file arrangement given by model L; the coupling of Models L and I further reduces the possibility of easy nonresearch appropriation of files. Of course, if respondents can be persuaded in the initial contract to use the joint identifier consistently, then it is possible for the broker and research agency to destroy their own code linkage files, and so destroy any capacity to identify responses.

The feasibility of this last model has not been tested in the field. Nonetheless it may be useful in any scenario characterized by mutually distrustful agencies. Conservative legislators may conduct longitudinal surveys of their constituencies, using a system in which the conservative group develops part of an identifier and a liberal group, the remainder. The benefit, so long as there is no collusion, is anonymity for the respondent and longitudinal data. Similarly, a community group may find researchers unworthy of full trust and so may be satisfied by providing one portion of identifiers and having the researcher provide the remainder.

VARIATIONS ON THE RESPONDENT-GENERATED ALIAS THEME

The procedures implied by models E through H have not been utilized often in survey research, and they deserve more attention. Their effectiveness depends on accomplishing two objectives: respondent generation of a private and unique alias, and the consistent use of the alias by the respondent. Ideally, the method used to generate the alias must produce identifiers that are virtually unique, unchanging, and easily reconstructable only by the respondent. In practice, these criteria seem less difficult to meet in research on small to moderately large samples with short intervals between one survey and the next. It does not take much effort to encourage respondents to create a distinctive alias, and when given some clues about how to do so, respondents are likely to react accordingly. The more easily remembered aliases might be based, for example, on the names of public places, personal acquaintances, and the like. They might be based on material products, events, or any other reference system that delineates a large pool of virtually unique and arbitrary identifiers. Nonunique aliases are permissible only if the researcher is equipped to resolve the complicated problems inherent in analyzing data based on aggregates rather than individuals (see chapters 5 and 6).

For longer-term and larger-scale surveys, the researcher may need to exercise more control over alias generation in order to assure high quality data. The tactics that appear to be most feasible in these circumstances include random selection of numeric identifiers and requiring the use of special algorithms to generate a numeric alias. In interview surveys and especially in studies conducted in group settings, for example, there seems to be no great difficulty attached to having the respondent privately choose a card (or coin or other physical device) containing an alias identifier from a large pool of such cards (see Barna 1974, for instance). It may be possible to use letter combinations, the so-called "nonsense syllables" often employed by learning psychologists, and machine-generated names, rather than numbers, to facilitate memorization of the alias. The alias so chosen is then used as a consistent identifier by the respondent in completing questionnaires, in reporting through self-initiated telephone calls, and so forth. Given the respondent's willingness to respond consistently under the alias, responses remain anonymous with respect to the researcher, but they can still be linked to support longitudinal data analysis.

Assuring that the identifier is maintained and used by the respondent is crucial, but appears to us to be no more (or less) complicated a problem than that of encouraging cooperation in any large-scale research. Monetary rewards and other incentives have been useful in compensating for far more severe demands on the respondent's time and effort. No systematic research appears to have been done on respondent willingness to maintain and use aliases in social surveys. However, some interesting work on the construction of numeric identifiers, which can be checked for error easily and which may be simple to memorize, has been done for administrative applications (see Holmes 1975).

Physical surrogates for alias identifiers have been used by journalists, police officials, and others but seem not to have been used often in social research. Basically, the alias takes the form of a commonly available material object with unique features—a dollar bill, a lottery ticket, a page from a magazine. The respondent chooses the object, and each time a contact with the researcher is made, he gives up part of the object. Segments of the lottery ticket (or whatever) might, for example, be included each time the respondent answers and turns in a questionnaire, and the segment is used to match questionnaires from the anonymous respondent. That the tactic is feasible for very small samples is evident: it is used by police departments to link an informant's initial tip with his later claim for reward, and in other informant-inquirer situations. It is an unmanageable tactic in most large-sample applications. And its major benefit in research settings, as a memory booster for respondents, might be gained in other ways, such as offering material rewards for the consistent use of an alias.

Usually the researcher has at hand listings of potential respondents to whom he directs inquiries. In special cases, no such lists may exist and the alias approach might be used to facilitate a crude level of contact without breaching privacy. For example, individuals often contact television or radio stations by telephone to ask questions about a program, especially if it bears on a sensitive topic, such as the detection and treatment of disease, physical or otherwise. Usually, such inquiries are referred to professionals or professional groups (e.g., a local medical association). To detect the effect of programming or the directions to seek professional counsel, it is necessary to follow up on callers. Callers may wish to remain anonymous and so assigning them an alias or encouraging them to choose and use an alias in any subsequent contact with the station or professional counsel can provide the basis for simpler forms of follow-up. Similar tactics might be used with so-called telephone hotlines, for child abusers or potential child abusers, alcoholics, etc., whose effectiveness is a matter for research.

SECONDARY COSTS OF USING THE PROCEDURES

These strategies help to preserve anonymity of response in longitudinal surveys, and so avoid one major shortcoming of the techniques described for cross-sectional studies. But they engender other problems that are identical to those encountered earlier.

For instance, the strategies based entirely on respondent-generated alias make it more difficult to assure validity of sampling, to gauge validity of response, or to link the data acquired under these models with outside data on the same sample of respondents. The strategies based on multi-agency generation of link file identifiers, or those requiring that a neutral broker generate alias identifiers or code linkage identifiers are also subject to these problems. Some remedial strategies have already been described. If, for example, the respondent can be persuaded to verify that he has indeed responded, independently of his anonymous response, then the analytic problem of accommodating nonresponse will be more tractable. Consistency checks nested in a set of inquiries can be helpful in assuring and gauging the validity of response, but this usually demands more time of the respondent. Similarly, repeated observations made over a very short time period will normally permit one to determine the severity of the random error in response, and though this tactic also makes an increased demand of the respondent, it does not present any more difficulty here than it does in conventional direct surveys. For most of the procedural strategies, it will often be desirable on scientific grounds that a subsample of respondents be reinterviewed or resurveyed under clearly identified conditions. The subsample may be essential to better establish validity of response or to link various sources of information for statistical analysis. Other procedural arrangements to assure confidentiality of response for these identified individuals must then be applied, a matter that complicates the management of the research and is likely to increase costs a bit.

These difficulties are irrelevant to situations where the quality of data is virtually guaranteed by the circumstances or where concerns about the quality of data are little more than nominal. In some studies of the aged, for example, a high level of cooperation can sometimes be predicted beforehand, because of the topic (i.e., the problems of the aged are of interest to the aged), the target population (who, being members of a group peculiarly isolated socially, are often delighted to be asked a question, let alone to answer one), or the context of the survey (e.g., a study of institutionalized and easily identified groups). For different reasons, the quality of response is sometimes predictably high—for example, where the survey elicits information which is salient in memory and which, because of the anonymity of the response, is not susceptible to the distortion induced by social, cultural, or other similar influences. The additional difficulty of assuring quality of response under these procedural models is unlikely to be of serious concern to survey organizations that normally employ no validity checks at all. Nor is it likely to concern the parent-teacher associations, the community groups, newspapers, and public officials who are often remorselessly amateur in conducting survey research. For the better commercial surveys and for the better community-conducted surveys, assuring both the confidentiality of data and the quality of data under these models may be as difficult a problem as it is in surveys conducted for social scientific purposes.

For the basic link file approaches, quality control is easier to sustain since there is a brief period, between the acquisition of the data and its incorporation into a link system, during which identified responses are available to the researcher. This temporary identifiability presents an opportunity for short-term validity appraisals, for tests of alternative methods for assuring the validity and completeness of responses, and for linking these responses with other data sources. The variations on the link approach, or on the respondent-generated alias approach, which require the use of an intermediary as a anonymity-preserving device, may not afford the same opportunities.

Finally, the use of any of these procedures or their variations puts notable constraints on the methods used to elicit information. They are often feasible for mailed questionnaire surveys, questionnaire surveys in group settings, delayed-response telephone surveys, and delayed-response interviews. The confessional approach (physical screens and so on), taken in a few of the original Kinsey studies, is feasible with any of the procedures, when on-site interviews are necessary. But there are few large-sample research projects in which the maneuver is feasible or appropriate.

Research Using Multiple Data Sources: Intersystem Linkage

None of the strategies presented so far are at all helpful if there is some need to link research records on individuals in a particular sample with independently stored records on the same individuals. One might wish to establish such a linkage in law enforcement research, for example, where police department records on policemen's previous training might be coupled to the researcher's records on the their behavior in the field in order to understand the predictive value of training information. The department's regulations may prohibit an outside researcher's accessing police personnel records. And the confidentiality of the researcher's records on identifiable individuals must usually be maintained, suggesting that the police department staff should not be given access to those records. How then can one link the two kinds of information? The following remarks bear on alternative solutions to the problem.

Model M. A simple strategy that permits linkage of multiple sources of confidential data is represented in figure 6:M. The researcher

Figure 6. Schematic representation of procedural methods for assuring the confidentiality in research based on multiple information sources: Models M to Q.

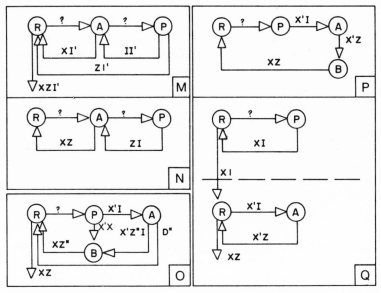

NOTE: The symbols are identical to those used in figures 2 and 3.

(R) elicits information from both the research participant *(P)* and from the data archive *(A)*, which already maintains data on the same individual. The participant provides information *(ZI')* with encoded identifiers—that is, an alias *(I')*—to the researcher and provides the key for decoding the identifier to the archival agency. The key consists of only two items of information—clear identification and the alias. The agency replaces clear identifiers in its own records with the encoded identifier and supplies the records *(XI')* to the researcher. The researcher matches the records of each type, *XI'* and *ZI'*, basing the linkage on the encoded identifiers *(I')* appearing in each record. As a result, the researcher can analyze linked data provided independently by both the archive and the respondent. The use of the alias and linkage strategy helps to assure that the researcher has no direct access to any identified records on any respondent, regardless of whether the respondent or the archive supplies the information. The confidentiality of information elicited by the researcher for research purposes is similarly assured with respect to the archive. The scheme can easily be generalized to multiple archives (Boruch 1972b). A related technique has been developed and demonstrated by Manniche and Hayes (1957) in their research on college students; the archive in this instance contained college student records.

Model N. In some cases, respondents may prefer to channel their responses through the archive. For example, in police research, the policeman/respondent may be reluctant to use an alias and may prefer to have his department remove identifiers. One might capitalize then on model N. The respondent forwards his identified responses *(ZI)* to the archive where the new information *(Z),* is linked to existing records *(XI),* stripped of clear identifiers, and finally submitted to the researchers in anonymous form *(XZ).* A variation of this strategy has been used in the Oklahoma Police Assaults study (Chapman and Swanson 1974) to assure that the researcher obtained all the data he needed in consolidated form without access to subject-created records or to archival records containing identifying information. Police advisors in the Oklahoma study did in fact react negatively to a suggestion to use aliases and model M; evidently policemen do not feel comfortable using aliases. Note that the subject-created record is not confidential with respect to the archive under model N.

Model O. To get around the problem of the archive's having access to clearly identified responses in model N and of a participant's reluctance to use an alias in Model M, one might instead require that participants encode their response cryptographically. The respondent first uses a personal encoding scheme to encode his identified responses on a questionnaire *(X'I).* He then sends the encoded information with clear identification to the archive and sends the decoding scheme to a trustworthy decoding agency *(B).* The archive links its own records *(ZI)* with those supplied by participants, and then cryptographically encodes the archival portion of the total record, transforming ZI to $Z''I$, to maintain confidentiality with respect to the decoder.[1] The linked, encoded records *(X'Z''I)* are then sent to the decoder, who uses the decoding scheme supplied by the respondent to decode the relevant section of the linked record; the partially decoded record is then stripped of identifiers and sent to the researcher. The researcher uses a decoding scheme *(D'')* supplied by the archive to decode the remaining section of the record and to obtain XZ, the decoded, linked, and anonymous records.

Model P. The strategy just described is a bit complicated, and having subjects create their own encoding scheme will not always be feasible. The decoder agency might then supply a uniform scheme to each subject. The subject encodes his responses and submits his questionnaire plus clear identification to the archive for linking with archival records. The decoding agent receives linked records (stripped of identifiers) from the archive, decodes the relevant section of the record, and forwards the anonymous joint records to the researcher.

Model Q. Model Q represents a variation on the insulated data bank strategy actually used in some research to link a researcher's records on identified individuals with Internal Revenue Service files on the same individuals (Schwartz and Orleans 1967), or with Social Security files (Steinberg 1970). The researcher encodes the information elicited directly from participants and submits it with identifiers to the archive for linkage with other records. The archive links the researcher's records *(X'I)* with archival records *(ZI)* on the basis of clear identifiers *(I)* appearing in each, strips identifiers from each record, and supplies the product to the researcher. The encoding by the researcher is done to preserve confidentiality with respect to the archival agency. The system can be generalized easily to the multiple-archive case, and it does preserve confidentiality with respect to particular contents of records and particular agencies. (See Boruch 1972b for details.) The feasibility of the original strategy, developed by Schwartz and Orleans, was demonstrated in their experiments designed to compare the relative effectiveness of various methods for encouraging taxpayers to report their incomes honestly. Specifically, a variant on model Q was used to link the research data on an individual to his Internal Revenue Service records, without violating either regulations concerning the confidentiality of IRS records or the promise of confidentiality made to research participants.

Variations on the same strategy have also been used in appraising the validity of survey subjects' reports of their savings, using bank records as the standard (Robert Ferber, personal communication, 1974), in appraising the effect of education on earnings, using Social Security records as an information source (Sewell et al. 1972), and in other studies.

Model R. In some cases, the *only* sources of information bearing on a particular research question are archives that prohibit direct access even to legitimate researchers. For example, to investigate the statistical relations between schizophrenia and various personal characteristics of individuals, the researcher might need to link archival records maintained by a psychiatric institute, records maintained by a family planning clinic, and those held by an insurance record system. It may be impossible for the researcher to obtain even identification of schizophrenics whose records are maintained by the institute, much less the contents of the records.

One approach to the problem of the economical use of archives in such a situation has been developed by Huxley and Radloff (1975). The first stage of a variant on their technique requires that the researcher contact various archives $(A_1, A_2, A_3$ in Figure 7) and elicit their cooperation in sending to a trustworthy broker the names of

Figure 7. Schematic representation of Model R, a procedural method for assuring confidentiality based on multiple information sources.

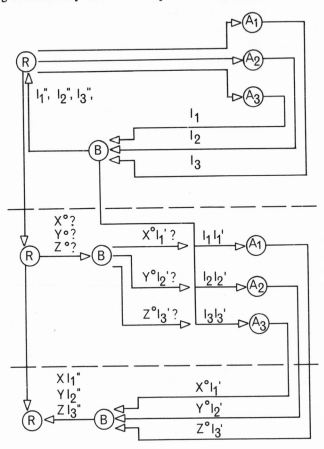

NOTE: The symbols A_1, A_2, A_3, represent independent information sources; $X°$, $Y°$, $Z°$, represent inquiries transmitted through the broker, to each archive. Other symbols are as defined earlier.

individuals (of a given age and sex, say) on whom they maintain records. The broker, who is not told of the specific objectives of the study, or of the sources of lists, receives and searches the lists for individuals common to each. A short list identifying the common individuals and giving an arbitrary identification number for each of them is then returned to each archive (I_1I_1', I_2I_2', I_3I_3'), all other lists being destroyed. The broker then sets up a second file containing two sets of arbitrary identifiers for each individual in the short lists ($I_1'I_1''$, $I_2'I_2''$, $I_3'I_3''$), to be used internally. The researcher is supplied with the second set of three arbitrary accounting numbers per person

(I''_1, I''_2, I''_3) which are used later in linking data elicited from the various sources.

During the second stage of the process, the researcher transmits three sets of inquiries, one set for each archive, to the broker; each questionnaire within a set is sealed in an envelope. The broker attaches an accounting number to each sealed questionnaire in the set and then transmits the document to the proper archive. The archival agent completes each questionnaire with respect to the individual whose identifying number appears on the document, and returns it, sealed again, to the broker.

In the third stage, the broker replaces one set of accounting numbers with a second set, then returns all documents to the researcher.

Using a system like this makes any outside illegal penetration of identified records very difficult if not impossible. Insurance against the use of covert identifiers or of deductive disclosure by the researcher is provided by the interposition of the broker. The use of sealed documents and monitoring by the researcher decreases the likelihood that the broker will corrupt the system (or be able to corrupt the system). Legal appropriation of the researcher's files or of the code linkage maintained by the broker would yield no interesting information. Only the appropriation or theft of records at their source, the archive, will yield useful information. The use of the double linkage scheme prevents illegal penetrators from profiting from access to *both* researcher records and any given archive's records.

A SPECIAL PROBLEM: IDENTIFIERS AS SENSITIVE INFORMATION

Usually a common list of identified individuals is necessary for record linkage. At times, however, even being a member of a list may constitute sensitive information and may make linkages for research difficult.

Consider a drug treatment center with an interest in the center's long-term effect on its clients' arrest rate following treatment. One convenient vehicle for follow-up study is arrest records stored routinely by state or local police agencies. To accomplish the study, client identifiers must be compared against and linked to the archive's records. However, the center may wish to avoid disclosing identifiers to an archive if it is supposed that the archive's staff might exploit those identifiers for nonresearch purposes. For example, if the names of the drug center's former clients are provided to the local police, the police may regard the information as an ingredient for its own files, for harassment of clients, etc. Several tactics used in combination with any of the models described may be appropriate here for linking records without indirectly disclosing information about a client:

1. Withholding information about auspices. When a drug center staff member presents a list of clients to the archive, there is an immediate implication that the list has something to do with drug use. To avoid the immediate implication, the center may simply use a broker (e.g., a university staff member) as an intermediary. The broker need not declare his relationship to the center, or the fact that the list contains the identification of drug center clients.

2. Withholding information about the reasons for linkages. If the archive's records are a matter of public information, then neither the center nor the broker need declare anything about the purpose of the linkage. Some very general information about the target population (e.g., an age range) and the problem may have to be provided, however, to assure cooperation. If there are several reasons for linkage, then the more innocuous ones might be offered to the archive; *innocuous* here means reasons unrelated to drug use.

3. Encoding or deleting other sensitive data. *Only* lists of identifying information should be provided to minimize accidental or deliberate appropriation of information in the center's records for nonresearch purposes.

4. Using dummy identifiers or trace identifiers. Inflating the basic list with names randomly selected from a telephone directory or the like will often help to depress the utility of the basic list of names to the exploitative archivist. The greater the inflation, the less useful the list, but the expense of searching the archive and matching names may put severe limits on this strategy. Some trace names, such as the names of center staff members, might be included in an inflated list to assure that if in fact the list is appropriated for some illegitimate purpose, the appropriation can be detected.

5. Obtaining the entire relevant archive. If archived records are a matter of public information, if they are conveniently filed (e.g., on magnetic tapes), and if the tape can be bought or leased, then the center can avoid most of the problems discussed above. The burden of purchasing and searching very large files can sometimes be reduced substantially by eliciting records on individuals with only certain demographic characteristics, e.g., age, sex, level of education, geographic residence.

Experimental Studies

To gauge the effectiveness of a new subsidized work program for former drug addicts, the Vera Institute has assigned eligible parolees randomly to either the special program or a regular parolee regimen. Information on the ex-addict's employment status, income, job performance, recidivism, and other variables is collected and used to judge the relative effect of the new program. Experiments like this generally yield a less equivocal estimate of program effects than many other research designs. Consequently, the approach is being used more frequently to evaluate social programs in education and training, rehabilitation, health care, and other areas.

When the program is designed to remedy a controversial social problem, experimental tests may require that sensitive information about program participants be collected. Studies of the effects of criminal rehabilitation programs, drug and alcoholism treatment, racial integration programs, and so on demand careful measurement of the human behavior that the programs are supposed to affect. Moreover, if the research records on identifiable individuals participating in research are disclosed, that disclosure may jeopardize the research participant and undercut the integrity of the research. The hazard here is illustrated by problems encountered in the Negative Income Tax experiment, an effort to test new income subsidy plans in the interest of a better national welfare policy (Orr et al. 1971). Early in that experiment, research staff assumed that they were legally protected against subpoena of their records on research participants. In fact, the records were not so protected; they were subpoenaed and used in a grand jury investigation of alleged fraud by the welfare recipients who participated in the research.

Experiments such as these can be important in appraising proposed solutions to critical social problems. But they can be badly disrupted if research records on identifiable respondents are appropriated for nonresearch purposes, legally or otherwise. It should be possible to avoid disruption in some experiments by using the confidentiality-preserving tactics described. Factors that influence the usefulness of these procedures are discussed next.

STRATEGIES AND THEIR BENEFITS

Almost all the procedural strategies described earlier are relevant to experimental tests if:

1. Only simple information about a large number of research participants is necessary for estimating program effects;

2. The information can be obtained impersonally: for example, through questionnaires, tests, inventories, specially designed telephone surveys, and the like;

As a concrete example, consider the evaluation of manpower training programs supported through federal revenue sharing. The Comprehensive Employment and Training Act of 1973 requires that these programs be mounted at the local (city or regional) level and be evaluated with respect to their effectiveness. The evaluation raises confidentiality issues of several kinds.

Some of the data obtained about program participants will, of course, be a matter of public record. The fact that an individual enrolls (or does not enroll) in a new program must, for example, be available to designated state and federal administrators. Otherwise program developers cannot be held accountable, in even an elementary way, for the public funds they receive. Other information, though not a matter of public record, will doubtless be essential for the internal management of the program and for external accounting by state and federal program monitors. For example, maintaining the program participant's attendance record is often necessary to assure that participation in the program is not merely nominal.

These data and other information about program participants must also be made available for the outside research analyst to evaluate the program's effects. Some of the better local programs will be willing to disclose such data, in some form, since they recognize the abuses that can be created by closed bureaucracies (see Gordon et al. 1973, and Divorski et al. 1973, for a discussion of problems in assuring access to governmental records).

The performance of trainees and of their control-group counterparts during or after manpower training is not necessarily public information. Nor is performance data necessary to assure fiscal accountability. Both innocuous and sensitive data on performance will, however, usually be essential for accumulating evidence on the program's relative effects. Where assurance of confidentiality of performance records is desirable, then a variety of the procedures described above can be used. To gauge the short-term impact of program variations, for example, completely anonymous questionnaires and inventories (model A) or the alias strategies can be useful, so long as the respondent also reports on the particular program in which he is enrolled. These strategies have been applied in previous manpower training efforts (e.g., Neighborhood Job Corps) to obtain data concerning participants' satisfaction with the program, their aspirations and anxieties, and even criminal activities during training. Similarly, the alias-based approaches represented by models E through H can be used to elicit information bearing on the longer-term effects of program variations on family life, antisocial behavior, and other characteristics, without seriously depreciating the individual's privacy or exposing research records to unwarranted threats to the confidentiality of data maintained therein. The insulated data bank approaches described earlier (model G) may be especially useful if local program developers wish to maintain some control over the kinds of information released to an outside analyst, without undermining intolerably the outsider's need for reliable information on program participants.

We can capitalize on model P, for example, to link the identified respondents' self-reports of (say) employment status with more sensitive information from restricted access program records on (say) the trainee's grades, without abridging rules regarding access to the program files and without violating promises of confidentiality made to the trainee who furnishes information on his postprogram employment status. The use of an intermediary or intermediaries such as community groups may in any case help to routinize data collection and, if the process is set up well, to enrich the data base available for evaluation.

COSTS, LIMITATIONS, VULNERABILITY

Most field tests of innovative programs require considerably more information about the respondent than can be obtained through simple questionnaires and from existing data archives. An evaluation of an innovative program for minimizing child abuse, for instance, may require that diagnostic information be elicited directly from families and from children. In-depth and periodic observation of the program participant is usually essential for monitoring complex effects of the program, and close observation is crucial for programs that have subtle or weak effects. Even with blind measurement, participants must usually be identified, physically observed, and engaged in face-to-face interviews, making complete anonymity with respect to the researcher impossible to maintain. Further difficulties stem from the needs for validity of response and validity of sampling experiments, prerequisites for detecting subtle program effects. Insofar as the procedural strategies limit one's ability to assure the quality of observation and of sampling, they can undermine the quality of research critically.

Whether any of the procedural methods presented here are appropriate for assuring confidentiality in an experiment, then, depends heavily on the experiment's scale, style, and purpose. In evaluations of major social programs, for example, the need for direct and intensive observation argues against any wholesale application of a single procedure. Piecemeal applications are more likely to be useful. Specifically, the needs-assessment surveys, which should ordinarily precede program installation and evaluation, often rely on more impersonal modes of response from a large sample of individuals. And so one of the procedural methods might be used to minimize the degradation of privacy during this stage of the evaluation. Similarly, the economic constraints on an experiment may warrant the use of existing data archives; again, some privacy-related problems engendered by such use can be resolved by adapting a procedure to that feature of the experiment.

In evaluating very compact programs or treatment regimes whose effects can be detected readily with impersonal measurement techniques, the applicability of the procedures is often clear. The Schwartz-Orleans experiment described earlier is an interesting illustration of small-scale applied research that capitalized neatly on confidentiality-preserving methods. Many of the methodological studies conducted by the U.S. Census Bureau, the National Opinion Research Center, and so on have used one or another procedure to guarantee privacy. The objective of most of these experiments has been limited in scope—testing various interview techniques, assessing the validity of alternative information sources—and in measurement approach; so the procedures can be easily tailored to suit the research demands. Also relevant here are small-scale experiments designed to advance social or psychological theory rather than to test a program. Many of these have no fundamental need for identifiability of the research subject, nor for highly personalized observations. And in the interest of eliminating discomfort ascribable to concerns about privacy, investigators have applied some of the procedures described earlier.

Notes

1. For reviews of technical work on encryption, see Dalenius and Silverstein (1978), National Central Bureau of Statistics (1976), and Carroll and McClelland (1970), Turn (1973), and Turn and Shapiro (1972).

Statistical Strategies in Direct Inquiry

And, after all, what is a lie? 'Tis but the truth in masquerade.

BYRON, *Don Juan*

A remarkable variety of statistical methods has been developed to preserve the confidentiality of response to a social researcher's inquiry. Their use eliminates any direct link between the respondent's identity and his or her true condition even in face-to-face interviews. Yet the resulting data can be subjected to useful, though limited, statistical analyses.

The methods have been designed to elicit discrete bits of information, such as income, rather than narrative testimony. Aside from such mechanical limitations on use, there is some penalty for the assurance of privacy given to the respondents. Larger samples may be necessary to sustain confident judgments about the incidence and character of a sensitive trait, for example. Statistical analysis is generally a bit more complex, and some specialized analyses will be very difficult or impossible to carry out.

In the next section, the rudimentary statistical strategies for assuring confidentiality in interviews are discussed, and their benefits, limitations, and costs examined briefly. The two succeeding sections concern the special demands of longitudinal research, record linkage, and experimental tests. Recent research and development, including field tests of the methods and some technical issues, are described in the last section.

Cross-sectional Research

Four related classes of strategies can be used for research based on a cross-sectional design. Three of them—contamination methods, randomized response, and microaggregation of response approaches—can be applied in direct interviews and in telephone or mail surveys. The fourth, microaggregation of the sample, is more appropriate for mail surveys and other impersonal methods of eliciting information. Each class is, in principle, applicable to longitudinal, experimental, and other research designs.

CONTAMINATION METHODS

We begin with the contamination approach because it is simple, albeit less efficient than some other methods. The approach requires that each respondent inoculate his or her response with a random error. The *general* character of the error is controlled by the researcher, so that while it is impossible to tell whether any particular response is accurate, it is still possible to estimate important statistical parameters from a *large* sample of respondents. Developed independently by Boruch (1972a), the method was clearly implied in Warner's (1965) earlier report on the first randomized response approach.

To be specific, suppose we want to estimate the proportion of students in a large sample who have used a particular drug. The question "Have you tried cocaine?" is presented to the respondent along with the choice of permissible prescribed responses: e.g., Yes or No. The respondent is instructed not to answer the question directly but to use a randomization device, such as a die, to determine whether he or she will give a true or false response. If a die is used, the respondent is asked to answer falsely if, for example, a one shows. If two, three, four, five, or six shows on the die, he would be required to answer truthfully with a Yes or No response. The respondent does *not* inform the researcher which number actually turns up on the die, but merely answers Yes or No in accord with the instructions. Under these conditions, one-sixth of all responses will be false, and the researcher cannot know which particular responses are true or false. Given these known parameters for error, and having the proportion of the sample say Yes in response to the question, it is easy to develop an unbiased estimate of the proportion who have actually tried the drug, $\hat{\pi}$:

$$\hat{\pi} = (\hat{P}_y - \phi_p) / (1 - \phi_p - \phi_n) \qquad \phi_p + \phi_n < 1, \qquad \phi_p < \hat{P}_y$$

where $\hat{P}_y$ = observed proportion of Yes responses, and

$\phi_p = \phi_n = 1/6$ (in this example) = specified probability
of false positive
and false negative response

So, for example, the researcher who finds that 40 percent $(\hat{P}_p)$ of his respondents say Yes under this scheme will estimate that in fact about 35 percent $(\hat{\pi}_m)$ have tried cocaine. The variance of this estimator is:

$$V(\hat{\pi}) = \frac{\hat{P}_y\,(1 - \hat{P}_y)}{N} + \frac{P_y\,[\phi_n\,(1 - \phi_n) - \phi_p\,(1 - \phi_p)]}{N(1 - \phi_p - \phi_n)^2}$$

$$+ \frac{\phi_p\,(1 - \phi_p)}{N(1 - \phi_p - \phi_n)^2}$$

which, for a sample size of $N = 200$, yields a standard deviation of about .04. Note that the variance is greater than one would obtain under direct questioning if completely candid responses were elicited by simple direct questions. The random error introduced only to protect confidentiality (without increased candor) produces an estimate that is less efficient than the regular estimate.

In preserving confidentiality, the method has an obvious benefit: there is no clear linkage between an identified individual's response and his true state. He may or may not have used cocaine, regardless of the fact that his recorded response is Yes. It is not a very difficult strategy to implement, judging from pilot studies. And, moreover, the researcher can obtain valid estimates of the true proportion of respondents who have used cocaine or have some other potentially stigmatizing characteristic. This is true *provided* that the respondent adheres faithfully to the procedure. Studies designed to determine whether respondents adhere to instructions and to assess the consequences of failure of the method are discussed later in this chapter.

The contamination method does have some important disadvantages. Since they are similar to those of the randomized response methods, they are discussed later.

RANDOMIZED RESPONSE METHODS

There are two general classes of randomized techniques: the related question method, invented by Stanley Warner (1965, 1971), and the unrelated question method, suggested by Walt Simmons and extended creatively by Greenberg, Horvitz, and others in the United States and by Dalenius, Bourke, and others in Sweden. These techniques are related to the contamination method just described, but they are more flexible, better developed, and better tested.

Warner's (1965) original proposal for a *related question* technique involves presenting the respondent with two complementary statements: "I have used cocaine" and "I have not used cocaine." The respondent is asked to use a randomization device to choose a statement and provide a True or False response. Again, the interviewer is not told which statement is used, nor is the die shown to him or her. Simple probability rules can be used to construct an unbiased estimate of the true proportion of individuals who have used cocaine, $\hat{\pi}$:

$$\hat{\pi} = (\hat{P}_y - \phi - 1) / (2\phi - 1) \qquad\qquad \phi < .5,$$

where ϕ is the probability of selecting one or the other statement, and $\hat{P}_y$ is the proportion of respondents who say "True" in response to the question. An expression for the variance of the estimate is:

$$V(\hat{\pi}) = \frac{\hat{\pi}(1 - \hat{\pi})}{N} + \frac{\phi(1 - \phi)}{(2\phi - 1)^2 N}$$

In a simple variant of the *unrelated question* technique, the researcher presents each respondent with two questions. Assume that the first question is of primary interest to the researcher and is likely to generate a social or legal risk to the respondent should disclosure occur: for example, "Did you read a pornographic magazine last month?" The second question, answerable in the same format as the stigmatizing question, must be at least innocuous and at best flattering: for example, "Did you use a public telephone last week?" For the simplest analysis, responses to the latter *must* be statistically unrelated to responses to the stigmatizing item. That is, there must be no inherent relation between people's reading a pornographic magazine and their weekly use of a public telephone. The respondent is then instructed to select one of the questions randomly and to answer it truthfully without revealing which item was chosen. In using a die as a randomization device, the researcher specifies that (say) a one indicates the first question must be answered, and two, three, and so on indicate that the second question should be answered. Again, the researcher is not shown the result of the die throw. Given the probabilities of choosing either question, $\frac{1}{6}$ and $\frac{5}{6}$ respectively in this example, the observed proportion of Yes responses (P_y) is equal to:

$$\hat{P}_y = 1/6 \; \hat{\pi} + 5/6 \; \hat{P}_m$$

where $\hat{\pi}$ represents the proportion of people who did read a pornographic magazine and $\hat{P}_m$ represents the proportion of people who used a public telephone the previous week. We can obtain an estimate of $\hat{P}_m$ from an independent survey sample, and knowing $\hat{P}_m$ and $\hat{P}_y$, we can solve for $\hat{\pi}$. The variance of the estimate is:

$$V(\hat{\pi}) = \frac{\hat{P}_y(1 - \hat{P}_y)}{N_1\phi^2} + \frac{\hat{P}_m(1 - \hat{P}_m)(1 - \phi)^2}{N_2\phi^2}$$

where N_1 represents the sample size used as a basis for generating the estimate $\hat{\pi}$, and N_2 is the size of the independent sample used to obtain $\hat{P}_m$.

Where individual privacy and confidentiality of response are important, a major benefit of these methods is that even in interviews, there is no clear linkage between an identified individual's response and his or her actual condition. Indeed, the researcher cannot know which question was asked, much less what the true response is to either question. Despite this, the data analyst can obtain unbiased estimates of proportions that reflect the incidence of an embarrassing characteristic in the population.

The feasibility of the techniques has been examined in large field experiments, as well as smaller pilot tests, in the United States, Taiwan, Sweden, and elsewhere. The questions at issue concerned drug abuse, child abuse, antisocial behavior, fertility control, and other sensitive topics. Results of such tests, reviewed in the section on new research and development in this chapter, suggest that the methods engender no insurmountable problems in implementation, that they are as likely as ordinary direct interviews to elicit gross (ostensible) cooperation, and they are sometimes more likely than direct interviews to elicit candid responses. Because the methods can be applied in face-to-face interviews, they reduce the problem of how sampling validity can be appraised, a difficulty in using some of the procedural methods described earlier. To assay the validity of response and the respondent's adherence to the strategy, special side studies can be developed [see Bourke and Dalenius (1974b), and O'Brien and Cochran 1977 and later sections of this chapter].

A final benefit of the randomized response methods is that they are quite flexible. A wide range of techniques, discussed later, has been developed for dichotomous response categories (e.g., Yes or No), for multinomial responses (e.g., Yes, No, Do not know), and for continuous responses (e.g., number of antisocial acts, salary level). Like the contamination methods, they can be used in conjunction with questions that are direct; that is, in the same interview, some questions are answered under the randomized-response paradigm, while others are answered directly.

LIMITATIONS, COSTS, AND VULNERABILITY

Some crude limitations are obvious. These methods do not appear to be adaptable to narrative responses. Nor do they appear to be appropriate for situations in which the actual behavior of the research participant must be observed directly. They are applicable in principle to telephone surveys, but we have found no demonstrations of the methods' feasibility in these settings.

Other costs engendered by the statistical methods can be grouped into two categories, one bearing mainly on statistical issues and one bearing mainly on the social psychology of the interview setting. We describe them briefly here and discuss solutions more thoroughly in the section below on recent research and development.

The statistical costs and limitations of the method will depend on the nature of the research effort. The most important for many applied researchers concern the sample size required by the method, the estimates of parameters that characterize a sensitive trait and its properties, and the increased technical sophistication required in using the methods. Small samples are generally inappropriate for these methods for two reasons. First, the methods' usefulness hinges on our being able to specify the rate of contamination or rate of choosing a given question (e.g., $\phi = \frac{1}{6}$ in the example given earlier). In a very large sample, or in repeated use in numerous small samples, we can be very confident that the unobservable sample value will be close to the theoretical value; large discrepancies are more likely in a single small sample. The odds on different types of discrepancy can be computed from tables or theory for a binomial frequency distribution function. The second justification for large samples is that the variance of estimates for the incidence (say) of a sensitive trait will be large compared to the variance of an estimate based on candid responses to simple direct questions. That is, the cost of providing privacy is a decrease in the precision or stability of the estimate, unless the new statistical method induces more candor. As a consequence, larger samples would be necessary, relative to direct questioning, to achieve a given level of confidence in an estimate. Recent attempts to improve the efficiency of estimates take a variety of forms. They include construction of tables that show how efficiency varies as a function of sample size, and configuration, and design parameters such as ϕ: for example, Warner (1965), Greenberg, Horvitz, and Abernathy (1974). More general theory of optimal designs for some of these methods has been developed by Moors (1971), Loynes (1976), Dowling and Shachtman (1975), and others. Repeated application of the simple methods can enhance efficiency as well (Liu and Chow 1976a).

Building an understanding of the properties of estimates based on randomized response methods is crucial for both user and theorist. Contrary to reports in earlier work, for example, the estimators presented here do not have maximum likelihood properties (Singh 1976; Devore 1977). It is possible, for example, to obtain an estimate that lies outside the permissible range of parameters—a proportion may be computed that is negative or greater than 1.00 for instance. Bourke and Dalenius (1974a) present tables that can be used to guide the choice of design parameters (sample size and ϕ in the simplest case) so as to reduce the probability of the awkward outcome to a negligibly small value. More generally, it is possible to construct restricted estimators which can have a small bias, but which do have maximum likelihood properties, and which do force estimates to fall within a prescribed range (Devore 1977; Sen 1974).

Finally, enlarging on the randomized methods, developing theory to identify risks to the respondent, and enhancing the usefulness of randomized response data have received a good deal of attention from the statistician. These matters are discussed later.

The social psychology of the interview process can be complex, especially if the topics of inquiry are sensitive or controversial. It is not unreasonable to expect novel statistical methods to complicate the interview process further and to have unwanted side effects. The first obvious potential problem is confusion. In using one variation of the randomized response method, for example, researchers for the Illinois Institute of Technology Research Institute and the Chicago Crime Commission (1971) elicited what appears to be reasonably valid information on crime in Illinois but noted that errors did occur due to the respondent's misunderstanding instructions or failing to implement the procedure correctly, and due to awkward handling of the interview by the interviewer. Shimizu and Bonham (1978) and Zdep and Rhodes (1977) also note mechanical problems and the need to solve them. A second, related difficulty is that the same respondents may fail to follow the researcher's instructions because the strategies provoke rather than reduce suspicion, or because they would not respond in accordance with instructions in any event. The hostility or indifference that can characterize *any* method of inquiry can, of course, jeopardize the usefulness of these special methods as much as ordinary ones. Experimental tests by Chi and his colleagues (1972), among others, suggest that these kinds of problems will not always obtain in randomized respondents' applications. They have found, for example, that women are more willing to admit that they have had abortions under the randomized response paradigm (relative to direct questioning), and that female respondents in this fertility control research are not unduly suspicious of or confused by the method. Other empirical investigations, however, suggest that certain classes of respondents in other types of research will have different reactions. For example, pilot studies on servicemen's use of marijuana led us to speculate that a respondent's adherence to instructions in the randomized response method is partly a function of the military rank of the respondent and other variables (Brown and Harding 1973). We are aware of no investigations of how social psychological theory can be used to explain or explore adherence to instructions and reactions to the novel statistical methods of inquiry.

MICROAGGREGATION OF RESPONDENT SAMPLE

Microaggregation methods have been suggested by Feige and Watts (1970, 1972) as a device for assuring the confidentiality of archive data. They are also potentially useful for eliciting information directly from individuals in survey situations. In the following remarks, we review the early application of this method, enumerate its costs and benefits, and generalize the method in direct interviews.

To understand the procedure, consider its original application to proprietary records on call reports and income of commercial banks. The records are maintained by a centralized data archive, which is prohibited from releasing anything but statistical summaries of information contained in the records. Even anonymous individual records cannot be released for outside statistical analysis. The Feige and Watts view is that to permit sophisticated outside analysis of the data, the archive could create and release statistical data on aggregates of records rather than unit records. So, for example, 1,000 sets of 3 records each might be constructed from a sample of 3,000 records. The 1,000 records would contain averaged information on call reports, assets, liabilities, and so forth of three banks within each aggregate. The archive can supply these aggregate records to *any* outside economic analyst without breaching legal regulations against disclosure of sets of anonymous unit records.

The benefit of the technique, then, is that the risk of deductive disclosure stemming from the release of unit data can be reduced considerably and eliminated for all practical purposes. Yet the outside researcher can compute meaningful descriptive statistics to characterize the data. Whether and how well the outsider can do more sophisticated analyses depends largely on how records are aggregated. For the cost of aggregation is that imprecision and (possibly) bias are introduced to the analysis. In particular, if we obtain only an average asset (say) for each aggregate, we lose information on the assets of banks within the aggregate. Any aggregation reduces effective sample size, and so estimates of statistical parameters in linear regression models, for example, will be susceptible to relatively high sample-to-sample variation (Orcutt, Watts, and Edwards 1968). The resultant uncertainty about parameters can be crucial to the research, and various strategies have been developed to ameliorate the problem. One general class of strategies involves setting up rules for aggregation that reduce imprecision but avoid systematic biases. The researcher must choose an aggregation criterion that is independent of the error variance of the statistical model. Doing so is difficult at best, and if unit record data are not available at some stage for testing biases induced by aggregation rules, it may be impossible. Feige and Watts, for example, have had to develop crude rules for aggregation by empirically comparing statistics based on disaggregated data with statistics computed from aggregated data on the same sample of banks. Searching for aggregation criteria that do not undermine the precision and accuracy of estimates is not an easy task, and for this reason, microaggregation is likely to be more useful for panel studies than for one-time-only research.

It is also possible to adapt the idea to preserve privacy in direct inquiry. One variant is a straightforward generalization of the banking example: microaggregation of members of a target sample in a cross-sectional study. A second and more useful variant involves microaggregation of each respondent's reply to inquiries rather than microaggregation of respondents, and this approach is examined in the following section. To make the first approach concrete, consider the problem of eliciting information on the legal problems of a population of (say) 2,000 physicians. We might randomly allocate them into 100 aggregates of 20 individuals each, and then designate one representative per aggregate to receive anonymous responses, to average them, and to provide resultant group means (on age, number of malpractice suits of a particular type, etc.) to the researcher. Responses of anonymous individuals might sometimes be supplied directly to the researcher, of course. But with reference to confidentiality, the benefit of microaggregation is that the possibility of deductive disclosure by the outside researcher can be reduced or eliminated. Confidentiality of unit records is maintained with respect to the outsider, since he or she receives only aggregate data. Confidentiality of anonymous unit records is maintained with respect to the designated representative only if collateral information cannot be used to discover the identity of a respondent.

The aggregates can be determined by a formal lottery set up by the researcher, by natural (nearly) random processes, or by prescribed rules. Membership in an aggregate can be determined by birth date, birth month, or week of birth, for example. Naturally occurring groups may also serve as aggregates *provided* that there is no un-specifiable relation between the grouping criteria and the sampling error underlying the model used to analyze the data. In a study of malpractice suits against physicians, for example, using physician age as the criterion for aggregation is likely to yield biased estimates of parameters for unit-level data since incidence of malpractice cases is likely to be correlated with age. Some variable such as the birth month of a friend of the physician or some other unverifiable, innocuous, and unrelated criterion would be more appropriate. The most appropriate variables for aggregation, which reduce imprecision relative to random grouping and induce no bias, often cannot be specified beforehand. Side studies or pilot research on unit-level records, then, will normally be helpful in discovering such variables. More generally, if good aggregation criteria are known to coincide with natural groupings (police departments in studies of policemen, youth gangs in studies of delinquency, etc.), then microaggregation methods may be exploited for making inferences about unit-level phenomena from aggregate data.

With respect to confidentiality, microaggregation of respondents has the benefit of eliminating direct disclosure of identifiable information to the researcher. Even if the researcher knows the identity of individuals within the aggregate, the threat of deductive disclosure is small insofar as the aggregate is large. The tactic is most promising for situations in which respondents will not or cannot cooperate directly with an outside researcher but an intermediary (the representative) is available. For a cross-sectional study, neither the representative of the aggregate nor the researcher needs to know the identity of other members except in side studies (see discussion below).

The statistical costs of using microaggregates rather than individual response as a basis for data collection and analysis are similar to, but more severe than, those encountered in the contamination and randomized response methods. It can be a very inefficient technique in the sense that larger samples are necessary to achieve the levels of confidence obtained in analysis of individuals rather than groups. The statistical technology available for analyzing data based on aggregated samples is well developed in some respects, notably for simple statistical models (see Fisher 1969, Freund 1971, and Hannan 1971). That technology will require extension if the aggregated data must be analyzed under more complex models. Moreover, unless the same functional model used as a basis for generating aggregates is also used to analyze the data, new analyses (models) may produce misleading results (see chapter 2). Of course, checking the validity of sampling within the aggregate for the aggregated-sample approach and the validity of reporting within the aggregate for both aggregated-sample and aggregated-response approaches is impossible unless the social researcher conducts a side study on small subsamples within the larger target group. Linking aggregated data with aggregated records from other data files on the same individuals is possible only if identification of each individual within each aggregate is available.

AGGREGATION OF RESPONSE FOR EACH INDIVIDUAL

Consider a situation in which the researcher presents each individual in a sample with two questions, each question being answerable with a numerical response. For simplicity, let one question be innocuous and the other sensitive. The respondent is enjoined *not* to furnish a response to each individual item but rather to add up the numerical value corresponding to the proper response to each and to furnish the total value to the researcher. So, for example, each respondent might be asked about incidence of telephone usage and of petty theft. A given respondent would then add the number of times he engaged in petty theft (say, 1) to the number of times he used the telephone (say, 3), in a specified period. The total, 4, is the only response supplied to the researcher. Proceeding in exactly the same way for each respondent in a random sample, the researcher can compute the average numerical answer to the questions, $\bar{Y}_1$. That average can be described in terms of a single equation in two unknowns. If the average response is 5, for example, we have

$$\bar{Y}_1 = 5 = \bar{X}_1 + \bar{X}_2$$

where $\bar{X}_1$ represents the unobserved average incidence of theft and $\bar{X}_2$ represents the unobserved average incidence of telephone use. We are, of course, interested in determining the numerical values of $\bar{X}_1$ and $\bar{X}_2$, and this single equation is insufficient for doing so. To obtain estimates of the rates of telephone use and theft, the researcher takes a second random sample from the population and asks each respondent in the sample to subtract (rather than add) numerical values for his responses. An average response of 1 might be obtained, and this, too, can then be described in terms of a second independent equation in two unknowns:

$$\bar{Y}_2 = 1 = \bar{X}_1 - \bar{X}_2$$

The two equations based on the two independent samples are sufficient for estimating values of $\bar{X}_1$ and $\bar{X}_2$:

$$\bar{X}_1 = (\bar{Y}_1 + \bar{Y}_2) / 2 = 3, \quad \bar{X}_2 = 2.$$

That is, the average weekly incidence of telephone use in the sample at hand is 2; members of the sample engage in petty theft about three times a week.

Two subsamples are sufficient for estimating variances and covariance of petty theft and phone use. We have three independent equations and three unknowns:

$$\text{Var}(Y_1) = \text{Var}(X_1) + \text{Var}(X_2) + 2\text{Cov}(X_1X_2)$$
$$\text{Var}(\bar{X}_1) = \tfrac{1}{4}\text{Var}(\bar{Y}_1 + \bar{Y}_2)$$
$$\text{Var}(\bar{X}_2) = \text{Var}(\bar{Y}_1 - \bar{Y}_2)$$

The manipulation of these equations will yield an estimate of the covariance, and we have our estimates of the variances. To estimate other parameters, additional sample data must be obtained. We may, for example, simply ask members of a third independent subsample to report on their telephone use; and having an estimate of the variance of X_1, Var (X_1), we can compute an estimate of the variance of X_2, Var (X_2). Or we may run through the entire procedure with a new subsample, requesting that they provide a weighted response to obtain (for example):

$$\bar{Y}_3 = \bar{X}_1 - 2\bar{X}_2$$

providing us with the third equation necessary for estimating the parameters.

No general theory for response aggregation has been developed. And given the variety of ways in which responses can be combined and questions for combination chosen, and the need to set up subsamples and combinations that are sufficient to generate estimates of parameters, a coherent framework would be useful to make the process orderly. One recent attempt to present such a framework capitalizes on a technology in statistical design of experiments. Raghavarao and Federer (1973), Smith, Federer, and Raghavarao (1974), and Dalenius (1974b) have proposed adopting technology for balanced incomplete block designs to facilitate the combination of questions. The basic adaption, which Raghavarao and Federer label as the Block Total Response (BTR) method, requires each respondent to sum responses to each item in a prescribed block of questions and present the result to the interviewer. A modified version requires that the respondent choose a set of questions *randomly* from a list of sets, and then sum responses and report the total to the interviewer (Smith, Federer, and Raghavarao 1974); the randomized choice establishes a kinship with the randomized response methods described earlier. No arithmetic aside from addition is required of the respondent in the Smith et al. approach; both addition and subtraction are exploited by Dalenius (1974b).

The BTR approach requires that the researcher specify some design parameters, and then choose a configuration from the configurations laid out by Cochran and Cox (1957), Kempthorne (1952), and others as a basis for the survey. If, for example, a set of seven questions is of interest, then configurations in which two, three, or four questions are added by the respondent are available. A configuration involving four questions, which produce a sufficient number of equations to solve for unknown values of the incidence of sensitive traits,' X_1 and

X_2, and nonsensitive ones, X_3, X_4, . . . , X_7, can be adopted directly from a plan given in Cochran and Cox (1957). The plan involves constructing seven blocks of questions, each containing four items; a block is presented to each respondent in a subsample of respondents. The arrangement of blocks follows this pattern order to provide estimates of parameters bearing on each question that are possible and equally precise:

Block 1	3	5	6	7
Block 2	1	4	6	7
Block 3	1	2	5	7
Block 4	1	2	3	6
Block 5	2	3	4	7
Block 6	1	3	4	5
Block 7	2	4	5	6

So, for example, each of the first 20 respondents in a sample of 140 reacts to Block 1, the second 20 react to Block 2, and so on. The configuration generates a system of seven independent equations in seven unknowns. That is, if $\bar{y}_1$, $\bar{y}_2$ . . ., $\bar{y}_7$ represents the average total response observed for each block, and $\bar{x}_1$, $\bar{x}_2$ . . ., $\bar{x}_7$ represents the unobserved average incidence of the traits of interest, then one can solve the equations for each unknown; e.g.:

$$\bar{X}_7 = [(\bar{y}_1 + \bar{y}_2 + \bar{y}_3 + \bar{y}_5) - (\bar{y}_4 + \bar{y}_5 + \bar{y}_6)] \, / \, 4.$$

Variances of the estimates can be computed directly using a components of variance approach, along the lines illustrated by the earlier example, provided that the characteristics X_1, X_2, . . ., X_7 are independent. Other layouts, for cases in which each respondent can be presented with up to nine questions, are presented in Cochran and Cox (1957).

The potential benefit of the response aggregation methods is protecting the respondent's privacy. The privacy protection is imperfect to the extent that combinations of methods permit crude deductive disclosure; for example, all questions concern sensitive traits, and some combinations permit deductive disclosure for questions within a set (see remarks below). The technique appears to be simple to use, at least for individuals who have no difficulty with addition, and Smith, Federer, and Raghavarao report no remarkable problems in their small pilot test. The ability to use the methods in mail, telephone, and interview surveys is an advantage over most of the procedural methods described in chapter 4. But no major field tests in any of these settings have been undertaken.

The main limitations and costs attached to the BTR technique bear on its use in the field, the level of protection afforded the respondent, and on the need to develop estimators and understand their properties. Microaggregation of response appears to us to be a bit more demanding than the methods described earlier, at least for the respondent and possibly for the interviewer. The arithmetic required will be tolerable to many respondents, but it carries a potential for error in following instructions. Both tolerance and accuracy might be enhanced by using inexpensive electronic calculators, for example.

Response aggregation methods that employ prescribed numerical responses, rather than open-ended responses, pose risks to respondents. In particular, if in a sensitive question about drug use the responses 0, 1, 2 (times a week) are prescribed as legitimate, and in an innocuous question about telephone use, the numbers 0, 1, . . ., 10 are permissible, a response of 11 or 12, which sums drug and telephone use, immediately informs the interviewer that the respondent has the sensitive trait. Altering the arithmetic operations in simple ways or reversing scales does not eliminate the problem. However, putting no restrictions on response, or fixing upper bounds that make it unlikely that a response will be extreme, virtually eliminate the problem. If each response range for each block of items in a *randomized* response aggregation is the same, and not all blocks contain a sensitive item, then the possibility of deductive disclosure is for most practical purposes negligible; one does not know which block of questions was presented to the respondent. Whether respondents recognize this, in forming a preference for the randomized aggregation method over the direct response aggregation, is not clear, though the small pilot test conducted by Smith, Federer, and Raghavarao (1974) suggests that this is the case (see also chapter 3).

Generally speaking, the variance of an estimate based on response aggregation will be larger than the variance of an estimator based on the randomized response methods. The reasons are twofold. In the aggregation approach, additional noise is introduced into the system through the use of multiple questions. The variance in response to those questions, in practical applications, is likely to be greater than the variance induced by contamination, for example. Moreover, the basic sample must be split up into numerous subsamples to accommodate each block of questions in the response aggregation approach. The use of a single sample randomized response is more efficient in producing estimators with small variance; double sample approaches are likely to be more efficient as well.

Finally, and perhaps most importantly, the simplest BTR methods require the researcher to construct sets of questions that concern traits which are stochastically independent. That demand is likely to be difficult in most research: we often do not have sufficient advance information to specify sets of variables that are independent and yet still of interest to the researcher. Indeed, most exploratory research is dedicated to finding relations among the variables. Partly as a consequence, the existing BTR approaches are unlikely to be very useful except in studies of the raw incidence of a sensitive trait when relations among variables are well understood.

Longitudinal Research

The value of these statistical strategies in longitudinal research must be judged in terms of the typical purpose of that research: monitoring or describing the changes in individuals. The important needs here are for linkage of individual records collected over time, assurance of confidentiality, and the precision and accuracy of statistics based on the resultant data.

Linkage of records accumulated periodically under many of the statistical strategies is operationally simple, since clear identification is always coupled to a response to inquiry. This simplicity is valuable where the procedural approaches to providing confidentiality are not feasible and where it is difficult to maintain contact with a target group. The opportunity to use either interviews or mail as a device for eliciting information in long-term research is an advantage over most of the procedural techniques, which require depersonalized contacts. That the confidentiality of identifiable records can be enhanced is clear. Despite the linkage between a response and an identifier, the individual's state cannot be inferred by the interviewer or by anyone else, including the data analyst. Furthermore, since the methods can be focused on a single question or cluster of questions, one does have the opportunity to use more direct methods for collecting information about the more innocuous characteristics of the respondent.

An obvious limit on the methods' usefulness is characteristic of any research that relies solely on answers chosen from a list of possible answers. Narrative information and case studies of at least a few respondents add flesh to the statistical bone provided by surveys, and the statistical methods of assuring confidentiality are not useful in protecting case-study material.

The main cost of using these statistical methods in longitudinal work is that the methods generally reduce effective sample size. This reduction means that we will be less certain of the actual magnitude of any detected relation between characteristics of individuals at two points in time. Suppose, for example, that there is no change in the relative frequency of illegal methadone use in a target group of a hundred individuals for two points in time. Suppose further that there are many consistent users; that is, most individuals using methadone at one time are also using it the next. Our ability to detect that consistency will be reduced by the methods insofar as they induce random noise in the data and do not induce more candid responses. Estimated upper and lower bounds on the size of the relationship will increase accordingly. The theoretical framework for estimating the damaging effects of induced variability on the power of statistical tests for categorical data is given in an article by Assakul and Proctor (1967). Increasing sample size is a common mechanism for offsetting the induced error.

Systematic biases in estimates of important population parameters may also obtain, depending on the particular analysis strategy and on the particular parameter being estimated. For example, simple product moment correlations between repeated measures of continuous characteristics, such as incidence of antisocial behavior, will decrease in absolute value with the contamination method and can increase artificially with microaggregation. Since the error rates in the contamination approach are fixed by the analyst, it will be possible to adjust sample statistics upward or downward to reflect the induced bias. In fact, with population data, adjustment of biases may exploit well-known techniques (e.g., correction for attenuation). We can rely on a substantial technology in theory of measurement error to make such adjustments to simpler analyses (e.g., Lord and Novick 1968; Bross 1954; Murray 1971; Stroud 1974; and others). In general, the problems in this context have been better explicated for contaminated data than for microaggregated data.

Research Using Multiple Data Sources

The statistical devices permit one to couple the identity of the interviewee to his or her response. Consequently, there are no remarkable problems in linking research records obtained under randomized response methods with other identifiable records maintained on the same individuals. Moreover, because the research record cannot be exploited to determine the state of the particular individual unambiguously, there is no direct threat of disclosure of personal information. It must be made clear, however, that the records are not informative, in order to avoid naive efforts to appropriate them for nonresearch purposes.

To assure confidentiality of the archival record (vis-à-vis the researcher) in a linkage with research records, both the procedural and statistical strategies can be used. For example, the linked records returned to the data analyst through an insulated data bank arrangement can be inoculated by computer with small amounts of controlled random error, processed through a simulated randomized response paradigm, or microaggregated. These processes reduce the possibility of deductive disclosure of the archival records. The joint use of procedural and statistical techniques in linking records provides a stronger assurance of confidentiality than the use of procedural methods alone (see chapter 6). But because the statistical methods do influence effective sample size, and may introduce some systematic biases into analyses of linked data, their use must be planned beforehand. The technical expertise required for planning will increase the cost of linkage. The primary criteria for judging whether the methods can be or should be adopted at all are the ability to anticipate imprecision and bias and to adjust for them where necessary, and the logistical support necessary for the procedures.

Experimental Studies

The main objective of an experimental test of a social program is usually to obtain a fair estimate of the program's effect in a way that permits us to quantify the reliability of the estimate. This normally involves comparing average differences between the responses of persons to alternative programs. Outcome variables here, for example, may include the incidence of drug use, theft or cheating, or the violation of medical standards in programs designed to reduce the incidence of these phenomena. Detecting program effects is usually difficult because social programs are often weak to begin with, and outcome variables that reflect the programs' effects are often susceptible to uncontrollable measurement error.

Using the statistical strategies may help to ameliorate the problem of uncontrollable systematic bias in response to the extent that they eliminate the fear of disclosure and embarrassment usually associated with a respondent's providing sensitive information about himself. And because the record reveals nothing about the exact state of the individual on whom the record is maintained, confidentiality is preserved. These strategies substitute controllable error for the uncontrollable, however, as a device for sustaining privacy. Insofar as the controllable error is large, tests of program effects based on such data may then be unnecessarily insensitive. That is, the analyst may fail to detect program effects, not because they are absent, but because the methods used to assure confidentiality also degrade the sensitivity of the experiment. How the power of statistical tests is affected by the use of the statistical strategies is a matter that requires both theoretical and empirical work.

To illustrate the problem, consider an experiment in which we compare the quality of medical care rendered by physicians with that rendered by nurse-practitioners to equivalent groups of patients with a particular disease. The observations may be simple—for example, judges' ratings of whether the care rendered by a particular individual was very good, unremarkable, or poor. Judges may prefer to render anonymous responses to avoid embarrassment or libel suits. Identifiers may be used with one of the statistical methods described earlier to assure the confidentiality of their responses. Because either method decreases effective sample size, our ability to detect a difference between (say) the proportion of physicians rendering good care and the corresponding proportion for nurse-practitioners is weakened. A failure to detect a true difference would be critical here, since we may erroneously adopt the nurse-practitioner program under the assumption that failure to find a difference means that no difference exists.

In general, any true difference between proportions will be reduced by error in classification, induced or otherwise. Because the general character of the induced error is known, however, it is possible to anticipate reduction in the power of statistical tests applied to the data. Doing so is not easy, but we can rely on work done already by Assakul and Proctor (1967), Cleary, Linn, and Walster (1970), and Levy (1976a), to increase power in such situations. One must increase the size of the program effect, reduce the level of (usually uncontrolled) error in the observations, reduce the contamination deliberately introduced into the system through the randomized response methods or microaggregation, or increase the sample size. The first two actions may be difficult if not impossible. The third action must be taken, and we have good methods for accomplishing this. The last —increasing the size of the sample—will be costly. See the next section for further discussion.

Recent Research and Development: Randomized Response

During the 1970s, work on statistical methods for assuring privacy expanded dramatically, stimulated by professional eagerness to accommodate public interest and by the challenge of working on interesting problems. In the following remarks, we outline some of the recent work conducted in the United States, Sweden, and elsewhere. Most of the research concerns randomized response methods.

FIELD TESTS AND APPLICATIONS

The feasibility of randomized response methods has been examined in a variety of research settings. So, for example, information about abortion and fertility control has been obtained without breaching women's privacy by Abernathy, Greenberg, and Horvitz (1970) in North Carolina; by I-cheng, Chow, and Rider (1972), Liu and Chow (1976a, 1976b), and Liu, Chen, and Chow (1976) in Taiwan; by Krotki and Fox (1974) in Canada (see also Krotki and McDaniel 1975); and by Shimizu and Bonham (1978) in national surveys in the United States. Researchers who have tested the methods in field studies of drug, alcohol, and amphetamine use include Goodstadt and Gruson (1975) among Canadian adolescents; Brown and Harding (1973), Brown (1975), and Reaser, Hartsock, and Hoehn (1975) among U. S. military servicemen; Barth and Sandler (1976) among Nashville high school students; Berman, McCombs, and Boruch (1977) among Nebraska college students (see Boruch 1972a also); and Dawes (1974) among college students. Zdep and Rhodes (1977) focused their attention on child abuse. Locander, Sudman, and Bradburn's (1976) study concerns a variety of sensitive characteristics, including arrests for drunken driving and occurrence of bankruptcy. A study described by Folsom (1974) and Folsom, Greenberg, Horvitz, and Abernathy (1975) attends to drinking and driving behavior. Eriksson's (1976a) small investigation involved welfare-subsidy recipients. Sexual behavior among college students has been investigated, using randomized response methods, by Dawes (1974), Fidler and Kleinknecht (1977), and Berman, McCombs, and Boruch (1977). The methods have been tried out in surveys on illegal gambling by the Illinois Institute of Technology and the Chicago Crime Commission (1971) and in an omnibus survey designed partly to assay the incidence of shoplifting (O'Brien, Cochran, Marquardt, and Makens 1976). All these studies, except Brown and Reaser, Hartsock, and Hoehn, involved personal interviews. The two exceptions were mail surveys.

Crude response rates, in each study that permits a comparison, suggest that gross cooperation is no less likely for randomized response methods than for standard interviews with the same interview topic and target population. Most of the field experiments listed in table 3 were designed to assay the extent to which using randomized response methods facilitates candid reporting from respondents. The last column of the table summarizes their results. Over half the studies designed to get at reporting bias obtained a notable reduction in bias. The remainder yielded inconclusive results. That is, individuals may be indifferent to or skeptical about the level of assurance offered by the method; the study may be insensitive to subtle changes in candor;

Table 3

Results of field studies undertaken with randomized response methods

	Sample size for RR method	Rounded percentage response to RR	Rounded percentage response to standard	Notable reduction in Response bias (crude)
Abernathy, Greenberg, Horvitz	3,113	97	NR	YES
I-cheng, Chow, Rider	1,021	89	89	YES
Liu, Chen, Chow	353	85	NR	YES
Krotki and Fox	352	97	73	INC
Shimizu and Bonham	9,797	99	NR	YES
Goodstadt and Gruson	431	95	87	YES
Brown and Harding	1,100	NR	NR	INC
Brown (mail)	2,114	18–50	32–65	INC
Reaser, Hartsock, Hoehn (mail)	2,400	23	26	YES
Barth and Sandler	64	100	NR	YES
Berman, McCombs, Boruch	156	100	100	INC
Dawes	270	100	NR	NR
Zdep and Rhodes	995	98	75–85	YES
Locander, Sudman, Bradburn	233	60–78	48–90	INC
Folsom	423	100		
Eriksson	76	97	NR	INC
Fidler and Kleinknecht	132	100	100	YES
Illinois Institute of Technology	1,200	100	NR	INC

Note: The gross number of respondents involved in a survey using the methods is reported in the first column. Cooperation, registered by crude response rate, is indexed in the second column for the randomized response sample. When an estimate of response rates for direct questions is available and reported, that is listed in column three. *NR* implies that the information was not included in the report. The fourth column contains a judgment, based on the published report, as to whether the use of randomized response led to reduced bias in reporting by respondents. *INC* indicates that results are inconclusive; *YES* indicates a clear reduction in bias, relative to a standard. A blank indicates that the study was not designed to provide the information. See the text for citations and topics covered in each study.

VARIATIONS ON THE RANDOMIZED RESPONSE METHODS

For the field researcher, a useful catalogue for these methods can be based on the type of response elicited, and on the methods' special functions and operating characteristics. So we adhere to a conventional response typology: dichotomous; multinomial; and continuous. Within each type, special functions, such as improving efficiency, or special operating characteristics, such as the use of single or multiple samples, provide additional dimensions for a typology. For the statistician, the more useful and interesting basis for cataloguing involves unifying mathematics.

Dichotomous response: single sample. In each of the dichotomous response variants, the objective is to estimate the proportion of individuals in two mutually exclusive and exhaustive categories: the proportion of those who are type A, π_A. A physical randomization device (cards, dice, spinner, etc.) must be used to generate the random choice, and the odds on a choice are fixed beforehand.

Warner's (1965) method, the precedent, requires that the interviewer present two statements to each respondent: "I am a member of A"; "I am not a member of A." The respondent is then asked to respond (saying True or False) to the first statement with probability ϕ_w and to the second statement with probability $1 - \phi_w$. The respondent may be instructed, for example, to cast a die and to respond to the first question if a one turns up: $\phi_w = \frac{1}{6}$. A response to the second statement is made if two, three, etc. turn up on the die. Liu and Chow (1976a) developed and field tested a multiple-trial modification of the Warner approach: each individual repeats the entire pattern, including die toss, three times and provides a response each time. The resulting estimates of abortion rate, in their study, are subject to considerably less sampling variation than estimates based on a single administration. Liu and Chow report no remarkable suspicion of the method among respondents for their field trial in Taiwan.

Boruch's (1972a) contamination method, a variant of Warner's methods, requires that the respondent be presented with only one statement: "Are you a member of A?" He or she is then told to respond truthfully with probability ϕ_P and to say No if he is A with probability $1 - \phi_p$. Small sample results are reported in the reference.

Lanke (1975a) and Drane (1975) proposed a single sample variation that requires the interviewer to present a question: "Are you a member of A?" and a statement: "Say Yes." The respondent chooses the question with probability ϕ_L and the statement with probability $1 - \phi_L$. The variation is simple, and can be very efficient in the sense of reducing variance of the estimate of π_A to a bare minimum. The tactic can be regarded as a special case of Simmon's (1970) model and of the contamination method. It has been field tested by Reaser, Hart-sock, and Hoehn (1975) in studies of the attitudes of U.S. Army officers. In Eriksson's (1973a) device, three options are presented to each respondent in the sample: "Are you a member of A?" "Say Yes"; and "Say No." The choice is determined by a randomization device, so that the probability of answering the question is ϕ_2, the probability of saying Yes is ϕ_2, and the probability of reacting to the No statement is $\phi_3 = 1 - \phi_1 - \phi_2$. Test results for a small sample are given in the author's dissertation. An identical method has been field tested by Fidler and Kleinknecht (1977) in a small study of some sexual behaviors of college students. Finally, Warner (1971) proposed a contamination approach that is more flexible than the preceding ones, in the sense that greater control over the general character of induced error can be obtained, and a higher proportion of Yes responses can be used to estimate the incidence of a sensitive trait. The respondent chooses one of three sets of questions randomly and reacts to the set chosen:

1. If A, report not A.
   If not A, report A.
2. If A, report not A.
   If not A, report not A.
3. If A, report A.
   If not A, report not A.

Efficiency is said to be slightly poorer than in the unrelated question methods, for the configurations examined by Greenberg, Horvitz, and Abernathy (1974).

In the single sample variations of the Simmons (1970) and Greenberg et al. (1969) approaches, the respondent is presented with a sensitive question: "Are you a member of A?", for which a proportion must be estimated, with probability ϕ_S. A second, innocuous question, presented with probability $1 - \phi_S$, concerns a trait B, whose relative frequency in the population, π_B, is known.

In Swensson's (1975, 1976a) strategy, rather than respond to one of two statements, the individual responds to a single question that involves several attributes: "Do you belong to A or B?" where A is sensitive and B is not. In the simplest case, the traits A and B are stochastically independent, and the population parameter π_B, concerning the proportion who have trait B, is known. The minor variations include asking whether the individual belongs to A or not to B, and asking whether the respondent belongs to:

A and B or $\bar{A}$ and $\bar{B}$

The first two variations give equal efficiency under equal levels of protection; the third is least efficient. Swensson (1976b) also appears to be the only researcher to have outlined the mathematics for permitting the respondent to choose the variant he or she prefers from a short list of variants.

Dichotomous response: multi-sample. Simmons (1970) and Greenberg, Abul-Ela, Simmons, and Horvitz (1969) have produced an unrelated question model based on the original randomized response idea. In it, the interviewer presents two questions to each respondent: "Are you a member of *A*?" and "Are you a member of *B*?" In the first of *two* independent samples of individuals, each respondent chooses the question randomly with probability ϕ_1 specified by the researcher. The second question is chosen with probability $1 - \phi_1$. In a second sample, the probabilities are altered to ϕ_2 and $1 - \phi_2$ respectively. The traits *A* and *B* must be independent for simple application. The variation often yields more efficient estimators of the incidence of the sensitive trait than the Warner approach. When the relative incidence of the innocuous trait, π_B, is known for the population, then the technique is notably more efficient.

Folsom, Greenberg, Horvitz, and Abernathy (1975) developed a variation, suggested by D. T. Campbell, to increase the statistical efficiency of the original unrelated question randomized response method. In the first of two independent samples, respondents are asked to use a randomization device to choose between two questions: "Are you a member of *A*?" and "Are you a member of *B*?"; they are asked to respond directly to a third question: "Are you a member of *C*?" *A* is sensitive; *B* and *C* are not. In the second sample, respondents choose randomly between questions concerning *A* and *C*, and they are asked to respond directly to the question about *B*. The use of two innocuous questions, *B* and *C*, in this instance, permits a more precise estimate of the incidence of the sensitive characteristic *A*, when population parameters for the alternative innocuous items π_B and π_C are unknown. A field test, concerning alcohol consumption, is reported in the paper. The occurrence of *A, B,* and *C* in the population must be independent in normal applications. Again, the motive for the invention of the method is to lay out a novel alternative that would require smaller sample size than the original Warner approach to obtain precise estimates of π_A.

These two-sample variants can be reduced to one-sample variations if the parameters associated with traits *B* and *C* are known or can be fixed (Greenberg, Horvitz, and Abernathy 1974). They may be known, for example, from published census statistics on the population at hand. They may be fixed by using as trait *B*, for example, in the Greenberg et al. variant, the statement "Say Yes." Or they may be fixed by using an additional randomization device—a second flip of a coin for instance—to determine the response to the second item.

The two sample approach is likely to be useful only where information about the relative frequency of the auxiliary traits, B and C, is unavailable and is itself useful. The unrelated question technique is a risky approach if the assumption of the independence of traits A and B is untenable: estimates of π_A will then be biased if the regular formulae are used.

Multi-proportion and discrete quantitative response. The basic problem is to establish a reasonable idea of the proportion of people who are of type 1, type 2, and so on.

Abul-Ela, Greenberg, and Horvitz (1967) formalize the problem in estimating the proportion of individuals in each of k related but mutually exclusive categories: $\pi(A_1)$, $\pi(A_2)$, . . ., $\pi(A_k)$. In their approach, k-1 independent samples must be taken. In the first sample, any given individual is asked to respond Yes or No (True or False) to one of the k statements bearing on group membership. The statement is randomly chosen. The probability of responding to the statement regarding A_1 in the first sample is ϕ_{11}, the probability for A_2 is ϕ_{12}, etc. In the second sample, the proportions are fixed at different values: $\phi_{21}, \phi_{22}, \ldots, \phi_{2k}$. For each sample, i, the sum of the probabilities must be 1.00:

$$\sum_{j=1}^{k} \phi_{ij} = 1,$$

and so on, down to the k-1 sample. Field test results from a study of pregnancy and abortion are given in the reference.

Warner's (1971) proposal is an extension of his earlier work. In estimating proportions for three mutually exclusive categories, for example, one constructs six sets of three statements; each set contains a permutation of assignment of the following form:

- if you are a member of A_i, report A_j
- if you are a member of A_j, report A_k
- if you are a member of A_k, report A_i,

where $i, j, k = 1, 2, 3$, and $i = j, f, k$. The odds on a respondent's selecting any three-statement set $\phi_1, \phi_2, \ldots, \phi_6$ are fixed by the researcher and constrained so that $\Sigma\phi = 1.00$.

In the Bourke and Dalenius (1973) variation, the problem is again to estimate the proportion of individuals in mutually exclusive and exhaustive categories $A_1, A_2, \ldots, A_k$. The solution is a single sample variation on the Abul-Ela et al. model just described. Each member of a target sample is told to select one of three cards, each containing questions about A; the probability of selecting each card is prescribed by the researcher $(\phi_1, \phi_2, \ldots, \phi_k)$. Each card contains k numbered statements: ϕ_1 of the cards enumerate as follows: $1 = A_1$, $2 = A_2$, $\ldots, k = A_k$; ϕ_2 of the cards enumerate in a different pattern: $1 = A_2$, $2 = A_3$, $3 = A_4$. The respondent, having selected a card, just declares the number of the statement corresponding to his or her status. The pattern is fixed and conforms to a Latin square.

Bourke's (1974a) systematic extensions of this work involve a half dozen novel designs that are based on an unrelated question framework similar to that used in the original Simmons (1970) and Greenberg et al. (1969) approaches. They require only one sample, but some variations require two or more stages of randomization. In the simplest case, for example, the respondent reacts to one of two sets of questions, the set being selected randomly. One set concerns the attributes $A_1, A_2, \ldots, A_k$, and the respondent merely indicates which number corresponds to his status. The second set of questions refers to an unrelated set of categories $B_1, B_2, \ldots, B_k$, and if that set is chosen randomly, the respondent again merely reports a number.

The Liu, Chow, and Mosley (1975) variation is appropriate for discrete quantitative data or categorical data. The interviewer presents the respondent with a long-necked bottle containing colored or numbered beads, the color of each bead corresponding to a group: color 1 indicates group A_1, color 2 indicates group A_2, etc. The neck of the bottle is graduated so that the beads fall into a single line and the order of the beads from 1 to m is evident from markings on the neck. The respondent is asked: If you are a member of A_1 (say), indicate the position in the neck which your bead occupies: first from bottom, second from bottom, and so on. The interviewer is not allowed to see the bottle's neck during the process. Estimates of the proportion of a sample of size N belonging to exclusive categories $A_1, A_2, \ldots, A_k$ are obtained from the observed proportion of designations of each bottleneck position, P_y, and the preselected probability of each color of bead falling into the bottleneck position. The probability of the ith color bead $(i = 1, 2, \ldots m)$ is computable from information about the total number of beads, and the number of beads of each color, m_i. A small sample, physical feasibility test is described in the paper. The method is complicated; its merit lies partly in the fact that split samples need not be used.

Quantitative response. Greenberg, Kuebler, Abernathy, and Horvitz (1971) cast the problem in terms of estimating the population parameters of a variable, for example, mean number of abortions. In the original variant, two independent samples are required. Within a sample, any given individual is presented with the first (sensitive) question with probability ϕ_1 and the second question with probability $1 - \phi_1$, the choice of question being made randomly. The questions should be answerable using a numerical response: for instance, "How many pornographic magazines have you bought this week?" (Z_A) "How many times did you compliment someone this week?" (Z_B). The mathematics have been worked out for the simplest case, in which traits A and B are unrelated in the population. Members of a second, independent sample are asked the same questions, but with probabilities ϕ_2 and $1 - \phi_2$, to provide sufficient information for estimating mean levels of the traits, μ_A and μ_B, and variances.

As in other two-sample variations, the second sample is unnecessary and the procedure is more efficient when the population parameters for the innocuous question are known. Several other variations on the theme have been proposed. In the first, each respondent is asked to add the numerical responses to each question $(Z = Z_A + Z_B)$ and to provide that information to the interviewer. This is itself a simple variant on the microaggregated response tactics discussed earlier and is characterized by the same benefits and problems. A second tactic involves multiplying the numerical values of the responses; the respondent reports only $Z = Z_A \cdot Z_B$. Pollock and Bek's (1976) analysis suggests that the additive response model can be set up to be more efficient than the single sample randomized response method for $\phi < 0.7$. Recall that values of $\phi > 0.7$ in the randomized response approach generally yield better efficiency relative to direct questions. The multiplicative model's efficiency is difficult to assay, since it requires good guesses about the mean and variance of the sensitive trait being examined. Poole (1974) presented an alternative variation: the respondent selects a random number (using a roulette wheel with positive and negative numbers), multiplies it by the value of a sensitive trait (e.g., number of antisocial acts), and presents only the product to the interviewer. Estimating the distribution of responses is simple using Poole's approach. However, if any nonzero incidence of the trait is regarded as sensitive, then the majority of nonzero responses will be generated by individuals with the sensitive trait. The jeopardy level may be unacceptable to the respondent or to the researcher considering the multiplicative variations.

In Eriksson's (1973b) single sample variant, the options presented to each individual are: "To what degree do you possess the trait A?" and "Say that you possess the trait to the degree A_j." The probability associated with the question is fixed at ϕ. The probability of reacting to a specific statement about level A_1, level A_2, etc. is fixed at $\phi_1, \phi_2, \ldots, \phi_j$, so that:

$$\sum_{j=1}^{J} \phi_j = 1 - \phi.$$

The randomization device suggested is a deck of cards: ϕ of them concern the question; ϕ_1 of them concern a statement about level

A_1; ϕ_2 concern A_2; and so on. Each respondent selects a card from a complete, shuffled deck, and responds accordingly. Used in a single sample, the technique permits one to estimate the mean and variance of the level of trait A, and to estimate the proportion of individuals at each level $A_1, A_2, \ldots, A_k$.

Other variations on those methods have been developed to accommodate the researcher's need to establish relations among variables. They are described below.

RANDOMIZATION DEVICES: USE IN THE FIELD

Whether any of the randomized response procedures is effective depends partly on the way a random choice is generated. It is reasonable, then, to examine a few standards for evaluating randomization devices.

Physical characteristics of the randomization device will influence the duration, convenience, and complexity of an interview. Contemporary research suggests that a variety of devices are acceptable at least insofar as they present no remarkable handling problems. Barth and Sandler's (1976) respondents flip coins. Locander, Sudman, and Bradburn (1976) use little boxes containing colored beads, an adaption of devices used earlier by Greenberg et al. (1969). Chi, Chow, and Rider (1972) shake a bag of colored stones; Abul-Ela et al. (1967) and Brown and Harding (1973) shuffle cards. Fidler and Kleinknecht (1977) use a transparent globe containing colored balls, of the sort used in bingo games. Reaser, Hartsock, and Hoehn (1975) use a paper target containing numbers in randomly assigned positions; the respondent, to whom the questionnaire and target are mailed, pokes the target with a pencil without looking at it. In a few instances, telephone numbers whose statistical properties are established *beforehand* have been used—for example, by Goodstadt and Gruson (1975). Takahasi and Sakasegawa (1977) created a strategy parallel to Goodstadt and Gruson's to eliminate the need for a randomization device. They suggest first asking the respondent about his or her preference for, say, color or season, and then having the respondent answer one question or another depending on the (secret) color preference. An independent and presumably large sample must be used to obtain the color-preference parameter.

The respondent's attitude toward a randomization device may be a bit more important, and again, no obvious problems have been reported. Most devices can be built to conform with local culture: Chi, Chow, and Rider's (1972) black and white stones, used in Taiwan, are similar to those used in the game of Go; dice, coin flipping, etc. are familiar randomization devices in many societies. A few respondents in any given sample are likely to announce their suspicion that the dice are fixed, that the cards are marked, or that they would like to eat one of the little colored balls. But the reported incidence of these attitudes is very low, and their influence on a respondent's behavior is unknown. No research on the respondents' view of the credibility of various randomization devices appears to have been carried out. Small experiments are easy to design and implement, and should help to verify the statistician's intuition that devices do not differ markedly in their attractiveness, persuasiveness, and so forth for the respondent.

Most analysts assume that the respondents have an understanding, perhaps imperfect, of the probability of their being asked to respond to a sensitive question or tell the truth. None of the field tests assay that understanding, though side studies are possible. The topic is discussed below in the section on respondent views of probability.

The statistical properties of numbers generated by various randomization devices have not received much attention. Cards are usually assumed to have been shuffled well, bead bags are assumed to have been shaken vigorously, and so on. The North Carolina work on bead boxes is one exception. According to Greenberg, his colleagues have attempted to establish that their simple device has a demonstrable ability to generate numbers with well-understood properties. The Reaser et al. (1975) test is another interesting exception. They maintain that numbers picked blindly by a respondent from a randomly numbered paper target are distributed even more uniformly than the numbers obtained in die throws. However, no other properties of the obtained numbers are reported. The assumption that the numbers generated by the randomization devices are indeed random may not always be warranted, judging from other social endeavors in which randomization procedures have been found wanting. The military draft lotteries of the late 1960s, for example, were not random selections as they were advertised to be, in part because the procedure used for generating random choices was faulty.

Using "naturally occurring" numbers as a basis of randomization is an attractive prospect, in that the physical device might be eliminated. But the tactic poses more serious difficulties. For example, one might ask a respondent to use the fifth digit of an unnamed friend's telephone number as the basis for making a random choice, under the *assumption* that the population distribution of the numbers is uniform. Contrary to some expectations, however, the distribution of the numbers appearing in any given position (digit) of telephone numbers is usually not uniform. Even the fifth digit, which is more likely than others to be free of systematic influences, does not contain numbers that are uniform in distribution for the telephone directories we have examined. Similarly, many naturally occurring serial numbers have sticky subsets; that is, pairs or triplets go together more often than one would expect on the basis of chance alone. Further, Paul Lavrakas (1975) confirmed what we would expect to find in asking people to "think of ten random numbers." The numbers so generated deviated considerably from a uniform distribution (people favor numbers ending in zero). Furthermore, numbers can be predicted imperfectly from numbers appearing earlier in a sequence, from numbers in the sequence, and from phone numbers and addresses of the individuals in the study. On the other hand, when the properties of a population of naturally occurring, recorded numbers are well understood or a large enough sample can be taken to specify their properties well, they can be a more convenient randomization device. Goodstadt and Gruson (1975), for example, counted the incidence of the numbers 0, 1, . . . , 9 appearing as the last digit of telephone numbers in a large sample, developed a reasonable statistical characterization of the numbers, and then successfully used that characterization as a basis for estimating the incidence of drug abuse from randomized responses. Moreover, it is reasonable to expect no relation between the probability of one or another question's being asked under this approach, and the probability that the respondent has the sensitive trait. The idea can be adapted to digits in social security numbers, serial numbers on paper money, lottery tickets, credit cards, and so on, provided the population distribution and its parameters can be specified. O'Brien et al. (1975) used different types of naturally occurring numbers for different questions in a single questionnaire, an effort that must have astonished if not amused some respondents. They provide no information on the distribution of such numbers, however. Using "naturally occurring" preferences for seasons, colors, and animals as a substitute for randomization, along the lines suggested by Takahasi and Sakasegawa (1977), is less likely to be satisfactory. It must be known beforehand that preferences are unrelated to the sensitive trait, and the mean population preference must be specifiable.

CHOICE OF AN INNOCUOUS QUESTION

The general class of unrelated question randomized response methods, developed by Greenberg, Abul-Ela, Simmons, and Horvitz, requires that a second question, dealing with a nonsensitive trait, be used as a foil for the question about a sensitive trait. The usefulness of any such question depends on:

- the absence of any inherent relation between the occurrence of the sensitive and nonsensitive traits, for conventional applications
- the nonsensitive trait's attractiveness versus its innocuousness
- the nonsensitive trait's potential use in deductive disclosure.

All of the methods discussed here, and the mathematics underlying each, involve the assumption that the occurrence or level of the sensitive trait is not related to the occurrence of the nonsensitive one: they are supposed to be stochastically independent. It is possible, of course, to generate methods that permit an association, but they will be more complex. To guarantee the independence of the innocuous trait, one might exploit birth dates ("Is your mother's birthday in April?"), telephone numbers ("Is the fifth digit of a friend's number 2?"), and other traits that intuition suggests are independent of a sensitive one. That a choice based on intuition can be risky is clear, however. Shimizu and Bonham (1978), for example, used this nonsensitive question in one of their studies: "This time last year, did you live in a different county or state than this one?" The sensitive question dealt with abortion. It is not unreasonable to argue that the likelihood of abortion is indeed related to migration behavior; women from middle-income families, who incidentally move across county lines often, may find it easier or cheaper to have an abortion than women from low-income families, who incidentally do not move across county lines very often. A second risk in exploiting intuitively appealing nonsensitive traits is tied to memory. Shimizu and Bonham, for example, also used "Was your mother born in April?" for their nonsensitive question, as others have done. They had the good sense to do a side study on a subsample and discovered that just over 8 percent of the group admitted that they could not recollect the month. Identical problems have cropped up in using procedural methods of assuring confidentiality (see the section on birthday-based aliases in chapter 4). If the impact of memory failure is random, the problem is more tractable. But memory lapse is more likely to be systematic, and, if so, it will exercise systematic effects on estimates of the incidence of the sensitive trait. That influence might be negligible, but we simply do not know enough about it. Where the evidence is ambiguous and the issue crucial, we think it is best to adopt one of the randomized response techniques that require no auxiliary unrelated question or to mount prior pilot tests to determine the nature and magnitude of memory failure.

The second concern is that a respondent's view of the attractiveness of the nonsensitive trait may influence cooperation. Suppose that the sensitive question bears on reading pornography and the nonsensitive one bears on having eaten a bar of candy. The negative affect associated with the sensitive question may override the neutrality of the second, and the respondent may say No, regardless of what he or she is instructed to do. So, for example, Zdep and Rhodes (1977) stress that the "innocuous" item should involve an attractive or socially desirable trait. Their pilot tests and experimental results, using attendance at PTA meetings as the foil for their questions on punishing children, seem to bear that out. The symmetrical randomized response approaches (e.g., Warner's related question and the Bourke 1974b inventions) consitute a logical circumvention of the problem, but it is not clear to us that respondents attach the same emotional value to the alternatives. Two areas of psychological research have an indirect bearing on this topic, but they have not yet been adopted as a frame of reference for pertinent laboratory research or field studies. The first area, illustrated by Hamblin's (1974) work, attends to the form of the relation between one's liking for a trait and the physical character of the trait; that is, ratings of one's liking (or dislike) for having x martinis per day are elicited, and then plotted against values of x. The relationship is a power function for a variety of such traits, suggesting that the emotional weight attached to high magnitude of a sensitive trait is not a mirror image of the emotional value attached to the negative extreme of the same trait. The second are of research falls under the general rubric of "direction of wording" investigations, and "Yea saying" versus "Nay saying" studies of personality inventories and attitude scales.

No rules as robust as power laws have emerged from the research, and the effect of experimental manipulation appears generally to be small. Nonetheless, adopting the designs of such research and some of the findings seems reasonable for exploring analogous effects in randomized response methods (see Robinson, Rush, and Head 1974 for an introduction).

Finally, the topic of the innocuous question may lend itself to deductive disclosure of other information. Consider the question about whether the respondent's mother's month of birth is April, used in the abortion study cited earlier. If it is possible for the interviewer to determine mother's birth month for the particular respondent, as it usually is in principle if not in practice, then deductive disclosure is possible. A Yes response implies the respondent had an abortion, if it is determined later that her mother's birthday was in August. A No response would imply having no abortion, if it is determined that the birthmonth is April. A Yes is "safe" only for children of April's child. It is reasonable also to expect that some respondents will recognize the problem, as they have in other research (see chapter 3). We are aware of no studies of randomized response that address the issue.

RESPONDENT VIEWS OF PROBABILITY

The assumption implicit in many randomized response applications is that at least some respondents understand the probabilistic nature of the methods. That assumption underlies the argument that when the methods are used respondents may respond more truthfully than they otherwise might. It bears on the statisticians' recommendations that we fix the probability of asking the sensitive question as high as one "dares," or as high as "possible," to achieve an efficient characterization of the trait under scrutiny (Lanke 1975a). And the assumption serves as justification for mathematical research on respondent "jeopardy"—roughly speaking, the probability of his or her having a sensitive trait given a Yes or No response to a randomized response statement (Leysieffer and Warner 1976). Yet we know very little about measuring understanding itself in this context, much less about respondents' actual understanding of the procedure and of the relevant probabilities.

Alternative frames of reference for gauging understanding are easy to propose, and each may bear on respondent cooperation. It is reasonable to suppose, for example, that trust supplants understanding for many respondents in this setting, just as it does in surveys that employ pleasant, well-trained interviewers, and that the trust will be enhanced by the technical veneer of instructions. If understanding is indexed by the accuracy of respondents' recollections of the interviewer's instructions, that understanding is likely to be imperfect, judging from other research on respondent recall (see chapter 3). It is also reasonable to suppose that understanding as indexed by knowledge of the simple mathematics underlying the method is low, judging from National Educational Assessment studies of high school populations. Furthermore, it is likely that the language of probability is imperfectly understood or at least susceptible to substantially different interpretation, judging from Kruskal's (1978) and Kruskal and Mosteller's (1977) studies. Finally, it is reasonable to suppose that respondents' views of numerical statements of probability will not always be coherent or accurate, judging from research on subjective estimates of magnitude. Little of the previous work has been adapted (or even recognized) by the statistician who toils in this vineyard, so we consider some of it briefly in the following remarks.

The probability of having to react to a sensitive statement is one of the small, if crucial, elements of information that is presumed to be understood by the respondent. We ought not to expect it to influence cooperation nearly as much as other factors in the scheme, such as interviewer demeanor. But since the objective of most applications is to identify small improvements in large samples, work on the topic is warranted. Further, insofar as basic research and theory can be exploited to guide our understanding, we can help to enlarge the theory. For the experimental psychologist, it is natural to put the process into a stimulus-response framework, where the statement or implication of probability serves as stimulus and an attitude, judgment, or behavior serves as response. Normally the controllable variables are the way the statement of probability is presented, or, if it is not presented directly, the randomization device and the probabilistic implication it carries. The variations on how to tell the respondent about probability are not especially numerous. One might present a statement of the form: "The sensitive question will on average appear 10 times out of 100." We might present the odds against its appearance, 9:1; a fraction, such as $^{10}/_{100}$, $^{1}/_{10}$, or $^{100}/_{1000}$; or a percentage. We would expect some variation in respondents' subjective views (perceptions) of the probability as a function of these "different" modes of presentation. More importantly, it is plausible to expect the subjective judgments about the acceptability of the probability and its magnitude in literal terms ("high" versus "low") to be a simple function of the actual magnitude. This supposition stems from a large research literature on the form of the relation between subjective statements or guesses about magnitude and the objectively measured magnitude.

The same approach can be more profitably exploited in assaying understanding when the numerical value of the probability is not stated, and instead, the respondent infers its magnitude from the randomization device and instructions. The device itself and the objective probability serve as stimuli, and this immediately suggests studies to assay the character of perception as a function of each. The structure of examination need not be complicated. So called multi-trait-multimethod matrices can be constructed from respondent judgments, repeatedly elicited for various randomization devices (methods) and various traits (alternative levels of probability). The response surface is most likely to be described best by power functions, judging by both theory and data on subjective estimation of magnitude (Hamblin 1974). Assaying only the distributions of opinions about magnitude relative to actual distributions is not unreasonable for the decision theorist. And judging from Mosteller's (1977) reports of work by Alpert and Raiffa, we would expect the differences between the two to be notable, especially at the extremes of the distribution. Moriarity and Wiseman's (1977) tests have some bearing on this. They found that most respondents underestimated the actually low probability of various outcomes in die tossing and random choice of playing cards, in contrast to what one might have expected from the Alpert-Raiffa studies: that is, overestimation of frequency in the tails of the distribution. Accuracy of perception did indeed depend on the randomization device in Moriarity and Wiseman, but the tests were small enough and complicated enough to justify replication studies and exploitation of the theory of magnitude estimation. Finally, no parallel research has been undertaken on respondents' perception of respondent jeopardy: that is, some function of the probability of having (or not having) a sensitive trait conditional on a Yes (or No) response. We would expect from some theories of arithmetic learning that the steps involved in such a computation are independent and that accuracy of responses is a multiplicative function of the accuracy of conception and execution at each step. This suggests that perceptions will deviate considerably from actual values if respondents think about jeopardy at all and develop an idea of conditional risk.

Aside from adding to what we know about the respondents' understanding, such small studies can occasionally be exploited in choosing design parameters for the methods. Moriarity and Wiseman (1977), for example, argue that one might capitalize on respondent ignorance by choosing the particular device and parameter value in which the respondent is most likely to underestimate odds on being asked a sensitive question (dice in their laboratory test). Further, if the relation between subjective estimates of probability is indeed a power function, it would make more sense to choose among sizable probability intervals—say .05–.30, .31–.60, .61–.95—instead of discrete numbers in designing methods, since respondents do not assay probability to any closer tolerance. If institutional regulations about respondents being "informed" are demanding, then choosing the interval in which respondents are most accurate is possible, given such data.

Finally, the probabilistic nature of the methods evidently carries the implication for some respondents, some of the time, that adhering to instructions (responding as prescribed) is less important in surveys that exploit these methods than in surveys based on more direct questions. Some direct evidence that respondents make the inference is available from studies by Berman, McCombs, and Boruch (1975). Judging from their recommendations on using the methods, O'Brien et al, (1976) encountered a similar phenomenon. To the extent that the attitude prevails, the usefulness of the technique is diminished. But we have neither formal theory nor sufficient data to establish the severity of the problem.

PILOT STUDY, SIDE STUDY, AND ADHERENCE CHECKS

The statistical strategies may be used for at least one of two purposes: to assure that the respondent's privacy is sustained; and to sustain privacy and so encourage more accurate responses. Regardless of the purpose, it is essential that the quality of data obtained under the models be examined.

If the only objective of using the methods is to sustain privacy, then the problems of assessing quality turn around the novelty of the methods. Beyond the ordinary problems of interviewing, the methods are less familiar and more complicated for both interviewer and respondent and so may engender confusion; it is less likely, in our judgment, but still possible, that the methods provoke suspicion on account of their novelty. To reduce the mechanical problems engendered by novelty, pilot testing prior to the survey and checks employed during and after the main survey are warranted. More elaborate planned experiments are warranted if an additional objective is to increase candor in response or establish increased suspicion. The results of pilot tests undertaken before a main survey are rarely reported in scholarly journals. However, Zdep and Rhodes (1977) provide some guidance based on their presurvey research on the use of the unrelated question randomized response technique. They recommend that to increase the effectiveness of the method, one should: (1) employ a nonsensitive question bearing on an attractive trait rather than an innocuous one; (2) instruct respondents in the format orally, before any written material or questionnaires are furnished; (3) minimize the instructions so as not to confuse the respondents; and (4) use a randomization device and a prescribed probability of selecting the sensitive question that have face validity for the respondents. As in ordinary surveys, they emphasize the training of the interviewers as well. Neither pilot tests nor training regimen are reported for the Illinois Institute of Technology's (1971) study of crime, or for Shimizu and Bonham's (1978) research on abortions, and their absence may account for the difficulties both report. Post-interview interrogation of interviewers and respondents, regarding their confusion about the methods, their certainty about the protection offered, and so on, has been helpful for these studies and others. However, the information ought to be more systematic than the informal anecdotal reports that characterize the IIT study and others: it is impossible for the outsider to gauge the severity of problems from informal interrogation.

The second objective, inducing more candor in response by increasing privacy, demands both pilot work on the mechanics of the technique and planned research on validity of response. In some cases, prior information may be useful basis for gauging quality of response. In their research on abortion, for example, Krotki and Fox (1974), Liu and Chow (1976b), Shimizu and Bonham (1978), and others used earlier surveys of abortion rate, which employed direct questions, to assay the results obtained under randomized response methods. Their criterion for judgment is that estimates of abortion rate under the new method must exceed rates estimated under the ordinary methods for the new one to be declared successful. Similarly, one might use as a standard the level of distortion in response reported in studies of nonsampling error in surveys; bibliographies on these studies have been published by the U.S. Bureau of the Census (1974), and by Dalenius and Lyberg (1970), and others, and research on the subject has been synthesized by Sudman and Bradburn (1974). Such data may be suitable only for crude comparisons against newer methods, since they may be obsolete, may concern target populations that are dissimilar from the one sampled using the new approach, and so on.

Less ambiguous comparisons have been based on randomized field experiments. Half the sample members are assigned randomly to one of the statistical methods for assuring confidentiality, and the remaining identified individuals are asked questions directly. Estimates of the level or incidence of the sensitive trait will be higher under the first condition than under the second if the statistical method does persuade respondents to be more candid; similarly, the estimated rate of affirming a socially desirable trait, such as contribution to charity, voter registration, and so on, should be reduced. This sort of comparison characterizes most of the tests listed in Table 3. Zdep and Rhodes (1977), for example, found that the rate of admitting corporal punishment of children under a randomized response approach was notably higher than the rate of admission under superficially anonymous conditions: 15 percent versus 4 percent. Likewise, respondents may be assigned to a statistical method in which they are identified, or to a condition in which no identification is possible, for example, a mailback questionnaire, or an anonymous questionnaire response in a large group setting. The comparison then focuses on whether an estimate of the incidence or level of a sensitive trait matches the corresponding estimate based on anonymous data. The only test of this sort available involved a sample size that was too small to yield conclusive results (Berman, McCombs, and Boruch 1977).

A different, direct method of comparison can be exploited when public records on presumably sensitive characteristics of individuals are available. Locander, Sudman, and Bradburn (1976), for example, used voter registration records, bankruptcy records, and records on arrests for drunk driving as a basis for sampling, and elicited the same information from the individuals in a personal interview using a randomized response method. Where records are up-to-date and accurate, comparison of the estimated incidence of the sensitive trait against the records can be informative. Locander, Sudman, and Bradburn found, for example, that the unrelated question randomized response method was not effective in reducing overreporting of traits like voter registration and library membership. The verifiable distortion rate was lowest under the randomized response method, relative to a self-administered questionnaire, when questions about bankruptcy and drunk driving were asked.

PROTECTION LEVEL

When correctly applied, none of the statistical methods permit the interviewer or anyone else to know with certainty that a respondent has a particular characteristic. True information about the respondent remains private and known only to the respondent.

Information about the respondent is, however, disclosed in a probabilistic sense rather than a deterministic one. Suppose, for example, that in using the contamination method, the researcher fixes the probability of controlled lies at a very low level: only one out of fifty respondents is required to lie. If respondents adhere faithfully to the instructions, most of those affirming the sensitive characteristic will be telling the truth, and so most will be in jeopardy. That is, a respondent's saying Yes immediately implies to the interviewer that the respondent *probably* has the sensitive characteristic.

The problem, probabilistic disclosure, warrants investigation for several reasons. First, probabilistic jeopardy is a form of risk. In the interest of building better research designs *and* providing protection, the analyst needs to learn how that risk can be controlled. Second, probabilistic information about an individual can be regarded as a form of circumstantial evidence; control over the risk level may then have a direct bearing on the use of research records in litigation. Finally, the respondent's perception of probabilistic jeopardy may be quite crude, even erroneous, and still be important. Building a framework for the control of the jeopardy level can then help us to understand respondents' reactions to these methods.

Though there are a variety of ways to characterize the problem, only the mathematical approaches have advanced very far (see our earlier remarks on respondent views). These focus almost entirely on translating the idea of protection into probabilistic form and exploring how the idea might be used in applying randomized response methods. We follow that line of development here.

The simplest index of protection or jeopardy is a conditional probability, representing the likelihood, $P(A|Y)$, that an individual who says Yes (Y) to the inquiry does in fact have the stigmatizing characteristic (A). Defining the level of jeopardy this way makes intuitive sense. If $P(A|Y)$ is very high, then the actual protection for the respondent is low: a Yes response means "chances are high that the individual has the characteristic in question."

The general formulae for conditional probabilities are easy to develop for the simple randomized methods. Using the fact that $P(AY) = P(A|Y) \cdot P(Y)$, and given the expected values of $P(AY)$ and $P(Y)$ in symbolic form for the Warner method, we have:

$$P(A|Y) = P(AY) / P(Y) = \frac{\phi P_A}{1 - \phi + P_A(2\phi - 1)}$$

for the simplest contamination method:

$$P(A|Y) = \frac{P_A(1 - \phi)}{P_A(1 - 2\phi) + \phi}, \qquad \phi_p = \phi_n = \phi \neq .5.$$

and for the simplest Simmons method:

$$P(A|Y) = \frac{\phi P_A + (1 - \phi)P_A P_B}{\phi P_A + (1 - \phi)P_B}, \qquad P_{AB} = P_A \cdot P_B, \ \phi \neq .5.$$

Here, ϕ represents the probability of choosing the stigmatizing question, and the subscript B refers to the innocuous question.

The index is simple and, in some respects, misleading. We accept it tentatively for purposes of illustration, and because it is quite possible that this index alone may be used intuitively by a respondent in gauging the risk of response. That is, regardless of its shortcomings, the index may be found in empirical tests to be useful in anticipating or understanding the cooperation rate. Accepting the index for the moment, then, how might it be used?

- An upper bound on the permissible values of the index might be established; then any statistical approach that will not exceed the level prescribed can be used in a survey.

- The index, computed for each possible method of questioning, can be used to compare methods and to select the one with the highest level of protection.

- When different designs can be set up to yield identical levels of protection, the choice can be made with respect to other criteria, notably the efficiency of each method, its attractiveness, and so on.

So, for example, we may specify that in a study of racism, the level of jeopardy ought not to exceed .50. That is, a Yes response to a question concerning one's racist attitude implies that one has the attitude with a probability of ½; a Yes response is no more informative than a judgment based on a toss of a fair coin. If we speculate that the proportion having the stimatizing characteristic is $P(A) = .20$, we can then construct a table of $P(A|Y)$ as a function of ϕ for, say, the Warner method:

ϕ_w	.10	.20	.30	.40	.45	.55	.60	.75	.80	.90
$P_w(A|Y)$	.027	.059	.097	.143	.170	.235	.273	.369	.501	.693

If the analyst, the respondent, or the courts rely *only* on $P(A|Y)$ as an index of jeopardy, then any of the ϕ values in the range .10–.80 are acceptable. Each yields a $P(A|Y)$ less than the .50 criterion set earlier.

Where a choice must be made between two methods—for example, Warner's versus Simmons's—then a similar table can be constructed for the competitor. Supposing in the Simmons approach that P_B for a mandatory innocuous item is known to be .20, we get

ϕ_B	.1	.2	.3	.4	.45	.55	.60	.70	.80	.90
$P_B(A|Y)$	.28	.36	.40	.52	.56	.64	.68	.76	.84	.92

Since the levels of jeopardy under this design, $P(A|Y)$, are generally higher than protection under the one considered earlier, one might then choose the Warner approach over the Simmons method in this instance.

Lanke (1975) shows that for $\phi_w > .50$, the Simmons and Warner methods will yield $P_W(A|Y) = P_S(A|Y)$ if ϕ_s is specified such that:

$$\phi_s = \frac{P_B(1 - 2\phi_w)}{P_B(1 - 2\phi_w) + \phi_w - 1}$$

In general, the index $P(A|Y)$ is too simple a basis for judging probabilistic jeopardy, for a Yes response may also predict *not* having the trait A. Further, a No response may be jeopardizing, as in the contamination and Warner methods, and we ought to attend to that possibility as well. Leysieffer and Warner (1976) have developed the most general schema for organizing the problem. They focus on two indices, one of which is $P(A|Y)$ and its relation to $P(\bar{A}|Y)$. The latter represents the probability of a respondent's not having the sensitive trait A, when we know that the response to the inquiry was Yes. The ratio $P(A|Y)/(P(\bar{A}|Y)$ reflects the weight of evidence for speculating that an individual has trait A rather than $\bar{A}$. If the ratio is near 1.00, a Yes response implies only that the chances of his having A or not having A are equal. A high ratio indicates that Yeses in the long run will be associated with persons who have A rather than not A. They *also* focus on the states that are probabilistically associated with a No response, $P(\bar{A}|N)/P(A|N)$, since a No may be jeopardizing. For simplicity, the Leysieffer-Warner jeopardy functions are cast in the following general terms:

$$g(R,A) = \frac{P(R|A)}{P(R|\bar{A})} = \frac{P(A|R) \cdot \pi}{P(\bar{A}|R)(1 - \pi)}$$

where R represents either a Yes or a No response.

The jeopardy of a Yes response with respect to A is then:

$$g(Y,A) = \frac{P(Y|A)}{P(N|A)}$$

Note that $g(N,\bar{A}) = 1/g\ (N,A)$ and $g(Y,A) = 1/g\ (Y,\bar{A})$.

The new indices can be used in much the same way as the simpler $P(A|Y)$ and will generally be less misleading. In particular, we may set up criterion values of $g(Y,A)$ and $g(N,\bar{A})$ and choose methods and design parameters that will meet those criteria. We may subsequently use another criterion, notably efficiency, to choose a particular method of eliciting sensitive information, or to choose values of controllable parameters for a particular method.

We observed earlier that the mathematical approaches to defining protection level have been the ones best articulated. To go much further, some empirical research is essential. We speculate, for example, that the perceived probability is not a linear function of the actual probability. Whatever the shape of that function, we know little about actual cooperation rate as a function of the conditional probabilities. Small studies at the university level to establish the linkage between perceived and actual probabilities seem warranted to build a dossier on reactions. Side studies in large surveys on the way behavior depends on perceived and actual probabilities need to be done to permit generalization of the laboratory work and theory development.

TESTING HYPOTHESES

When data are gathered using a randomized response scheme, it is still possible to test hypotheses by adapting existing testing apparatus. The simplest case involves forming opinions about the equality of two proportions π_1 and π_2 where estimates of each, $\hat{\pi}_1$ and $\hat{\pi}_2$, are based on independent samples 1 and 2. Suppose that one or both estimates are based on a randomized response approach. To assay whether a direct question about alcohol abuse in sample 1, for example, yields the same mean result as a Warner randomized question used in an independent sample 2 of the same population, we might test

$$H_o : \pi_1 = \pi_2 \qquad H_a : \pi_1 \neq \pi_2$$

at some prescribed level of significance. Under null conditions, a useful test statistic is:

$$Z = \frac{\hat{\pi}_1 - \hat{\pi}_2}{\sqrt{\text{var}(\pi_1) + \text{var}(\hat{\pi}_2)}} \sim N(0,1)$$

where variances of the estimates, $V(\hat{\pi}_1)$ and $V(\hat{\pi}_2)$, are computed using the ordinary estimator for sample 1 and the Warner estimator respectively. Simple pairwise comparisons of this sort are the basis for Krotki and Fox's (1974) experiment on methods for collecting data about pregnancy and abortion in Canada. That the statistic is distributed normally in large samples is based on the argument that $\hat{\pi}_1$ and $\hat{\pi}_2$ are independent maximum likelihood estimators of parameters for the binomial (Levy 1976a). That many such estimates are not maximum likelihood is now clear; but it is not unreasonable to suppose that the large-sample distribution of the test statistic is close enough to the theoretical to justify its use.

To form an opinion about the equality of three or more proportions, $\hat{\pi}_1, \hat{\pi}_2, \ldots, \hat{\pi}_k$, each based on an independent sample, Levy (1976b) argues that a chi-square statistic can be employed. He suggests that under the null hypothesis

$$H_o : \pi_1 = \pi_2 \ldots = \pi_k$$

the test statistic

$$\chi^2 = \sum_{k=1}^{K} (\hat{\pi}_k - \hat{\pi}_o)^2 / V(\hat{\pi}_k)$$

is distributed as chi-square with $K - 1$ degrees of freedom. The $\hat{\pi}_k$ and $V(\hat{\pi}_k)$ are computed using the pertinent formulae, and the weighted mean based on the equality assumption is:

$$\hat{\pi}_o = \sum_{k=1}^{K} \frac{\hat{\pi}_k \, V(\hat{\pi}_k)}{V(\hat{\pi}_k)}$$

The argument that the statistic is distributed as advertised is based on the additive property of the chi-square and the fact that the squared maximum likelihood estimates of the parameters for the binomial are themselves distributed as a function of a chi-square.

Tests about the relatedness of traits are also possible. Drane (1975) and Clickner and Iglewicz (1976), for example, show that the usual computations for testing a relation in a 2×2 table are pertinent. Their argument hinges on the idea that an individual's responses to two different randomized response questions will be independent only if the two underlying traits A and B are independent. Moreover, the randomized response methods developed by Warner and others will introduce no additional association between traits. A test that

$$H_o : \pi_{AB} = \pi_A \pi_B \qquad H_a : \pi_{AB} \neq \pi_A \pi_B$$

where π_{AB} represents the true joint relative occurrence of traits A and B, and π_A and π_B represent true relative frequencies of A and B, can be obtained by testing

$$H_o : \lambda_{AB} = \lambda_A \lambda_B \qquad H_a : \lambda_{AB} \neq \lambda_A \lambda_B$$

where λs represent the relative frequencies observed under a randomized response method.

For continuous data, a null hypothesis of the form

$$H_o : \pi_1 = \pi_2 \qquad H_a : \pi_1 \neq \pi_2$$

suggests a statistic such as

$$t = \frac{\hat{\pi}_1 - \hat{\pi}_2}{\sqrt{V(\hat{\pi}_1) + V(\hat{\pi}_2)}}$$

if estimates of π_1 and π_2 are based on independent samples. Previous investigators have assumed that if estimates of either π_1 or π_2 or both are obtained under randomized response methods, then the statistic is distributed approximately as Student's t. Variances may have to be stabilized, using a log transform as Goodstadt and Gruson (1975) do in their drug-abuse studies, and sample sizes restricted to be equal in order to accommodate heterogeneous variances. Conventional analysis of variance of a single response variable and multivariate analysis of variance are also pertinent. So, for instance, Locander, Sudman, and Bradburn (1976) analyze the proportion of distorted responses as a function of five question types (e.g., randomized response, archival record search) and four levels of sensitivity of the inquiry, using ordinary analysis of variance of both raw and transformed data.

Three issues, commonly attended in normal applications of tests such as these, are especially important when data are collected under the randomized response approaches. First, outliers or observations falling outside the plausible range need to be eliminated. So, for example, in asking about mean level of drug abuse, Goodstadt and Gruson (1975) expunge unreasonably high reports before undertaking tests. Criteria for plausibility are admittedly subjective, and so they must be explicit. The second consideration concerns analysis of data on any rare trait. The distribution underlying observations is often skewed badly, and variances based on different methods of eliciting information may differ notably. Though tests based on means are robust against deviations from some of the assumptions underlying the tests, transformation of raw observations may still be desirable. So, for example, Locander, Bradburn, and Sudman (1976) use an arcsin transform to stabilize variances in their analysis of variance of randomized response data. Goodstadt and Gruson (1975) use a log transform of raw observations to stabilize variances and eliminate some of the skewness of the observations on alcohol and drug use obtained under randomized response and direct questions.

The task of designing sensitive tests can be facilitated in several ways. Published reports, for instance, can be exploited to anticipate the study at hand. This includes compendiums on response error, such as the one produced by Sudman and Bradburn (1974), and other studies cited earlier, which cover both systematic bias and random misreporting. And it includes research on the randomized-response methods. Table B summarizes studies that compared the randomized approach to a reasonably clear standard, for example, direct interviews. Variances are generally larger under the randomized approach, as one would expect. In Goodstadt and Gruson's study of alcohol use, for example, the standard error under the randomized scheme is four times that under direct questioning, but incidence estimates are much higher under the novel approach. There are exceptions, like the reporting of bankruptcy in the Locander, Sudman, and Bradburn study.

The task can also be facilitated by building little power tables that help one understand the likelihood of rejecting hypotheses when the data have been gathered under these methods. The power tables may be based partly on existing tabulations of mean square error of randomized response estimators (e.g., Horvitz, Greenberg, and Abernathy 1975; and Leysieffer and Warner 1976. Or they may be constructed from scratch, using available machinery to expedite computations.

Suppose, for instance, that one used the contamination technique or some related approach in eliciting information about trait A or B, or both. To gauge the power of a conventional chi-square test of the association between A and B, one may construct a power plot of the following sort. Calculate the noncentrality parameter, λ, that one would obtain under truthful direct responses (say) and the λ one would obtain under a randomized response method with specified parameters. In terms more familiar to the psychologist, the parameter λ is related to the common phi coefficient for a relation between two dichotomous variables, ϕ_D, and to the sample size, N, in large samples by the formula $\lambda = N\phi_D{}^2$. The influence of a contamination approach on ϕ_D and hence λ can be determined by using a conventional formula for determining ϕ_D from relative frequencies in a 2×2 table when reporting is perfect, and an analagous formula for $\phi_D{}'$ when data are contaminated.

$$\phi_D = \sqrt{\frac{\pi_{AB} - \pi_A \pi_B}{\pi_A \pi_B (1 - \pi_A)(1 - \pi_B)}}$$

$$\phi_D' = \sqrt{\frac{\lambda_{AB} - \lambda_A \lambda_B}{\lambda_A \lambda_B (1 - \lambda_A)(1 - \lambda_B)}}$$

where πs refer to the perfectly accurate observations and the terms are defined as above. The formula for the joint probability observed with contamination is given in the section on estimating relations. The last step is simply plotting values of power against values of λ for different significant levels. So, for example, if all the marginal relative frequencies in a 2×2 table of true states are .30, the true phi coefficient is .50, and the contamination approach results in a misclassification rate of 10 percent in both rows and columns, then the observed phi coefficient will be about .20. With a sample size of 100 and a significance level of $\alpha = .05$, the power associated with a test that $H_o : \pi_{AB} = \pi_A \pi_B$ drops from .72 to .28.

ESTIMATING RELATIONS AND MULTIVARIATE ANALYSIS

Existing statistical methods for determining the association between variables, and for summarizing relations among variables, can be adapted to randomized response data. Moreover, some new response methods have been invented to accommodate better the researcher's interest in multivariate data. The state of the art is still fragmentary, however, and requires development and testing. Here, we examine three new approaches to eliciting data when the objective is to form opinions about relatedness of variables: multitrial applications of a given method, joint-trait methods, and vector response methods. A fourth category of research concerns the adoption of conventional analytic methods to such data.

The *multitrial approach* involves independently applying a randomized response scheme to each trait in a set of traits. For example, in using the Eriksson method, a die is tossed for a question about trait A, it is tossed again for a question about trait B, and so on, for each respondent. The probabilistic underpinnings for the approach have been worked out by Clickner and Iglewicz (1976) for repeated application of Warner's unrelated question method; by Drane (1976) for the Warner, Simmons, and Lanke-Drane (forced Yes) approaches; and by Bourke (1976a), who developed a more general framework. The mathematics can get a bit complicated, and technical assistance may be essential in adopting a new method. However, the principles can be illustrated easily.

Suppose that the researcher elicits reports about racial prejudice from each respondent, using a contamination method, and reports about the level of each individual's reading habits, using a direct question. The proportion of prejudiced respondents can be estimated using the formulae given earlier; the proportion of frequent readers can be estimated directly. To estimate the cells in a 2×2 table—for example, the proportion who are both prejudiced (A) and frequent readers (C)—some algebra is necessary. The point of most such algebra is to express the cell entries in terms of the fixed design parameters such as the contamination rate, and the observed relative frequencies. For the case at hand, the proportion actually having attributes A and C can be computed using:

$$P(AC) = \phi \pi_C \pi_{A|C} + (1 - \phi) \, \pi_C \pi_{\bar{A}|C}$$

where the contamination rate $\phi = \phi_P = \phi_N$, π_C is the observed proportion of frequent readers, $P(AC)$ is the observed proportion of respondents who say Yes to both questions, and $\pi_{A|C} = \pi_C - \pi_{\bar{A}|C}$ is the quantity to be estimated. The true proportion of people who are prejudiced, frequent readers is $\pi_{AC} = \pi_C \pi_{A|C}$. Similarly, for Eriksson's method, in which the respondent tells the truth with probability ϕ and says Yes with probability $1 - \phi$, the corresponding probability is:

$$P'(AC) = \phi \pi_C \pi_{AK} + (1 - \phi) \pi_C$$

The approach can be generalized easily to the case in which both A and C are measured using a randomized response method. Clickner and Iglewicz (1976) give a more sophisticated treatment, deriving maximum likelihood estimates of joint frequencies such as $P(AC)$, variances and covariances of the estimators, and distribution theory for tests of hypotheses based on the data.

The second class of approaches, *joint-trait methods*, is related, but focuses on eliciting information simultaneously, rather than sequentially, on the joint occurrence of traits. In Bourke's (1974a) proposal, one begins by constructing a set of statements such as the following and putting them all on a card or a page of a questionnaire.

This week:

1. I have read a pornographic novel and a church newsletter.
2. I have not read a pornographic novel, but I have read a church newsletter.
3. I have read a pornographic novel, and I have not read a church newsletter.
4. I have read neither a pornographic novel nor a church newsletter.

Assume, for simplicity's sake, that "pornographic" is defined beforehand; the categories are also supposed to be mutually exclusive and exhaustive. A second set of statements is constructed by merely renumbering items, and similarly for a third and fourth set. In symbolic form (P for pornography, C for church), four cards contain:

	I	II	III	IV
1.	PC	$\bar{P}C$	$P\bar{C}$	$\bar{P}\bar{C}$
2.	$\bar{P}C$	$P\bar{C}$	$\bar{P}\bar{C}$	PC
3.	$P\bar{C}$	$\bar{P}\bar{C}$	PC	$\bar{P}C$
4.	$\bar{P}\bar{C}$	PC	$\bar{P}C$	$P\bar{C}$

The researcher reproduces the cards and fixes the proportion of type I cards at ϕ_I, the proportion of type II cards at ϕ_{II}, and so on. Each respondent picks a card from the shuffled deck and declares the number of the statement that best describes himself or herself. If the relative frequencies of joint traits are designated π_{PC} and so on, and the observed proportions of Yes responses to each statement are designated $P(Y_1)$ and so on, then the observed proportions can be expressed as a function of known parameters and the unknown joint probabilities:

$$P(Y_1) = \phi_I \pi_{PC} + \phi_{II} \pi_{P\bar{c}} + \phi_{III} \pi_{\bar{P}C} + \phi_{IV} \pi_{\bar{P}\bar{c}}$$

$$P(Y_2) = \phi_I \pi_{P\bar{c}} + \phi_{II} \pi_{PC} + \phi_{III} \pi_{\bar{P}\bar{c}} + \phi_{IV} \pi_{\bar{P}C}$$

$$P(Y_3) = \phi_I \pi_{\bar{P}C} + \phi_{II} \pi_{\bar{P}\bar{c}} + \phi_{III} \pi_{PC} + \phi_{IV} \pi_{P\bar{c}}$$

$$1 = \pi_{PC} + \pi_{P\bar{c}} + \pi_{\bar{P}C} + \pi_{\bar{P}\bar{c}}$$

When the ϕs are fixed properly, the equations will be independent and the πs estimable. The technical constraint on properness is given by Bourke (1974a).

DeLacy's (1975) interest lies in a related problem: asking conditional questions. In his proposal, two sets of questions are presented, the choice of a set being random, and each set bearing on traits that are independent. The first would be set up as:

- Did you punish your child this week?
- If so, did you strike the child?

The second set would be:

- Is the last digit on a dollar bill that you hold a 0, 1, . . . , or 6?
- If so, is it a 5 or a 6?

The permissible responses then are: No; Yes, Yes; Yes, No. Responses to the items generate a little system of simultaneous equations involving three proportions of respondents who report permissible responses, the unknown parameters about child punishment, the known parameter for serial numbers on a dollar bill, and the odds on presenting either question. DeLacy derives maximum likelihood estimates of proportions, variances, and covariances, and suggests that the technique can be generalized easily to several conditional responses.

The vector response designs produced by Bourke (1974c) are very similar to the joint-trait methods. Here the respondent is presented with a numbered series of statements about traits and complements of traits. For instance, a card or page of a questionnaire might contain:

1. I drank at least six beers yesterday.
2. I drank less than six beers yesterday.

3. I made a contribution to charity last month.
4. I made no contribution to charity last month.
5. I graduated from high school.
6. I did not graduate from high school.

The ordering of each set of traits within a series is permuted—for example, in symbolic form:

I	II	III	IV
1. B	1. $\bar{C}$	1. C	1. $\bar{B}$
2. $\bar{B}$	2. C	2. $\bar{C}$	2. B
3. C	3. B	3. $\bar{B}$	3. $\bar{C}$
4. $\bar{C}$	4. $\bar{B}$	4. B	4. C

A stack of cards for each series is made up, the proportion of cards of each type (I, II, III, IV) being fixed by the researcher. The respondent picks a card from the combined pile of cards, and then declares the position number (1, 2, 3, 4) of the statements that best describe him or her. The mean number of responses of any type can then be estimated through this tactic. It has been illustrated for questions with a dichotomous response, and it is generalizable in principle to multi-category response (see Bourke 1974c) and to quantitative response.

□ 6 □

Secondary Analysis and Audit

of Social Science Data*

As long as Francis and I remained closed out from the experimental data, the best course was to maintain an open mind. So I returned to my thoughts about sex.

James Watson,
The Double Helix

So far, we have focused on methods for assuring the confidentiality of data elicited from identifiable individuals by a researcher. In this chapter, the focus is on a different but related problem: assuring that scientific and administrative records can be made available for reanalysis without depreciating the privacy of the individuals on whom the records are kept.

The chapter begins with a brief justification for reanalyzing data and an explanation of the confidentiality-related problems engendered by the process. Some approaches to resolving the problems in secondary analysis of social research data and in conventional audits of research projects are presented next. The final section discusses administrative review of clinical records.

Justification for Reanalysis and Audit

Reanalyzing archival data for scientific purposes will be referred to here as *secondary analysis*. The process typically involves the statisti-

*Excerpts of this chapter have been presented at the U.S. General Accounting office Conference on Social Experimentation in 1976, and have been included in a report of the Social Science Research Council's Committee on Evaluation Research (1978) on the GAO role in social experiments.

cal review of a group of records (microdata) to confirm earlier analyses, to test new hypotheses, or to use the data as a test bed for developing new theory or new analytic methods. In the social sciences, these uses are exemplified by the Moynihan and Mosteller (1972) reanalysis of Coleman's data on the effects of schooling on children, by the Wortman–St. Pierre (1975) reanalysis of the Rand Corporation's evaluation of the Voucher Program, and others. Routine secondary analysis of data stemming from social program evaluations is relatively novel. But the idea is an old one, dating from pre–Civil War examinations of erroneous census data on "insane Negroes" and from Madison's concern about the credibility of census data (see Davis 1972, and Regan 1973). Reanalysis of records from conventional administrative archives is also important in this context. Here the emphasis is on *statistical* examination of records to conduct, plan, or evaluate social programs to which the administrative records pertain.[1]

Examination of records on participants in social research may also be required by an audit agency. For example, the U.S. General Accounting Office has been given responsibility for appraising the quality of federally supported program evaluations. This mandate is justified not so much on the grounds of detecting fraud in the conduct of research as on the more general grounds of monitoring the scientific quality of research. Any audit agency may also take the responsibility for conducting intensive secondary analysis of data to check and verify earlier conclusions based on the data. For the GAO, this is a legally mandated activity and a desirable one, given the cost and difficulty of evaluating innovative social programs.

The benefits of reanalysis are clear, if limited. There are some distinctive privacy problems, however, and it is these we describe next.

Confidentiality-Related Issues

The information stored in a social science data archive will typically have been collected under a promise of confidentiality. Most nonprofit and academic research groups, for example, make a promise to the respondent that if his or her record is maintained in identifiable form, it will remain confidential with respect to any outside group. Similar assurances, required by law if not by professional ethics, cover some administrative record systems. Unless exceptions are made clear to the respondent beforehand, any disclosure of a respondent's record in *identifiable form* to an outside secondary analyst can be regarded as a violation of the initial promise at best and a violation of law at worst.

So, for example, in 1976 we filed a request under the Freedom of Information Act with the Drug Enforcement Agency for the names of researchers who received a grant of testimonial privilege under the Drug Abuse Act of 1970 (Cecil and Boruch 1977). We intended to interview the researchers in order to determine, among other things, how helpful the privilege was in protecting their records on identifiable respondents against inquiry by law enforcement agencies. DEA initially refused to disclose the researchers' names on the grounds that disclosure might violate the Privacy Act of 1974 and in any event would breach the researchers' privacy. A more dramatic conflict occurred in 1975 over the actual disclosure of identified records on Medi-Cal recipients to a researcher at the University of Southern California's Medical School. The purpose of release was legitimate statistical research. But state officials under a new political administration claimed that the release violated the law, regardless of the worthiness of the research goal, and the files were returned (*Sacramento Bee,* 2 February 1975; *Los Angeles Times,* 2 February 1975; Brian 1975a, 1975b). Two points about the illustrations should be noted. First, even under law it is reasonable to argue that identifiable records can and perhaps should be disclosable for research purposes. Second, in both principle and practice, refusal to disclose records does not mean that research cannot be undertaken. In these and other cases, a good deal of research can be done using records from which identifiers have been deleted. We consider both points in this chapter.

When release of identifiable records is unnecessary or clearly prohibited by law or regulation, even the release of anonymous records may present a problem, for anonymous records can, under certain conditions, be used to deduce information about the individuals on whom the records are maintained. To be specific, consider the Drug Enforcement Agency case just cited. Following the DEA's refusal to release the names of researchers, we asked for and received general information about each project for which a grant of testimonial privilege had been made. That information, coupled with information obtained over the telephone from staff at the host institutions for the research, was sufficient to permit us to deduce the identities of over 75 percent of the individual grantees (Cecil and Boruch 1977). Simultaneously, we appealed the original DEA refusal of our Freedom of Information request, and eventually received the complete listing. Aside from what we regard as an incorrect decision at the lower levels of DEA, the point to the illustration is that protecting individuals against deductive disclosure can be quite difficult, especially if the number of individuals involved is small and the amount information on them is substantial.

The problems of assuring the confidentiality of individual responses in audits are similar to those generated by the secondary analysis of raw records. A fair audit may require disclosure of information on identifiable individuals, thereby breaking an initial promise of confidentiality. Even if a limited promise of confidentiality is made initially to respondents, for the sake of later audit, the limits on the promise may confuse them. And the investigatory tone of an audit may reduce individual's willingness to participate in the research. Whether these problems occur at all and their severity if they do occur are considered in the following remarks.

Secondary Analysis of Archival Records

Suppose that a researcher or data analyst wishes, for legitimate research purposes, to reanalyze data held in an archive. It will often be the case that identifiers are completely unnecessary for the analysis, and this situation is considered first.

WHEN IDENTIFIERS ARE NOT REQUIRED

When the secondary analyst requires only anonymous records, the factors that must be recognized by the archivist before releasing the records include:

- the availability (to the outside analyst) of a listing of individuals whose records are on file, which facilitates deductive disclosure
- the availability of collateral information on the individuals whose records are on file
- the number, content, and form of descriptors in any given record
- the number of individuals in the sample on whom records are released and the size of the population from which the sample was drawn.

These factors determine whether anyone, including the outside analyst, can use the anonymous records as a basis not for statistical research, but for building a dossier on a particular individual from the anonymous records. Here we take the position that because most social research records contain innocuous information, they will provoke no interest in a dossier builder, and, if they do, the benefits of deductive disclosure are negligible. It may be possible to read a set of anonymous records and deduce that Freddy scored a quarter standard deviation below the mean on an achievement test, but it is not likely to be worth the trouble to an interrogator. Further, there are no material risks to Freddy, though the deduction may be annoying. As a matter of principle, however, the problem is worth considering even for such innocuous data, since some simple solutions to the problem are available. As a matter of practice, deductive disclosure of sensitive information is more important to us, and justifies more complicated solutions.

In the simplest case, the procedure for the safe release of microdata will be straightforward—delete identifiers from records and then hand the records over to the analyst. In our judgment, this procedure is sufficient for most social research projects. However, the deletion of identifiers is necessary but insufficient for preserving anonymity in all instances. The action will be sufficient provided that there is no way for the outside analyst to determine if a particular individual's record is one of those disclosed to him. This determination can be prevented by withholding a list of individuals whose anonymous records have been disclosed, or it may be prevented by the absence of collateral information sufficient to uniquely identify an anonymous record. These conditions will often be fixed, for example, by the archive so that the outside analyst cannot know or determine the personal identity of individuals whose records are maintained by the archive. For example, Yinger, Ikeda, and Laycock (1977) made their evaluation data on a program for disadvantaged youth available to outside analysts for reanalysis without any risks to the respondents. They simply deleted the names of students and the names of their schools from the files. Even a list of students would not have been sufficient to allow anyone to link the names with the statistical records.

At the other extreme, listings of individuals on whom records are maintained may be readily available, and collateral information may be sufficient to build a dossier based on the anonymous record. In this instance, one of the simplest strategies is to have the archive agency conduct all data analyses for the outside researcher and then supply statistical summaries to the researcher for further analysis. So, for example, anonymous records on a hundred drug abusers might be withheld from the analyst by program staff. In the interest of providing access to at least some data for scientific reasons, the agency might compute means, covariances, variances, and similar statistics, and then supply these to the analyst for further scrutiny. A typical difficulty here is assuring that the agency can and will provide statistics according to the outside analyst's prescription, especially if the statistics required are unusual. The strategy is reasonable if the agency is supported or mandated to provide a service for secondary analysis. The cruder types of statistical summary, notably simple counts and cross tabulations, can still yield identifiable information. The possible remedies are described in chapter 7.

Between the two extreme situations—those in which simple deletion of identifiers and release of records is sufficient, and those in which only analysis by the archive and subsequent release of statistics will do—there is considerably variety. No simple prescription seems to be uniformly applicable. The following tactical rules of disclosure extend those enumerated by Campbell et al. (1975). They are described in roughly the order of their complexity. Rule B is not employed if A is sufficient; rule C is not employed if A and B are sufficient; and so on.

A. Deleting identifiers and withholding listings. Clear identifiers ought to be routinely separated from raw records and not generally disclosed to outside analysts. Some research archives may also find it possible to withhold or keep secret the identities of individuals whose anonymous records have been disclosed. The tactic makes it difficult if not impossible for an outsider to conduct a deductive interrogation of anonymous records for dossier-building purposes. If the archive's function is primarily administrative, withholding a list of identifiers may be impossible; that is, the identity of the individual may be a matter of public information.

B. Adjusting the number of records disclosed: subsampling. When the number of records in the basic archive is quite large, the needs of the outside research can at times be met by a random subsample of the complete file. This will reduce the likelihood that any particular individual's record is actually included in the released data and can reduce the possibility of useful disclosure markedly. The small ratio of released sample records to the total number of records in the population is, for example, one reason why the 1 percent samples of records released by the Census Bureau and the work history samples released by the Social Security Administration are innocuous with respect to privacy threats.

C. Decreasing the number of items disclosed. Usually not all the information in an original record is necessary for outside analysis. If information is unnecessary, it should not be disclosed. This tactic reduces possible collateral information in the file and consequently the probability of deductive disclosure. The tactic will often also reduce unique information, so reducing the record's usefulness for dossier building should deductive disclosure occur accidentally. Particular *kinds* of variables might also be deleted purposefully. For example, deletion of some or all public variables reduces the incidence of collateral information and the likelihood of deductive disclosure. The side effect of these tactics is that they may undercut some important functions of secondary analysis. That is, some partial redundancy is essential for checking the internal consistency and accuracy of the record, and some variables essential for testing new statistical hypotheses may not be specifiable beforehand. Finally, some variables that are essential to a planned secondary analysis may be deleted only because they are associated with a very low probability of deductive disclosure.

D. Adjusting the exactness of response category. At times, the outside analyst can be satisfied with cruder information than appears in the record; for example, rather than obtain exact information on salary, it may be sufficient to obtain salary range. Released records covering not exact data but cruder ranges of data reduce the likelihood of deductive disclosure based on exact collateral information and the exactness of the unique information that may be disclosed. In some cases, the implications of less exact contents for statistical analysis can be anticipated and action taken to minimize problems. Generally, the effect of using cruder categories is less precision in analysis, suggesting that bounds must be placed on the crudeness introduced into records prior to release. Using a range of incidence of child abuse or of driving while intoxicated instead of an exact number, for example, is likely to dilute the quality of analysis based on exact numbers of these relatively rare events.

E. Adjusting the reliability of response content. The contamination method described in chapter 5 can be used to reduce the probability of deductive disclosure. Random errors whose general parameters are known can be introduced into anonymous records prior to their release, at a level sufficient to prevent deductive disclosure, but low enough to permit good analysis. The analyst is given information about the general character of the error (e.g., parameters) so that he may adjust his statistical analyses accordingly, but he is not told whether any given response contains error, nor is he told the magnitude of any error within any given record. This tactic is especially degrading to effective analysis if the sample size (i.e., number of records) is small, the phenomenon under examination in the secondary analysis is weak, and the data at hand are not very reliable to begin with. In the last case, the records inoculated with even low-level random error might well be useless.

F. Microaggregation of records. Random contamination of records may be unacceptable at times. As an alternative, the archive can consider combining sampling units into small clusters, and then releasing data on clusters rather than on individuals. The mean, variance, etc., on clusters constitutes statistical information that, if membership in clusters is not disclosed, is virtually impregnable against attempts at deductive disclosure. As we noted in chapter 5, however, the rules for combination must be carefully thought out, since, if microaggregation is not implemented properly or if the analyst does not recognize the pitfalls of analyzing microaggregated data, severe statistical biases can easily be generated in the analysis.

Generally, any analysis of microaggregated or contaminated records will be more cumbersome because less familiar techniques must be used by the secondary analyst to extract meaning from the data. The analysis must, for example, recognize the possibility of biases in estimates of important parameters, biases induced directly or indirectly by the microaggregation or contamination process. Precision may also be reduced, though this problem can be ameliorated by increasing the number of records analyzed, by refining the analytic models, and so forth. Anticipating and adjusting for statistical biases, especially when novel models are imposed on the data, is difficult. To better accommodate both problems, a three-stage record analysis process can be justified.

G. Multistage adjustment prior to release. In the first stage, the outside analyst obtains anonymous archival records in contaminated, microaggregated, or otherwise adjusted form. The second stage involves analysis of the adjusted records, including tests of models presumed to underlie the data, and estimation of important parameters. The main presumption of these analyses, however they are conducted, is that the results (estimates of parameters and inferences) are identical to those one would obtain if conventional analyses were conducted on the unadjusted data. And to assure that this presumption is met in fact, it is reasonable to proceed to a third stage. The outside analyst presents his final prescription for analysis (models) and results (or tests and estimation) to the archive. The archive then uses the prescription to reanalyze the unadjusted records to verify the outside analyst's results. The primary reason for this tertiary stage is to verify that there are no biases in the secondary analysis. Also, it may be much easier to conduct the tertiary analysis on a larger sample, perhaps even the population, enhancing precision. The requirement that the archive engage in confirmatory analysis is demanding. But it is far less demanding than requiring that the archive go through a whole sequence of analysis of raw records under instruction from the outside analyst.

H. Secondary analysis by prescription. If archival records are few in number and extraordinary in their sensitivity, and if no procedural or statistical approach reduces the possibility of deductive disclosure to an acceptable level, then the only way to permit secondary analysis with no risk of deductive disclosure is complete analysis of the records by the archival agency. The plan for analysis would have to be prescribed fully by the secondary analyst to suit his or her research needs. And to be conducted easily, the analysis cannot be of a very unconventional sort. This is the most expensive option, and archives will be entitled to support for routine analyses by prescription. The tactic may be ineffective where analyses must be performed sequentially. But recent research by American, Canadian, and Swedish census bureaus suggests that the potential for deductive disclosure through sequential statistical inquiry can be reduced to an acceptable level with sophisticated monitoring (see also chapter 7). A similar tactic can be used in primary analysis of administrative records, of course.

WHEN IDENTIFIERS ARE REQUIRED

Some secondary analysts require completely identified records. For example, identifiers may be necessary to verify the contents of original records, since verification often implies reinterviewing the original respondents or cross-checking records from different sources. Similarly, identifiers may be thought necessary for longitudinal study of individuals on whom records are maintained. This is especially crucial in socio-medical studies where early medical treatments have been found harmful, and follow-up of individuals is essential for understanding treatment effects and producing a remedy.

Under these conditions, several options ought to be considered. First, it is reasonable to argue that disclosure of identified records to the legitimate researcher is justified. For, after all, material risks to the respondent are negligible: there have been no reported abuses of records so released for statistical research (Privacy Protection Study Commission 1977). And if a principle of confidentiality applies at all, it can be accommodated by informing the respondent, at the time the record is constructed, that the record will be disclosed and used only for purposes of research. Regardless of whether the respondent is informed beforehand, the principle may be overridden by the likely benefits of the research and the absence of material risk. This last line of thinking led to the Internal Revenue Service's release of certain taxpayers' addresses to medical researchers during the 1950s and 1960s, to permit longitudinal research on veteran's disabilities and changes in their prognosis and treatment. The view has not been adopted as policy by relevant governmental and private agencies, and even the IRS procedure has been suspended under the Tax Reform Act of 1976. It has, however, been articulated by the Privacy Protection Study Commission (1977), and it has been incorporated into the commission's recommended changes in the Privacy Act of 1974.

The second option involves capitalizing on strategies that avoid direct researcher access to identified records or identifiers, while still permitting good research to be undertaken. The procedural strategies, such as contamination, have been described in the preceding section and in chapter 5. These approaches may be unacceptable for the reasons discussed earlier: they are complicated and may yield, in a particular setting, lower-quality data than more direct methods. It would then be appropriate for the researcher to seek permission to access records from the individuals on whom the records are kept. The problem of obtaining their consent does not differ much from the more common problem of eliciting the cooperation of individuals in research. It is discussed briefly in the section below on informed consent and access to records.

Satisfying Audit Requirements

This section concerns requests by a government auditor for research records on identifiable respondents. The auditor's need for the information stems partly from a responsibility to oversee the integrity of the research process and the data. That need may conflict, or at least appear to conflict, with the researcher's interest in preserving the confidentiality of respondent records, since a promise of confidentiality is generally thought to facilitate candor in reporting and cooperation in the research. The issue has emerged in two national experiments, and because it is both important and likely to persist, we attend to it here.

To make matters concrete, consider a situation in which the U.S. General Accounting Office requests records concerning identifiable respondents in a social experiment. Suppose further that the agency supporting the experiment is the Department of Housing and Urban Development (HUD). The department has in fact supported a major experiment to estimate the relative effects of new housing subsidy plans on subsidy recipients (the poor) and on the housing market. Designed to understand the effects of a new national housing program, the experiment is an expensive, long-term, and congressionally mandated research effort. To encourage the cooperation of participants in the experiment, HUD promised respondents that their identifiable reports to the researchers would remain confidential.

The GAO's mandate to review the conduct of this and similar projects is explicit in the Budget and Accounting Act of 1921. Under the law, the agency's mission is to investigate "all matters relating to the receipt, disbursement, and application of public funds." The mandate was strengthened notably by the Congressional Budget and Impoundment Control Act of 1974 (Pub. L. 93-344), which stresses the GAO's responsibility to evaluate federal programs. Most states have analogous legislation to delimit the power of state audit agencies. The authority for investigation is broad and, as far as the social sciences are concerned, limited only by a few explicit laws that prevent nonresearch uses of research information. These laws include the testimonial privilege statutes described in chapter 8. Otherwise, the scope of any investigation is at the discretion of the audit agency. For the case at hand, the discretionary power includes determining whether reinterview of all respondents, rather than a sample of respondents, is warranted; whether reinterviews ought to cover all initial questions, or just a part of them; and whether to conduct reinterviews at all.[2]

Conventional audit of the fiscal management of a project generally raises no privacy-related problems. More recently, federal audits have covered the design, conduct, and analysis of social research. These activities also involve no privacy problems, though there has been some discussion of how to accomplish such reviews more effectively. For federally supported research, the most serious problem concerns the auditor's interest in establishing the quality of respondent reports through reinterview. The problems and strategies for reconciling the needs of the auditor and those of the research team, when confidentiality of respondent records is at issue, are discussed in the following remarks.

REINTERVIEWS: PURPOSES AND PROBLEMS

For the auditor with an interest in establishing the quality of interview data, wholesale reinterviews are a natural option. The tactic has some scientific merit in the crude sense that independent observations of the same phenomenon are generally desirable. They have some institutional merit, too, since for a naive public, reinterviews may be the only acceptable device for quality assessment.

But the scientific benefit of reinterviews will, for *some* research projects, be marginal. In the first place, the well-designed study will have included a side study on validity of response, perhaps using archives as the standard in assessing factual responses. And it will have included side studies to gauge the reliability and construct validity of measures of attitude and opinion. It is possible for an audit agency to participate in the design of this type of side study and to oversee its operation without direct contact with respondents. Second, any major study will generate a file of data whose quality can be assayed, up to a point at least, without reinterview. The researcher's procedure for editing records, internal checks on the consistency of the information provided by a respondent, and comparisons of the researcher's statistical data with similar data from prior studies can be reviewed by an auditor without disrupting survey operations.[3] The third and perhaps most important issue is that outside reinterview can yield ambiguous results. For example, even if interview tactics for researcher and auditor are identical, the investigative tone or the auditor's sponsorship of the survey may produce systematic differences in results. Ordinary measurement error will, of course, produce random differences in the data yielded by the two types of survey. Differences in the time of interview and reinterview may also produce systematic differences in results. Finally, where the interviewing skills of the researcher and those of the auditor differ notably, there are likely to be remarkable differences in interview results.

Despite all this, assessment by audit agencies is warranted. Not all research projects are good, and the oversight of an audit agency may help to avoid or detect gross incompetence. Similarly, because the price of such research can be high and because money may increase the likelihood of fraud in this sector to the levels achieved in the political sector, the auditor's attention to quality may help to prevent gross impropriety.

Accepting the idea that auditor scrutiny is justified despite its limited scientific benefits does not imply that reinterview is warranted. In fact, it is reasonable to expect an auditor's reinterview of research respondents to have negative effects. With a few exceptions, commercial and governmental auditors are not trained to handle surveys, nor do they often have the manpower at hand to do the job well. Moreover, even if the skills are available, the respondent may view the auditor-sponsored survey as threatening, and certainly as less innocuous than the original research interview. As a consequence of the reinterview, the respondent may refuse to cooperate further in the research or may change his style of response (e.g., become less candid) in subsequent contacts with the researcher.

This is the *worst* possible case. We expect problems to be much less severe to the extent that the interview skills of the audit agency are notable, the audit agency is viewed as researcher rather than as administrative agent, and the rewards for participation in research override the costs associated with reinterview.

The evidence on whether auditor contact with research participants poses some risk to the research or threat to the respondent is indirect and certainly not uniform. Pertinent material on the need to assure respondents of confidentiality can be drawn from chapter 3.

- Some case studies reveal that some respondents involved in controversial research refuse to participate further when a governmental agency with an investigatory mission threatens to examine identifiable records—for example, the ACE Study of Campus Unrest, Spergel's evaluation of the Woodlawn training project. But there are also cases in which the effect of investigation and record disclosure has been negligible—for example, the Negative Income Tax Experiment.

- Experimental tests on different methods of assuring confidentiality suggest that the greater the level of protection, the higher cooperation will be. The effect for innocuous research is weak—privacy is often not a salient issue, and people are usually trusting. But the influence of the protection level has been notable in army research on drug abuse and racism, in epidemiological research on abortions, on industrial research on employee morale and attitudes, and in the recent Census Bureau studies of refusal rate and confidentiality assurance, described by Goldfield (1976). Evidence for the idea that an assurance of confidentiality influences item response rate in surveys and that requiring a signature of respondents affects cooperation has been obtained by Singer (1978a).

- Available survey data can be used to argue along the same lines. Confidentiality is not usually a salient issue for most respondents. However, researchers who can assure respondents of confidentiality have detected higher incidences of socially undesirable activity relative to administrative surveys when there are risks attached to the administrative surveys, as in the drug abuse studies cited earlier. Most respondents in the recent census surveys believe that assuring people of confidentiality for income reporting has the benefit of encouraging more accurate response. On the other hand, many of the same respondents cannot recollect census assurances of confidentiality and believe that census records can be turned over to investigatory agencies; yet they still cooperate in the surveys.

None of these studies bear directly on reinterview by a governmental auditor. The evidence is, however, sufficient to warn us that some research participants will be sensitive to a third-party's interrogation of research records and, in some instances, less cooperative in research. So it behooves us to recognize this type of intervention as a *potential* hazard, and to develop strategies that minimize the risks involved. We discuss those strategies next.

CLASSIFYING INFORMATION AND PRIOR AGREEMENTS

It is not possible to reconcile audit objectives with social research aims without specifying the kind of records that might be of interest to an audit agency. Delaying the process of identification and of agreement about what data ought to be accessible to an auditor until research is in progress can disrupt the project's management, as it did in the case of the Negative Income Tax Experiment. Discussions prior to research may be unproductive where bureaucratic imperatives rather than an interest in the quality of data underlie negotiation, but this need not imply that the research plan should be abandoned. It does imply that the research agency must develop methods for collecting information so as to minimize the negative effects, if they are expected, of legitimate audit on the conduct of legitimate social research.

Whether an element of information can be or should be regarded as disclosable depends partly on the character of the research. If, for example, an experimental program is viewed as a strict prototype for a real social program, then it can be argued that the rules governing access to records must also be prototypical. Any information that would normally be collected by an auditor in the anticipated regular program would then be disclosable in the experiment. Any information collected solely for purposes of statistical analysis rather than individual audit would not be disclosable. Under this argument, identification of participants in the Housing Allowance Experiments should be made available for audit purposes, since identification of housing-allowance recipients would be a matter of public record if and when the program was adopted at the national level. Data on an identifiable individual's eligibility for services or subsidy would be similarly regarded as accessible to an auditor. Other information, which would not ordinarily be accessible—data on identifiable participants' attitudes, for example—would remain inaccessible. Individuals would, of course, be informed of the rules when they are invited to participate in the research.

A second basis for making decisions about the accessibility of records for audit is the view that the research project or experimental social program cannot be regarded as a strict prototype of a program. For a variety of reasons, it may have to be viewed as a partial prototype, a fragile pilot effort, necessarily under the extraordinary control of the researcher. The control may be essential for the careful surveillance of the phenomenon under study, or for the detection of subtle effects of the experimental program. Any interference that would jeopardize the integrity of control or examination could destroy the whole project. The level of control required here certainly detracts from the realism of the prototype, but it does make its performance simpler to track and evaluate.

So, for example, some research may require, at least temporarily, that even the identity of program recipients be kept confidential with respect to an audit agency. This may be especially necessary where the research is not secure against abrupt disturbances. In the case of the Housing Allowance Experiments, for example, the identity of a housing-allowance recipient may technically be a public matter, or at least legally accessible to an auditor. As a practical matter, however, publication of respondents' identities or disclosure to an audit agency *may* present a severe shock to the research. If the research is important enough to justify considerable expenditures in its support, and the probability of a shock is high, then disclosure may be unjustified.

The implied precedence of the research goal in this case does not mean that audit goals are to be ignored or abrogated. Researchers involved in the experimental tests of social programs can focus intensively on the audit-related status and behavior of the research participant. Checks on that behavior, constructed by the researcher in collaboration with the auditor, are critical if the experimental program is to be at all workable in the long run. In the short run, such checks may be essential in view of the opportunity that a novel subsidy program in welfare, aircraft construction, or any other area offers to the larcenous entrepreneur.

Identifying the information on research subjects that may be of interest to an auditor sets the bounds on the collaboration of researcher and auditor. It is a necessary but insufficient condition for minimizing problems of collaboration, however. A few strategies for resolving one problem—disclosure of information for use in auditor verification of sample and response validity—are discussed next. They include parallel sampling, the use of surrogate auditors, and subsampling for reinterviews.

Any prior agreement between auditor and researcher has implications for the quality of research, and they ought to be understood before agreements are made final. If, for example, certain classes of research information are disclosable, then would-be research participants must be informed of the fact. Will the chance of disclosure affect cooperation rates? If so, how much? If the chance is low, or if surrogate auditors are responsible for reinterviews, how does that affect the cooperation rates? We do not know the answers to these questions. We do expect that the answers have a critical bearing on the quality of the research. For that reason, we discuss pilot tests and side studies in more detail later.

PARALLEL SAMPLING BY AUDITORS

When a main objective of audit agency requests is to establish the validity of sampling and response, a reasonable strategy for accomplishing part of that goal without threatening the confidentiality of original records is to obtain an independent sample of the same target population used in the original survey. So, for example, GAO might adopt exactly the same sampling design and target population used by HUD in its original interview surveys to generate an independent, equally valid, and nonoverlapping sample of respondents. Comparing the estimates of population parameters from the GAO survey with those from the HUD survey gives an indication of the quality of the estimates generated in the original HUD research. The product of the strategy is the statistical means for judging the quality of the initial survey. The benefit is that one obtains the data without disrupting the original sample.

One might object to this strategy on the grounds that drawing a parallel sample is considerably more expensive than simply reinterviewing the original sample of respondents, but, in fact, most of the problems required by parallel sampling would have already been worked out for the original survey. Any parallel effort, for example, capitalizes on the original survey design, target population listings, and procedures worked out for sampling, callbacks, and so on. The additional cost of manpower for parallel interviews is likely to be marginal in comparison to the investment in original design. If there is a high risk of disruption of an expensive experiment through investigatory reinterview, the costs of such interviews are likely to be marginal and the benefits great.

SURROGATE AUDITORS

Direct reinterview of respondents in an ongoing social experiment can disrupt social research *if* the reinterviews are conducted by people whom respondents view with strong suspicion. In particular, some respondents who are able to distinguish between auditor and researcher will be less cooperative with the former, perhaps on privacy grounds. It may be possible to reduce this problem by using a surrogate interviewing agency to reinterview a subsample of the original respondents.

The surrogate might be the one already under contract to the experimenting agency; for example, the original contractor to HUD may service the information needs of both HUD and GAO. And if this approach is acceptable to the audit agency, perhaps all that is required is straightforward, but more intensive, reinterview on questions of interest to the audit agency. This approach is likely to be burdensome to the respondent insofar as the demands on his ability and willingness to supply information are increased. But with good pilot testing of questions and interviewer training, even that burden can be minimized. The main benefit is that the interviewing agency already under contract in the field has established some rapport with respondents, and respondents are less likely to feel uncomfortable with a familiar agency.

The point of many audits, however, is to verify the integrity of the original contractor's performance. So, for example, the GAO may need to establish that a contractor did indeed engage in interviews with individuals A, B, and C, and that the responses of those individuals were of a certain kind. Under this circumstance, a heretofore uninvolved third party may be an acceptable surrogate for the audit agency, insofar as the third party is more neutral or less suspect than the original contractor. The potential benefits of the strategy are that the process of verification can be removed a step from direct governmental investigation, and this may attenuate the problems generated by that process. A second benefit is tied to more general secondary analysis. Specifically, a research group whose primary mission is secondary analysis could, in some cases, also serve as surrogate for the audit agency. This outside research group would take primary responsibility for the reanalysis of the statistical data, and for verifying its internal consistency and the conclusions based on the data. And it would also take responsibility for, say, reinterviews with original respondents to verify the credibility of the original research records on those respondents. In this latter activity it fulfills an auditor function, except that it may provide no information on identifiable respondents to the audit agency. It can serve primarily as a neutral intermediary to estimate the statistical reliability of original reports. If the reliability of the data appears to be extraordinarily low—and "low" is defined beforehand—then the audit agency may intervene, remedial action may be taken by the research contractor, and so on.

SUBSAMPLE REINTERVIEWS BY AUDITORS

Direct reinterviews may on occasion be essential to accomplish audit agency goals. The GAO, for example, could choose to verify that interviews had indeed been conducted by the research organization in the HUD experiment, or that certain responses were indeed given, in order to check the integrity of the original interviewers. Parallel sampling is normally insufficient for accomplishing these goals. The use of a surrogate audit agency may be unacceptable.

One obvious approach to minimizing the disruption of the ongoing research here is to minimize the number of individuals who must be reinterviewed. The GAO, for example, might select a stratified random subsample from the extant HUD sample. The subsample would presumably be selected so as to be as representative of the target population as the main sample is. Members of the subsample would then be reinterviewed by GAO staff. At best, the audit agency that takes this approach will obtain the basic statistics necessary to establish the integrity of the data collection. And, again at best, it does so without a major disruption of the research effort. In addition, the audit agency records can be linked to earlier information collected by the experimenting agency on the same respondents, using some variation on the procedural strategies for assuring the confidentiality of sensitive records linked from independent archives. The normal purpose of such linkage is to compare average levels of agreement between original interview and audit-based interviews. Linkage can be accomplished without violating promises of confidentiality made by either the audit agency or the original research agency staff (see chapter 4).

The subsample involved in the audit agency reinterviews is unlikely to be of much use to the research agency if reinterviews provoke individuals to drop out of the study. But the loss need not be intolerable if the need for destructive testing is anticipated in the design of a large social experiment and sample size is increased accordingly.

One risk of subsampling for reinterviews by an auditor is the adverse effect of the reinterview process on the remaining members of the sample. If the reinterviews have the character of an investigation and if they are widely publicized, cooperation rates in the remaining sample are likely to decline. It is not clear how such publicity can be avoided, especially in controversial surveys. It is reasonable to expect that the effects of this can be reduced if participants are told beforehand that reports might be selected randomly for verification by an outside auditor, but the idea has not been tested.

OTHER OPTIONS

When the auditor's primary concern is verifying the factual accuracy of respondent records, then record linkage may be more appropriate than reinterviews. For instance, respondent reports of income to an interviewer may be better assessed by linking those reports with IRS records on the same respondents. The assessment can be better than reinterviews in the sense that lapses in memory and other factors may degrade reporting to interviewers, while IRS records may be regarded as a clearer standard by an auditor. Also, if verification against official records is the only objective and record linkage is adequate, the potential problems of reinterview can be avoided. Chapter 4 discussed procedural tactics for linking records from different sources without breaching rules governing disclosure. In this case, so-called insulated data file approaches are relevant. The researcher supplies a file of respondents plus reports of income to the IRS; the IRS links its data with the file reports, strips identifiers from the file, and returns the statistical file to the researcher. Variations on the tactic, also described earlier, are designed to enhance the system's efficiency and the protection it affords to the respondent.

The statistical strategies discussed in chapter 5 are also pertinent, especially when sample size is large, interview information is sensitive, and auditor access to identified records is judged unwise or inappropriate. The reader may recall that these tactics permit one to elicit sensitive information from identified respondents, even in interviews without establishing a linkage between the identity and the state of the individual. Reinterviews, using these techniques or simple direct methods, for the sake of establishing accuracy are specious. The random contamination of response by the interviewee, for example, makes verification of individual records irrelevant. Though verification of individual responses is not possible, one can still assay the credibility of the resulting statistics. Obtaining data on parallel samples, using exactly the same techniques, is one way of doing so without disrupting the main research. Otherwise, side experiments might be created to determine whether the novel statistical tactics yield more candid reports than (say) completely anonymous response by mail, or direct reports to auditors, and so on.

Finally, some research topics may justify the use of statutory devices for preventing disclosure. The researcher conducting studies of alcohol and drug abuse, for example, may regard any disclosure of respondent identity or of identified response as an unjustified threat to the respondent and to the research. He or she may then appeal to the legal privilege designed to protect respondents in this and a few other research areas. The privilege is limited; it depends on the research topic; and it usually constitutes only part of the solution to the problem of assuring that research records are used only for research purposes. Moreover, the relevance of the statutes is ambiguous: some make explicit provision for GAO access to general information, while others do not refer to GAO at all. Nonetheless, the approach is useful in some cases: relevant statutes, their shortcomings, and their benefits are discussed in chapter 8.

EVIDENCE, PILOT TESTS, AND SIDE STUDIES

Our justification for examining alternatives to direct reinterview is that reinterviews by an auditor of respondents in social research may discourage respondent cooperation. As we said earlier, the evidence on these problems is indirect and fragmented. it is certainly sufficient to conclude that cooperation rates and candor in reporting can be affected by an investigatory process. But neither evidence nor theory is sufficient to predict the effects accurately. This ambiguity in the evidence prompts us to consider pilot tests and side studies.

Pilot tests, mounted prior to the main research, can be helpful in establishing (1) whether auditor reinterview has a notable effect on cooperation rate and, if so, whether negative effects can be accommodated; and (2) whether auditor reinterview has a notable effect on candor in reporting and, if so, whether negative effects can be tolerated or eliminated. So, for example, a small experiment might be mounted to determine if direct auditor contact with especially sensitive members of the target population results in fewer volunteers or consenting participants than if surrogate auditors are used or if no outside reinterview are undertaken. Refusal rates under the audit interview condition may be found to be intolerable. The options that then ought to be examined include: termination of the research; withdrawal of auditor interviews; other experiments on methods for making auditor interviews palatable. If no marked differences in refusal rates turn up, then auditor reinterview would be accepted, recognizing that the small samples characteristic of pilot tests may be insufficient to detect weak effects of the auditor's involvement. Similarly, pilot experiments on the validity of response might be mounted to get at differences in candor of reporting as a function of whether auditors are involved.

Side studies, perhaps of a less formal type, can also be informative. They are likely to be essential where the audit generates publicity and where respondents find reinterviews offensive despite their willingness to cooperate initially. Side experiments on candor in reporting, adjoined to the main research, are justified if reinterviews are threatening to respondents. Though agreeing to cooperate, respondents may not respond candidly under reinterview conditions. It is possible to determine whether this is true by using a side experiment in which some respondents are subjected to auditor reinterview and some are not. Any finding of differences in reporting between two such groups forms the basis for a better understanding of reporting biases.

Both pilot tests and side studies are likely to be cumbersome and time-consuming. They may delay the implementation of the main research, and siphon resources away from the main problem during design and implementation. Consequently, the pilot tests are worth considering only for large-scale studies, where the cost of pilot tests and side studies will be marginal. They are useful only if the results can be generalized reasonably well to both the research at hand and similar projects.

SUMMARY ON AUDITS

Where time permits, it is essential that agreements between the audit agency and the researcher be reached before the research is mounted. Agreements should cover what identified information is disclosable to an auditor; whether and under what conditions the identities of respondents will be disclosed; whether and how auditor reinterviews of respondents will be undertaken.

Three standards in reaching agreements are important. The first concerns the fragility of the research and its probable benefits. If the research is a robust prototype, then information normally disclosable under a regular program would also be disclosable in the research. Information that would not normally be gathered in a regular program would not be disclosable under the prototype. If the program is very sensitive to destabilizing influences and its probable products are important, then, other things being equal, auditor access to respondents would be held to a minimum.

The second standard concerns the need for auditor contact with respondents in research. Reinterviews may be unnecessary if the researcher's quality control system is good. They may be irrelevant or misleading if the reinterviews concern unstable attributes—for example, attitudes—or sensitive traits. In the latter case, respondents may be less inclined to respond candidly to the auditor, and the results of the reinterviews will then differ notably from those of the original survey.

The third standard concerns the disruption of research by an audit agency. It is possible that individuals will refuse to respond or will respond less candidly if reinterviews are to be conducted by an audit agency. If that is a possibility, then negotiations ought to recognize it by considering alternatives to direct auditor contact, by determining *if* the concern is warranted through pilot tests, and by designing strategies to ameliorate the problem, if it is a problem, in the research at hand.

There are a variety of alternatives to direct reinterview of respondents by an audit agency. Obtaining a parallel sample from the same target population is feasible and is a natural device for satisfying the auditor's interest in the quality of sampling and the stability of results. Where the tactic is unacceptable, subsampling individuals in the original sample is feasible. Reinterviews in the subsample may be conducted either by the auditor or by a surrogate. If the sampling design anticipates the need for a subsample, and sample sizes are increased accordingly, then loss of the sample due to disruption is not likely to damage seriously the main research. At best, the results of the auditor survey can be pooled with the remaining data, and no disruption will occur.

Whether auditor contact with respondents will be disrupted cannot be predicted accurately from the data or theory at hand. The data are sufficient only to demonstrate that an investigative agency can influence cooperation in research negatively, but there are exceptions. This indirect evidence can be used to justify pilot tests prior to a major research effort, designed to assay the effect (positive or negative) of auditor involvement on refusal rates and candor in reporting. Where time and resources do not permit pilot testing, side studies can be designed to monitor the process, detect problems before they become serious, and establish why they occur.

It is reasonable for a researcher involved with some target populations to expect that misdemeanors or other minor illegal activity will occur. Since it is the research or program that presents the opportunity for such activity, it behooves the researcher to design systems for its early detection and termination. More importantly, since the opportunity is an incidental effect of the research, it does not seem equitable to take legal action against the individual participant. Just as roadside surveys may incidentally detect a drinking driver and have him driven home without sanction (Perrine 1971), so too can research on income-subsidy programs detect incidental irregularity and take corrective action. Taking formal action penalizes the research participant unnecessarily; it is a distraction from the main research; and sanctions may jeopardize the quality of the research data.

The use of some statistical strategies described earlier can reduce the likelihood of disruptive reinterviews, since in some of these, clear identifiers are not linked to individual status; thus, audits based on reinterview will be useless. The methods do not, however, prevent good auditing on statistical grounds. Also, procedural strategies such as the mutually insulated file systems permit audit without disclosure of identifiable records by the research agency. Disclosure of the identities of respondents will usually be necessary, however.

Informed Consent, Reanalysis, and Audit

Some laws and agency regulations require that informed consent be obtained from an individual before his or her record is disclosed in identifiable form to a researcher. The identified data or identification alone may be necessary for an analysis of existing data, for a follow-up study of individuals whose records are on file, or for other legitimate research purposes. They may also be required by an audit agency whose mandate includes checking the quality of the research. In these cases, the agency holding the records may serve as a vehicle for eliciting consent. For example:

- The Office of Research and Evaluation of the School District of Philadelphia generally requires that before student records are released for research, parental permission for disclosure must be obtained. The Division serves as an intermediary, sending a letter to the parents and asking for their consent to disclose identifiable records to the researcher.

- Research organizations that make a promise of confidentiality to their respondents forward outsiders' requests to use the records to the respondent in order to obtain permission for that use. The strategy has been used to permit the GAO to access some respondent records in the Experimental Housing Allowance Program.

- The Tax Reform Act of 1976 requires that the taxpayer's consent be obtained before tax return information can be disclosed for purposes other than administrative or judicial use. So, for example, the Secretary of the Treasury would have to elicit permission from the taxpayer, on behalf of the researcher, to disclose identified tax return data to the researcher for research purposes.

When it is essential that consent be obtained, using the archive as an intermediary can be a useful strategy, judging from the examples in chapter 4. But there is no guarantee that this strategy will be feasible, and, indeed, it will be inadequate in some research.

In particular, informed consent will often fail to be obtained from the parent, respondent, and so on, *not* because of any privacy concern, but for other reasons. The data available suggest that failure to reply to letters requesting consent will be attributable mainly to indifference, memory lapse, and similarly prosaic factors unrelated to a concern for individual privacy. Many, if not most, of the reasons for a nonresponse in this special setting are identical to the reasons for nonresponse in any ordinary survey. To the extent that these reasons prevail, an emphasis on assuring privacy with respect to the outside researcher is misplaced. To the extent that the use of an intermediary complicates or weakens efforts to elicit cooperation in research, the emphasis is damaging.

The influences on response rate in ordinary surveys are well documented. But direct evidence for our contentions, based on surveys that elicit formal consent, is fragmentary. That response rates can be low in school settings is clear, for example, from the use of the intermediary approach by the Philadelphia School District's Office of Research and Evaluation. Research projects are screened, and the office sends letters to parents eliciting their consent for their children's participation in dissertation-level research, or eliciting consent to disclose records for the same purpose. Michael Kean, a director of the office, reports that the response rate to mailed requests is usually between 20 and 30 percent, and when the request involves a study with obvious benefits to current students, the response rate may reach 70 percent. Bauman and Sage (1976) go a good deal further to establish the reasons for low consent rates. In their early research, they received responses from only 35 percent of parents from whom they sought consent for their children to participate in a drug abuse survey. In a follow-up study of nonrespondents, they found that about 75 percent of those individuals "were not against their children's participation in the survey." Their stated reasons for not responding include forgetting the letter of request, lack of interest in the research, failing to mail the consent form once it was completed, and other equally mundane reasons.

The U.S. General Accounting Office (1977) has conducted interesting exploratory work along the same lines. Their objective was to determine whether respondents in the Experimental Housing Allowance Program would consent to reinterviews by GAO staff. The purpose of reinterview was to obtain independent evidence on the reliability of information provided earlier by respondents to EHAP researchers. An accounting firm was used as an intermediary to elicit the consent of participants for reinterview, since respondents had been assured of confidentiality earlier by EHAP staff. To be specific, participants were asked to return a postcard if they would *not* consent to be reinterviewed. One would expect a slightly higher consent rate than in the Bauman-Sage or Kean examples since (1) failure to return the postcard implied consent in the GAO effort, but refusal in the other two; (2) the process of eliciting consent could be viewed by respondents as a natural continuation of their participation in EHAP; and (3) the reinterviews were conducted at the request of the federal government, and most people do trust the government. On the other hand, one can argue equally well that the consent rate would be decreased if GAO was seen by respondents as an investigatory agency and reinterview viewed as an intolerable burden; in fact, reinterview also meant on-site inspection of housing, for example. Evidently, this last argument was not crucial for the majority of respondents, since consent rate at each of three sites was relatively high: 76 percent in Pittsburgh, 65 percent in Green Bay, and 81 percent in Salem. This is a remarkably good result, compared with other cases we have examined, but it failed to satisfy some GAO staff members. Their criterion for sampling validity was 80 percent. The actual rate of reinterview is slightly lower, since some consenters later refused to cooperate with the interviewer. Of the identifiable reasons for refusal, most involved mechanical problems—respondents had moved, were ill, encountered scheduling difficulty, and so on. We can find no mention of concerns about privacy as the basis for refusal, though it is not clear how accurate the reasons for refusal are. Two out of three GAO subsamples of reinterviewed respondents were similar to the original target sample in demographic character. The third subsample, despite its being the one with the highest consent rate, differed from the target in average age, income, and sex ratio. Still, we regard the result as promising: absolute response rates are good if imperfect, and they can be improved with more planning time.

Levels of nonresponse much below 50 percent are usually intolerable, for they virtually guarantee that any sample drawn will be biased. The bias may make subsequent research worthless, irrespective of the rate of obtaining consent in the actual respondent sample. So improving the first-level response rate in the process of obtaining cooperation is essential. The simplest improvements capitalize on the state of the art in survey sampling. One may use multiple mailings, for example, rather than a single mailing, to request permission for record release or follow-up. Three waves of mailing were used to boost response rates from 20–30 percent to 70–80 percent in the National Academy of Sciences' Project on Computer Data Banks. Similar results are reported in Reeder et al. (1976) and by others for a variety of research programs. Material rewards for cooperating, such as cash payment and lottery tickets, can be very effective at times. High-quality letters of request, appeals through trustworthy sources, and so on are standard tools of the survey researcher and can enhance response rate, though not necessarily candor.

That these simple tactics can be insufficient is also clear. Bauman and Sage's (1976) efforts suggest that they could achieve a 60 percent response rate, far better than the initial 35 percent, but still intolerable if the remaining 40 percent of the target sample are very different from the respondents. In that case, for example, nonrespondents are likely to be from lower income levels, and if drug abuse among children is generically related to the family's socioeconomic status, analyses based on the 60 percent sample will be misleading. So telephone or personal surveys of nonrespondents, and of respondents who refuse to provide consent, may be necessary for identifying threats to the validity of the inferences based on the data. The methods chosen to increase response rate and so increase initial sampling validity, and the methods used to encourage consent rates, can be subjected to experimental tests, of course, to identify the better alternatives.

Notes on Advisory Boards and Audit of Clinical Records

The Experimental Day Health Care Programs underwritten by Public Law 92–603 were reviewed in 1976 by a special advisory board concerned with the programs' effectiveness. During their site visits, members of the board sought to obtain information on a small random sample of patients who received services under the new program. The request immediately raised a conflict between the board's need for review-related information and the patients' right to privacy vis-à-vis persons outside the immediate project staff. On the one hand, it was imperative in this and similar situations that a review group be able to review client records. For without tracking a client through the system, it is impossible to describe the typical client or the services he or she receives, and it is difficult to understand and evaluate the facility's information system and document flow, and to assess the internal consistency of a given record or cluster of records on a client. On the other hand, withholding records from the advisory group might be justified on legal grounds, since some privacy legislation could be construed as requiring that records be maintained as confi-

dential. Records might also be withheld because their release con-
flicted with a medical tradition that only treatment staff be accorded
access to patient records. At the time, there were no clearly relevant
federal regulations, no in-program rules, and no judicial precedent to
guide administrative action. The confusion engendered by the request
in at least one case produced a baldly schizophrenic reaction. The
program's director, a physician, told the assistant director to handle
the matter; the latter released records to an advisory group member
but refused to sign any formal authorization for release.

This type of conflict combines features of confidentiality issues in
secondary analysis and audit, and so it is not especially unique. Nor
is it atypical in the context described. Most, if not all, policy-relevant
social research programs, evaluative or otherwise, are subject to review by outside experts. Many require on-site visits to avoid egregious
errors in review or to better assess program objectives, staff skills, and
so on. Many do need to track document flow to complete their mission.

To reconcile conflicts, two approaches are possible. The first assumes that records made available need not contain client identification. To assay the internal consistency of a sample of records, to
obtain a feel for document flow, it is often sufficient to know only that
a set of records that vary in content refer to a single individual.
Identifiers can be deleted from (say) copies of records, and copies can
be consolidated for each of a few sampled clients before they are
turned over to an outside group. If records are randomly selected,
identifiers are deleted, and the outsiders are in fact experts interested
in evaluating the program rather than in making personal judgments
about clients, then the deductive-disclosure problem is negligible:
clients will be anonymous.

The second option involves the release of a small stratified random
subsample of fully identified records to competent members of the
review board. The principle here is that the board's interest coincides
with the client's, at least with respect to determining whether the
program is well run. Release might also be justified under the principle that no thorough review, at the level usually chosen by review
boards, is possible without identified records, since verification of
record contents will sometimes require comparison of those contents
with the client's oral testimony or with a staff member's testimony.
As a practical matter, the option helps avoid improbable but possible
forms of deception: inspection of "ideal" records on nonexistent clients, or of records selected opportunistically by program staff.

The approach preferred here is a variant of the approaches described earlier for secondary analysis and audit. If the program is
supported by the government, then governmental regulations must be
set up to permit the disclosure of a small sample of identified records

to review boards for program evaluation. Program policy and advisory-group policy must be explicit and reflect a similar intent. In all regulations, it should be made clear that disclosure will not disrupt program operations (at least no more than site visits usually do), and that if record verification is essential, then the verification process (e.g., an interview with a client) is legitimate, provided that it does not threaten the client's well-being. Finally, the program recipients and members of control or comparison groups (where they exist) must be informed that records are maintained as confidential but that advisory members as overseers of the program and related research may, along with relevant program staff, have occasion to review identifiable records. This is all under the proviso that where identifiers are not needed, they will be eliminated.

AUDIT OF CLINICAL RECORDS

At least one of the procedures suggested earlier may be generally useful in resolving conflicts between the auditor's needs and the need to protect a few classes of very sensitive records maintained for administrative purposes. Consider, for example, administrative records maintained on clients of a mental health clinic, for billing services and so on. Identifiers are often encoded, as they should be, to prevent the invasion of privacy by the nontherapist. For example, the agency accountant, who must have access to the content of the records for internal agency management, need have no access to identification plus content.

When an outside audit is warranted, then the outside auditor's need to access identifiable records must be reconciled with the therapists' interest in not disclosing identifiable records to the nontherapist. Such a conflict occurred recently at the Livingston Crisis Center (Geneseo, New York). The *interim* solution to the problem was developed independently, but it was along the lines of the surrogate model described above, and model C of chapter 4.

According to Dr. Cheryl Emlich, acting director of the Center in 1976, the Center's services were contracted for by the Office of Drug Abuse Services (ODAS) of the state of New York. In June 1976, the contractor asked for an audit review of files maintained on clients; that request was for both record content *and* for patient identification coupled with record content. Dr. Howard Meyers, then center director, declined the request on the grounds that the disclosures would constitute an invasion of patient privacy and would run contrary to the ethics of the profession. ODAS withdrew funding immediately. In the negotiation that followed, ODAS declined the Center's offer to pay an intermediary or surrogate to audit records, but did use one of its own psychologists to conduct the review. The review uncovered no evidence of irregular practices in the Center's financial affairs. The Center's contract expired in September 1976, and was not renewed until the Center brought the matter to court, asking that an injunction against contract termination be issued until the question of audit procedures was settled. ODAS, avoiding a court battle, renewed the contract and established a special committee to investigate the issues.

The conflict between principles here is not much different from the one encountered in the case of the social research-audit issue. It is a more serious matter in practice, though, since insurance fraud and irregularity of other forms of paid service are empirically more likely events than fraud in the conduct of research. So, we believe the interim solution reached by the Livingston Center and the ODAS is a reasonable one. Presumably, if no irregularities are uncovered by the independent psychologist-auditor, then no real invasion of privacy exists—the surrogate is a part of the therapy team, engaged in monitoring quality of treatment. Moreover, the psychologist-auditor is better qualified to review identifiable records than the auditor without therapeutic experience. If irregularities are uncovered and they are serious, then the records may be legitimately turned over to an audit agency under the proviso that *only* records in which irregularities appear can be scrutinized by therapeutically naive auditors.

Notes

1. For a more elaborate description of the reasons for and products of secondary analysis in social program evaluation, see Hedrick, Boruch, and Ross (1978), and Bryant and Wortman (1978). The unpublished testimony presented before the Privacy Protection Study Commission covers sociological, medical, and psychological views on the secondary analysis of data for research purposes. Some federal agencies have created formal written policies to make research data obtained under a government grant available to the research community: for example, the Law Enforcement Assistance Administration's internal memorandum "Special Conditions for Institute Grantees" requires the original researcher to guarantee outsiders access to data so long as individual privacy is not abridged. The results of a discussion among representatives of Swedish, German, Canadian, and American archive agencies on research uses of archived data and individual privacy have been summarized in a position statement for government agencies (see Flaherty 1978).

2. Discussions of the case are given in U.S. General Accounting Office (1976, 1977) reports. Similar problems emerged during the Negative Income Tax Experiments; Kershaw and Fair (1976) and Kershaw and Small (1972) provide the contractor's view of the argument.

3. Bailar and Lanphier (1978) describe pilot research, sponsored by the American Statistical Association, on assessing the quality of sample surveys. None of the approaches examined involve reinterviews of respondents.

Publication of Statistical Tables

He lay still, marveling at the carrying power of the widow's snores. He knew little of the late Mr. Benedetto, but he gathered now that he had been either a man of saintly patience, a masochist, or a deaf mute.

THEODORE STURGEON

Recall that it is possible, under certain conditions, to deduce personal information about an identified individual from a set of completely anonymous records, one of which refers to that individual. It is also possible, under similar conditions, to deduce information about the individual from a statistical summary of the records' contents. Deductive disclosure based entirely on statistical tables is more difficult, to be sure, and differs in character from disclosure based on anonymous records. In principle, it is no less important a problem.

This section begins with a simple illustration of the process, and then describes what we know about its incidence and character. There are stereotypical ways of accomplishing deductive disclosure based on count data, and some of these are described next. Strategies to reduce or eliminate the possibility of disclosure have been developed by computer scientists and statisticians in Germany, the United States, Canada, Sweden, and elsewhere, and these too are discussed.

A Simple Illustration

Suppose that a Parent-Teacher Association mounts a legitimate questionnaire survey of all the students in its school district to document the character and incidence of vandalism. To enhance the usefulness of the resulting data, some demographic information is also elicited:

for example, the student's level of education, his or her participation on an athletic team. The questionnaires, returned anonymously, are used to construct statistical tables, and are then destroyed. One such table, cross-tabulating athletic activity against level of schooling, might show that exactly forty seniors are team members. Because such things as the team membership and grade level of an individual are common knowledge and because all the students were surveyed, the thoughtful teacher will recognize that little Jerzy and his friends constitute that subgroup. Suppose, now, that another table is published, giving a count of all team members who are seniors *and* who admitted on their questionnaires engaging in property crimes. That count also turns out to be forty.

Assuming that all students responded to the survey and that their reports were honest, the conclusion that Jerzy and his cronies are vandals is inescapable. More to the point, we learned this from statistical tables containing no identifiers and a bit of supplementary information. In extreme cases, it may even be possible to deduce additional information about Jerzy himself. A parent may recognize that the single student who appears in a statistical table as a senior, a team member, and an immigrant, *and* who admits (anonymously) having derailed a locomotive can be none other than Jerzy, for he fits the first three descriptors. Even if there were two or three such students, nothing would prevent the curious teacher or parent or the local police from consulting their own mental dossiers on children to identify all of them. Finally, if each individual reported the level of his leisure activity and only two children fell into the category of railroad vandals, it is clear that Jerzy could compute his colleagues' vandalism rate exactly merely by subtracting his own rate from the total.

The example is simple, but it suggests some of the controllable (and uncontrollable) parameters of the problem; for example, we must know that Jerzy is in the sample, and we must have collateral information on the little fellow. It illustrates, albeit crudely, how the process works and implies how a more specific mathematical description of the problem and its solutions might be developed. It is realistic insofar as it shows that a great deal of information need not be available, in statistical tables or elsewhere, to accomplish deductive disclosure, provided that the conditions are met.

The Problem in Literal Description

Though the illustration is based on statistical data, it is obvious that information that is published entirely in literal form may be quite sufficient for deductive disclosure. Indeed, because deductive disclosure can be accomplished more easily with literal description, the problem has been a concern, for the past few years at least, to many anthropologists, political scientists, sociologists, and psychiatrists. Beals (1969), for example, reports that two persistent journalists managed to determine the identity of the ostensibly anonymous family described in Oscar Lewis's *Children of Sanchez* within months after the volume's publication. Mead (1968) strongly expressed her concern that despite vigorous efforts to purge anthropologists' reports of the idiosyncratic behavior of public officials in developing countries, the details that remain in scholarly reports might still be sufficient to permit the identification and embarrassment of some officials. Carroll and Knerr's (1975) case reports about forcible appropriation of social research records are terse, but not terse enough to prevent the knowledgeable outsider from identifying some of the cases and principals involved in them. In fact, the failure to identify some of them is puzzling, given that identical information is public. Similarly, Colvard's (1967) investigations of political conflicts in the Arkansas teacher certification controversy and the "Springdale Study" of small-town civic processes (see Katz, Capron, and Glass 1972) could not prevent deductive disclosure of information about principals, despite efforts to adjust reports to ensure anonymity. The psychiatrist's or physician's problem of disguising the identity of an individual described in a publishable case study that covers a few individuals is a chronic one. The result of failing to do so adequately has become a bit more complicated, if we may judge from the increasing number of civil suits brought against the psychiatrist.

No systematic statistical research on the incidence of deductive disclosure in case studies of these types appears to have been undertaken. Our own (weak) order of magnitude estimate, based on the number of articles published about deductive disclosure relative to total published reports on independent studies over a ten-year period, suggests that the probability of disclosure is very low—around .005 —even if only one out of every five disclosures is detected. We have discovered no papers that advance the state of the art in avoiding deductive disclosure in such studies, or in detecting disclosure.

The Problem in Statistical Description: National

Deductive disclosure based on statistical tables is difficult to detect, and because it may occur in *any* data-collection setting, private or public, we know little about its incidence. Nonetheless, the possibility has not gone unattended by statisticians or the affected publics. The need to reduce the probability of deductive disclosure, for example, underlies legislation enacted in 1910 that restricts publication of statistics from Census Bureau surveys of commercial organizations. Respondents lobbied for better statutory safeguards against accidental deductive disclosure of "private" facts about their firms. For the 1930 census, Congress took action to recognize the possibility of disclosure about both establishments and individuals (Eckler 1972 and Davis 1971). Now and then, claims that individual privacy has been breached through publication of statistical data will surface. Miller's (1971) often-cited example involves tabulations provided by the Census Bureau to the American Medical Association. Although no respondent identification was supplied with the statistics, one critic maintained that the income categories could be cross-tabulated against the medical specialty and the region of residence within the state. Since the latter information for identifiable physicians is also available from public sources and the number of physicians practicing certain specialties is small, Miller contended that disclosure of individual incomes was possible. The Federal Committee on Statistical Methodology's Subcommittee on Disclosure-Avoidance Techniques (1978) re-examined the Miller example, declared that Miller was confused, based on the evidence at hand, and that disclosure did not occur, based on the tabulations published by the Census Bureau.

The census bureaus of a half dozen countries have traditionally attended to the problem of deductive disclosure, and a good deal of what we now know about the topic stems from their efforts. Some exceptions to this institutional emphasis exist: the U.S. Social Security Administration, for example, through its Office of Research and Statistics, as a producer of statistical tables. One would guess that groups such as the Central Intelligence Agency attend to the topic as consumers of information on organizations, though we know of no remarkable work in this arena. Other government agencies have expressed interest more recently. These include both operations groups, such as the Internal Revenue Service and the U.S. Department of Agriculture, and research groups, such as the National Center for Health Statistics. Their common interest in the United States has led to the formation of a new Subcommittee on Disclosure-Avoidance Techniques (1978).

There are several obvious reasons for increased agency interest in Europe and North America. The most visible one is recent legislative stress on the individual's right to privacy exemplified by the Privacy Act in Sweden (Vinge 1973), the Privacy Act of 1974 in the United States and others (see National Central Bureau of Statistics 1976, and Müller 1978). Though the laws are ambiguous in detail, they are unambiguous in their prohibitions against direct disclosure of records on identifiable individuals, and, by implication, indirect (deductive) disclosure of the same information. It is reasonable to expect agencies to take responsibility for both, granted that the former is considerably more important in practice. Aside from meeting responsibility, however, the legislative action provided a unique opportunity for advancing the mathematical state of the art in this arena. The opportunity has been exploited in Sweden, for example, through the National Central Bureau of Statistics (1974, 1975) and through the Confidentiality in Surveys Project directed by Tore Dalenius. Similar research has been undertaken in the United States, Canada, and Britain; the topic is of interest in Israel (Bachi and Bar-on 1969) and Italy (Martinotti 1971, 1972) because systems of national identification generate information that is collateral with census records.

The new research on deductive disclosure problems is entrained in a broader stream of activity—providing information to the public. Indeed, the justification for such agencies depends partly on their production of detailed statistical tables. And the demand for such tables, at least in the United States, has increased as a result of other legislation, which uses regional statistics as a basis for the allocation of federal resources, revenue sharing, and the like. The increased production of detailed tables carries the risk of increasing opportunities for deductive disclosure, and so there is at least a nominal conflict between agency missions. Partly to resolve the conflict, at least in the sense of agreeing on principles, and partly to learn how to avoid self-serving and overweening emphasis on restricting the production of statistical tables, a group of government executives and researchers from several Western countries convened to issue the so-called Bellagio principles (Flaherty 1978). Those principles reflect the belief that the risks of deductive disclosure are generally low, that the risks are generally not notable in their consequences, and that the openness of the statistical system must be regarded as on a par with individual privacy, as a matter of policy.

The quality of the mathematical work notwithstanding, other features of deductive disclosure in this setting have not been vigorously examined. For example, very little systematic social research on the incidence of disclosure or on its consequences has been undertaken. The imbalance in treatment is at least as much a function of the skills of agency staff, largely mathematical rather than social scientific, as it is a function of the immediate character of the problem.

Local and Regional Producers of Statistical Descriptions

Neither state and local government agencies nor private data collection agencies have made any noticeable investment in examining the deductive-disclosure problem. It may well be that any such investment is unwarranted in view of the small risks involved, but we know virtually nothing about the risks of disclosure in this setting.

The less formal archives, because of their low visibility and sporadic activity, may also generate opportunities for disclosure. The illustration concerning Jerzy's privacy in an anonymous school survey is hypothetical but not implausible. It is also reasonable to expect deductive-disclosure problems to appear in other anonymous surveys of small populations about which much is already known. The graduate student of prison sociology who turns his statistics over to the cooperating warden may provide considerably more information than he recognizes if the cross tabulations are detailed. The military psychologist who surveys drug use on army posts, the personnel manager who surveys theft among anonymous employees, may publish statistics that, though they refer to no identifiable individual, might be detrimental to particular respondents.

The risks of disclosure and their consequences in these special cases may be quite negligible. We simply do not know. We do know that oversight of situations like these, by professional organizations, by community groups, by individuals, or by government, is nonexistent. There are no laws to deal with the (potential) problem, nor is any administrative action customary. In Sweden, because computerized data banks are licensed, it is possible to conduct the empirical research necessary to determine whether the problem is a negligible one. For the United States, no such licensing practice exists, so any formal research is likely to be difficult. In lieu of detailed, reliable information, we assume for the remainder of the discussion that the context of the problem is wide open, and any data collector, private or public, professional or otherwise, might produce statistical tables that permit deductive disclosure.

Problem Specification

The lesson we draw from the material reviewed so far is that *actual* deductive disclosure and improper exploitation of the resultant information do not serve to justify interest in the topic. The possibility of deductive disclosure, however, does justify interest for the variety of reasons we have suggested. A good deal of the work undertaken is preventive, rather than remedial or even diagnostic. Furthermore, it is, as we have said, largely mathematical in character, and for that reason, parochial. As in any preventive research, we ought to be sensitive to the fact that in trying to cosh the goblin, we may annihilate our friends. In particular, restrictions on the production of tables, in the interest of preventing an unlikely event whose consequence is of dubious nature, will also restrict the research community's ability to exploit data for legitimate purposes.

Espousing a few definitions is in order, partly because the independent efforts of computer scientists, mathematicians, and statisticians have produced a gallimaufry of key words. We lay these out first, and then consider some of the recent work on the topic.

Exact deductive disclosure refers here to the process of using statistical summaries about a sample of individuals and collateral information on some or all of those individuals to learn that some identified individuals have a particular heretofore-unrecognized attribute. *Probabilistic deductive disclosure* refers to a similar process in which one learns that all or some identified individuals very probably have the attribute. It is sometimes helpful to talk about either process as *inadvertent direct disclosure,* or i.d.d. (Felligi 1972) and to distinguish between disclosures based on entries in a single table and disclosures based on (linear) combinations of the entries in several tables. The latter is labelled as *residual disclosure* by Felligi (1972) and *indirect disclosure* by Hansen (1971a).

The basic models for exact disclosure, already discussed in chapter 4, can be consolidated into symbolic form. Let the expression C_i $(A_1, A_2, \ldots, A_p)$ represent information available on each identified individual i. Let G_i *represent a sample that is known to contain the identified individuals, among others, and let*

$$G_i \ (A_1, A_2, A_3 \ldots A_p) = N_1$$

represent the count (N_1) of all individuals in the sample who possess attributes $A_1, A_2, \ldots, A_p$. If a new table is developed to identify the number of individuals who possess traits $A_1, A_2, \ldots, A_p, A_{p+1}$, we represent the count as:

$$G_i \ (A_1, A_2, A_3 \ldots A_p, A_{p+1}) = N_2$$

Exact deductive disclosure occurs if $N_1 = N_2$, for one can then conclude that i not only has the traits $A_1, A_2, \ldots, A_p$, but has the trait A_{p+1} as well. The inference is one-directional, since if $N_1 \neq N_2$, nothing can be said with certainty about i's possession of A_{p+1}. Probabilistic disclosure occurs if N_1 and N_2 are about equal. If $N_1 = 10$ and $N_2 = 9$, for example, we infer that there is a high probability that the individual possesses the trait A_{p+1}, but we cannot be certain.

When only a single individual has traits $A_1, A_2, \ldots, A_p$—that is, $N_1 = 1$—the process is slightly more informative in that inferences are bi-directional. For is $N_2 = 1$, we infer without doubt that the individual in question has trait A_{p+1}, and if $N_2 = 0$, we infer with equal surety that he or she does not have the trait. That it is not implausible to expect a single person to have a peculiar set of traits can be illustrated neatly with an example borrowed from Morris Hansen. If traits are either present or absent, uniformly distributed in a sample, and independent of one another, a questionnaire survey of 10,000 persons each reporting the presence or absence of only ten traits would yield a cross tabulation with, on the average, about one person in each cell. If trait patterns for each individual are known beforehand and the survey contains an eleventh item that is unique and unknown, such a table could provide all the information necessary to learn whether any identified individual has the trait.

The report by Bell, Mugge, and Dalenius in the Subcommittee on Disclosure-Avoidance Techniques (1978) reports on disclosure and sketches other nice examples; it is marred a bit by peculiar labeling of count data in tabulating nominal and interval information. See reports by the National Central Bureau of Statistics (1974, 1975), Dalenius (1977a), and Schlörer (1975) for other clever illustrations. The subcommittee report also contains examples of approximate deductive disclosure and probabilistic disclosure based on statistical tables.

Now consider the situation in which a single table plus supplementary information is insufficient for exact deductive disclosure. The availability of several tables facilitates deductive disclosure if, when all tables are combined, some cells contain zero entries. To make matters concrete, suppose that the data from a PTA survey of all the students in a school are summarized and we are given two-way tables with counts bearing on student membership on an athletic team (A_1), his or her commission of an act of vandalism (A_2), and twelfth-grade education (A_3). Overbarred letters below represent students who are not athletes $(\bar{A}_1)$, and so forth.

	A_1	$\bar{A}_1$		A_1	$\bar{A}_1$		A_2	$\bar{A}_2$
A_2	8	3	A_3	6	5	A_3	9	2
$\bar{A}_2$	4	7	$\bar{A}_3$	6	5	$\bar{A}_3$	2	9

Nothing about particular individuals can be deduced from any one of the tables. The important questions then become: Can the tables be combined to yield a larger table with counts of students in category $A_1A_2A_3$, $A_1A_2\bar{A}_3$, and so forth? And will this larger table permit deductive disclosure?

The fact of the matter is that a new table of the following form can be laid out to answer the first question by trial and error:

	A_1		$\bar{A}_1$	
	A_3	$\bar{A}_3$	A_3	$\bar{A}_3$
A_2	X_{11}	X_{12}	X_{13}	X_{14}
$\bar{A}_2$	X_{21}	X_{22}	X_{23}	X_{24}

One can write out the possible values of each entry, beginning with the smallest. The cell labeled X_{13}, for example, must contain a number between zero and three, since that cell plus its neighbor on the right must equal the total number of students who have trait A_2 and do not have A_1, a total fixed at three by the relevant two-way table. Continuing the cycle for each cell, using all three two-way tables, shows that the only possible cell entries are:

	A_1		$\bar{A}_1$	
	A_3	$\bar{A}_3$	A_3	$\bar{A}_3$
A_2	6	2	3	0
$\bar{A}_2$	0	4	2	5

The trial-and-error computation is a bit tedious; it can, of course, be assisted by computer and made more efficient by using an iterative approach.

It is clear that the elaborated table permits exact deductive disclosure. The number of senior students A_3 who are team members (A_1) is six. All six of these individuals are, according to the table, vandals (A_2). We may also infer that all of the students who are not seniors and who are not team members have not committed acts of vandalism; that is:

$G_i (\bar{A}_1, \bar{A}_2) = 5$ and $G_i (\bar{A}_1, \bar{A}_2, \bar{A}_3) = 5$.

In general, there is no guarantee that the larger table can be produced from the smaller two-way tables of the kind presented here. For example, if each cell of each 2×2 table contained five individuals, there is no unique solution to the problem of constructing the three-way table. In fact, there are about two hundred patterns of numbers which could be entered into a three-way table and which are completely consistent with two-way tables whose cell counts are identical. Whether one can determine a unique set of entries for the three-way tables from the two-way data depends on the empirical pattern of numbers in the two-way tables.

If one has the option of obtaining a single entry in the three-way table (e.g., element X_{11}), then, of course, the entire table can be computed from this element and the two-way tables. If one has the option of obtaining the sum of two elements in the three-way table, then that sum ought to be a function of an interaction term; for example, given marginal totals, two cross tabulations of the form

$G_i (A_1, A_2)$ and $G_i (A_1, A_3)$,

and the interaction

$G_i (A_1, \bar{A}_3 | A_2 + \bar{A}_1, A_3 | A_2)$,

then the proper set of entries for the three-way table can be computed.

A crucial point here is that attempting a solution is not worthwhile unless it is expected that zeros or low counts will appear in the more elaborate table. We know of no mathematical preconditions that will guarantee a unique solution with one or more zero entries.

The problem can be cast in terms of higher-order tables. Trial and error methods can be used here, too, though computer support is necessary for the zealous inquirer. Dalenius (1977c), for example, shows how the diagnosis of tables can be made tidier and more thorough by mapping table entries algebraically. Independent computations (sums) on various attributes can be used to generate little sets of simultaneous equations, which can then be used to solve for missing cells, which in turn may lead to deductive disclosure. The Dalenius paper, as well as papers by the Subcommittee on Disclosure-Avoidance Techniques (1978), Olsson (1975), National Central Bureau of Statistics (1974), Cox (1976), and the references they cite, contains other illustrations of indirect disclosure.

Prophylactic Measures

Embedded in the disclosure situations described above are four major factors that influence the possibility of exact deductive disclosure. The factors, together with their manipulable or observable features, include (1) the sample used as a basis for statistical tables, characterized by a sampling ratio, sample composition, and sampling validity; (2) the attributes or traits considered in the tables, characterized by their exactness, number, uniqueness, and sensitivity; (3) the reports (in tabular form) elicited from survey sample respondents, characterized by their validity; and (4) the tabulations themselves, characterized by type, number, attribute coverage, and cell entries. These factors, arranged roughly in order of their importance in controlling deductive disclosure, are discussed below. Here, the symbol i is used to refer to an identified individual or group of individuals about whom unique information is desired.

Sample. Recall that one of the conditions necessary for exact deductive disclosures about i to occur is that i be a member of the group of individuals on which statistical tables are based.

If the tables are based on an entire prescribed population, then i's report will be included, and the inquirer will recognize this and can proceed to investigate the relevant tables systematically. If a sample from the population is drawn and used in tabulation, and the inquirer has access to the sample membership list, the same is true. This immediately suggests that in local research settings, the tabulator ought to keep secret the population or sample listing, so as to reduce the possibility of inadvertent deductive disclosure. So, for example, a psychologist may keep secret the identity of drivers interviewed during a highway survey. An anthropologist may withhold the identities of women interviewed in a study of the emotional effects of abortion. It will, of course, be impossible to maintain the secrecy of lists in other situations, where lists are a matter of public information—for example, surveys of all prisoners in a prison, all police in a precinct, and so forth. In still other cases, it will be easy for an inquirer to verify independently that i is in fact a member of the basic sample: the individual might simply be asked about participation. Nonetheless, maintaining list confidentiality is a simple and effective device in many, perhaps most, research settings.

When sample or population lists are public, the tabulator can reduce the possibility of deductive disclosure by issuing statistics based (say) on a random subsample of the basic group involved in the survey. For example, a statistical report issued on the homosexual behavior of prisoners in a state facility might be based on a random 80 percent of the sample or population actually surveyed. Naturally, the membership of the subsample must not be publicized. To the extent that the sampling ratio is small, the likelihood that i is in the sample is also small. The strategy is entirely inappropriate where some of the traits under examination are rare (e.g., machinist skills among felons) and the published table must speak to those traits. And it does not protect against the exceptional case in which i has a very peculiar set of attributes, i happens to be included in the random subsample, and i's membership in the subsample can be deduced because tables refer to those attributes. (See the section on attributes, below.)

A similarly convenient tactic can be developed by recognizing that for any disclosure to occur on the basis of multiple tables (or an elaborated table), the sample on which the tables are based must be the same. That is, the tabulation of

$$G_1 (A_1, A_2 \ldots A_p) = N_1 \text{ and } G_i (A_1, A_2 \ldots A_p, A_{p+1}) = N_2$$

must, with one exception, be based on the same sample to make deductive disclosures possible. To eliminate the condition, the tabulator can use one random subsample of the basic population to generate one table, then take a second random sample with replacement to generate the second table. Even if i does appear in each sample, the fact will be generally impossible for an outsider to verify. And the fact that $N_1 = N_2$ will yield no unique information. The exception here is that by chance one table contains all the individuals known to possess certain attributes. This problem is not likely to occur if subsampling ratios are small to moderate. And it can be controlled, as Felligi (1972) suggests, by building the higher-order tables from low-order tables each based on *independent* subsamples of the population or main sample. Drawing independent subsamples and using each as a basis for a different table of counts is *not* generally useful for local applications, where sample sizes are small (say not over 500) to begin with. Any appreciable number of published tables would in this case be based on rather small samples.

When target sample listings rather than actual sample listings are public, the naturally imperfect validity of the sample can help to reduce the possibility of deductive disclosure. Suppose, for example, that the overlap between the target sample, whose membership is known, and the actual sample is small. The actual sample membership may be kept confidential: as far as the inquirer is concerned, i may not be in the sample at all. If there is no indirect way to verify membership, then deductive disclosure based on relevant tables is virtually impossible. Indirect verification requires not only collateral information on i but also a 100 percent cooperation rate by all is in the survey. Many local surveys, however, by school districts, legislators, newspapers, etc. are characterized by considerably lower response rates—in the 25–50 percent range. Consequently, inept sampling offers a kind of natural protection from exact deductive disclosure. Low validity is generally antithetical to research standards, and it is an undependable feature of the research process.

Attributes. A great many social research projects involve structuring permissible responses as categories to facilitate data collection and consolidation. For example, a respondent is often asked to acknowledge one of several alternative income intervals rather than to report an exact amount. The researcher's control over the size of the interval of response suggests the notions of approximate and exact disclosure. In making the distinction, Hansen (1971a) asserts that interval size is an important parameter insofar as disclosure of exact confidential information about an individual is often more threatening than disclosure of approximate information, and furthermore, some levels of approximate disclosure leave so much room for interpretation that they constitute virtually no disclosure at all. In fact, varying the size of the interval in the scale of permissible responses in the original survey, or the interval size on released records or statistical data, is one of several methods of decreasing the sensitivity of a response (see the earlier remarks on crude report categories). Hansen defines *approximate disclosure* as publication of count data for interval A_q such that the range of interpretation (of inferring that individual i has property A_q) is of the order of A_q's magnitude. Order of A_q has evidently been defined heuristically by Census Bureau statisticians as $.75\ A_q - 1.5\ A_q$ (Hansen 1971b). So, for example, if we find from published data that i's dividends are in the $3500–5500 range when in fact they are $4000, then approximate disclosure occurs. For a larger interval, say $3000–6000, disclosure does not occur, but this grouping may be too large to be informative or useful to the legitimate statistician.

Distinctions between "common" or "public" attributes and uncommon ones, and between sensitive and innocuous attributes are generally made in this context. The idea is that to establish what collateral information might be used for deductive disclosure the designer of statistical tables must be able to identify commonly held knowledge or public information about an individual. And if it is then possible to identify especially sensitive attributes, then the designer adapts disclosure-prevention devices to tables that refer to those variables. One might then impose restrictions on the type of attributes covered by a table; the categorical exactness of an attribute might be altered to permit only approximate disclosure. The sensitivity of an attribute might also be deliberately decreased by changing its exactness or intrusiveness in published categories, or the variable might be eliminated entirely from a table. Actions of this sort, however, cannot be taken independently of the contents (cell entries) of the tables, since restrictions might be irrelevant or unnecessary. It may also be inappropriate to impose gross restrictions, because they denigrate the tables' usefulness.

One of the major problems in viewing commonness or sensitivity as controllable features of published tables is that too little is known about these concepts. Commonness might easily be defined by fiat, for example, as legally public information. But this is patently inadequate when statistical tables are supplied to agencies such as banks, hospitals, credit bureaus, and the like, which may have a large store of common and uncommon information under this definition. Sensitivity in this context is even less well defined, but some preliminary work by the census bureaus of Sweden and the United States is promising. Rapaport and Sundgren (1975) report that the National Central Bureau of Statistics is using expert panels of judges to screen tables that might yield disclosures in order to assure the harmlessness of the information so disclosed. We have been told that a waiver system in use by the United States Census Bureau permits census staff to ask a manufacturer for permission to publish important tables that *might* yield sensitive manufacturer-related information, on the grounds that the industry's influence in an area is simply too dominant to be disguised in a table.

Commonness, sensitivity, or uniqueness could be defined empirically as well as by fiat. A crude definition of level of publicity or commonness of information concerning an attribute A_1, for example, might be the ratio of the total number of times data about A_1 appears in a record on i relative to the total number of formal records maintained on i. Or one might simply ask i whether trait A_1 is a matter of common knowledge. The matter has not been explored empirically even by groups that have had a relevant mission—privacy commissions at the state or federal level—to estimate how much information, on the average, is maintained on a particular individual by all data archives. In the absence of such information, we rely on more idiosyncratic, personal notions of what is likely to be commonplace knowledge and what is sensitive.

Whether common or not, information may also be characterized by its uniqueness with respect to the individual. A street address, a cell designation, a hospital room, or similar information constitutes *de facto* identification of an individual at least at one point in time. Tabulated material is generally not so specific, but when such material is cross-tabulated against age, marital status, and the like, and when that information is easily accessible from other sources, then opportunity for deductive disclosure is greater. For local research, it is not difficult to avoid the problem, provided that such attributes have no policy implications or are of no theoretical interest: one simply does not publish tables in which these attributes are cross-classified by some other new attribute. It is a considerably more difficult problem if the attributes are fundamental to theory. Neighborhood residence and other demographic variables are basic to some urban planning studies, police patrol strategy research, sociological theory of crime incidence and deterrence. Reducing the likelihood of deductive disclosure from tables would, we believe, normally have to rely on tactics other than increasing the crudeness of reporting categories, subsampling, and eliminating counts based on these attributes.

Reports. Natural influences on the possibility of deductive disclosure include the validity and stability of reports made by respondents to a survey. What has been said so far assumes, by and large, that responses are near perfect or at least perfectly stable across reporting systems. But this will rarely be the case. In the illustrative survey of vandalism among high school students, for example, it is unlikely that students will report their vandalous behavior with perfect accuracy even when assured of anonymity. Some students will underreport because they are suspicious about the survey. Some will overreport if vandalism is regarded locally as a social merit badge. Their responses will be more variable to the extent that "vandalism," despite what one might think, is not a well-defined activity. The result of this noise in the system is that count data will be faulty, and if the researcher does his job well, the average fault level will have been estimated in a side study. A verifiably low level of fault will not necessarily vitiate the analysis of the overall data, but it will almost certainly impede exact deductive disclosure. If only a few students lie in denying vandalism, if a few fail to report accurately any of the relevant items in the questionnaire, then exact disclosure is impossible. Temporal instability of an attribute exerts a similar influence. An individual's income, attitudes, and so on vary from one time to the next, despite the fact that the data generally display orderly patterns when the entire group is considered. Even if collateral information on attitudes is available, for example, the information is often guaranteed to be obsolete for a sizable number of individuals.

Depending on either feature of reports to avoid deductive disclosure is not sufficient protection, of course. But it does make matters simpler if average error rates can be estimated. The inquirer who knows that 20 percent of reports are inaccurate will also know that the possibility of exact deductive disclosure is reduced accordingly. Neither inaccuracy of response nor temporal instability of responses appears to have been exploited systematically in developing disclosure-avoidance techniques.

Tables. If opportunities to exploit tables for deductive disclosure are recognized prior to their publication, then it is generally possible to adjust table structure or entries to reduce or eliminate the problem. Much of what is known about adjusting tables for this purpose stems from work by the national census bureaus. In particular, the National Central Bureau of Statistics in Sweden, Statistics Canada, the U. S. Bureau of the Census, and Britain's Office of Population Censuses have laid much of the groundwork because the scale and levels of detail covered in their published products can lead to inadvertent deductive disclosures. The remarks that follow draw heavily from their efforts.

The main objective of table adjustment in this context is to reduce the possibility of disclosure without unnecessary and naive abridgment of the statistical data that can be made available to the public. Meeting the objective when numerous tables at varying levels of detail are published requires the solution of several basic problems. The first is development of overarching schemes for searching and adjusting publishable tables for possible disclosures. Nested in the first task is a second: the need to develop specific search tactics and adjustment options to reduce or eliminate disclosures. The third task is the development of feedback mechanisms to assure that the main objective— disclosure reduction without intolerable loss of information—is met.

The national bureaus have generally built their search schemes around regional hierarchies that underlie the collection and consolidation of their data. The idea is that since statistics based on very large regions (e.g., national counts of unemployed by race, sex, etc.) present negligible problems in deductive disclosure, few if any adjustments on relevant tables need be made. On the other hand, since tables that concern very small regions (e.g., number of unemployed Indians in a census tract) present the highest risks, then more attention must be focused on these. Region of residence is, for example, an elementary piece of collateral information that an inquirer might use in deductive disclosure.

The regional hierarchy also happens to coincide with a second contemporary hierarchy, that of political importance. National parliaments and executive offices normally attach greater import to national than to local statistics, so the current overlap in hierarchies is convenient. If data must be suppressed, they are then to be suppressed at local levels rather than at the national level, the latter being more important on general policy grounds and less critical on privacy grounds. The perspective is not especially elegant, but it has been useful. The problems it raises for policy makers, researchers, or commercial consumers of data at the local levels can be difficult, however.

At a given level of the hierarchy, such as the census tract, the relevant tables can be searched to determine whether one or more, alone or in combination, can yield unique information on identifiable individuals. As a heuristic device, region of residence (census tract, or enumeration district), sex, race, and other pieces of commonly held knowledge are identified as collateral information in the search. Though these seem appropriate, it is still not yet clear whether other variables ought to be regarded as key collateral variables in this context as well. Newman (1975), for example, has expressed a strong concern that for population surveys in Britain, there may be a good deal more collateral information than is generally recognized. What is sensitive is similarly defined heuristically. In the U.S. Census of Manufacturers, "value of shipments" is designated as a key variable bearing on institutional privacy; total sales is designated sensitive in table searches based on the Census of Business (Barabba and Kaplan 1975). For the population censuses, cultural differences show up, for instance, in the U.S. designation of race, the British designation of age, the Swedish designation of welfare recipient status as sensitive in bureau documentation. In the search for possibilities for deductive disclosure, such variables are pivotal. The search itself can be mechanized, at least up to a point; the computer-programmable tactics are based roughly on the ideas covered earlier, and more formally on algorithms developed from mathematical statements of conditions under which deductive disclosure is possible (e.g., Felligi 1972; Felligi and Phillips 1974; Rapaport and Sundgren 1975).

Once a disclosure risk is identified at the lowest level of regional aggregation, the relevant table or tables are adjusted so as to minimize the negative effects of adjustment at that level and at higher levels of aggregation. The main adjustment tactics used at the lower levels include interval expansion, elimination, contamination, and rounding. All of these can be illustrated with a simple example in which, say, the number of individuals in a given region is classified by race and quality of housing (example 1).

Example 1.

	Low	Medium	High
Caucasian	46	17	28
Black	1	0	0
American Indian	4	2	0
Asian	10	10	10

The table suggests that if one found the single black in this neighborhood one would know that his or her housing was poor. Furthermore, any more elaborate table, giving (say) income level, would be equally revealing.

Interval expansion is an obvious way to accommodate the problem: one "collapses" (if one is British) or "rolls up" (if one is Swedish) two categories to avoid disclosure. In this case, we might choose the two smallest categories to produce a table similar to example 2.

Example 2.

	Low	Medium	High
Caucasian	46	17	28
Black and			
American Indian	5	2	0
Asian	10	10	10

Though exact deductive disclosure is reduced, the fact that there are only five people in low housing and most are either black or Indian may be sufficiently threatening to individual privacy to justify collapsing categories for blacks, American Indians, and Asians.

Complete elimination of the entries offers some additional possibilities. One blanks out or erases the particular entry and others that permit computation of the deleted entry. The result is a table like example 3. Finding that the number of blacks can be computed from marginal totals, one then suppresses related statistics to obtain example 4. Marginal counts are preserved under the assumption that they are more important than internal entries.

In fact, both the U.S. and the British census bureaus suppress data similarly whenever cell counts fall below some acceptable level. For

Example 3.

	Low	Medium	High	
Caucasian	46	17	28	91
Black	*	*	0	1
American Indian	4	2	0	6
Asian	10	10	10	30
Total	60	29	38	128

Example 4.

	Low	Medium	High	
Caucasian	46	17	28	91
Black	*	*	0	1
American Indian	*	*	0	6
Asian	10	10	10	30
Total	61	29	38	128

example, according to Barabba and Kaplan (1975), racial-subgroup/ housing data based on a particular (small) region of enumeration are suppressed if the number within a racial subgroup is less than five. Entire tables, especially those concerning a small number of institutions in a small district, may be suppressed on similar grounds. Regular cross tabulations for enumeration districts (census tracts) in Britain go unpublished if the district contains no more than twenty-five persons or households.

The foregoing illustration is oversimplified: tables that are higher in the publication hierarchy and those lower in the hierarchy may also lend themselves to deductive disclosure, and diagnostic and prophylactic action must recognize that. Given a large number of such tables, all of whose entries are linearly related and based on the same sample, and the members of the sample are known, it is reasonable to seek a general strategy for table adjustment rather than flail away at the individual, potentially publishable arrays. Some work on more coherent approaches has in fact been undertaken at the U.S. Census Bureau, especially by Cox (1976, 1977), for tabular count data on commercial establishments. The Cox approach exploits Boolean algebra to organize the set of potentially publishable arrays at each level in a hierarchy, and so it can be mechanized. It permits derivation of explicit theorems to identify conditions that are sufficient to eliminate disclosure, and it has been designed to minimize the overall number of cell suppressions in tables. The approach does not recognize imperfect sampling validity or response validity, exploits only cell suppression as a device for preventing disclosure, and depends in a fundamental way on numerical definitions of "sensitive" information and "disclosure." The definition of "sensitive" is a bit peculiar—any attribute or cluster of attributes that very few establishments have—but at least it is explicit. Different forms of approximate disclosure, as well as exact disclosure, are handled under the algorithm. For instance, suppression is automatic for small cells dominated by a few establishments: the so-called n-respondent, k percent rule of dominance applies routinely.

Contamination or error inoculation involves adding a very small amount of random error to tables prior to publication so as to undermine their use for deductive disclosure without destroying the data's integrity. In Britain, for example, detailed tables are regularly constructed on wards or parishes, a ward generally being made up of several enumeration districts. If only two or three districts make up a particular ward, even the aggregated data may pose some risks of disclosure with detailed tables. To eliminate the possibility, tables on all the districts within the ward are constructed first, and then each district is paired arbitrarily with another. A number is randomly selected from 1, 0, and -1 and assigned to each independent cell in the cross tabulation for one randomly selected member of the pair. So, for example, if counts for income levels in district 1 were found to be:

Level	0	1	2	3	4
Actual Count	1	21	30	59	21

then the assignment process might yield:

Level	0	1	2	3	4
Adjusted Count	2	20	30	60	20

The complementary number is then added to counts for the second member of the pair, yielding, say:

Level	0	1	2	3	4
Actual	1	15	26	70	19
Adjusted	2	14	26	71	18

The rules for number assignment are set up to prevent the embarrassment of a negative number in a cell or in the aggregate data. The sum of the data for the two districts *in this case* yields a table aggregated to the ward level and containing no biased marginal totals. However, this is not always the case. When the second member of a pair is selected for adjustment, no complementary adjustment is made to the first member's data. As a consequence, the adjusted total ward level counts will differ from the actual counts. Evidently, the difference is small, amounting to no more than .1 percent for the smallest wards to which the technique has been applied (Newman 1975).

The technique has been generalized for use in responding to requests for district-level data aggregated in unusual ways. For example, a health care planning commission may ask that districts or parts of districts be separated out into medical service areas defined a priori by the commission. The districts or parts of districts so aggregated would yield count data that are slightly imprecise but contain no serious bias and protect against deductive disclosure. The exact level of bias, though small, is not computable except under some special conditions. This can be a distinct disadvantage, and we consider the problem in a bit more detail below.

Note that in principal, at least, a microlevel contamination approach is possible. One may inject error into individual records prior to table computation, and then construct tables based on these. The adjusted tables offer protection against disclosure when small-area statistics are published, and the computation of long-run bias in unusual aggregations is simpler. However, the method may lead to more variable tables than the approach currently in use by the British. There appear to be no data on the comparative statistical efficiency or integrity of these approaches.

In practice, rounding table entries to avoid deductive disclosure has taken one of two forms. The deterministic form has been used by the British in their 1971 census for adjusting all tables other than small-area statistics. The technique is simple to apply: one merely rounds the last digit to some number under a formal prescription. According to Newman (1975), the prescription used on British statistics includes the following: if the last digit in a cell count or marginal total is:

- 0, 1, or 2, then replace it by an asterisk (*)
- 3, 4, 5, 6, or 7, then replace by the number 5
- 8, 9, or larger numbers ending in 0, 1, or 2, replace the last digit by the number 0.

There are special rules to accommodate impossible entries. The device is used generally to protect against the possibility of disclosure based on detailed cross tabulations on even a large subgroup in the population.

The second form of adjustment, stochastic or random rounding, has been used by Statistics Canada to adjust published tables stemming from the 1971 census (Nargundkar and Saveland 1972). The basic technique involves making a random decision for each cell entry as to the direction of rounding (round up or round down), and computing under a prescription the level of rounding (roughly speaking, the magnitude of numbers added to or subtracted from the rounded number). The probability of rounding up or down is fixed to assure that there is no long-run bias in cell entries so adjusted. The approach requires a bit more initial investment than deterministic rounding, but it offers a higher level of protection against disclosure, and the statistical properties of resulting tables are clearer at this point. In principle, for example, any deterministic rounding rule could be learned by an inquirer and used in searching tables for opportunities for deductive disclosure. The same is not true of stochastic rounding, since the direction of rounding for any given cell is impossible to predict.

Both random and deterministic rounding introduce additional variation into tables. To the extent that the variation is small, the loss of information and the difficulty of interpreting the tables will also be small. There is no bias introduced by the random method in cell counts or marginal counts for the table in which it is applied. However, the added noise in the table may reduce the clarity of relationships among the tabulated attributes. The reduction is likely to be negligible for tables in which basic cell entries are large and the rounding algorithm does not yield extreme adjustments. Deterministic rounding will generally induce small bias into cell counts and marginal counts. Because very little is known about the (small) level of bias or imprecision induced by deterministic rounding, some new research on the topic is being mounted in Britain and Sweden.

One of the negative effects of rounding is that it can confuse the student of published count data. Marginal tabulations and cell counts are inconsistent in some British tables because each table is adjusted independently. The same problem could occur in using the stochastic rounding method unless adjustment is confined to cell entries at the lowest levels of aggregation of published tables.

FEEDBACK AND CONTROL MECHANISMS

Most well-thought-out adjustments to large-area statistics are unlikely to have much effect on the tables' interpretation. Cell entries are usually large and heterogeneous enough to sustain the induced noise without difficulty. Tables covering lower levels of aggregation, especially where cell entries must be suppressed or modified, are a bit more of a problem. Weak trends or relationships may be rendered considerably less visible, despite a guarantee of no bias in the average cell entry or marginal tabulation. Moreover, even if published tables only appear to depreciate in quality as a result of adjustment, that appearance may lead to a loss of public confidence in the tables and to frequent, if spurious, complaints among data users.

These issues suggest that formal feedback mechanisms ought to be set up to assay the impact of table adjustment on users. Less formal systems now exist, of course. Conferences and individual action have, according to census bureau staff, revealed some complaints by regular users of tabulated information (e.g., Barabba and Kaplan 1975; Newman 1975). But the information stemming from this irregular approach is often unavailable to the outside critic of census operations, and, more importantly, the information itself may be misleading on account of its informality. We expect, under Naval Lore, that 10 percent of users will never get the word, and of the remainder, 20 percent will fail to understand it. Complaints may be devoid of justification; legitimate criticism may not surface.

Only the Swedes appear to have experimented with a formal mechanism for feedback. The National Central Bureau of Statistics has conducted small surveys to gauge user reaction and problems stemming from its adjustment strategy. Though the survey results are inconclusive, they do furnish groundwork for better appraisal. This approach immediately suggests to us that one should not only solicit user's opinions but also document the behavioral aspects of use. User decisions or predictions based on adjusted data may differ from those based on unadjusted data. Simple double-blind experiments with real or simulated data can be used to compare the impact of various adjustment methods on user decisions. Comparative studies like these need not be expensive or elaborate, even with long-term follow-up. But they can notably enlarge our understanding of whether the reactions of users to the adjustment of tables are legitimate, and, more generally, our understanding of the quality of their interpretation of the data. Finally, the specific uses and users of social statistics have rarely been the subject of systematic research. Yet better information on each is essential for justifying the production of reports and balancing privacy demands against demands for data. The formal feedback work proposed here fits nicely into a larger program of empirical research on the topic.

The adjustment of tables produced less regularly or at the request of an outside data analyst warrants more elaborate control. This is especially true where, for example, the data concern rare events or traits and suppression or random modification can be very damaging. In these cases, the three-stage process described in chapter 6 can improve the scientific usefulness of published adjusted tables while reducing the possibility of harmful disclosures to a low level. The first stage is production of adjusted tables, where the adjustment strategy may be any of those described here and in the references cited earlier. The second stage consists of an examination of published adjusted tables by outside scientists exploring a particular set of hypotheses. Presumably they will use some limited set of adjusted tables as a basis for constructing evidence concerning the hypotheses of interest. However, the scientist cannot be entirely sure that the unadjusted tables will lead to the same conclusions or to exactly the same estimates of key statistical parameters. And this doubt leads us to the third and final stage of the process: an analysis of unadjusted tables done by the census agency but according to the outside researcher's prescription. The information given to the researcher from this analysis might be a simple verification of his initial conclusions, or it might be a statement of the existence, direction, and perhaps the magnitude of bias in the researcher's initial estimates of key parameters. Certainly this third stage may raise a few more problems of confidentiality, but the information supplied can be restricted and yet still useful to the outside researcher. At the very least, he or she is informed that statistical conclusions based on adjusted tables are consistent with conclusions based on more perfect tables.

This last strategy is not an unreasonable one for research institutions that seek to make the data collected useful to the social science community. It is cumbersome, but where sample lists are public and collateral information plentiful, there appear to be few options. Given the time lag in journal publication rates, it is unlikely to impose an intolerable hardship on the analyst, provided that the institution's analysis can be completed between the submission of the report and its publication. The strategy is likely to be useless for small-scale projects or for temporary research organizations. A good many research groups have neither interest in nor capability for tertiary analysis of this sort; many do not have a long life in any event. So some other agency, to which the data are entrusted, would have to take responsibility for the third stage.

Legal Assurances of Confidentiality

A state without the means of some change is without the means of its conservation.

EDMUND BURKE

In his book *The Natural History of Iceland,* the Danish historian Horrebow included a chapter entitled "Concerning Snakes," the entire text of which read: "No snakes of any kind are to be met with throughout the whole island." Such brevity provides a tempting model for the contents of this chapter. While some legal protections for confidential research information do exist, in relation to the breadth of social science inquiry these protections are quite limited. This chapter reviews the justifications for legal guarantees of confidentiality and the forms such legal protection has taken.

Our general purpose is to inform social scientists of the extent to which their promises of confidentiality will be upheld in the courts. Two cautions are in order. First, in exploring the boundaries of legal protection for research information, the discussion sometimes becomes rather technical, more suited to lawyers than to social scientists. Second, and more importantly, the information in this chapter may become dated rather quickly. Federal agencies are becoming more aware of the need for legal protection, and so legislative and regulatory changes can be expected. This chapter, then, should serve more as an overview of the various issues, than as a final statement regarding them. Those who wish to inquire further into this area

---

*Portions of this chapter have been presented at the Conference on Privacy Legislation and Social Research, organized by Paul Müller at the University of Cologne, under the auspices of the Committee of European Social Science Data Archives (CESSDA) and the International Federation of Data Organizations (IFDO).

should see Boness and Cordes (1973), Nejelski and Peyser (1975), Duncan (1976a), and others on whose work we have capitalized.

The Need for Protection

At least six arguments have been advanced to justify legal protection of confidential research data. The ethical and practical justifications have been mentioned earlier in connection with the development of statistical and procedural approaches to confidentiality. Advocates of legal protection also point to the inadequacy of existing means of protecting research information, the constitutional right to gather and communicate information, the trend toward increased protection for participants in research, and the relative benefit to society of protecting research information. Each of these arguments is reviewed below.

The ethical codes of most social science disciplines (see chapter 1) state that information obtained under a promise of confidentiality ought not be revealed without the permission of the respondent—a promise made ought to be kept. These ethical codes also discourage the use of one's professional position in a way that would result in harm or injury to persons who cooperate in furthering scientific inquiry. In this regard, legal recognition of promises of confidentiality merely formalizes ethical professional behavior.

The practical reasons for legal protection are closely related to the ethical reasons. Researchers depend on voluntary participation in their research. Since usually there are very few direct benefits to the individual respondents, researchers can offer little more than a promise of confidentiality as an inducement to participate. Without such assurances, some persons will be unwilling to cooperate in research. The empirical evidence summarized in chapter 3 indicates that a breach of a promise of confidentiality may result in reduced participation in research, or less valid responses by some members of the sample. Of course, this adverse impact on research is most dramatic when sensitive information is sought. By providing adequate protection for research information, researchers may obtain greater cooperation from research participants.

Legal protection for promises of confidentiality is also a necessary supplement to the existing means of protecting sensitive research information. As we indicated in chapters 4 and 5, procedural and statistical techniques provide sufficient protection for the research participants in some instances, but they are inadequate in others. Statistical procedures are not always appropriate; they can be complicated and expensive, and may be less attractive or impressive to the respondent than legal protection. Procedural devices, such as aliases, are not always feasible, can be very complicated, and are suitable only for depersonalized types of research. Legal protection, especially through legislation, can avoid some of these problems. Further, rather than relying on a single technique, one can integrate procedural and statistical solutions with legal protection to provide more comprehensive protection.

Some commentators have argued that the legal foundation for the protection of promises of confidentiality might be found in the constitutional right to gather and communicate information (Nejelski and Lerman 1971). Journalists were the first to contend that the constitutional guarantees of freedom of press and speech permit them to withhold the identities of their sources, arguing that their sources would be unavailable without such protection and the flow of news and ideas protected by the Constitution would then be disrupted (Beaver 1968). Legal scholars and researchers have extended this argument, contending that a breach of a researcher's promise of confidentiality will discourage participation in social research, thereby impeding the flow of research information protected by the Constitution (Nejelski and Lerman 1971; Blasi 1976). Recent court cases have cast doubt on the validity of this argument. The extent of the constitutional protection for research information is summarized in the following section on judicial protection.

Researchers also point to increasing legal obligations to protect the privacy and well-being of research participants in order to justify legal recognition of promises of confidentiality. Federal regulations require full and frank disclosure of foreseeable risks to the participants in research. This implies that the participant in social research must be informed of the risk that the sensitive information he shares with the researcher may be released to others and possibly used to his detriment. Keeping sensitive information confidential narrows the risk of subsequent harm to the participant. Further, the researcher's explicit promise of confidentiality becomes part of the agreement under which the respondent consents to participate, and obligates the researcher to honor this promise or suffer personal liability for the consequences of its breach. Legal protection of promises of confidentiality would allow researchers to collect sensitive information without increasing the risk of adverse consequences to the participant.

Recent federal statutes have also recognized the right to privacy of research participants. The Privacy Act of 1974 requires federal agencies to protect the privacy of the individuals on whom they have identifiable records, including research and statistical records. Recently proposed changes in the Privacy Act would strengthen privacy protection for research participants (Privacy Protection Study Commission 1977). Educational researchers working within the public schools face similar obligations, imposed by the Family Educational

Rights and Privacy Act of 1974 (Pub.L. 93-380). Under the Drug Abuse Office and Treatment Act of 1972 (Pub.L. 93-282), researchers in drug-abuse treatment centers now must maintain the confidentiality of patient information. In light of these increased legal obligations, many researchers feel that their assurances of confidentiality should be honored as a means of providing protection in similar areas of research.

Advocates of protection of research information have argued that greater societal benefits are to be obtained by permitting research information to remain confidential than by requiring disclosure through a subpoena. These arguments are frequently raised when identifiable records on research participants are subpoenaed. Prosecutors, grand juries, legislative bodies, civil litigants, and administrative agencies all can use their subpoena powers to compel disclosure of confidential research information. However, exercise of this power is rare.

A recent sample survey of members of nine social science professional organizations identified seventeen instances within the past twelve years in which researchers were confronted with subpoenas demanding information regarding research subjects, research data, or both (Carroll and Knerr 1976; Knerr 1976). In twelve instances, researchers resisted the subpoena. Even in these cases, other investigatory means of judicial inquiry could have continued. The rarity of subpoena for research information and the courts' ability to exploit alternative sources suggests that research information may clearly be placed beyond the reach of the subpoena process without severely impeding judicial inquiry.

One might turn the argument around to contend that the rarity of subpoenas for research information implies that such a remote threat to the research process does not justify a broad immunity from judicial inquiry. But this argument ignores the fact that we expect but cannot predict with certainty, based on the evidence at hand, that the research project will be disrupted by a subpoena, and that it will be difficult or impossible to adjust for biases introduced into the data as a result of disruption. The available evidence is covered in chapter 3 and a parallel problem is covered in chapter 6. Furthermore, this argument ignores the effects of a subpoena that are distal rather than proximal. The chilling effect on researchers other than the one subject to subpoena can be severe, judging by the reluctance of some well-regarded organizations to do research on controversial topics (U.S. Senate Committee on Labor and Public Welfare 1970). The threat of a subpoena has been used for harassment and intimidation by law enforcement officials seeking sensitive research information. For example, a 1973 survey of drug treatment centers by McNamara and Starr (1973) found that almost one-third of the centers responding to the survey reported at least one instance of difficulty in protecting the confidentiality of their records. The most frequently cited difficulty concerned requests for information from the police; almost 10 percent of the centers had actually been threatened with a subpoena. Similar instances have been reported by Nejelski and Lerman (1971) and by other authors cited in chapter 3. As the research community becomes aware of the risks of subpoena, funding agencies and institutional research review boards are likely to become less willing to support research in which the confidentiality of the information may be compromised. Considering societal interests in understanding social phenomena, then, the danger of chilling research activities may outweigh the interest of providing evidence in the context of individual litigation.

Researchers are understandably confused by these apparently conflicting demands; professional ethics and federal statutes encourage researchers to protect the privacy of their research participants while courts permit forced disclosure of confidential research information. If the researcher offers assurances of confidentiality to research participants, is presented with a subpoena and refuses to release the confidential research information, he or she faces the prospect of time-consuming litigation and possibly incarceration for contempt. Only by understanding the extent to which the law will protect sensitive research information can the researcher avoid jeopardizing the interests of research participants.

Since the forms that legal protection may take vary greatly, only major types are described here. They include protection through executive discretion, protection through the power of the judiciary to control admission of evidence, and legislative protection through special statutes.

Protection of Research Data through Executive Discretion

The most persistent and intimidating threats to researchers' assurances of confidentiality stem from the possibility of criminal prosecution of the research participants. Since the executive branch of government exercises broad discretion in criminal prosecution, some commentators have suggested that this discretion might be exercised to honor the confidentiality of research information (Nejelski et al. 1971, 1973, 1975). Under this form of protection, an officer of the executive branch of government agrees to permit the research to continue unhampered by the threat of a subpoena for criminal information.

Occasionally the executive branch has given immunity from prosecution to those providing the information to special research and investigatory efforts. A number of investigatory commissions have been offered executive assurances of immunity from prosecution. In 1972 then Governor Nelson Rockefeller appointed a commission to investigate the Attica prison riots. To encourage candid testimony, the commission members were given executive assurances that they would be immune from subpoena. This immunity was challenged when the New York State Attorney General's Office issued a subpoena for the commission's complete records while investigating the criminal liability resulting from the riot. In *Fisher* v. *Citizen's Committee* [339 N.Y.S. 2d 853 (1973)], the court found that the commission's records were protected by a "public interest privilege" and quashed the subpoena. Similarly, researchers working with the President's Commission on Civil Disorders, investigating the race riots of 1967, were assured that their information would be privileged. In each instance of such protection, there was a decision before data collection began that the information was sufficiently valuable that it could be excluded from the normal judicial process.

Related protection of research through executive discretion is found in some Alcohol Safety Action Programs supported by the Department of Transportation in the 1970s. These were state efforts to examine the problems associated with driving while intoxicated. Many states conducted highway surveys to measure the incidence and degree of driver intoxication. In Vermont, the surveys included both interviews with the automobile driver and breath sampling, requiring the assistance of the state police. Obtaining cooperation of motorists could have been difficult, since drivers found to have been drinking could have been prosecuted. To encourage cooperation, the governor of Vermont extended immunity from prosecution to motorists who participated in the survey. Instead of being arrested, the intoxicated driver was driven to his or her destination by the police, and no reports or criminal charges were filed (Perrine 1971).

Executive discretion to protect research information has also been exercised by local law enforcement officials. Such protection requires that the law enforcement community first be convinced that the benefits derived from the research are more important than criminal convictions. Then, formal or informal agreements may be reached with local prosecutors, exempting research information from use in criminal investigations. Nejelski and Lerman (1971) report that such agreements were made to protect drug research prior to the passage of federal legislation.

At the national level, similar protection could be sought in the form of prosecutorial guidelines for subpoenaing researchers. The Department of Justice has already issued guidelines governing subpoenas issued to news reporters (28 C.F.R. §50.10). Similar guidelines for researchers would recognize the importance of restricting law enforcement access to research information and would specify the limited situations in which such access would be permitted (Nejelski and Peyser 1975).

While such guidelines would reduce the uncertainty of the threat of a subpoena, this form of protection would still be inadequate for a good deal of social science research. In a large research project extending over several jurisdictions, the same agreement must be reached with all of the law enforcement officials involved. Otherwise, a different standard of protection will exist for research participants in different jurisdictions. Also, federal guidelines may not be honored by some state and local prosecutors who are less concerned with the long-range benefits of such research. Finally, such executive guidelines provide no protection against subpoenas originating with other branches of government; legislative and administrative subpoenas may still be issued. Similarly, the judiciary may permit a subpoena for research information in a civil (rather than criminal) lawsuit.

James Roegge has suggested that the formal doctrine of executive privilege be extended to protect research information collected by individuals engaged in governmental research (Note 1970). The executive branch exercises broad authority to promulgate regulations to promote efficient administration. Since such authority can be extended to govern the use of agency records, it was suggested that the agency could claim a privilege for agency records if subpoenaed. This source of protection would be most applicable in special cases where the research is associated directly with an executive agency mission. No instances have been found in which executive privilege was invoked to protect research information.

In any event, executive privilege is unlikely to be an important source of protection for researchers. Recent federal statutes, such as the Freedom of Information Act (Pub. L. 89-554), restrict the instances in which such a privilege could be asserted. The doctrine of executive privilege is in a state of flux, and the courts are cautious about acknowledging a privilege that has no clear statutory basis (Sofaer 1977).

In summary, executive discretion may still be an important source of protection for a few research studies of peculiar character, high visibility, and broad public support. However, such discretionary protection has been extended only in exceptional circumstances and does not provide adequate protection for the broad spectrum of social research activities. To the extent that it remains informal and limited to individual cases, executive discretion will be too idiosyncratic in its protection to offer much comfort to the research community. Protection of research through executive discretion is best regarded as a final alternative when protection through judicial or legislative means is unavailable.

Judicial Protection of Research Data

When a social scientist is confronted with a subpoena for confidential research information, a conflict may exist between the researcher's interest in preserving the confidentiality of the information and societal interests in obtaining evidence for the resolution of legal disputes. A court may issue a subpoena at any stage of the proceedings to compel either testimony by individuals or the production of records. The power of a court to issue a subpoena is somewhat restricted by the Constitution, statutes, and judicial precedent, but within these limits broad discretion exists in determining whether or not a subpoena should be issued (Nejelski and Lerman 1971). This section will examine the manner in which the courts have exercised this discretion when confronted with common law, constitutional, and evidentiary claims of privilege for researchers.

COMMON LAW RECOGNITION OF RESEARCH PRIVILEGE

Some researchers might expect the courts to protect confidential communications between the researcher and the research participant with the same professional privilege that the courts have recognized for communications between an attorney and his or her client. In expecting such a privilege, the researcher in fact is asking that the information he or she obtained from the research participant be excluded from the evidentiary fact-finding process that the judiciary must conduct. The courts must, in turn, weigh the professional obligation of the social scientist to the research participants against the duty of all citizens, including social scientists, to participate in the fact-finding process.

Traditionally, the judiciary has been reluctant to acknowledge any evidentiary privileges not recognized by federal or state legislation. Yet in rare instances the judiciary has recognized certain privileged relationships on its own authority. In his treatise on evidence, Wigmore (McNaughton Rev. 1972) expressed the four standards for judicial recognition of an evidentiary privilege as follows:

1. The communications must originate in a confidence that they will not be disclosed.

2. This element of confidentiality must be essential to the full and satisfactory maintenance of the relation between the parties.

3. The relation must be one which in the opinion of the community must be assiduously fostered.

4. The injury that would inure to the relation by the disclosure of the communications must be greater than the benefit gained from its contribution to the disposition of the litigation.

Though these criteria have no formal legal standing, they have been used as a guide in deciding whether an item of information ought to be made available to the court.

Confidential information offered by research participants appears to meet the first three standards for an evidentiary privilege. The communications between the researcher and the subjects are normally predicated upon assurances of confidentiality offered by the researcher, thereby meeting the first standard. The evidence cited in chapter 3 lends support to the belief that assurances of confidentiality, explicit or implicit, are essential to maintaining the relationship between the researcher and the research participants, thereby meeting the second standard.

The third standard is more difficult to assess, since the "opinion of the community" toward the confidential relationship between the researcher and research participants cannot be directly assessed for every piece of research. There is, to be sure, a substantial body of historical evidence bearing on public concerns about the confidentiality of U.S. Census records, and the development of census law to accommodate those interests (Davis 1971; Eckler 1972; and chapters 1 and 3). The customarily high response rates in public surveys bearing on health, economics, and manpower, and others described in chapter 2, and contemporary legislative mandates for evaluative surveys are indirect evidence of public interest in the relation. The research community's efforts to construct statistical and procedural devices to protect confidentiality reflect the researchers' view of the relationship. Empirical evidence on the public's attitudes suggests the attitudes are mixed. Public awareness of the need for confidentiality *and* the absence of concern among some groups have been demonstrated in recent field tests by the U.S. Census Bureau, by the Swedish Central Bureau of Statistics, and by Singer (1978a, 1978b). Post interview debriefing in both the U.S. Census research and Singer's work suggests that even if the assurance of privacy is not explicit, respondents expect the information to remain confidential. Evidence of the expectation that the information will remain confidential can be combined with evidence of the broad public approval for social science research to provide some support for meeting Wigmore's third standard.

The fourth standard presents the most difficult obstacle to a common law research privilege—the importance of the researcher-subject relationship must be weighed against the interest of a more informed litigation. In striking this balance, courts have generally favored correct disposition of the litigation over the creation of any privileges other than the attorney-client privilege. While an attorney-client privilege is considered an essential part of the advocacy process, courts are reluctant to permit other claims of privilege that would "shut out the light." Such evidentiary privileges frustrate the principle that every person is obligated to provide all relevant evidence in his or her possession upon subpoena. In a few notable instances, the judiciary has recognized a privileged relation between a priest and a penitent, between a social worker and a client, and between a psychiatrist and a patient, but the general attitude of the courts is that judicial recognition of professional privileges other than that between an attorney and his or her client should be avoided unless expressly established by statutory law or by the Constitution (Note 1970). Thus, the researcher can expect little sympathy from the courts in asserting a common law right to an evidentiary privilege.

Because of the poor prospects for recognition of a common law privilege for researchers, some have sought other means of justifying judicial recognition of promises of confidentiality. Two arguments have been advanced: first, that such a privilege is protected by the Constitution; and second, that courts may honor such a privilege under the broad judicial discretion permitted by the federal rules of evidence. The following remarks examine these two approaches in terms of two stereotypical cases—*U.S.* v. *Doe (Appeal of Samuel Popkin,* 460 F.2d 328 (1st Cir. 1972), *cert. denied* 411 U.S. 909 (1973), and *Richards of Rockford* v. *Pacific Gas and Electric* (71 F.R.D. 388 (N.D. Cal. 1976).

THE CONSTITUTIONAL BASIS OF EVIDENTIARY PRIVILEGE—*U.S.* v. *DOE* (APPEAL OF SAMUEL POPKIN)

An evidentiary privilege based on the Constitution would be more advantageous to a researcher than a common law privilege. Even if recognized, a common law privilege would be determined by the courts on a case-by-case basis. In each case, the judge would have to decide whether the social value of the particular research project was more important than the contested information in the particular context of the litigation. Since the outcome of such a process would be uncertain at the time the researcher was recruiting the participants, any assurances of confidentiality would have to be well qualified.

A constitutional basis for the protection of social research would avoid this discretionary aspect of a common law privilege. If a researcher's assurances of confidentiality were within the protection of the Constitution, the constitutional dimension of the privilege would require that the research information always be withheld, without regard to the importance of the evidence to the litigation. Thus, assurances of confidentiality could be more straightforward.

Samuel Popkin, a political scientist at Harvard University, was the first defendant to assert a constitutional basis for protecting confidential communications to a scholar. In 1972 Professor Popkin was called before a grand jury investigating the release of the "Pentagon Papers" and asked to reveal certain information he obtained while involved in his research on the war in Indochina. He refused to answer questions relating to conversations with individuals to whom he had promised confidentiality, arguing that the breach of these promises would threaten his scholarly research. Because of his refusal to identify those with whom he had spoken, Popkin was cited for contempt and jailed for eight days, until the grand jury was dismissed.

In appealing the contempt citation, Popkin asserted that the Constitution protected scholarly information under the first amendment guarantees of freedom of the press and freedom of speech. He claimed that in the course of scholarly research it is sometimes necessary to promise that the identities of those who provide sensitive information will not be revealed. To permit a grand jury to breach these promises of confidentiality would deter other sources from furnishing such information, thereby restricting the free flow of information protected by the First Amendment of the Constitution. The First Circuit Court of Appeals recognized this interest in noting:

His privilege, if it exists, exists because an important public interest in the continued flow of information to scholars about public problems would stop if scholars could be forced to disclose the sources of such information. Appellant is a political scientist. As is true of other behavioral scientists, his research technique rests heavily on inquiry of others as to their attitudes, knowledge, or experience. Often such inquiry is predicated on a relationship of confidence.

Nevertheless, the appellate court rejected Popkin's constitutional argument, pointing out that the underlying rationale for such a claim lies not in the importance of protecting the sources per se but in the importance of preserving the flow of information from the sources, via the scholars, to the public domain. This rationale would not immunize a scholar from testifying about conversations with those who are *not* his or her sources. Since the questions Popkin declined to answer involved conversations with other scholars, the court held that even if the First Amendment claim were recognized, Popkin would have still have been obligated to answer the questions of the grand jury.

A later Supreme Court case concerning newsmen, *Branzburg* v. *Hayes* [408 U.S. 665 (1972)], clarifies the extent to which the courts will honor a First Amendment claim of an evidentiary privilege. In

Branzburg, three news reporters appealed the contempt citations they received upon refusing to identify informants who had given them confidential information concerning criminal activities. All of the reporters contended that the grand jury's interest in obtaining the information was outweighed by their need to preserve confidential relationships. They argued that compelling newsmen to testify before grand juries disrupts a free flow of information to the public and abridges the freedoms of speech and the press guaranteed by the First Amendment. In a five-to-four decision, a majority of the Supreme Court rejected these arguments and ordered the reporters to appear and testify before their respective grand juries. Justice White, speaking for the majority, stated:

We perceive no basis for holding that the public interest in law enforcement and insuring effective grand jury proceedings is insufficient to override the consequential, but uncertain, burden on newsgathering that is said to result from insisting that reporters, like other citizens, respond to relevant questions put to them in the course of a valid grand jury investigation or criminal trial.

The Court tempered this position somewhat by permitting newsmen to refuse to answer irrelevant questions and questions asked in bad faith, and suggested that in certain other situations such a burden on the freedom of the press might not be justified.

Justice Powell, who cast the fifth and deciding vote, noted that a newsman could ask the court to dismiss the subpoena when:

the newsman is called upon to give information bearing only a remote and tenuous relationship to the subject of the investigation, or if he has some other reason to believe that his testimony implicates confidential source relationships without a legitimate need of law enforcement.

While this case concerns newsmen rather than research scientists, it has direct implications for researchers seeking to justify an evidentiary privilege based on the First Amendment to the Constitution. Researchers have assumed many of the same functions as journalists, causing some observers to characterize researchers as "slow journalists" (Nejelski and Lerman 1971; Blasi 1976). Both professions involve the communication of ideas. The concept of academic freedom combines many of the fundamental concepts of freedom of speech and freedom of the press enshrined in the Constitution. The Court noted in *Branzburg:*

Freedom of the press . . . is not confined to newspapers and periodicals . . . [but includes] pamphlets and leaflets [and] comprehends every sort of publication which affords a vehicle of information and opinion. . . . The information function assured by representatives of the organized press in the present cases is also performed by lecturers, political pollsters, novelists, academic researchers and dramatists.

Thus, if the privilege for researchers corresponds to the privilege afforded newsmen in *Branzburg,* researchers will be compelled to disclose information in situations where the questions are relevant and material to criminal activity and are asked in good faith. Only in instances of bad faith or harassment, or where the information sought is irrelevant to the investigation, does the Constitution protect such confidential communications. Of course, this determination will not be made until the case has been heard in court. As Justice Powell noted in his concurring opinion in *Branzburg:* "The balance of . . . vital constitutional and societal interests on a case-by-case basis accords with the tried and traditional way of adjudicating such questions." Such a narrow and indefinite privilege is unlikely to satisfy research participants who seek assurance that their communications will not be used against them.

The *Branzburg* decision also provides guidance to researchers who wish to establish stronger protection for research information. First, the court in *Branzburg* simply was not convinced that the flow of information to the public would be constricted in the absence of a newsman's privilege. If researchers can provide persuasive evidence that the absence of a privilege disrupts the flow of research information, that research participants are unwilling to provide necessary information without some firm assurance of confidentiality, one of the barriers to obtaining such a privilege for researchers might be removed. Second, the court in *Branzburg* also placed great emphasis on society's interest in obtaining incriminating evidence in a judicial proceeding, feeling that this interest was greater than the need to have press reports from confidential sources. Again, it appears that researchers must be able to demonstrate that social science research is sufficiently important to override the need for disclosure of confidential information on identifiable research participants in a court of law.

More importantly, the Court pointed out that Congress has the authority to determine whether a statutory privilege is necessary and to fashion the standards for one. Nejelski and Finsterbusch (1973) have viewed this as a reminder to the social science community that it has the right to lobby for researchers' privilege in the state and national legislatures.

JUDICIAL DISCRETION TO ADMIT EVIDENCE—*RICHARDS OF ROCKFORD* v. *PACIFIC GAS AND ELECTRIC*

The refusal of the Court in *Branzburg* to acknowledge a broad evidentiary privilege for newsmen (and, by analogy, for researchers), is consistent with a trend in the judiciary to avoid inflexible determinations and grants of absolute privilege. Such sweeping privileges are thought to be inappropriate for resolving the variety of problems in which the interests of confidentiality conflict with the evidentiary needs of the courts.

Instead, the courts prefer some form of the balancing test mentioned earlier in the context of a common law privilege. Such a standard affords the courts discretionary power to admit or reject evidence based on the particular facts of the case. Trial judges have broad discretion in supervising the admission of evidence into the record. The exercise of this discretion requires the courts to reconcile the interests of the private litigant in obtaining the research information with the interests of the research community in maintaining confidentiality.

A case that demonstrates several features of this judicial discretion is *Richards of Rockford* v. *Pacific Gas and Electric* [71 F.R.D. 388 (N.D. Cal. 1976)]. In that instance, Richards brought a civil suit against Pacific Gas and Electric for the latter's refusal to make final payment on equipment supplied by Richards, and for allegedly defamatory statements made by employees of the utility company. The utility company had refused to pay, claiming that the requirements of the contract had not been met. Coincidentally, a Harvard professor and his research assistant had been conducting interviews with company employees to determine how public utilities develop policy on environmental quality. Richards, in attempting to collect evidence that might strengthen his defamation case, requested that the researchers supply a list of the employees interviewed and information from the interviews. When the researcher refused, pointing out that the employees had been promised that the information would remain confidential, Richards asked the court to issue a subpoena for the information. The researchers' attorneys objected to the subpoena, again arguing that statements made in confidence to the researcher were protected by the Constitution against forced disclosure.

In assessing the case, the court examined the professor's academic position, the purposes of the research, and the journal publications emanating from the specific research project in order to establish the general credibility of his claim to be a researcher. Rather than examine the case in terms of an absolute privilege based on the Constitution, the court acknowledged the analogy between researchers and newsmen and turned to another Supreme Court case, *Baker* v. *F & F Investment Co.* [470 F.2d 778 (2d Cir. 1972)], to guide its decision. The *Baker* decision was handed down shortly after *Branzburg* and establishes a qualified privilege for newsmen in civil litigation. In *Baker,* the Court noted:

While we recognize there are cases—few in number to be sure—where First Amendment rights must yield, we are still mindful of the preferred position which the First Amendment occupies in the pantheon of freedom. Accordingly, though a journalist's right to protect confidential sources may not take precedence over the overriding and compelling interest, we are still of the view that there are circumstances, at the very least in civil cases, in which the public's interest in nondisclosure of a journalist's confidential sources outweighs the public and private interest in compelled testimony.

In considering the journalist's right to maintain the confidentiality of his or her sources, the *Baker* court inquired about the nature of the proceeding, whether the journalist was involved directly in the litigation, whether the information was available from other sources, and whether the information sought went to the central issue of the litigation. The Court held that in this instance the First Amendment rights asserted by the newsman outweighed the rights of the private litigant and permitted the newsman to withhold the identity of his source.

In the *Richards* case, the Federal district court relied on very similar standards, balancing the "plaintiff's interest in satisfying the discovery request" (i.e., obtaining information which could help his case) against the "public interest in maintaining confidential relationships between academic researchers and their sources." The court found that neither the researcher nor his assistant was a party to this civil action, that the requested information was not relevant to the central issue of the case (breach of a contract), and that alternative means of obtaining the requested information did exist. Thus, the court found the balance to be in favor of honoring the researcher's pledge of confidentiality. The court was careful to observe that it is within a district court's customary authority to compel or not to compel a researcher's testimony, and that its decision to honor the promises of confidentiality did not rest on a constitutional theory of a researcher-subject privilege. Of course, the courts are much more likely to grant subpoenas for data on anonymous respondents when adequate means have been taken to protect their identity and there is no real need for identifiers. See *Lora* v. *Board of Education of the City of New York* [74 F.R.D. 565 (E.D.N.Y. 1977)].

So in some instances, at least, the courts may exercise their discretion to exclude evidence derived from a confidential research relationship, finding that the social costs in compelling disclosure override the interest of the individual litigant in obtaining the information. Most likely, courts will honor assurances of confidentiality by a researcher in instances of civil litigation in which the researcher is not a direct participant, in which the information is not directly relevant to the central issue of the litigation, and in which the information may be obtained through other means. However, as mentioned earlier, this is a very narrow privilege that must be decided on a case-by-case basis as a matter of judicial discretion. The uncertainty of such a privilege will be difficult to explain to many research participants and virtually impossible to explain to some groups. Any attempt to provide an accurate, detailed statement regarding confidentiality is unlikely to encourage cooperation; the detail and language may be sufficiently formidable to provoke suspicion or confusion. Both problems are amenable to experimental tests.

Statutory Protection of Confidential Research Information

Statutory protection of confidential research information has several advantages over the judicial protections just discussed. A statutory privilege permits a uniform standard of protection that can be drafted to correspond to a legislature's specific policy interests. Furthermore, a statutory guarantee of confidentiality gives tangible assurance to research participants that sensitive information would not be revealed, explicitly informing researchers and participants of the limits of its protection. Knerr (1978) and Madden and Lessin (1978) provide a review of state laws that protect research. Here, we cover the federal statutes pertinent to social research:

- the Privacy Act of 1974;
- Section 303(a) of the Public Health Services Act, as amended in 1974;
- Section 502(c) of the Controlled Substances Act;
- Section 408 of the Drug Abuse Office and Treatment Act of 1972, as amended in 1974;
- Section 524(a) of the Crime Control Act of 1973;
- other selected federal statutes.

EVALUATIVE CRITERIA

Because existing statutory protection is so varied, it is helpful to establish several criteria for assessing the quality of such protection. In proposing a model privilege statute for researchers, Nejelski and Peyser (1975) have suggested a number of important characteristics of statutory protection. The following list of questions extends their results to provide a framework for evaluating the adequacy of the protection afforded by the various statutes. The evaluative criteria have been divided into four general topics: scope of protection, materials protected, persons protected, and procedural issues.

A. Scope of protection (qualified or absolute privilege)

1. To what extent does the statute permit the social scientist to resist a subpoena for confidential research information?

2. To what extent does the statutory protection interfere with subsequent research activities? Does the statutory protection provide for the release of identifiable information to permit independent secondary analysis of the results? Does it permit record linkage and similar mechanisms used in extensions of the research? Are the obligations of the secondary researchers in protecting the privacy of the research participants specified by the statute?

3. Does the statute permit specialized and nondisruptive audit of the research activity, including verification of information from identified respondents? Does it specify the auditor's responsibility in protecting the privacy of research participants?

Questions regarding the scope of the statutory protection are critical, since the answers determine the extent to which the confidentiality of the research information can be assured. The scope of protection offered by a statute may be either an absolute privilege, which protects the research information under all circumstances, or a qualified privilege, which specifies the circumstances under which the information is not protected. As Nejelski and Lerman (1971) have noted, almost all privileges are qualified to some extent. Frequently, statutes permit disclosure of information to law enforcement personnel or when a subpoena has been issued by a court of proper jurisdiction. The extent of statutory protection can be defined by identifying the circumstances in which protection will be denied.

The first question concerns the extent to which information may be withheld when release is sought for reasons unrelated to research, the fundamental issue of statutory protection. However, statutory protection may also be analyzed in terms of the extent to which it interferes with subsequent research and auditing activities. These issues are raised by the second and third sets of questions. An absolute privilege permits the primary researcher to withhold the information from all who seek its release, including those who wish to gain the maximum research benefit from the data either by extensions of the research or by reanalysis of the existing data set. Managerial audits by governmental agencies are also restricted by an absolute privilege. Thus, by examining all three sets of questions, it is possible to determine the extent to which confidential research information is protected from disruptive inquiry while permitting access for subsequent research and audit activities.

B. Material protected by the statute

1. In which stages of data processing is the confidential research information protected by the statute: Raw data with

individual identifiers still attached? More refined research products, which cannot be associated with individuals? Drafts of manuscripts to be submitted for publication?

2. Are certain kinds of information—such as the identities of the research participants or the research data itself—excluded from protection?

3. Is incidental information collected in the course of the research but not directly relevant to the research goal within the protection offered by the statute?

The second set of criteria bears on the variety of research materials that might be subpoenaed. At the earliest stages of the research, raw data will normally include both the respondent's identifying information and substantive research information. At subsequent stages, the identifiers are separated from the raw data, the data are consolidated in statistical form, and general conclusions are expressed in a published report. It is important to know which stages of the research process are protected by the statute. The greatest vulnerability may be in the early stages of the research process, soon after the sensitive information has been gathered but before any steps have been taken to remove the individual identifiers. The later stages of the process, involving drafts of unfinished manuscripts, notes, and memoranda, may pose little threat to the individual participants in the particular instance. Nevertheless, where it is physically possible to recreate the linkage between identifier and substantive data, risks may still be present. A statute may protect all research information, or it may limit protection to the unprocessed raw data.

Similarly, a statutory privilege may extend only to certain kinds of information. For example, it may protect the identities of the research participants but permit release of the unidentified research data. Or a statute may protect the research data while permitting access to the names of those individuals participating in the study. Finally, a statute may permit the release of both names of participants and unidentified individual research data, so long as the two cannot be linked.

Occasionally, the research staff will uncover sensitive information that is beyond the strict bounds of the area of research inquiry. For example, in the course of responding to a field interview, a participant may incidentally confess some past criminal action, even though such information was not being solicited. If the statutory protection is construed narrowly to include only the formal research data set, any sensitive information that does not fall within the anticipated area of research will be vulnerable to a subpoena. In *People* v. *Newman* [32 N.Y. 2d 379 (1973)] for instance, the doctor-patient privilege was interpreted as protecting only the information communicated to the doctor in the course of actual medical treatments, not information obtained in the nontherapeutic aspects of the professional relationship. Similarly, a statute could be narrowly construed to protect only information pertinent to the goal of the research or to protect only recorded research data, and not the informal verbal communications or observations that go unrecorded.

C. Persons protected by the statute

    1. Which persons are authorized to exercise the statutory privilege for research information: The researcher? The research participant? Both?

    2. Does the statute attempt to define "researcher"?

    3. May members of the research staff other than the principal investigator exercise the privilege? May anyone having knowledge of sensitive research information exercise the privilege, whether or not this person is part of the research staff?

The third topic concerns the specifications of persons authorized to exercise the statutory privilege. Although the statutory protection is provided for the benefit of the research participants, there are compelling reasons why the researcher should be the one to exercise the privilege. In instances where the purpose of the subpoena is to learn the identity of a research participant, only the researcher can properly protect the identity of the participant. Even in instances where the identity of a participant is already known, the researcher should be the one to exercise the privilege to withhold information, since he or she controls access to the information. Thus, it becomes important to examine the statutory definition of "research" or "researcher," for it is only in this context that assurances of protection under the statute may be properly offered.

Protection may be defined in very narrow terms, extending to persons working only in specific agencies or on specific research topics, or only to persons meeting certain requirements such as academic degrees. Or, broader protection may be extended to all individuals working in a specific area of research, whether or not they meet the stricter personal qualifications mentioned above. In specifying which individuals will be permitted to exercise the privilege, the statute must attempt to provide adequate protection for research while assuring that the privilege will not be abused by counterfeit researchers.

Assuming that protection can properly be limited to legitimate researchers and research projects, one must determine which individuals in addition to the principal investigator should be permitted to exercise the privilege. A privilege that protects the principal investigator but permits compelled testimony by the research assistants is useless. The privilege might also extend to other research scientists who become involved in auxiliary research efforts that employ the sensitive information.

D. Procedural issues

    1. What administrative procedures exist to award or grant

statutory protection? If an application for the statutory privilege is required, are the application procedures clear? How is the application verified? Is administrative discretion in awarding the privilege exercised fairly?

2. How is the statutory privilege enforced? What protections exist to guard researchers and participants against harassment and informal threats? What sanctions apply against researchers who abuse the privilege, or against outsiders who penetrate records in violation of the statutory protection?

3. How is the right to statutory protection waived?

The final list of questions concerns the procedural mechanisms for implementing the statutory protection. Examination of such procedural mechanisms is crucial, since adequate statutory protection may be rendered ineffective if it is difficult to obtain, awarded unevenly, or lacks the measures for enforcement.

The first set of criteria concerns the way in which the researcher obtains the statutory protection. If it is extended to a broad class of researchers having certain qualifications or working in certain areas, then the research data they collect can be protected automatically. More likely the protection will be more restrictive, requiring a researcher to apply for the privilege. In this case, the extent of the protection should be clear and unambiguous, the application process must be efficient, and if administrative discretion is necessary to approve the application, this discretion must be exercised in a fair manner. A means of verifying the information contained in the application should also exist.

The second set of criteria concerns the enforcement of the protection. Usually the statute will permit the researcher to refuse to honor a court-ordered subpoena, the statute barring any contempt proceedings. But this may be ineffective in guarding against informal threats. The statute might contain sanctions for such harassment. Sanctions might also be included for researchers who abuse the protection.

Finally, some means of waiving the privilege should be noted. Since the protection is for the ultimate benefit of the research participant, it seems reasonable that this power be vested in the participant, but the researcher may also be involved in the waiver process.

Although these evaluative criteria are presented in the context of an analysis of statutory protection of research information, they may also be employed to analyze the characteristics of judicial protection or protection through executive discretion. These issues are introduced in the context of a discussion of statutory protection because the statutes are more explicit in describing the limits of the protection. Several federal statutes will be examined. Rather than analyze the statutes point by point in terms of these evaluative criteria, we will discuss only the particularly notable attributes of the protection offered by each statute.

PROTECTION UNDER THE PRIVACY ACT OF 1974

For the most part, statutory protection of research information is limited to federal statutes that have been drafted with attention to the specific problems of research records. Before considering several of these, it is worthwhile to consider the extent to which research data is protected by the Privacy Act of 1974 (Pub.L. 93-579, codified at 5 U.S.C.A. §552a). Though not drafted for the explicit purpose of protecting research records, the Privacy Act regulates all record systems maintained by federal agencies, including research and statistical record systems. Careful analysis of the extent to which it protects research information is merited, since it is a cornerstone of federal statutory protection of individual privacy.

The Privacy Act of 1974 attempts to protect a citizen's right to privacy by regulating the collection, management, and disclosure of personal information maintained by government agencies. It permits individuals to learn of personal information maintained by federal agencies, to gain access to these records, and to challenge information that may be incorrect. It also restricts the kinds of identifiable information that an agency may collect and maintain. Finally, and perhaps most importantly, the Privacy Act regulates the disclosure of personal information by federal agencies. By requiring written consent for disclosure of identifiable research records, the Privacy Act could be an important source of protection for research records. We do not attempt to evaluate the broader purposes of the Privacy Act. Rather, this analysis examines the extent to which the Privacy Act protects sensitive research data by restricting the disclosure of information. (See generally Cecil 1978, chapter 15 of Privacy Protection Study Commission 1977 and Hulett 1975).

The scope of protection offered by the Privacy Act is narrow. The Act regulates only records maintained by federal agencies, prohibiting disclosure of any individually identifiable record to a person or another agency without the written consent of the individual to whom the record pertains. Thus private record systems or those maintained by state or local governments without federal assistance are exempt from these restrictions. Furthermore, most research record systems developed through federal funding (contracts or grants) but not directly maintained by the funding agency are beyond the protection of the Privacy Act. Only if a federal agency subcontracts for a record system that the agency itself would otherwise have established and maintained is the nonfederal record system regulated by the Privacy Act.

Protection for research records is further narrowed by eleven exceptions to the general rule that written consent must be obtained for the disclosure of agency records. Some of these exceptions permit intrusions that have been of particular concern to researchers. For example, the Privacy Act permits disclosures "pursuant to the order of a court of competent jurisdiction." Consequently, the Privacy Act offers no immunity to research records that may contain information on illegal activities and that may be subject to subpoena. In fact, another exception permits disclosure of records to other agencies for law enforcement purposes without the formality of a subpoena. Identifiable records also may be transferred within an agency to employees who need the record to perform their duties, without regard to the purposes for which the record was obtained. Presumably this would permit research records to be used by agency personnel for administrative purposes. Finally, an exemption for "routine use" of identifiable records is sufficiently vague to permit access even by nonfederal employees to specified record systems.

The greatest problem with the Privacy Act is that its restrictions are difficult to enforce. This is especially true in the case of confidential research records. The Privacy Act grants standing to an individual suing for damages in federal court whenever an agency "fails to comply with [the restrictions on disclosure] . . . in such a way as to have an adverse effect on the individual." Such a remedy does not permit the researcher to sue for enforcement of the act on behalf of research participants, does not permit injunctive relief to prevent or forestall improper disclosure, and requires proof of an "adverse effect," and proof that the agency acted in a manner that was "intentional and willful." Therefore, the Privacy Act, with its narrow scope, numerous exceptions, and ineffective enforcement mechanism, offers little protection to research records that may contain sensitive information.

Nevertheless, the restrictions of the Privacy Act are sufficient to impede researcher access to agency records for social research activities.[1] Unless the researcher can invoke one of the exceptions to the Privacy Act, access to identifiable agency records is forbidden unless the consent of the individual is obtained. While exceptions to the Privacy Act may restrict protection of confidential research records, they also represent the only means by which researchers may obtain access to regulated record systems. The exception most likely to aid researchers permits agencies to disclose information for purposes of statistical research if the record is transferred in a form that is not individually identifiable. In fact, records that are not individually identifiable are not regulated by the Privacy Act. This suggests that the statistical and procedural techniques discussed in chapters 4 and 5, which permit meaningful analysis of data while preserving the anonymity of the respondents, can be employed when the Privacy Act restricts the release of identifiable records (see also Jabine 1975).

Merely removing the name or individual identifier from the record usually will be a sufficient guarantee of anonymity to permit disclosure under the exemption for statistical research. However, this may be inadequate if public records are available to aid in identifying the anonymous data. The exemption states that disclosure is permitted only if the record is "in a form which is not individually identifiable." The Office of Management and Budget guidelines for the Privacy Act interpret this restriction to mean that the identity of the individual cannot be deduced from tabulations or other presentations of the information. Where such deductive disclosure is a threat, the agency will have to take precautions beyond the simple deletion of individual identifiers (see chapters 6 and 7).

When the research requires identifiable agency records, other excemptions to the disclosure restriction can aid the researcher in obtaining their release. For example, the Privacy Act contains an exception for disclosures of information required by the Freedom of Information Act. Prior to the implementation of the Privacy Act, researchers were able to obtain identifiable records from federal agencies unless the disclosure involved a "clearly unwarranted invasion of personal privacy," a more lenient standard than the strict prohibition of the Privacy Act. Under this exception, the researcher could obtain the release of identifiable records by showing a compelling public interest in the research and a minimal invasion of privacy for the identified individuals. *(Getman* v. *NLRB* [450 F.2d 670 (D.C. Cir. 1971)], *Department of Air Force* v. *Rose* [425 U.S. 352 (1976)]. However, reliance on the Freedom of Information Act to gain access to identifiable data assumes that the disclosure policies under the Freedom of Information Act have remained unaffected by the implementation of the Privacy Act. The impact of the Privacy Act on the Freedom of Information Act is still a matter of speculation, with observers divided on whether the adoption of the Privacy Act will result in greater restrictions on disclosure under the Freedom of Information Act.

The "routine use" exception mentioned above diminishes the protection of research data, but it could also be used by researchers to access identifiable agency records. If an agency was to define "research and statistical analysis" as a routine use of an agency record system, researchers outside the agency could gain access to identifiable records without obtaining the consent of the individuals to whom the records pertain. In fact, in its Privacy Act regulations, the Department of Health, Education and Welfare acknowledges statistical analysis by qualified individuals as a "routine use" for some record systems [Title 45 C.F.R. §5, Appendix B (101)]. If this designation is extended to the record system of interest to the researcher, and if he or she is found to be "qualified" by the secretary of HEW, the researcher may have access to the identifiable agency record system for research purposes without obtaining the consent of the individuals.

Another exemption that may assist the researcher seeking identifiable information permits the transfer of identifiable agency records to the Census Bureau. This exception allows the Bureau to accept identifiable agency records to perform certain statistical analyses for researchers outside the Bureau who are unable to gain access to these records. The Interagency Record Link Study described in chapter 2 is an example of such a procedure. Under the Privacy Act, the Bureau is permitted to continue to act as a brokerage agent to perform such research (Jabine 1975).

The Privacy Act also permits the release of agency records to the General Accounting Office for audits of agency programs. The Privacy Act, in permitting a broad exemption for auditing purposes, offers no guidance in finding ways to minimize the intrusions into the privacy of research participants.

Except for disclosure under the Freedom of Information Act, all of the methods of disclosure discussed above are at the discretion of the agency maintaining the records. Since the agency may wish to maintain the confidentiality of the research records, disclosure to researchers under these exceptions can be successfully resisted by the agency. Because the cooperation of the agency is critical, the Privacy Act does little to assure uniform access to agency records for research purposes.

Once the agency transfers the record to another agency, or to an individual researcher, the agency loses all control over the manner in which the record is maintained. The Privacy Act does not require the transferees to maintain the record in such a way as to protect the confidentiality of the research participant. While this may be cited by an agency in support of its refusal to release data, it is also an indication of the lack of consideration by the Privacy Act of even the elementary needs of research record systems.

Although most of our discussion concerning the Privacy Act has been directed toward the first evaluative criterion—the scope of the protection—the other issues deserve some comment. As mentioned above, the Privacy Act protects only research records that contain a name or other identifying characteristics assigned to an individual. Agency records without identifying characteristics are not regulated by the Privacy Act and may be obtained through normal agency channels (see Jabine 1975 for examples) or through the Freedom of Information Act. The Privacy Act protects individual citizens having identifiable records with federal agencies; and either the agency or the individual may invoke the protection to avoid an improper disclosure.

The Act established criminal penalties against officers or employees of any agency who knowingly and willingly disclose confidential information without the consent of the individual. Agencies failing to meet the standards set by the Act are subject to civil suits. Criminal penalties are also provided for persons who knowingly request information under false pretenses. Each is discussed in detail by Nycum (1976).

We have examined the effectiveness of the Privacy Act only in terms of its impact on research records. Although the Act restricts access to records for research purposes and fails to protect confidential research information adequately, this was an unintended consequence. The Privacy Act was drafted with primary attention to the problems of administrative record systems rather than research record systems. Since no distinction was made between identifiable research records and administrative records, the single set of regulations extends to each. Consequently, some of the regulations that are sensible when applied to administrative records seem ill-conceived when applied to research records. The Privacy Protection Study Commission (1977) recently suggested that separate systems of regulation be established for administrative and research record systems. Establishing a clear boundary between research and administrative records will permit regulations to be tailored to assure adequate protection and access for both kinds of record systems.

PROTECTION UNDER THE PUBLIC HEALTH SERVICES ACT AND THE CONTROLLED SUBSTANCES ACT

The statute most frequently cited as providing protection for nongovernmental social science research is found in §303(a) of the Public Health Services Act (Pub. L. 91-513) as amended in 1974 [Pub. L. 93-282, codified at 42 U.S.C.A. §242(a)]. This statute permits the secretary of Health, Education and Welfare to:

authorize persons engaged in research on mental health, including research on the use and effect of alcohol and other psychoactive drugs, to protect the privacy of individuals who are the subject of such research by withholding from all persons not connected with the conduct of such research the names or other identifying characteristics of such individuals. Persons so authorized to protect the privacy of such individuals may not be compelled in any Federal, State, or local civil, criminal, administrative, legislative, or other proceedings to identify such individuals.

The scope of protection offered by this statute is still open to interpretation. The recent federal regulations [44 *Federal Register* (4 April 1979, pp. 20382–20387)] do not define "mental health research," but do define "research" broadly to mean any "systematic study directed toward new or fuller knowledge of the subject studied." This, of course, will include most scientifically designed mental health studies, surveys, and evaluations. Within these areas, unless the participant agrees to the release of the information or release is required by a medical emergency, a researcher who has received a "confidentiality certificate" from the secretary of Health, Education and Welfare, may refuse to comply with a subpoena issued by any branch of government.

The regulations also define which research materials are protected; the researcher can withhold "names or other identifying characteristics" of the research subjects. The regulations are quite thorough in protecting the identities of research participants. In addition to withholding names and addresses, researchers may withhold "any other item or combination of data about a research subject which could reasonably lead directly or indirectly by reference to other information to identification of that research subject." This broad definition of "identifying characteristics" will protect those research data which could lead to the deductive disclosure of the identity of the research participant.

Still, the statute protects only identifying information and not the research data themselves. Little comfort is offered to those researchers who collect sensitive or incriminating information from persons known to the authorities. A prosecutor who knows the name of a research participant can obtain a subpoena for the release of all research information pertaining to that person (Knerr 1976). The statute does not provide an explicit assurance of confidentiality in such a situation, and it is up to the courts to determine whether such protection was intended by Congress. In the only case to address this issue, *People* v. *Still* [369 N.Y.S. 2d 759 (1975)], the court interpreted a similarly worded statute to protect only identifying information. The court upheld a subpoena requesting all of the records at a methadone-treatment clinic associated with an identified patient who had been charged with illegal possession of methadone. However, the court also noted that the defendant had waived any privilege that existed, since he claimed that the methadone had been issued as part of the treatment program and thereby identified himself with the program. Without such a waiver, courts may interpret this statutory protection more broadly.

The obligation of the researcher to protect the research participant under the Public Health Services Act remains unclear. The Act permits the researcher to protect identifying information, but the researcher is under no statutory obligation to do so. The statute does not restrict voluntary disclosure of identifying information by researchers. When confronted with a subpoena, the researcher may choose to disclose the identifying information, thereby waiving the protection without seeking the permission of the research participant. While there is no known instance in which a researcher having access to such a privilege yielded to a subpoena, the possibility of such an occurrence is disturbing. The regulations attempt to overcome this limitation in two ways. First, the recipient of a Confidentiality Certificate must provide the secretary of HEW with written assurances that the Certificate will be used to protect the identities of research participants. Second, the research participants must be informed of the extent to which the researcher will protect their identities. Such assurances will certainly make researchers more aware of their obligations under the statute. However, the sanctions to be imposed against a researcher who violates the terms of this agreement are not clear. Neither the regulations nor the statute provide criminal sanctions. Presumably, the research participant who is harmed by the improper release of identifying information will have to pursue his or her own civil remedy. However, such remedies are difficult to enforce (Teitlebaum, 1979), and may be invoked by a research participant only after the harm has occurred. The statute provides no means of preventing the release of identifying information.

The regulations require the release of identifiable information when needed to conduct a program evaluation or audit, and further require those persons conducting the evaluation or audit to maintain the confidentiality of the information. Since the regulations do not restrict the "voluntary disclosure" of identifying characteristics of research participants, the regulations permit release of identifying information for secondary analysis. However, the regulations place no obligation on the recipient of such information to resist a subpoena for the identities.

Another major criticism of the Public Health Services Act is that protection is not automatically conferred. Instead, the privilege must be secured by a discretionary grant from federal officials. If the research is controversial, the decision to extend the protection might be influenced by considerations other than the merits of the research project. The validity of such concern was demonstrated when a research project was terminated following intense public controversy. The project, designed to study the influence of marijuana on sexual activity, had received funding and was awaiting Justice Department approval to use controlled drugs in the research when it was singled out by several politicians and newspapers as an example of the wasteful spending practices of the federal government. Soon after the controversy began, the United States attorney for the district urged that the Justice Department withhold the grant of immunity it customarily provides to such research projects. Without this grant of immunity, the researcher and the participants would be subject to criminal prosecution for the possession of marijuana if they commenced the research. Rather than approve the grant of immunity, the Justice Department returned the proposal to the funding agency, asking that the agency review its decision to approve the study (*Chicago Tribune,* 25 January 1976). Though the Justice Department was never forced to take action on the immunity request (Congress rescinded funding in the interim), its actions demonstrate the potential for abuse when protection rests with the discretion of an administrative agency.

Since the research privilege permitted under the Public Health Services Act requires approval by the secretary of Health, Education and Welfare, it is vulnerable to similar abuses of administrative discretion. This limitation has caused some commentators to question the adequacy of such discretionary protection (Knerr 1976; Nejelski and Peyser 1975). Since protection under the Public Health Services Act has only recently been fully implemented, it remains to be seen whether abuses of discretion will occur. However, insight into the likelihood of such abuse can be gained by examining administrative practices under a similar statute which permits the attorney general to extend an evidentiary privilege to drug research projects. Section 502(c) of the Controlled Substances Act [Pub. L. 91–513, codified at 21 U.S.C.A. §872(c)], empowers the attorney general to:

authorize persons engaged in research to withhold the names and other identifying characteristics of persons who are the subjects of such drug abuse research. Persons who obtain this authorization may not be compelled in any Federal, State, or Local civil, criminal, administrative, legislative, or other proceeding to identify the subjects of research for which such authorization was obtained.

This statute is very similar to the Public Health Services Act, requiring discretionary action to extend protection to research participants. Recent changes in the implementing regulations of the Controlled Substances Act have restricted this protection to a narrow range of law enforcement studies (21 C.F.R. §1316.21 (1978), and 21 U.S.C.A. §872(a) (2–6). Before these changes, protection under the Controlled Substances Act was available to a broad range of social research studies investigating issues of drug use. Any research which was even remotely relevant to drug use was considered eligible for "grant of confidentiality" by the Drug Enforcement Administration, the agency administering the program.

The implementing regulations of the Public Health Services Act recognize the threat of abuses of discretion, and attempt to minimize intrusive review of the merits of the research. The secretary of HEW is not specifically required to consider the soundness of the purposes or methods of the research project. Instead, the secretary is required to determine whether the project constitutes "bona fide 'research' " within the scope of the regulations. If an applicant is affiliated with an institution, the secretary will consider the review and approval of research by the institution as evidence to be weighed in determining whether a project is "bona fide" research. If the application for a

Confidentiality Certificate is denied, the letter denying the Certificate will set forth the reasons for such denial. These precautions indicate an awareness of the potential for abuse of the discretion by the secretary, and a sincere effort to award the protection on some principled basis. Material obtained through periodic Freedom of Information requests should permit a means of reviewing this exercise of discretion. According to information obtained through a Freedom of Information Act Request to the Drug Enforcement Administration, approximately eighty-five requests for grants of confidentiality were received over a five-year period (1971–1975), and not one request was refused. Occasionally the DEA asked researchers to provide more information, and, in one case, referred the researcher to another agency which provided a more appropriate form of protection. Our review of the correspondence between researchers and the agency and subsequent telephone interviews with researchers revealed no obvious abuses of discretionary power (Hedrick, Nelson, and Cecil 1979). These preliminary findings suggest that administrative review of applications for the research privilege by the secretary of HEW is indeed fair and proper, but some means should be available for periodic review of this exercise of administrative discretion.

The implementing regulations of the Public Health Services Act recognize the threat of abuses of discretion, and attempt to avoid intrusive review of the merits of the research. The secretary of HEW is not specifically required to consider the soundness of the purposes or methods of the research project. Instead, the secretary is required to determine whether the project constitutes "bona fide 'research' " within the scope of the regulations. If an applicant is affiliated with an institution, the secretary will consider the review and approval of research by the institution as evidence to be weighed in determining whether a project is "bona fide". If the application for a Confidentiality Certificate is denied, the letter denying the Certificate will set forth the reasons for such denial. These precautions indicate an awareness of the potential for abuse of the discretion by the secretary, and an effort to award the protection on some principled basis. Material obtained through periodic Freedom of Information requests should permit a means of reviewing this exercise of discretion.

PROTECTION UNDER THE DRUG ABUSE OFFICE AND TREATMENT ACT OF 1972

In 1972 Congress passed section 408 of the Drug Abuse Office and Treatment Act (Pub. L. 92-255, amended in 1974 by Section 303 of Pub. L. 93-282, codified at 21 U.S.C. §1175a), establishing a long-term federal commitment to combat drug abuse. Congress included the following broad assurance of confidentiality in the statute:

Records of the identity, diagnosis, prognosis, or treatment of any patient which are maintained in connection with the performance of any drug abuse prevention function conducted, regulated, or directly or indirectly assisted by any department or agency of the United States shall, except as provided in subsection (e) of this section, be confidential and be disclosed only for the purposes and under the circumstances expressly authorized under subsection (b) of this section.

Implementing regulations for this statute [42 C.F.R. §2.1 et. seq. (1977)] broadly define "drug abuse prevention function" to apply to research as well as drug-related education, training, treatment, and rehabilitation. Subsection (e) of the statute permits an exception for records of the Armed Forces and health-care records of the Veterans' Administration from this statutory protection. However, a later section requires the administrator of Veterans' Affairs to abide by this legislation to the extent possible.

Subsection (b) specifies the circumstances under which drug treatment records can be disclosed. Of course, disclosure is permitted when the patient gives his written consent, thereby waiving the privilege. Other exemptions permit information to be revealed without consent in cases of medical emergencies, for purposes of research, audits, and evaluations, and when disclosure is authorized by an appropriate court order. Information contained in the treatment records may not be used to initiate criminal charges against a patient unless the information was gained through a court order. Criminal penalties are established for violation of this statute. In 1974 Congress passed almost identical protection for alcohol-abuse research (Pub.L. 93–282, codified at 45 U.S.C.A. §4582a).

Protection under these statutes differs in a number of ways from the discretionary research privilege described above. First, the protection of confidentiality authorized by the Drug Abuse Act is self-executing, in that the protection is effective without administrative action. However, the participants' rights to privacy under this statute are sharply limited by the exemptions, especially the one that allows the privilege to be set aside by court order. This exemption reads:

[T]he content of such record may be disclosed . . . [i]f authorized by an appropriate order of a court of competent jurisdiction granted after application showing good cause therefor.

Since this statute applies to all drug-abuse prevention functions, including research, the protection it provides can overlap with the protection provided by the confidentiality provisions of the two statutes permitting a discretionary privilege. If the alcohol or drug researcher protected under the Drug Abuse Act does not have an explicit grant of testimonial privilege from the attorney general's office, or a similar grant from the secretary of Health, Education and Welfare, the research information might still be vulnerable to a court-ordered subpoena. But if a researcher has such a discretionary grant of confidentiality, he or she may resist a subpoena despite the exception contained in the Drug Abuse Office and Treatment Act.

In the case of *People* v. *Newman,* this interpretation of the relationship between the two confidentiality statutes was tested and affirmed. A witness to a murder in New York City told police she had seen the killer in the waiting room of a methadone clinic. Subsequently, Dr. Robert Newman, director of the clinic, was ordered by subpoena to produce photographs of patients at a methadone maintenance center. Dr. Newman possessed a grant of confidentiality from the attorney general and refused to produce the photographs. The district attorney contended that the directors of methadone programs may be compelled, pursuant to the Drug Abuse Office and Treatment Act, to produce identifying records upon court order. Nevertheless, the Court of Appeals found that Dr. Newman was privileged to withhold the information under the grant of confidentiality from the attorney general.

Another notable exception to the restrictions on the disclosure of information on drug-abuse patients permits the release of information without the consent of the individual for purposes of scientific research and program evaluation. The implementing regulations indicate that the purpose of this section is:

To facilitate the search for truth, whether in the context of scientific investigation, administrative management, or broad issues of public policy, while at the same time safeguarding the personal privacy of the individuals who are the intended beneficiaries of the process or program under investigation.

In referring to the participants' right to privacy, the regulations note:

The courts have spoken of a right to privacy in a wide variety of contexts, but they have repeatedly and explicitly rejected the notion that anyone has a right to go about his daily affairs encapsulated in an impenetrable bubble of anonymity. They have been careful to weigh the competing interests, and the social interest in valid research and evaluation is clearly of sufficient moment to be considered in this process.

In recognizing the need for identified information in such secondary research efforts, the regulations make clear the responsibility of the secondary analyst to maintain the confidentiality of the identified information he has received. In fact, in discussing the qualifications necessary for release of the information for research purposes, the regulations indicate that not only must the secondary research personnel be qualified in terms of training and research experience, but they must also perform such work with adequate administrative safeguards against unauthorized disclosures. The privacy of the patients is protected by limiting further disclosure of identifying information by the secondary researcher.

Further recognition of the special nature of records used for secondary research is found in the way the regulations restrict the authority of the courts to demand disclosure of such records. While the statute indicates that courts have the authority to issue orders authorizing the disclosure of patient records, the regulations interpret this authority as extending only to the primary records maintained by treatment or research programs, and not to secondary research records resulting from the disclosure of the primary records to researchers or evaluators. As noted in the regulations:

[T]here must not be any question whatsoever about the legal inviolability of [the records'] confidential status in the hands of the researcher. Granted, there may occur rare occasions when the original records are for some reason not available, where a [court] order would lie as to the original records, and where there would seem to be some advantage in the administration of justice for such an order to permit disclosure of identifying information by the researcher. But compared to the damage which the mere potentiality for access does to the whole research enterprise, the advantage in terms of ability to deal with rare and anomalous cases seems almost trivial. Even in those cases, denial of access to the party seeking the information leaves him in no worse position than if the research or evaluation, which was certainly not undertaken for his benefit, had never been done at all.

The regulations further note that it would be permissible for a court to force the release of secondary records generated in an audit or examination of a program if the secondary records were for use in research and evaluation. In such an instance the court must weigh the need for the research against the privacy rights of the individual patients.

The implementing regulations that deal with scientific research are noteworthy for their lack of detail concerning the exemption for research and evaluation. Since no instances of abuse by persons acquiring identified information on patients for purposes of research were found, the drafters of the regulations thought it best to leave the rule as it is stated in the statute, permitting development on a case-by-case basis by those seeking the information.

Several weaknesses in the 1972 Act should be noted. The most obvious omission is coverage of verbal communications made by the addict during treatment (McNamara and Starr 1973). The confidentiality provisions of the 1972 Act mention only "records," which seems to include only written reports actually on file. Equally in need of protection are the verbal communications of the patient within the treatment or research setting. The interpretative regulations suggest that coverage extends to all information about patients, whether or not it's recorded. While this interpretation has not been tested in court, it may be overruled as going beyond the authority expressed in the statute.

The 1972 Act also lacks adequate procedural protection for the rights of patients participating in drug research. The patient need not receive notice or a hearing when a subpoena application for disclosure is made to the court. The patient also has no legal course of action to enforce his or her rights under the 1972 Act. While a person who discloses records unlawfully is liable to fine under the act, if the government chooses not to prosecute for the disclosure (a likely circumstance, since the prosecutor's office is often the recipient of the disclosed information), there is no effective penalty (McNamara and Starr 1973).

SECTION 524(a) OF THE CRIME CONTROL ACT OF 1973

Research data concerning criminal activities are especially vulnerable to forced disclosure by court-ordered subpoena. The courts' unwillingness to exercise discretionary power to bar researchers' evidence of criminal activity has resulted in federal statutory protection for criminal justice research. Section 524(a) of the Crime Control Act of 1973 (Pub. L. 93–83 codified at 42 U.S.C.A. §3771) provides that identifiable research and statistical information may only be used for the purpose for which it was obtained, and cannot be admitted as evidence or used for any purpose in any judicial or administrative proceeding without the consent of the individual research participant. The legislation states that:

Except as provided by Federal law other than this chapter, no officer or employee of the Federal Government, nor any recipient of assistance under the provisions of this chapter shall use or reveal any research or statistical information furnished under this chapter by any person and identifiable to any private person for any purpose other than the purpose for which it was obtained in accordance with this chapter. Copies of such information shall be immune from legal process, and shall not, without the consent of the person furnishing such information, be admitted as evidence or used for any purpose in any action, suit, or other judicial or administrative proceedings.

The implementing regulations for the statute [28 C.F.R. §22.1 et. seq. (1977)] acknowledge that one of the purposes of providing such protection for criminal justice research is to increase the credibility and reliability of federally supported research and statistical findings by minimizing subjects' concern over subsequent uses of identifiable information.

The scope of protection under this statute is quite broad, extending to research and statistical information obtained either directly or indirectly by the Law Enforcement Assistance Administration, or under any agreement, grant, or contract awarded under the Omnibus Crime Control and Safe Streets Act. Such a relationship can be demonstrated for almost all federally sponsored criminal justice research.

Protected information may be used only for statistical or research purposes and may not be used as evidence in judicial or administrative proceedings. However, the statute leaves research information vulnerable to a legislative subpoena, an exception the LEAA considers to be a shortcoming (Madden and Lessin 1978). Also, the statutory protection does not extend to information concerning future criminal conduct.

Research is broadly defined by the regulations to include any conceivable social science research project. The regulations define "research or statistical project" to include any project "whose purpose is to develop, measure, evaluate, or otherwise advance the state of knowledge in a particular area." By requiring only that the purpose of the project be to advance knowledge, the statute could extend protection to journalists, novelists, and other "teaching" professions, if the proper affiliation with LEAA can be established. The only specific exception to this generous protection is "intelligence activities" in which information is obtained directly for purposes of enforcement of criminal laws.

However, this statutory immunity extends only to research and statistical information; it will not protect a researcher's incidental observations. As an illustration, Madden and Lessin (1978) relate the following incident. A researcher initiated a study on defendants shortly after their arrest and again after the disposition of their case. The district attorney's office advised the researcher that should a defendant who had been interviewed shortly after his arrest enter a plea of guilty by reason of insanity, his office would subpoena the questionnaire and the interviewer. The questionnaire and the observations of the interviewer would be material to the validity of an insanity defense. Under such conditions, the statute would immunize the actual questionnaire, but no protection would be given to the observations of the interviewer as to the mental condition of the defendant during the interview. If questioned, the researcher would be required to testify about his unrecorded recollections or be cited for contempt of court.

The regulations define "identifiable information" in such a way as to protect research participants from deductive disclosure as well as from direct disclosure. The protection extends to any information that can be reasonably interpreted as referring to a particular individual. Information from which the identity of an individual may be deduced can be revealed only if the individual consents or has been informed that the findings cannot be expected to conceal his identity totally.

The regulations include special provisions for access to identifiable information by secondary analysts and auditors. Identifiable information may be released without the consent of the individual for any subsequent research or statistical use. However, the party requesting secondary access must demonstrate that the information is needed in identifiable form. Where the objectives of the subsequent research can be accomplished through the use of anonymous or coded data, release of the information in identifiable form is precluded.

The immunity offered by the statute is self-executing, requiring no act of administrative discretion. However, these protections are formalized through a series of certification procedures. A "Privacy Certificate" is required of all applicants for either direct or indirect LEAA support for projects with research or statistical components. The certificate must describe the project and contain assurances that access to identifiable information will be limited in accord with the regulations. The researcher must specify the precautions that will be taken to assure that identifiable data will remain secure, such as deleting names and coding. All employees who have a need for the identifiable information must be advised, of procedures and agree in writing to comply with them.

The regulations also set out the notification procedures that must be followed prior to collecting information directly from an individual. The respondent must be told that the information will be used only for research or statistical purposes, and that his or her participation is entirely voluntary and may be terminated at any time. It is left to the researcher to decide whether to inform the research participant that the information will be immune from legal process. Of course, the information provided by the research participant is protected whether or not he or she is informed of the immunity. These notifications may be omitted where information is obtained through field observation, and the researcher determines that such notification would disrupt the research.

Protection for research participants after information is transferred for secondary analysis or audit purposes is assured through a transfer agreement required to be signed by the requesting party. The transfer agreement must state that the information will be used only for statistical or research purposes, and that records of identifiable individuals will be returned without the copies retained upon completion of the project. Furthermore, the transfer agreement must specify the physical and administrative precautions that will be used to assure the security of the identifiable information.

Specific sanctions are provided for violations of the Act. If the Privacy Certificate or the transfer agreement is violated, the research contract or grant may be terminated, and responsible individuals may be fined up to $10,000.

OTHER FEDERAL STATUTES PROTECTING RESEARCH INFORMATION

A number of other federal statutes offer protection to record systems that may occasionally be used in social scientific inquiries. Some statutes offer protection for special categories of data. The Health Services Research, Health Statistics, and Medical Libraries Act of 1974 [Pub. L. 93-353, Section 308(d) codified at 42 U.S.C.A. §242m(d)], for example, provides subpoena immunity to National Center for Health Statistics researchers collecting data in health surveys and health-related program evaluations. A model statute that outlines immunity provisions and permits disclosure of health data for legitimate research has been developed by the National Center for Health Statistics (1977) for state legislatures. Special statutes protect census data (13 U.S.C.A. §§8, 9) and social security data (42 U.S.C.A. §1306), but these protections generally extend only to federal researchers and to outside researchers hired temporarily as agency personnel (see Eckler 1972, and Jabine 1975 for examples).[2]

Another form of federal statutory protection extends to specific topics of research. Federal surveys concerning venereal disease have received statutory protection. Information derived from programs for treating venereal disease can be released for statistical or research purposes only if the identity of the individual program is not disclosed [42 U.S.C.A. §247c(d)(5)].

Statutory protection has even been provided for specific research projects commissioned by Congress. For example, when authorizing a comprehensive statistical survey of runaway youth, Congress indicated that identifiable records gathered in the course of the survey could not under any circumstances be disclosed (42 U.S.C.A. §5731).

BENEFITS AND LIABILITIES OF STATUTORY PROTECTION

The benefits of statutory protection of confidential research information are clear. Most importantly, the privacy of research participants will be protected by restricting governmental or private appropriation of the information they provide. Statutory protection should increase the rate of cooperation in research on sensitive topics, where even small increments in cooperation notably enhance the quality of the research. Furthermore, an unambiguous statutory privilege will permit researchers to avoid disruptive legal confrontations. As researchers gain experience with the privilege and gain skill in assuring that information will remain confidential, sensitive information of higher quality and greater social importance should become more accessible.

Though a statutory privilege has some notable benefits, liabilities can also be anticipated. A statutory privilege may frustrate secondary analysis of research data. Original investigators may wrongly interpret the privilege as forbidding all third-party access, even for legitimate research, or as leaving a decision entirely to his or her discretion. Incompetent, dishonest, or fraudulent researchers may rely on the privilege to prevent discovery of their misdeeds. To avoid these difficulties, the statute should indicate the situations in which third-party access is permitted and provide for extension of the privilege to secondary researchers.

The emergence of two additional problems may also accompany any broad statutory protection. Some researchers may respond to statutory protection of research information by asking unnecessarily sensitive questions. Institutional review committees for research can guard against obvious abuses.

The second risk is that statutory protection will be viewed as a panacea for the problems of confidentiality in research. However, a statutory privilege alone will be an insufficient guarantee of confidentiality for some target populations, notably those indifferent or hostile to research and its user. Judging by the evidence discussed in chapter 3, a statutory privilege will be insufficient to guarantee cooperation in social research. Further, the statutes demand very little in the way of physical protection for the data. Consequently, the naive researcher will not recognize that legal protection is no substitute for physical protection of confidentiality. Finally, a possible consequence of a privilege is reduction in the exploration, development, and use of other, perhaps better, devices for assuring confidentiality and minimizing privacy intrusions.

Notes

1. The Privacy Act was developed during a period of controversy over domestic intelligence, police spying, and assorted political chicanery at the national level. Those activities influenced the passage of the law, to be sure; despite the atmosphere in which it was developed, the law is remarkably thorough in its treatment of administrative records and individual rights. The attention to research records and researcher use of administrative records is superficial, however. The sins of the administrative record-keeper and of intelligence organizations have, in this case, been visited on the research

community. Evidence of record abuse justified the act's creation in the first instance; but such evidence is absent or meager for research records. Neither the original hearings nor the Privacy Protection Study Commission cites specific abuses of records by researchers.

2. Though the economic researchers have no general legal protection against nonresearch uses of data they may collect, some economic microdata obtained by government for statistical research do have that protection. For example, the Bureau of Labor Statistics obtains anonymous data through the Census Bureau, employing the Census as a broker and archive insulated by Title 13 of the U.S. Code. The information on identified businesses, collected directly by BLS, is legally exempt from the provisions of the Freedom of Information Act, which would otherwise permit disclosure. In 1975 a bill was proposed to bring the level of this protection up to the standard implied by Title 13 (Yates 1975).

Perspective, Summary, and Policy Implications

Verily, when the day of judgment comes, we shall not be asked what we have read, but what we have done.

THOMAS Á KEMPIS

The detail in this monograph reflects our interest in adhering to reasonable standards of evidence, analysis, and reporting. The detail is also sufficiently rebarbative to justify summarizing both content and policy implications. The summary undertaken here is organized to conform roughly with the chapter sequence, but is not confined to chapter contents.

Perspective and Working Assumptions

We have adopted two basic principles to guide the research underlying this monograph. The first is that depreciation of privacy in research should be minimized; the second, that constraints on the conduct of research should be minimized. That the two principles need not be inimical is fundamental to our thinking. To get much beyond the principles, for each has been espoused with more piety and less work by others, we have adopted an engineering-science approach to implementing the principles.

That approach stresses the fundamental nature of the problem, the

*Portions of this chapter have been presented in testimony before the Privacy Protection Study Commission's Hearings on Research and Statistics, on behalf of the American Psychological Association.

quality of solutions, and the evidence. It serves partly as a prophylactic for the rhetoric that characterizes some political approaches to arguments about privacy. It also helps to avoid the academic trap of confusing obscurity with profundity and arrogance with expertise in discussing these matters.

That there is some need for a monograph of this sort seems clear. Despite the belief of one of our reviewers, for example, a good deal of the material is either not known to or not used by many social scientists. To illustrate, if we examine the set of proposals recently tendered by twelve major research firms in response to the government's requests for bids on new manpower surveys, we find only two recognizing statutory constraints on data collection, difficulties in record linkage, or procedural and statistical approaches to resolving problems. The absence of attention to multiple solutions, *other* than testimonial privilege, is evident in formal testimony before the Privacy Commission during the 1970s, in court cases such as *Merriken* v. *Cressman,* in Institutional Review Board arguments over the propriety of university-based research, and in other cases discussed earlier. Beyond meeting the immediate need for a better description of the state of the art, the methods discussed here form a small but essential technology of research methods. They are beginning to be taught at the graduate level, and we expect new texts in research design to attend to the approaches and their shortcomings.

We have attempted to be catholic in this examination for several reasons. Every social discipline, from psychology and marketing to statistics and epidemiology, yields illustrative cases, problems, and approaches to their solution. The simultaneous involvement of many institutions—government, community groups, academe, for-profit and nonprofit research institutes—is more typical than not. The problems are nothing if not international in their appearance, and solutions have been advanced by researchers from most Western countries. Nor is there any justification for temporal parochialism. Almost every difficulty discussed here, and elements of almost every tactic suggested for its resolution, can be found in the early history of social research, notably in sanitation surveys and in censuses.

The emphasis on multiple solutions reflects the belief that no single approach will meet problems in this sector. The diversity in research topics, in the beliefs of respondents, and in customs and law governing privacy is simply too large to expect a single approach to work equally well in all settings. The emphasis also represents a reaction against the view, taken by some legislators and some scientists, that law is the primary mechanism, a panacea, for accommodating public interests in the privacy sector.

Finally, theory has been put in a secondary role for several reasons. The consolidation, synthesis, and analysis of information undertaken here is, we believe, a requisite for development of good theory. Earlier discussion of the topic has often been characterized by theory that is often supported by evidence only incidentally and ignores controllable features of problems almost entirely. It is partly in reaction to this phenomenon—in the political arena, among both liberals and conservatives; in the social science arena, among some economists, psychologists, and sociologists—that theoretical analyses have been put aside. There are, to be sure, a variety of theories that might be exploited, but that task demands another book. The relevance of self-disclosure theory in social psychology or of crude theory of social desirability of response in psychometrics, for example, has not yet been well explored, though the evidence presented here suggests that it can be established. No ties between the statistician's unique methods of assuring confidentiality and the experimental psychologist's interest in subjective estimates of magnitude have been examined systematically, though the evidence discussed in this monograph suggests that the effort would be productive. No formal theory of bureaucracy has been used to organize the way we look at public and individual interests, court action, and federal regulation in the context of privacy and research. But here, too, the prospects for refining theory seem to us to be good. It is also reasonable to expect the economist to investigate problems in this arena despite the profession's insularity. For at both the individual and the aggregate level, the link between motives for participating in the interview or in research and the costs and benefits attached to the process are unclear. Nor has any economic theory been generated as a framework for guiding research on the generation of privacy law.

The Need for Identifiers in Research

Despite political rhetoric, the identification of a respondent ordinarily serves as a simple accounting device in social research, rather than as a vehicle for making judgments about an individual. The need for identifiers is most obvious in longitudinal research of the kind described in chapter 2: individuals must be tracked over time in medical research to establish the course of a disease and the effectiveness of a cure; in educational research to assay social development and the impact of special intervention programs; in clinical psychology to understand the origin, progress, and tractability of mental illness; and so on. Substitutes for longitudinal design, which are said to avoid privacy problems, are often inadequate. The material in chapter 2 shows how cross-sectional studies, which may not require respondent identification, for example, can lead to dumb conclusions. Cribbing a

New Yorker illustration, we observe that cross-sectional surveys of Miami Beach will, in the absence of any other information, lead us inevitably to the conclusion that one is most likely to be Cuban at infancy, to transform one's self to White, Anglo-saxon, and Protestant at middle age, and to be Jewish near terminus. It is also easy to use other examples given in chapter 2 to show how relying on published aggregate data, rather than more pertinent surveys that may engender privacy issues, can be similarly misleading.

Some, but not all, research that involves linking samples of records from different archives requires identifiers. The research may be dedicated to assaying the quality of multiple sources of data, as is true of the current linkage of samples of records from the Census Bureau, Social Security Administration, and Internal Revenue Service archives. It may focus on enlarging the data base for better prediction and higher quality research, as in the development of the Wisconsin Income and Assets file for economic research. And it may be used to determine whether and how much one can reduce the reporting burden in surveys: for example, the Census Bureau research on the usefulness of different rating systems for housing quality.

The longitudinal and correlational research discussed here is based on samples rather than populations, so depreciation in privacy is typically minimized in that respect. It can be minimized in other respects, too, by exploiting methods described in previous chapters. However, none of the major projects reported in chapter 2 resulted in any detectable abuse of identifiers, accidental disclosure, or harm to individual respondents as a result of the collection of identifiable information.

As a matter of public policy, the fact that identification of individual respondents in large-scale field research is usually fundamental to the quality of research and does *not* serve as a device for making judgments about individuals ought to be recognized explicitly and consistently in law. That in many, but not all, large-scale research projects, privacy and confidentiality are *not* a crucial public issue also ought to be recognized explicitly in policy and regulation. The attention dedicated to the topic is not commensurate with the level of the problem, at least with respect to some major research projects.

The review of longitudinal studies and record linkage has two implications for research policy. The first turns around the fact that our information on the demography of longitudinal and record linkage studies is inadequate. Information about how often they are carried out and what their principal results have been is simply not available in consolidated form for all the social sciences. Yet we should understand both scope and character of these studies when privacy legislation is at issue. Commission and legislative hearings on privacy often cannot catalogue all the necessary information, though it clearly bears on their interests. The social science community is typically ill-equipped to handle requests for consolidation on short notice. The value of the information lies only partly in monitoring the costs and benefits of research with respect to privacy. For the scientific community, it is at least as important as a device for understanding the scope of long-term studies of human development, for identifying gaps in what we know, for planning, and for allocating resources. The vehicles for meeting the aim include periodic, rather than one-time-only, studies of such research, perhaps along lines similar to those proposed by the American Statistical Association (1977) for a study of survey quality. They may involve invention and routine publication of social science indicators that enumerate and describe studies.

The second implication concerns the need for better enumeration and description of the uses to which the data are put. It is difficult for the research planner, let alone for a public concerned about privacy, to attach value to the product without some specific indicators of its use. Yet no formal system exists within any government agency or foundation for monitoring and documenting governmental requests for social scientific information, the uses of such data in agency management, legislative planning, appropriations, and evaluation, or in judicial decisions, or the use of the data by the social research community itself. The development of a technology of utilization and a coherent theory of the social use of social information is a reasonable prospect; a monitoring system can make that prospect considerably less difficult to explore. At the very least, we can advance a step or so beyond the current reliance on illustration, anecdote, and testimonial. We ought not to expect information on utilization to be exploited consistently even when it is available. The Privacy Protection Study Commission's (1977) remarks on educational research fail, for example, to cite any pertinent survey research or experiments, and refer to no systematic examination of the benefits of research, despite the commission's emphasis on balancing public interests in research against public interests in privacy. We expect that better documentation of the incidence, costs, and benefits of such studies will *gradually* increase the public's ability to identify the high-quality ones.

Assuring Respondents of Confidentiality and Privacy

The need to assure confidentiality can be argued on a variety of grounds, including the idea that cooperation in research will decrease with decreasing protection of privacy. Pertinent evidence has received less attention than it deserves, mainly because it is fragmented. That, in turn, has led to grand claims that assurance of confidentiality is essential in obtaining cooperation in research. The evidence provided in chapter 3 is quite sufficient for warning us that threats to the confidentiality of respondent reports can degrade cooperation in the research at hand. But it is as yet insufficient for predicting the occurrence or level of disruption with any real precision.

Case studies, for instance, illustrate that arguments about privacy are usually entangled with other issues, such as the propriety or legitimacy of the research topic and the governmental uses of resultant *statistical* data rather than individual records. The likelihood of disruption, judging from these cases, is greater to the extent that: news coverage is sensational and inaccurate; research participants or their representatives actually read; and principals or institutions that serve as hosts for the research are timid, ignorant, or confused about its purposes. Field experiments on different methods of assuring confidentiality constitute another form of evidence, and these generally support the intuition that for innocuous research topics and trusting respondents, privacy concerns will be minimal. The respondent's trust is itself normally determined by potentially misleading factors, such as the manner of the interviewers, and sometimes determined by more pertinent factors, such as the nature of the confidentiality assurance, the sensitivity of the elicited information, and the risk of records being disclosed for nonresearch purposes. Survey evidence bearing on respondent demands for assurance of confidentiality and on public concerns about privacy exists, but it is more difficult to interpret. It is clear that the attention accorded privacy has not *dramatically* affected cooperation rates in major social research projects. The public is evidently less influenced by this issue than by active trust or by acquiescence to legitimate social research. It is also clear that for a minority, privacy concerns are more than a novelty or diversion, and they are well informed.

The cases support the idea that it is alarmingly simple to exploit privacy concerns to accomplish other goals. Had they erred in doing so, Richard Nixon and Neil Gallagher would doubtlessly be regarded as champions of privacy law. Some journalists and other spokesmen are reckless in their attitude toward competent reporting on social research. It is also true that unnecessary conflicts have been generated by poor program design, especially predictive studies which, though advertised as administrative devices, are actually sustained by very little data, and which do not justify the collection and use of identifiable records for making judgments about individuals.

As a matter of research policy, the privacy problems engendered by research ought to be regarded as a legitimate topic for theoretical and applied social research. The topic has until recently not been routinely treated as such. As a consequence, case studies are sparse, field experiments have often been small and isolated from both theory and live controversy, and surveys have been less well tied to policy or science than they might be. The policy can be supported in part by maintaining adequate scientific logs that document, among other things, privacy-related problems. Also as a matter of research policy, pilot tests or side studies on the topic should be incorporated into major research programs. Perceptions and behavior relevant to confidentiality concerns will vary with changes in public, political, and journalistic interest, and with new laws or regulations. It is doubtful that a few static studies, to the exclusion of routine side study, will be sufficient to build adequate theory or basis for prediction.

There is an analogous need for formal research on the production of privacy law and special statutes for the protection of research records. The sources of ideas, the law's construction and legislative history, the character of political support and opposition to the law, and the sophistication and catholicity of the process deserve the social scientist's attention. Research on implementation of new law, privacy-related or otherwise, is still in its infancy. Indeed, we know of only one survey designed to assay the performance of new statutes for the protection of research records. No time-series analyses of these or other privacy laws appear to have been undertaken, though small case studies are available. Nor are we aware of field experiments, other than those mounted by Singer and the Census Bureau, to estimate the effects of new law on the conduct and quality of social research.

As a matter of research practice, the researcher should expect irrelevant but damaging arguments, errors, and distortions in reporting to emerge in controversial research, and should anticipate efforts to capitalize politically, professionally, or journalistically on ethical concerns. These efforts can be vigorous and justify the development of tactics to deal with them.

Procedural Strategies for Assuring Confidentiality

Procedural strategies refers here to nontechnical methods for eliciting information from individuals or archives without degrading privacy. Many of the devices, described in chapter 4, are simple and especially feasible in small studies. They include: alias, brokerage, and link file systems for longitudinal research; insulated file systems for settings in which information from different sources must be linked; and brokerage systems when an intermediary is necessary to screen the respondent from the researcher.

The first of two major benefits of the techniques is that they depress the researcher's need to access and maintain identifiable records on individuals. Second, they permit one to obtain data where privacy law, social custom, or regulation of data collection might otherwise prevent the process. The methods are helpful in protecting records that are archived in numerical rather than narrative form.

There are two major limits on the usefulness of the procedures. The first is that the procedures are cumbersome and may affect the quality of research. Certainly many of the methods are more complex, and demand more time and care in their use, than do direct methods of inquiry. More importantly, some of the methods prevent good appraisals of the validity of samples, the validity of response, or the validity of the archive records on which research is based. The methods can sometimes be altered, or coupled with side studies, to accommodate the need for quality control. In either case, maintaining and assuring the quality of the data is a bit more difficult, and the ostensible simplicity of the methods is misleading in this respect.

The second major limitation concerns the vulnerability of records generated under these procedures. Under each procedure, access to identified records is reduced or eliminated, and the risk of accidental disclosure of an identified record or theft is similarly reduced. On the other hand, the protection will sometimes be less complete than circumstances demand. For instance, it is possible to deduce identified information from anonymous records under certain conditions. The task is difficult enough to make the problem a negligible one for most research on innocuous topics. But for very sensitive information, more sophisticated protection devices must be brought to bear. Further, strategies such as the link file system provide only limited protection against legal appropriation. The legal vulnerability of the strategies is not entirely clear because there has been no example of legal appropriation of files developed under any of the methods. That they have satisfied some publics and that they can meet government and private regulations on researcher access to data is clear. The ambiguity in the legal status of some procedures suggests that they be augmented with statistical or statutory protection for records.

As a matter of public policy, the usefulness of procedural devices for satisfying privacy demands, and the devices' shortcomings and costs, ought to be recognized explicitly. Reference in law and regulation to the availability of such devices should help to avoid unnecessary managerial problems in implementing them, and to inform a public that they do exist. The history of their use ought to be recognized as well, and it serves in arguing against anecdotal evidence on alleged impropriety in social research. Further, where such devices are inappropriate, some provisions in institutional rule and law must be made to permit the legitimate researcher access to identifiable records when such access is essential.

As a matter of research policy, the idea that access to identifiable data can often be minimized without severely degrading the quality of research should be recognized explicitly. It is one vehicle for making concrete the task of balancing the privacy interests of the individual and social needs for information. Also, as a matter of research practice, it is plain that such procedures are useful but primitive devices for achieving that balance. The uses of the methods, their benefits and shortcomings in the particular instance, ought to be routinely documented in research papers, and should be regarded as a small but legitimate topic in research methodology. In the absence of such a policy, it is likely to be difficult to improve methods and get them tested routinely in the field.

That the procedures can be complex and cumbersome ought to be recognized by research support agencies and researchers. They can increase the cost of research and in some instances will make the research less timely than it might otherwise be. Additional financial support will also be required to reduce the limitations of the procedures, notably those that make it difficult to assure the quality of sampling and the quality of response.

Statistical Methods for Assuring Confidentiality

A wide variety of statistical methods have been developed to permit a researcher to elicit information directly from identified individuals, and yet maintain respondent privacy. The methods include a large class of randomized response methods, microaggregation of response, and microaggregation of sample units. Roughly speaking, they protect privacy by requiring that a respondent inject his or her response with random error whose specific value is unknown to anyone but whose statistical properties are controlled by the researcher. The benefit is that the individual respondent's status cannot be determined from the response, but the average induced errors can be accommodated at least partially in statistical analysis of the group data. Regardless of their assurance of privacy in principle, the methods may also help to increase cooperation rate by decreasing the sensitivity of the question and the embarrassment associated with a response, but this advantage must be verified in side studies. Because identifiers are coupled to the response, record linkage is possible.

The main practical limit of current methods is that they are suitable only for large samples, and only for questions that can be answered using a categorical or quantitative response. Further, they require more technical expertise to use, especially in analytic studies that employ complex multivariate and nonlinear models. They, like any method for eliciting information in research and especially new methods, must be pilot tested before being adopted in major research.

These costs must be evaluated against gains in accuracy of estimation, and, independently, against increased respondent privacy.

The techniques have been field tested in the United States, Sweden, Canada, Taiwan, Germany, and elsewhere, and they have been tested in a variety of target populations and on a variety of topics. The latter include drug and alcohol abuse, attitudes about race, illegal activities, abortion, bankruptcy, and other sensitive characteristics of individuals. The field tests have been promising in the sense that no grave problems in application have been uncovered. More importantly, the field tests suggest that estimates of population parameters obtained under these methods are usually no less accurate, and often more accurate, than estimates obtained using direct-interview methods for eliciting sensitive information. As a matter of public policy, the existence, limitations, and benefits of these techniques ought to be recognized explicitly in regulation. They do, after all, represent one concrete class of approaches to satisfying public interest in privacy without severely truncating research interests.

As a matter of research policy, these strategies should be routinely considered as an option for large-sample research in which a few questions are sensitive. Institutional Review Boards with responsibility for overseeing the ethical character of research should be familiar with the benefits, limitations, and costs of the methods. Also as a matter of research policy, pilot tests and side studies on the methods should be adjoined routinely to research employing the methods. This is consistent with good practice in using any novel method or any standard method in novel circumstances. Pilot tests should be directed at establishing the accuracy and precision of statistical estimates so obtained and at the respondent's attitudes toward the methods.

The mathematics of these methods have developed, as usual, considerably faster than application and behavioral research. There is an obvious need for field research on how respondents perceive the integrity of the methods: research on variation in cooperation rate as a function of sensitivity of response, the level of probabilistic protection, and other factors. The methods have not yet been linked to more traditional theory in psychology, notably that on social desirability of response, self-disclosure, and respondent perceptions of probability.

These methods will not be adequate or appropriate in small-sample research, case studies, and the like. Even where large samples are available, it will not generally be desirable to frame every question, in a long sequence of questions, in accordance with the methods. Other methods for assuring privacy and confidentiality must play a role. The supplements may be procedural or statutory, or both. The combination of methods should be a legitimate topic of research: we know little about which combinations are optimal and about nonstatistical criteria for judging optimality.

On the Publication of Statistical Tables

We believe that the likelihood of deductive disclosure is at least as high, probably higher, in news reporting, case studies, and other narrative description as it is in publication of statistical tables. We further believe the incidence of deductive disclosure concerning individuals for any large-scale survey is quite low. The low incidence for major studies is doubtless influenced by the fact that most research information is innocuous, that any given item of information is likely to be available elsewhere in more accessible form, that deductive disclosure is a technically demanding task, and, finally, that large samples of analyses typically involve publication of tables with very large entries. Sophisticated studies based on small-to-moderate samples of a large target population generally involve publication of statistics *other* than counts and cross tabulations, and these are not susceptible to deductive disclosure.

As a matter of policy, the ordinarily low likelihood of deductive disclosure and the tractability of the problem ought to be recognized explicitly in regulation. As a matter of research practice, tables ought to be routinely checked for the possibility of deductive disclosure. The screening need not be elaborate for sample surveys on innocuous topics, given the bounds on the problem—inaccurate, obsolete, or incomplete information—and given simplicity of control. But the researcher must bear responsibility for disclosure based on tables. The procedures that have been developed to understand disclosure, and the methods that reduce its likelihood, ought to be used routinely. In decreasing order of simplicity, the procedures include: publication based on independent subsamples and nondisclosure of respondent lists; use of crude report categories; consolidation and elimination of small cell frequencies; controlled contamination or capitalization on normal measurement error in the data.

Secondary Analysis and Audit

Secondary analysis refers to competing analysis of research data, for the sake of assuring the credibility of conclusions based on an earlier analysis, or for the sake of testing new hypotheses. *Audit* refers to government examination of a research project, including its conduct and products.

Neither secondary analysis nor audit ordinarily requires disclosure of identifiable records on research participants. Most secondary analysis requires no identifiers, since the analysis focuses traditionally on statistical data or anonymous records. Similarly, most audits focus on management and operations and so require no direct contact with research participants. These practices are likely to continue.

In either category, two privacy-related problems may emerge: accidental deductive disclosure, and direct planned disclosure where identifiers are thought to be required. The first problem is generally tractable. The risk of deductive disclosure can often be controlled with simple tactics: for example, controlling access to lists of respondents, microaggregation, construction of crude report categories. The second problem emerges where research participants must be reinterviewed and where new information must be linked with records collected earlier. For the secondary analyst, follow-ups may be necessary to enrich the original data pool or to appraise the validity of sampling or of response. In many, if not all, of these cases, the procedural tactics we have described, such as insulated file linkage, can be used to enlarge the data set without compromising earlier assurances about the confidentiality of records. For the auditor, access to identified records and to respondents may be thought necessary for similar reasons. The various procedural methods for checking the validity of sampling and of response, designed to avoid conflicts between the need for confidentiality of research records and the needs of the auditor, are pertinent: they include parallel sampling, the use of brokers as intermediaries, and others.

In a minority of cases, it will be imperative that records be disclosable in identified form. Respondents ought then to be informed beforehand when this is feasible; seeking permission after data collection is complete can be more cumbersome. In either case, the tactics for eliciting consent appear to differ little in spirit from those ordinarily used in obtaining high response rates: multiple appeals for consent, adequate justification, and so on. There is little empirical evidence on the way cooperation rates in these settings will be affected by consent requirements, however.

It is reasonable to expect that an audit whose purpose is to acquire information and make administrative judgments about individual respondents will be disruptive. But here, too, evidence is scanty. To the extent that auditor involvement is incompetent or not consistent with standards of research, the likelihood of disruption of a research project will increase. Insofar as auditor involvement carries no implication of sanction for the respondent and the audit is consistent with good practice in survey research, the likelihood of disruption is reduced.

As a matter of research policy, the tradition of secondary analysis for the sake of advancing scientific knowledge should be encouraged. Privacy-related problems do not emerge frequently in this context and certainly do not emerge often enough to impose a major constraint on this task. The newer practice implied by auditor involvement in research must be approached more circumspectly, partly because it is a new enterprise and its benefits and shortcomings are not yet well understood. For though no privacy-related problems typically emerge in conventional audit operations, they may emerge if research respondents must be reinterviewed or their records disclosed to an audit whose interest does not lie solely in assuring the quality of the scientific enterprise. Access to identifiable records must be minimized in audit, as in secondary analysis. Where disclosure is essential, the records should be accorded the same treatment as promised initially by the researcher. Where auditor contacts with respondent are warranted, they should be made with the same professionalism as in the original contact.

No secondary analysis or audit should be undertaken without an assessment for privacy implications. That assessment need not be elaborate, since problems are infrequent and anonymous data are often sufficient for high quality in either task. The exceptions require prior negotiation. They can and should be treated as a legitimate problem in the management, design, and audit of research.

There will at times be no recourse other than direct access to respondent or record. In these cases, the likely consequences ought to be established in pilot tests and side studies as a matter of research policy. The most crucial issues are the reduction of cooperation in research as a function of the threat attached to secondary analysis or audit, and the degradation of the privacy of the respondent. The first may be controllable if threats to the individual can be eliminated. The second may require that costs to privacy be balanced by material or other rewards, by minimizing the sample size and the offensiveness of inquiry, and other tactics. Procedural, statistical, and similar devices to assure confidentiality are not always appropriate or sufficient. Consequently, legal protection is and should remain a legitimate vehicle for protection.

Legal Protection of Research Records on Identifiable Individuals

Legal protection is defined here as statute, court decision, or executive action that prevents research records on identifiable respondents from being used for purposes other than research. The need for such protection is most clear in settings where records are likely to be appropriated by a governmental agency for use in administrative or legal action against an identified respondent. The incidence of formal subpoena is low, but the *possible* consequences are not negligible: they include disruption of research in the short term, and difficulty in eliciting cooperation in research in the long run. The problem can be especially severe if current rules on the protection of human subjects are interpreted as requiring that they be informed about the legal vulnerability of their responses; that information is likely to affect the cooperation rate.

Statutory protection is generally more desirable than judicial or executive action simply because it offers uniformity in application. However, current protection is very limited in the type of research to which it pertains and in the scope of protection given. The privilege statutes that exist concern research in drug and alcohol abuse, crime and delinquency, mental health, and health. Most economic and educational research, and political, psychological, and sociological research outside the protected areas, remains uncovered. The best statutes appear to us to be those bearing on research in crime and drug abuse, which cover identification of respondent and respondent records and copies of records, and render the information immune from subpoena by the courts and executive agencies.

There have been few cases in which courts have ruled on the admissibility of research records collected by a researcher under a promise of confidentiality. In civil litigation, *Richards of Rockford* v. *Pacific Gas and Electric* is an important decision, reiterating the court's interest in balancing its need for information against the negative consequence of disclosure for research. The interest in this balance, and decisions that are favorable to the researcher's maintenance of confidentiality, are much less well articulated for criminal cases. In any event, the courts have preferred to rule on a case-by-case basis, rather than to create a general mechanism that would prevent their using research records on identifiable individuals as a basis for judicial decision.

Executive powers have been used at times, at both national and state level, to provide protection. They are irregular in their appearance, having been employed in a few research projects on prison riots, civil disorder, and other topics. Further, the integrity of executive protection of the privacy of research subjects has not been fully tested in the courts, though executive privilege has been used at times to provide protection. Irregular in incidence and not uniform in application, it has promise where other protection is unavailable.

As a matter of policy, current federal statutes governing the privacy of the research participant are deficient and ought to be amended. Even the better ones, for example, do not provide the respondent's research record with protection from legislative investigation; nor is the researcher protected against having to testify from memory. The more deficient statutes fail to provide automatic protection and permit the researcher to disclose identifiable records without the permission of the respondent. More generally, the existence of several privilege statutes, each with different provisions and regulations, complicates matters.

National professional organizations have the right to argue for changes in law. To the extent that the law impedes or constrains research unnecessarily, they have the responsibility to do so. Little statutory protection exists in state law, and since most federal statutes cover only research projects supported by a federal agency, the gap in protection is large. With a few remarkable exceptions, state professional organizations have not been active in this quarter. So long as these groups or individual researchers fail to take some responsibility for constructing and submitting model statutes, the low level of protection will persist. At least, the development of manuals, better documentation on current protections and problems, and a system for monitoring the conception, adoption, and implementation of new law are warranted for both national and state offices.

The research community also has the right to argue for changes in privacy regulation and law that reduce impediments to the legitimate research use of administrative data and legitimate social science investigation. Professional organizations have become more competent in doing so, but the sheer number of new bills and their complexity make individual or professional action difficult. Moreover, an ex post facto examination of the effect of a law on the conduct of research, such as a commission or hearing, is less satisfactory than formal anticipation of problems. It is not unreasonable, then, to suggest that a mechanism, such as a legally required "research impact statement," be created. A device of this sort would provide that bills be routinely reviewed to determine whether they will affect the quality and usefulness of research operations; if they are likely to have an adverse effect, then they should be amended to eliminate impediments to research. The legally mandated and automatic process is likely to engender a more thorough review than is normally available through legislative hearings and better evidence on which to base amendment. To be effective, the device must be tied to both the capabilities of professional organizations and to the duties of privacy officers in federal and state agencies.

There is a clear need to capitalize on the experience already accumulated in avoiding the unnecessary impediments to research generated by privacy law. That need applies to local as well as state and federal regulation. It includes maintenance of the functional distinction between research and administrative record systems that was articulated in early discussions of conflicts between research and law, and reiterated recently by the Privacy Protection Study Commission.

The distinction is as important in the school district or health services unit as it is at the national level. The need includes formally assuring that devices, such as the insulated data bank or enclave approaches, can be used legitimately to access records without breaching law. It includes formal recognition that the statistical methods designed to protect respondents' privacy and the confidentiality of research records on identified respondents actually do so. And it includes special provisions for researcher access to identifiable records when mechanical protection devices for safeguarding records are inappropriate.

Education and Training

It is reasonable to surmise that the language of privacy, like Galbraith's language of economics, can be seduced by the unlearned, and its seduction may even be aided by the enfeebled intellect. This, of course, brings us to the possibility of educating ourselves and educating others.

A good deal of the material presented here accumulated under the first quaesitum. We admit that our understanding is imperfect but trust that our failures are also impermanent. The prospects of meeting the second objective are especially interesting for groups with the major responsibility for privacy concerns in research: Institutional Review Boards, graduate students of research, and government agencies. Institutional Review Boards have been established to assay the ethical implications of research. Their performance and effectiveness is controversial and justifies the research undertaken by the National Commission on Human Experimentation established under the National Research Act. Our concern is with the competence of such boards. In particular, it is not clear that they can be uniformly educated about either ethical problems or their solution, given their heterogeneous membership and short term of service. Nor is it clear that such boards have the time to become educated, given the task of reviewing every single proposal for research on human subjects that stems from an academic institution. It is certainly true that some have been incompetent in suggesting solutions to problems. As a matter of policy, it is not unreasonable to expect that board members be educated formally on the task to which they are assigned. In particular, they should be well informed about precedents in problems and solutions, about the limits and benefits of solutions, and about honorific appeals to privacy or confidentiality. Further, much of what we know about the quality of review board performance is based heavily on oral history. This style of knowledge building is characteristic of more primitive tribes, and we do not believe that review boards should espouse it. Written records, accessible to the research community at least, ought to be required. Where sufficiently detailed, they can help understand which problems are tractable and which are not, which methods of sustaining privacy are most palatable, when privacy concerns are gratuitous and when they are not, and so on.

One of the difficulties in capitalizing on research ethics courses at the graduate level is mechanical. Those courses generally do not consider the devices that may be employed systematically to actualize a set of ethics. The procedures and evidence discussed in this monograph can help to ameliorate the problem. For they are nothing if not concrete, and they do bear on ethical issues. More importantly, they add a new dimension to the process of obtaining high-quality information with integrity, and that ought to be part of conventional graduate education. The theoretical arena, as we have said, badly needs to be articulated and tested. Finally, we recognize that the technical material is demanding. This will perhaps have a salutary effect on the student, and if incorporated into licensing procedures, it may have the same effect on the supply of social scientists, lawyers, and statisticians.

Very little is known about the selection of government staff with responsibility for assuring adherence to the Privacy Act, the confidentiality provisions of the Tax Reform Act, and other privacy legislation. We know virtually nothing about their performance, though it is clear that in some instances, the staff member's lack of skill, and perhaps interest, in research has led to more truculence than was necessary. Some privacy officers feel comfortable enough about their new roles to meet periodically to exchange views. Others, who recognize that they can be penalized for violating the law but not for stupidity, employ an insular policy. Yet it is from these staff that we must learn about how privacy law can be accommodated without degrading research. Under these conditions, it is reasonable for the research community to encourage the development of staff skills and their understanding of research. That development can be facilitated through better organization and communication among staff members, through workshops in which they participate, and through their contributions to the research journals, case books, and monographs that periodically cover privacy-related issues.

Bibliography

Abernathy, J. R.; Greenberg, B. G.; and Horvitz, D. G. 1970. Estimates of induced abortion in urban North Carolina. *Demography* 7: 19–29.

Abul-Ela, A. A.; Greenberg, B. G.; and Horvitz, D. G. 1967. A multiproportions randomized response model. *Journal of the American Statistical Association* 62: 990–1008.

Acheson, E. D. 1967. *Medical record linkage.* London: Oxford University Press.

American Psychiatric Association. 1968. Confidentiality and privilege with special reference to psychiatric patients. *American Journal of Psychiatry* 124: 1015–16.

———. 1970. Guidelines for psychiatrists: Problems in confidentiality. *American Journal of Psychiatry* 126: 1543–49.

———. 1972. The need for preserving confidentiality of medical records in any national health care system. *American Journal of Psychiatry* 128: 1349.

———. 1973. Confidentiality of medical research records. *American Journal of Psychiatry* 130: 739.

American Psychological Association. 1973. *Ethical principles in the conduct of research.* Washington, D.C.: APA.

American Statistical Association. 1977. Report of the ad hoc Committee on Privacy and Confidentiality. *American Statistician* 31: 59–79.

Anderson, H. 1976. Estimation of a proportion through randomized response. *International Statistical Review* 44: 213–17.

———. 1977. Efficiency versus protection in a general randomized model. *Scandinavian Journal of Statistics* 4: 11–19.

Ash, P., and Abramson, E. 1952. Effect of anonymity in attitude and opinion research. *Journal of Abnormal and Social Psychology* 47: 722–23.

Assakul, K., and Proctor, C. H. 1967. Testing independence in two way contingency tables with data subject to misclassification. *Psychometrika* 32: 67–76.

Astin, A. W. 1968. Personal and environmental determinants of student activism. *Measurement and Evaluation in Guidance.* Fall: 149–62.

Astin, A. W., and Boruch, R. F. 1970. A "Link File System" for assuring confidentiality of research data in longitudinal studies. *American Educational Research Journal* 7: 615–24.

Bachi, R., and Bar-On, R. 1969. Confidentiality problems related to data banks. *Bulletin of the International Statistical Institute* 43 (Book 1): 225–48.

Bailar, B. A., and Lanphier, C. M. 1978. *Development of survey methods to assess survey practices.* Washington, D.C.: American Statistical Association.

Baltes, P. B., and Schaie, K. W. 1976. On the plasticity of intelligence in adulthood and old age: Where Horn and Donaldson fail. *American Psychologist* 31: 720–25.

Barabba, V. P., and Kaplan, D. 1975. U.S. Census Bureau statistical techniques to prevent disclosure: The right to privacy vs. the need to know. Paper presented at the 40th Session of the International Statistical Institute, Warsaw, 1–9 September.

Barna, J. D. 1974. Invasion of privacy as a function of test set and anonymity. *Perceptual and Motor Skills* 38: 1028–30.

Barth, J. T., and Sandler, H. M. 1976. Evaluation of the randomized response technique in a drinking survey. *Journal of Studies on Alcohol* 37: 690–93.

Barton, E. M.; Pleinons, J. K.; Willis, S. L.; and Baltes, P. B. 1975. Recent findings on adult and gerontological intelligence: Changing a stereotype of decline. *American Behavioral Scientist* 19: 224–36.

Bauman, K. E., and Sage, E. 1976. An assessment of informed consent procedures used in a pilot test of drug behavior among youth. Unpublished report. Chapel Hill, N.C.: University of North Carolina, School of Public Health.

Bauman, R. A.; David, M. H.; and Miller, R. F. 1970. Working with complex data files: The Wisconsin assets and income studies archive. In *Data bases, computers, and the social sciences,* ed. R. L. Biscoe, pp. 112–36. New York: Wiley-Interscience.

Baxter, R. 1969. The harassed respondent: Sales solicitation in the guise of consumer research. In *Current controversies in marketing research,* ed. L. Bogart, pp. 23–31. Chicago: Markham.

Beals, R. L. 1969. *Politics of social research.* Chicago: Aldine.

Beaver, J. E. 1968. The newsman's code: The claim of privilege and everyman's right to evidence. *Oregon Law Review* 47: 243–65.

Bejar, I. 1975. Substudy 1a: Secondary analysis of the Cali tests of the nutrition and cultural enrichment program. Evaluation Research Memo No. 1IIB. Department of Psychology, Northwestern University, Evanston, Ill.

Benson, L. E. 1941. Studies in secret ballot technique. *Public Opinion Quarterly* 5: 79–82.

Berdie, R. F. 1965. The ad hoc committee on social impact of psychological assessment. *American Psychologist* 20: 143–46.

Berger, R., and Gold, M. 1976. *Experiment in a juvenile court.* Ann Arbor: Institute for Social Research.

Berman, J.; McCombs, H.; and Boruch, R. F. 1977. Notes on the contamination method. *Sociological Methods and Research* 6: 45–62.

Birren, J. E. 1964. *The psychology of aging.* Englewood Cliffs, N.J.: Prentice-Hall.

Blasi, V. 1976. The newsman's privilege and the researcher's privilege: Some comparisons. In *Social research in conflict with law and ethics,* ed. P. Nejelski, pp. 155–61. Cambridge, Mass.: Ballinger.

Boeckman, M. E. 1976. Policy impacts of the New Jersey Income Maintenance Experiment. *Policy Sciences* 7: 53–76.

Boness, F. H., and Cordes, J. F. 1973. The researcher-subject relationship: The need for protection and a model statute. *Georgetown Law Review* 62: 243–72.

Boruch, R. F. 1971a. Educational research and the confidentiality of data: A case study. *Sociology of Education* 44: 59–85.

———. 1971b. Maintaining confidentiality in educational research: A systemic analysis. *American Psychologist* 26: 413–30.

———. 1972a. Relations among statistical methods for assuring confidentiality of data. *Social Science Research* 1: 403–14.

———. 1972b. Strategies for eliciting and merging confidential social research data. *Policy Sciences* 3: 275–97.

Boruch, R. F., and Creager, J. A. 1972a. Measurement error in social and educational research. ACE Research Reports, vol. 7, no. 2. Washington, D.C.: American Council on Education.

———. 1972b. Self-reports of protest activity and attitudes: A note on stability. *Measurement and Evaluation in Guidance* 5: 332–38.

Bourke, P. D. 1974a. Multiproportions randomized response using the unrelated question technique. Confidentiality in Surveys Report No. 74, Department of Statistics, University of Stockholm, Stockholm.

———. 1974b. Symmetry of response in randomized response designs. Confidentiality in Surveys Report No. 75, Department of Statistics, University of Stockholm, Stockholm.

———. 1974c. Vector response in randomized response designs. Confidentiality in Surveys Report No. 76, Department of Statistics, University of Stockholm, Stockholm.

———. 1976a. The generation of randomized response designs for multivariate estimation using design matrices. Confidentiality in Surveys Report No. 16, Department of Statistics, University of Stockholm, Stockholm.

———. 1976b. Randomized response designs for multivariate estimation. Confidentiality in Surveys Report No. 6, Department of Statistics, University of Stockholm, Stockholm.

Bourke, P. D., and Dalenius, T. 1973. Multi-proportions randomized response using single sample. Forsknings projektet, Fel I Undersokningar, Rapport Nr 68, Stockholms Universitet, Statistika Institutionen, Stockholm.

———. 1974a. A note on inadmissible estimates in randomized inquiries. Confidentiality in Surveys Report No. 72, Department of Statistics, University of Stockholm, Stockholm.

———. 1974b. Randomized response with lying. Confidentiality in Surveys

No. 71, Department of Statistics, University of Stockholm, Stockholm.

———. 1975. Some new ideas in the realm of randomized inquiries. Paper presented at the 40th Session of the International Statistical Institute, Warsaw, 1–9 September.

Bowers, R., and DeGasparis, P. 1978. *Ethics in social research.* New York: Praeger.

Brian, E. W. 1975a. Letter to the Editor, *Los Angeles Times,* 12 February.

———. 1975b. Statement on major charges in the Gnaizda letter. Unpublished. University of Southern California, Center for Health Services Research.

Brim, O. G. 1965. American attitudes toward intelligence tests. *American Psychologist* 20: 125–30.

Bross, I. D. J. 1954. Misclassification in 2 × 2 tables. *Biometrics* 10: 478–86.

Brown, G. H. 1974. Drug usage rates as related to method of data acquisition. HUMRO Technical Report 74-20. Arlington, Va.: Human Resources Research Organization.

———. 1975. Randomized inquiry vs. conventional questionnaire method in estimating drug usage rates through mail surveys. HUMRO Technical Report 75-14. Arlington, Va.: Human Resources Research Organization.

Brown, G. H., and Harding, F. D. 1973. A comparison of methods of studying illicit drug usage. HUMRO Technical Report 73-9. Arlington, Va.: Human Resources Research Organization.

Bruce, R. V. 1975. Alexander Graham Bell and the conquest of solitude. In Hearings of the Subcommittee on Census and Population, Committee on Post Office and Civil Service, House of Representatives. Hearings on H.R. 10686, A Bill to Amend Title 13 of the United States Code, Serial No. 94-50, 94th Congress, 17 November 1975, pp. 10–17. Washington, D.C.: U.S. Government Printing Office.

Bryant, E. C., and Hansen, M. H. 1972. Methods for cross-program comparisons. In *Evaluating the impact of manpower programs,* ed. M. E. Borus, pp. 13–20. Lexington, Mass.: D. C. Heath.

———. 1976. Invasion of privacy and surveys: A growing dilemma. In *Perspectives on Attitude Assessment: Surveys and their alternatives,* ed. H. W. Sinaiko and L. A. Broedling, pp. 70–77. Champaign, Ill.: Pendleton.

Bryant, F. B., and Wortman, P. M. 1978. Secondary analysis: The case for data archives. *American Psychologist* 33: 381–87.

Brymer, R. A., and Farris, B. 1967. Ethical and political dilemmas in the investigation of deviance: A study of juvenile delinquency. In *Ethics, politics, and social research,* ed. G. Sjoberg, pp. 297–318. Cambridge, Mass.: Schenkman.

Burstein, L. 1975. The unit of analysis in educational research. Paper presented at the Annual Meeting of the American Educational Research Association, Washington, D. C.

Campbell, C., and Joiner, B. L. 1973. How to get the answer without being sure you've asked the question. *American Statistician* 27: 229–31.

Campbell, D. T. 1975. Assessing the impact of planned social change. In

*Social research and public policies: The Dartmouth-OECD Confer-
ence,* ed. G. M. Lyons, pp. 3–44. Hanover, N.H.: University of New
Hampshire Press.

Campbell, D. T.; Boruch, R. F.; Schwartz, R. D.; and Steinberg, J. 1975.
Confidentiality preserving modes of access to files and to interfile
exchange for useful statistical analysis. Appendix A. In National
Academy of Sciences, the Committee on Federal Agency Evaluation
Policy, *Protecting individual privacy in evaluation research,* ed. A. M.
Rivlin, pp. A-1–A-25. Washington, D.C.: NAS.

Campbell, D. T., and Erlebacher, A. 1970. How regression artifacts in quasi-
experimental evaluations can mistakenly make compensatory education look harmful. In *Compensatory education: A national debate,* ed.
J. Hellmuth, pp. 155–225. New York: Brunner/Mazel.

Cannell, C. F., and Fowler, F. J. 1963. Comparison of a self-enumerative
procedure and a personal interview: A validity study. *Public Opinion
Quarterly* 27: 250–64.

Cannell, C., and Henson, R. 1974. Incentives, motives, and response bias.
Annals of Economic and Social Measurement 3: 307–17.

Caplan, N.; Morrison, A.; and Stambaugh, R. J. 1975. *The use of social science
knowledge in policy decisions at the national level.* Ann Arbor: University of Michigan, Institute for Social Research.

Carroll, J. D., and Knerr, C. R. 1975. A report of the APSA confidentiality
in social science research data project. *Political Science* (Summer):
258–61.

———. 1976. Law and the regulation of social science research: Confidentiality as a case study. Paper presented at the Symposium on Ethical
Issues in Social Science Research, Department of Sociology, University of Minnesota, 9 April.

Carroll, J. M. and McClelland, P. M. 1970. Fast "infinite-key" privacy transformation for resource sharing systems. Paper No. 191, University of
Western Ontario.

Cassedy, J. H. 1969. *Demography in early America: Beginnings of the statistical mind.* Cambridge: Harvard University Press.

Cassel, C. M. 1974. *On probability-based disclosures in frequency tables.*
Sweden: National Central Bureau of Statistics.

Cecil, J. S. 1978. Regulation of research record systems by the Privacy Act
of 1974. Research Report, Department of Psychology, Northwestern
University, Evanston, Ill.

Cecil, J. S., and Boruch, R. F. 1977. They're privileged and you're not: A note
on deductive disclosure of confidentiality grantees when the Privacy
Act prevents direct disclosure of their identification. Research Memo,
Psychology Department, Northwestern University, Evanston, Ill.

Chapman, S. G., and Swanson, C. G. 1974. A descriptive profile of the assault
incident. Research Report. University of Oklahoma, Assaults on Police Research Project.

Chi, I. C.; Chow, L. P.; and Rider, R. V. 1972. The randomized response
technique as used in the Taiwan Outcome of Pregnancy Study. *Studies
in Population Planning* 3: 265–69.

Clark, J. P., and Tifft, L. L. 1966. Polygraph and interview validation of self-reported deviant behavior. *American Sociological Review* 31: 516–23.

Cleary, T. A.; Linn, R. L.; and Walster, G. W. 1970. The effect of reliability and validity on power of statistical tests. In *Sociological Methodology,* ed. E. F. Borgotta and G. W. Bornstedt, pp. 130–38. San Francisco: Jossey-Bass.

Clickner, R. P., and Iglewicz, B. 1976. Warner's randomized response technique: The two sensitive questions case. In *Proceedings of the American Statistical Association: Social Statistics Section,* pp. 260–63. Washington, D.C.: ASA.

Cobb, S.; Clubb, J.; Davidson, T.; Gold, M.; Michael, D.; Morgan, J.; and Scott, J. 1971. Report of the Committee on Privacy. Mimeo paper. Ann Arbor: Institute for Social Research, University of Michigan.

Cobleigh, C., and Alvey, W. 1974. Validating reported social security numbers. *Proceedings of the American Statistical Association: Social Statistics Section,* pp. 145–54. Washington, D.C.: ASA.

Cochran, W. G. 1968. Errors of measurement in statistics. *Technometrics* 10: 637–65.

Cochran, W. G., and Cox, G. M. 1957. *Experimental designs.* New York: Wiley.

Cole, J. 1970. Statement of Dr. Jonathan Cole. In U.S. Senate Committee on Labor and Public Welfare. *Hearings.* 91–2, Part 2.

Colvard, R. 1967. Interaction and identification in reporting field research: A critical reconsideration of protective procedures. In *Ethics, politics, and social research,* ed. G. Sjoberg, pp. 319–58. Cambridge, Mass.: Schenkman.

Committee on Government Operations. 1966. *The computer and invasion of privacy: Report of the committee.* U.S. House of Representatives, 89th Congress (2nd Session), Washington, D.C.: U.S. Government Printing Office.

Corey, S. M. 1937. Signed versus unsigned questionnaires. *Journal of Educational Psychology* 28: 144–48.

Coronary Drug Project Research Group. 1973. The coronary drug project: Design, methods, and baseline results. *American Heart Association Monograph,* Supplement to vols. 47 and 48, issue 38.

Cox, L. H. 1976. Statistical disclosure in publication hierarchies. Confidentiality in Surveys Report No. 14, Department of Statistics, University of Stockholm.

———. 1977. Disclosure analysis and cell suppresion. *Proceedings of the American Statistical Association: Social Statistics Section,* pp. 380–82. Washington, D.C.: ASA.

Crabb, D.; Gettys, T. R.; Malfetti, J. L.; and Stewart, E. I. 1971. Development in preliminary tryout of evaluation measures for the Phoenix Driving While Intoxicated Reeducation program. Tempe, Ariz.: Arizona State University.

Crespi, I. 1976. Protecting respondent anonymity in multi-wave surveys. Report, Mathematika Policy Research, Princeton, N. J.

Dalenius, T. 1974a. The invasion of privacy problem and statistics production: An overview. *Sartryck ur Statistisk Tidskrift* 3: 213–25.

———. 1974b. Protecting confidentiality by means of weighing decisions. Confidentiality in Surveys Report No. 77, Department of Statistics, University of Stockholm, Stockholm.

———. 1977a. Towards a methodology for statistical disclosure control. Confidentiality in Surveys Report No. 19, Department of Statistics, University of Stockholm, Stockholm.

———. 1977b. Matching personal files: A threat to individual privacy? Confidentiality in Surveys Report No. 21, Department of Statistics, University of Stockholm, Stockholm.

———. 1977c. Data base insecurity and the statistical disclosure problem. Confidentiality in Surveys Report No. 24, Department of Statistics, University of Stockholm, Stockholm.

———. 1978. The Swedish Data Act and statistical data-II. Confidentiality in Surveys Report No. 28, Department of Statistics, University of Stockholm, Stockholm.

Dalenius, T., and Klevmarken, A. 1976. *Privacy protection and the need for data in the social sciences.* Stockholm: Swedish Council for Social Science Research.

Dalenius, T., and Lyberg, L. 1970. *Bibliography on non-sampling error.* Stockholm: University of Stockholm, Institute of Statistics.

Dalenius, T., and Silverstein, J. 1978. Public key cryptosystems: An elementary overview. Confidentiality in Surveys Report No. 29, Department of Statistics, University of Stockholm, Stockholm.

Dalenius, T., and Vitale, R. A. 1974. A new randomized design for estimating the mean of a distribution. Confidentiality in Surveys Report No. 78, Department of Statistics, University of Stockholm, Stockholm.

Davis, R. C. 1971. Confidentiality and the census: 1790–1929. Appendix C of Secretary's Advisory Committee on Automated Personal Data Systems. *Records, computers, and the rights of citizens,* pp. 178–201. Washington, D.C.: U.S. Government Printing Office.

———. 1972. Social research in America before the civil war. *Journal of the History of the Behavioral Sciences* 8: 69–85.

Dawes, R. M. 1974. Guttman scaling randomized responses: A technique for evaluating the underlying structure of behaviors to which people may not wish to admit. Mimeographed report. Oregon Research Institute, University of Oregon.

DeBakey, M. E., and Beebe, G. W. 1962. Medical follow-up studies on veterans. *Journal of the American Medical Association* 182: 1103–09.

DeLacy, P. 1975. Randomized conditional response. *Proceedings of the American Statistical Association: Social Statistics Section,* pp. 383–86. Washington, D.C.: ASA.

Deming, W. E. 1972. Code of professional conduct. *International Statistical Review* 40: 215–19.

Devore, J. L. 1977. A note on the randomized response technique. *Communications in Statistics* A6: 1525–29.

Director, S. 1974. Evaluating the impact of manpower training programs. Ph.D. dissertation, Northwestern University.

Divorski, S. 1971. An experimental evaluation of public access to information held by state and local agencies. M. S. thesis, Northwestern University.

Divorski, S. W.; Gordon, A. C.; and Heinz, J. P. 1973. Public access to government information: A field experiment. *Northwestern University Law Review* 68: 240–79.

Dohrenwend, B. S., and Dohrenwend, B. P. 1968. Sources of refusals in surveys. *Public Opinion Quarterly* 32: 74–83.

Dougherty, P. H. 1975. Advertising: Questionnaires and anonymity. *New York Times,* 10 November.

Dowling, T. A., and Schactman, R. H. 1975. On the relative efficiency of randomized response models. *Journal of the American Statistical Association* 70: 84–87.

Drane, W. 1975. Randomized response to more than one question. *Proceedings of the American Statistical Association: Social Statistics Section,* pp. 395–97. Washington, D.C.: ASA.

———. 1976. On the theory of randomized response to two sensitive questions. *Communications in Statistics Theory and Methods* 5: 565–74.

Duffy, J. 1968. *A History of public health in New York City, 1625–1866.* New York: Russell Sage.

———. 1974. *A History of public health in New York City: 1866–1966.* New York: Russell Sage.

Duncan, J. W. 1975. The impact of privacy legislation on the federal statistical system. *Public Data Use* 3(1): 51–53.

———. 1976a. Federal statistics—Recent legislation and activities affecting confidentiality. Paper presented at the Cooperative Health Statistics Workshop on Confidentiality, Atlanta, Ga., 3 March.

———. 1976b. Current and needed legislation relating to confidentiality in statistical programs. Paper presented at the 16th National Meeting, Public Health Conference on Records and Statistics, St. Louis, Mo. 15 June.

Duncan, O. D., and Davis, B. 1953. An alternative to ecological correlation. *American Sociological Review* 18: 655–66.

Eckler, A. R. 1972. *The Bureau of the Census.* New York: Praeger.

Edwards, A. L. 1967. *Edwards personality inventory.* Chicago: Science Research Associates.

Elinson, J., and Haines, V. 1950. Role of anonymity in attitude surveys. *American Psychologist* 5: 315.

Ellis, A. 1947. Questionnaire versus interview methods in the study of love relationships. *American Sociological Review* 12: 541–53.

Endicott, J., and Spitzer, R. L. 1975. Patient assessment and monitoring. In *Safeguarding psychiatric privacy,* ed. E. M. Laska and P. Bank, pp. 285–313. New York: Wiley.

Eriksson, S. A. 1973a. Randomized interviews for sensitive questions. Ph.D. dissertation, University Institute of Statistics, University of Gothenburg, Sweden.

———. 1973b. A new model for randomized response. *International Statistical Review* 41: 101–13.

———. 1976a. Applications of the randomized response technique. In *Personal integrity and the need for data in the social sciences,* ed. T.

Dalenius and A. Klevmarken, pp. 119–26. Stockholm: Swedish Council for Social Science Research.

———. 1976b. Regression analysis of data from randomized interviews. Confidentiality in Surveys Report No. 17, Department of Statistics, University of Stockholm, Stockholm.

Eron, L. D., and Walder, L. O. 1961. Test burning II. *American Psychologist* 16: 237.

Ervin, S. J., Jr. 1974. Civilized man's most valued right. *Prism* 2(6): 15–17, 34.

Eser, A., and Schumann, K. F., Eds. 1976. *Forschung im konflikt mit recht und ethik.* Stuttgart: Ferdinand Enke Verlag.

Fägerlind, I. 1975. *Formal education and adult earnings: A longitudinal study on the economic benefits of education.* Stockholm: Almquist and Wiksell.

Feige, E. L., and Watts, H. W. 1970. Protection of privacy through microaggregation. In *Data Bases, Computers, and the Social Sciences,* ed. R. L. Biscoe, pp. 261–72. New York: Wiley.

———. 1972. An investigation of the consequences of partial aggregation of microeconomic data. *Econometrica* 40: 343–60.

Felligi, I. 1972. On the question of statistical confidentiality. *Journal of the American Statistical Association* 67: 7–18.

Felligi, I., and Phillips, J. L. 1974. Statistical confidentiality: Some theory and applications to data dissemination. *Annals of Economic and Social Measurement* 3: 399–409.

Fidler, D. S., and Kleinknecht, R. E. 1977. Randomized response versus direct questioning: Two data collection methods for sensitive information. *Psychological Bulletin* 84: 1045–49.

Fischer, J. L. 1972. The uses of Internal Revenue Service data. In *Evaluating the impact of manpower programs,* ed. M. E. Borus, pp. 177–80. Lexington, Mass.: D. C. Heath.

Fischer, R. P. 1946. Signed versus unsigned personal questionnaires. *Journal of Applied Psychology* 30: 220–25.

Fisher, W. D. 1969. *Clustering and aggregation in economics.* Baltimore, Md.: Johns Hopkins.

Flaherty, D. H. 1972. *Privacy in colonial New England.* Charlottesville: University Press of Virginia.

———. 1977. Privacy and access to government microdata for research and statistical purposes. Unpublished report. University of Western Ontario, London, Canada.

———. 1978. Final report of the Bellagio Conference on privacy, confidentiality, and the use of government microdata for research and statistical purposes. *Statistical Reporter,* May, No. 78-8: 274–79.

Fligner, M. A.; Policelle, G. E.; and Singh, J. 1977. A comparison of two randomized response survey methods with consideration for level of respondent protection. *Communications in Statistics* A6: 1511–24.

Florman, S. C. 1976. *The existential pleasures of engineering.* New York: St. Martin's.

Folsom, R. E. 1974. A randomized response validation study: Comparison of direct and randomized reporting of DUI arrests. Final Report, 2550-807, Research Triangle Institute, Chapel Hill, N. C.

Folsom, R. E., Greenberg, B. G.; Horvitz, D. G.; and Abernathy, J. R. 1973. Two alternate questions randomized response model for human surveys. *Journal of the American Statistical Association* 68: 525–30.

———. 1975. Recent developments in the randomized response model for human surveys. Unpublished manuscript. Research Triangle Institute, Research Triangle Park, N. C.

Frankel, L. 1976. Statisticians and people—the statistician's responsibilities. *Journal of the American Statistical Association* 71: 9–16.

Freund, R. J. 1971. Some observations on regressions with grouped data. *American Statistician* 25: 29–30.

Gemmill, H. 1975. From the editor: The invisible ink caper. *National Observer,* 1 November p. 22.

Gerberich, J. B., and Mason, J. M. 1948. Signed versus unsigned questionnaires. *Journal of Educational Research* 42: 122–26.

Gerson, E. J. 1969. Methodological and interviewing problems in household surveys of employment problems in urban poverty areas. *Proceedings of the American Statistical Association: Social Statistics Section,* pp. 22–30. Washington, D. C.: ASA.

Gerstel, E. K.; Moore, P.; Folsom, R. E.; and King, D. A. 1970. Mecklenburg County drinking driving attitude survey. Mimeographed report, Research Triangle Institute, Research Triangle Park, N. C.

Gibbons, D. 1975. Unidentified research sites and fictitious names. *American Sociologist* 10(3): 191.

Gilmore, C. P. 1973. The real villain in heart disease. *New York Times Magazine,* 25 March, pp. 31–100.

Glaeser, W. S. 1976. Die Freiheit der Forschung. In *Forschung im konflikt mit recht und ethik,* ed. A. Eser and K. F. Schuman, pp. 77–99. Stuttgart: Ferdinand Enke Verlag.

Gold, M., and Reimer, D. J. 1974. Report No. 1, on the National Survey of Youth '72, to the Center for Studies of Crime and Delinquency. Ann Arbor: National Institute of Mental Health, Institute for Social Research.

Goldfield, E. D. 1976. Study of privacy and confidentiality as factors in survey response. Paper presented at the Executive Seminar on Expanding the Right to Privacy. Washington Public Affairs Center of the University of California, Washington, D. C., 14–15 October.

Goodman, L. A. 1959. Some alternatives to ecological correlation. *American Journal of Sociology* 64: 610–25.

Goodstadt, M. S., and Gruson, V. 1975. The randomized response technique: A test on drug use. *Journal of the American Statistical Association* 70: 814–18.

Gordon, A. C.; Heinz, J. P.; Gordon, M. C.; and Divorski, S. 1973. Public information and public access: A sociological interpretation. *Northwestern University Law Review* 68: 280–308.

Goslin, D. A., and Bordier, N. 1969. Record keeping in elementary and secondary schools. In *On record: Files and dossiers in everyday life,* ed. S. Wheeler, pp. 29–61. New York: Russell Sage.

Gould, A. L.; Shah, B. V.; and Abernathy, J. R. 1969. Unrelated question randomized response techniques with two trials per respondent. *Proceedings of the American Statistical Association: Social Statistics Section;* pp. 351–59. Washington, D. C.: ASA.

Greenawalt, K. 1975. *Legal protections of privacy: Report prepared for the Office of Telecommunications Policy.* NITIS Report No. PB-250-132. Washington, D.C.: U.S. Department of Commerce, National Information Service.

Greenberg, B. G.; Abernathy, J. R.; and Horvitz, D. G. 1969. Application of the randomized response technique in obtaining quantitative data. *Proceedings of the American Statistical Association: Social Statistics Section,* pp. 40–43. Washington, D. C.: ASA.

————. 1970. A new survey technique and its application in the field of public health. *Milbank Memorial Fund Quarterly* 68 (4, Part 2): 38–55.

Greenberg, B. G.; Abul-Ela, A. A.; Simmons, W. R.; and Horvitz, D. G. 1969. The unrelated question randomized response model: Theoretical framework. *Journal of the American Statistical Association* 64: 520–39.

Greenberg, B. G.; Horvitz, D. G.; and Abernathy, J. R. 1974. A comparison of randomized response designs. In *Reliability and Biometry* ed. F. Proschan and R. J. Serfling, pp. 787–815. Philadelphia, Pa.: SIAM.

Greenberg, B. G.; Kuebler, R. R.; Abernathy, J. R., and Horvitz, D. G. 1971. Application of the randomized response technique in obtaining quantitative data. *Journal of the American Statistical Association* 66: 243–50.

Grubert, H. 1971. How much do agencies know about error structure? In *Federal Statistics: Report of the President's Commission.* Vol. 2. Washington, D.C.: U.S. Government Printing Office.

Hamblin, R. L. 1974. Social attitudes: Magnitude measurement and theory. In *Measurement in the social sciences: Theories and strategies,* ed. H. M. Blalock, pp. 61–120. Chicago: Aldine.

Hamel, L., and Reif, H. G. 1952. Should attitude questionnaires be signed? *Personnel Psychology* 5: 87–91.

Hannan, M. T. 1971. *Aggregation and disaggregation in sociology.* Lexington, Mass.: D.C. Heath.

Hansen, M. H. 1971a. Insuring confidentiality of individual records in data storage and retrieval for statistical purposes. *Proceedings of the Fall Joint Computer Conference,* pp. 579–85. Montvale, N.J.: AFIPS.

————. 1971b. The role and feasibility of a national data bank, based on matched records and alternatives. *Federal Statistics: Report of the President's Commission.* Vol. 2. Washington, D. C.: U. S. Government Printing Office.

Hansen, M. H., and Hargis, B. J. 1966. Census Bureau uses of tax data. In *Proceedings of the American Statistical Association: Business and Economic Statistics Section,* pp. 160–64. Washington, D. C.: ASA.

Hartmann, E.; Isaacson, A. L.; and Jurgell, C. M. 1968. Public reaction to public opinion surveying. *Public Opinion Quarterly* 32: 295–98.

Hartnett, R. T., and Seligsohn, H. C. 1967. The effects of varying degrees of anonymity on responses to different types of psychological questionnaires. *Journal of Educational Measurements* 4(2): 95–103.

Hauser, P. M. 1975. *Social statistics in use.* New York: Russell Sage.

Heber, R., and Garber, H. 1973. The Milwaukee Project: A study of the effect of early intervention to prevent mental retardation in high risk families. Paper presented at the American Statistical Association and Allied Social Sciences Meeting, New York, 28 December.

Heber, R., et al. 1972. *Rehabilitation of families at risk for mental retardation.* Madison: University of Wisconsin.

Hedrick, T.; Boruch, R. F.; and Ross, J. 1978. On ensuring the availability of evaluative data for secondary analysis. *Policy Sciences,* pp. 259–80.

Hedrick, T.; Nelson, R. L.; and Cecil, J. S. 1979. Grants of confidentiality: A survey analysis of a statutory researcher-subject privilege. In *Proceedings of the conference on solutions to ethical and legal problems in social research,* ed. R. F. Boruch, J. S. Cecil, and J. Ross, pp. 200–230. Evanston, Ill.: Psychology Department, Northwestern University.

Heller, R. N. 1972. The uses of social security administration data. In *Evaluating the impact of manpower programs,* ed. M. E. Borus, pp. 197–201. Lexington, Mass.: D. C. Heath.

Herriot, R. A., and Spiers, E. F. 1975. Measuring the impact on income statistics of reporting differences between the Current Population Survey and administrative sources. *Proceedings of the American Statistical Association: Social Statistics Section;* pp. 147–58. Washington, D.C.: ASA.

Hilmar, N. A. 1968. Anonymity, confidentiality, and invasions of privacy: Responsibility of the researcher. *American Journal of Public Health* 58: 324–30.

Hoffman, L. J., ed. 1973. *Security and privacy in computer systems.* Los Angeles: Melville.

Hoffman, L. J., and Miller, W. F. 1970. How to obtain a personal dossier from a statistical data bank. *Datamation,* May, pp. 74–75.

Hofstetter, C. R. 1971. Salesmen as survey researchers: A note on fraudulent interviews. *Social Science Quarterly* 52: 991–94.

Holmes, W. N. 1975. Identification number design. *Computer Journal* 18: 102–7.

Horn, J. L., and Donaldson, G. 1976. On the myth of intellectual decline in adulthood. *American Psychologist* 31: 701–19.

Horvitz, D. G. 1966. Problems in designing interview surveys to measure population growth. *Proceedings of the American Statistical Association: Social Statistics Section,* pp. 245–49. Washington, D. C.: ASA.

Horvitz, D. G.; Greenberg, B. G.; and Abernathy, J. R. 1975. Recent developments in randomized response designs. In *A survey of statistical design and linear models,* ed. J. N. Srivastata, pp. 271–86. Amsterdam: North-Holland.

――――. 1976. Randomized response: A data gathering device for sensitive questions. *International Statistical Review* 44: 181–96.

Horvitz, D. G.; Shah, B. V.; and Simmons, W. R. 1967. The unrelated question randomized response model. *Proceedings of the American Statistical Association: Social Statistics Section,* pp. 65–72. Washington, D. C.: ASA.

Hulett, D. T. 1975. Confidentiality of statistical and research data and the Privacy Act of 1974. *Statistical Reporter,* June, pp. 197–209.

Huxley, M., and Radloff, R. 1975. Record linkage in mental health research. Memo. National Institute of Mental Health, Rockville, Md.

I-cheng, C.; Chow, L. P.; and Rider, R. V. 1972. The randomized response technique as used in the Taiwan outcome of pregnancy study. *Studies in Family Planning* 3: 265–69.

Illinois Institute of Technology Research Institute and the Chicago Crime Commission. 1971. *A study of organized crime in Illinois.* Chicago: IIT Research Institute.

Jabine, T. B. 1975. The impact of new legislation on statistical and research uses of SSA data. *Proceedings of the American Statistical Association: Social Statistics Section,* pp. 221–30. Washington, D.C.: ASA.

Jabine, T. B., and Rothwell, N. D. 1970. Split-panel tests of census and survey questionnaires. *Proceedings of the American Statistical Association: Social Statistics Section,* pp. 4–13. Washington, D. C.: ASA.

James, K. E. 1973. Regression toward the mean in uncontrolled clinical studies. *Biometrics* 29: 121–30.

Janson, C. G. 1975. Project Metropolitan: A longitudinal study of a Stockholm cohort. Research Report No. 1, Department of Sociology, Stockholm University (S-10405). Stockholm, Sweden.

Kannel, W. B.; Dawber, T. R.; Kagan, A.; Revotskie, N.; and Stokes, J. 1961. Factors of risk in the development of coronary heart disease—Six year follow-up experience, the Framingham Study. *Annals of Internal Medicine* 55(33).

Katz, J.; Capron, A.; and Glass, E. S., eds. 1972. *Experimentation with human beings.* New York: Russell Sage.

Kelman, H. C. 1968. *A time to speak: On human values and social research.* San Francisco: Jossey-Bass.

Kempthorne, O. 1952. *The design and analysis of experiments.* New York: Wiley.

Kershaw, D., and Fair, J. 1976. *The New Jersey income maintenance experiment.* New York: Academic.

Kershaw, D. N., and Small, J. C. 1972. Data confidentiality and privacy: Lessons from the New Jersey Negative Income Tax Experiment. *Public Policy* 20: 258–80.

King, F. W. 1970. Psychology in action: Anonymous versus identifiable questionnaires in drug usage surveys. *American Psychologist,* 25: 982–85.

King, L. S. 1971. *A history of medicine.* Middlesex: Penguin.

Kish, L. 1967. *Survey Sampling.* New York: Wiley.

Klevmarken, A. 1972. *Statistical methods for the analysis of earnings data.* Stockholm: Almqvist and Wiksell.

Knerr, C. R. 1976. Compulsory disclosure to the courts of research sources and data. Paper presented at the Annual Meetings of the American Psychological Association, Symposium on Privacy, Public Policy, and the Practice of Psychology, September. Available from C. R. Knerr, Department of Political Science, University of Texas, Arlington, Tex., 76019.

———. 1978. Confidentiality and behavioral research: What to do before the subpoena arrives. Paper presented at the Workshop on Research Ethics, Eastern Psychological Association Conference, Washington, D.C., 28–29 March.

Knudsen, D. D.; Pope, H.; and Irish, D. P. 1967. Response differences to questions on sexual standards: An interview-questionnaire comparison. *Public Opinion Quarterly* 31: 290–97.

Krotki, K., and Fox, B. 1974 The randomized response technique, the interview, and the self-administered questionnaire: An empirical comparison of fertility reports. *Proceedings of the American Statistical Association: Social Statistics Section,* pp. 367–71. Washington, D.C.: ASA.

Krotki, K. J., and McDaniel, S. A. 1975. Three estimates of illegal abortion in Alberta, Canada: Survey, mail-back questionnaire, and randomized response technique. Paper presented at the 40th Session of the International Statistical Institute, Warsaw, 1–9 September.

Kruskal, W. B. 1978. Formulas, numbers, words: Statistics in prose. *American Scholar* 47: 223–29.

Kruskal, W. B., and Mosteller, F. 1977. Representative sampling. Technical Report No. 47, Department of Statistics, University of Chicago.

Langlet, P. 1975. Survey of the sensitivity of personal particulars. Stockholm: National Central Bureau of Statistics (SCB).

Lanke, J. 1975a. On the choice of the unrelated question in Simmons' version of randomized response. *Journal of the American Statistical Association* 70: 80–83.

———. 1975b. On the degree of protection in randomized response. Paper presented at the 40th Session of the International Statistical Institute, Warsaw, 1–9 September.

———. 1976. On the degree of protection in randomized interviews. *International Statistical Review* 44: 197–203.

Laska, E. M., and Bank, R., Eds. 1975. *Safeguarding psychiatric privacy.* New York: Wiley.

Lauren, R. H. 1970. Reliability of data bank records. *Datamation* 16(5): 88–92.

Lavin, P. 1974. A necessary and sufficient condition for asymptotic masking of the Warner ML Estimate. Confidentiality in Surveys Report No. 00, Department of Statistics, University of Stockholm, Stockholm.

Lavrakas, P. J. 1975. A randomized response technique for assuring confidentiality of data in a group survey situation. Research Memo. Psychology Department, Loyola University, Chicago.

Levy, K. J. 1976a. Reducing the occurrence of omitted or untruthful responses when testing hypotheses concerning proportions. *Psychological Bulletin* 83: 759–61.

———. 1976b. Testing hypotheses about proportions. Manuscript, Psychology Department, State University of New York at Buffalo.

Leysieffer, F. W., and Warner, S. L. 1976. Respondent jeopardy and optimal designs in randomized response models. *Journal of the American Statistical Association* 71: 649–56.

Liu, P. T., and Chow, L. P. 1976a. The efficiency of multiple trial randomized response technique. *Biometrics* 32: 607–18

———. 1976b. A new discrete quantitative randomized response model. *Journal of the American Statistical Association* 71: 72–73.

Liu, P. T.; Chen, C. N.; and Chow, L. P. 1976. A study of the feasibility of Hopkins randomized response models. *Proceedings of the American Statistical Association: Social Statistics Section,* Part 2, pp. 561–66. Washington, D.C.: ASA.

Liu, P. T.; Chow, L. P.; and Mosley, W. H. 1975. Use of the randomized response technique with a new randomizing device. *Journal of the American Statistical Association* 70: 324–32.

Lobenthal, J. S. 1974. Designing research in corrections: An abbreviated tour guide. *Federal Probation* 38: 29–36.

Locander, W.; Sudman, S.; and Bradburn, N. 1976. An investigation of interview method, threat, and response distortion. *Journal of the American Statistical Association* 71: 269–75.

Lord, F. M., and Novick, M. R., with A. Birnbaum. 1968. *Statistical theories of mental test scores.* Reading, Mass.: Addison-Wesley.

Love, L. T., and Turner, A. G. 1975. The Census Bureau's experience: Respondent availability and response rates. *Proceedings of the American Statistical Association: Business and Economics Section,* pp. 76–85. Washington, D.C.: ASA.

Loynes, R. M. 1976. Asymptotically optimal randomized response procedures. *Journal of the American Statistical Association* 71: 924–28.

Madden, T. J. 1977. Testimony before the Privacy Protection Study Commission, 5 January. Washington, D. C.

Madden, T. J., and Lessin, H. 1978. Privacy and confidentiality of social research information. In *Proceedings of the conference on solutions to ethical and legal problems in social research,* ed. R. F. Boruch, J. S. Cecil, and J. Ross, pp. 55–60. Evanston, Ill.: Psychology Department, Northwestern University.

Magidson, J. 1977. Toward a causal model approach for adjusting for preexisting differences in the nonequivalent control group situation. *Evaluation Quarterly* 1: 399–420.

Magnusson, D.; Dunér, A.; and Zetterblom, G. 1975. *Adjustment: A longitudinal study.* Stockholm: Almquist and Wiksell.

Manniche, E., and Hayes, D. P. 1957. Respondent anonymity and data matching. *Public Opinion Quarterly* 21: 384–88.

Marks, E. S., and Waksberg, J. 1966. Evaluation of coverage in the 1960 Census of the Population through case by case checking. *Proceedings of the American Statistical Association: Social Statistics Section,* pp. 62–70. Washington, D.C.: ASA.

Marquis, K. 1970. The effects of social reinforcement on health reporting in the household interview. *Sociometry* 33: 203–15.

Martin, M. E. 1974. Statistical legislation and confidentiality issues. *International Statistical Review* 42: 265–81.

———. 1976. Report on activities: Committee on National Statistics. *American Statistician* 30: 21–23.

Martinotti, G. 1971. La difesa della "Privacy." *Politica del Diretto* 2: 749–79.

————. 1972. II. La difesa della "Privacy." *Politica del Diretto* 3: 59–106.

McKay, H.; Sinisterra, L.; McKay, A.; Gomez, H.; and Lloreda, P. 1978. Improving cognitive ability in chronically deprived children. *Science* 200: 270–78.

McNamara, R. M., and Starr, J. R. 1973. Confidentiality of narcotic addict treatment records: A Legal and statistical analysis. *Columbia University Law Review* 73: 1579–612.

Mead, M. 1968. Research with human beings: A model derived from anthropological field practice. *Daedalus* 98: 361–86.

Mednick, S. A., and McNeil, T. F. 1968. Current methodology in research on the etiology of schizophrenia. *Psychological Bulletin* 70: 681–93.

Mednick, S. A.; Schulsinger, F.; and Garfinkel, R. 1975. Children at high risk for schizophrenia: Predisposing factors and intervention. In *Experimental approaches to psychopathology,* ed. M. L. Keitzman, S. Sutton, and J. Zubin, pp. 451–64. New York: Academic Press.

Meyer, H. J. and Borgatta, E. F. 1959. *An experiment in mental patient rehabilitation.* New York: Russell Sage.

Meyer, P. 1973. *Precision journalism.* Bloomington, Indiana: Indiana University Press.

Millea, M. T., and Kilss, B. 1975. Exploration of differences between linked Social Security and Internal Revenue Service wage data for 1974. *Proceedings of the American Statistical Association: Social Statistics Section,* pp. 138–46. Washington, D.C.: ASA.

Miller, A. S. 1971. *Assault on Privacy.* Ann Arbor: University of Michigan Press.

Miller, H. P., and Hornseth, R. A. 1970. Cross-sectional versus cohort estimates of lifetime income. *Proceedings of the American Statistical Association: Social Statistics Section,* pp. 339–41. Washington, D.C.: ASA.

Moors, J. J. A. 1971. Optimization of the unrelated question randomized response model. *Journal of the American Statistical Association* 66: 627–29.

Moriarity, M., and Wiseman, F. 1977. On the choice of a randomization technique with the randomized response model. *Proceedings of the American Statistical Association: Social Statistics Section,* Part 2, pp. 624–26. Washington, D.C.: ASA.

Mosteller, F. 1977. Assessing unknown numbers: Order of magnitude estimation. In *Statistics and public policy,* ed. W. B. Fairley and F. Mosteller, pp. 163–83. Reading: Addison Wesley.

Moynihan, D. P., and Mosteller, F., eds. 1972. *On equality of educational opportunity.* New York: Vintage.

Mueller, G. O. W. 1976. Prestige and the researcher's accountability. In *Social research in conflict with law and ethics,* ed. P. Nejelski, pp. 111–22. Cambridge, Mass.: Ballinger.

Müller, P. J., ed. 1978. Proceedings of the CESSDA/IFDO international conference on emerging data protection and the social sciences' need for access to data. Cologne, West Germany: Zentral archiv für empirische Sozial Forschung.

Murray, J. R. 1971. Statistical models for qualitative data with classification errors. Ph.D. dissertation, University of Chicago.

Nargundkar, M. S., and Saveland, W. 1972. Random-rounding to protect statistical disclosures. *Proceedings of the American Statistical Association: Social Statistics Section,* pp. 382–85. Washington, D.C.: ASA.

National Academy of Sciences, Committee on Federal Statistics. 1979. *Report of the panel on privacy and confidentiality as factors in survey response.* Washington, D.C.: NAS.

National Center for Health Statistics. 1968. The influence of interviewer and behavioral variables on reporting in household interviews. *Vital and Health Statistics: Public Health Service Publication,* No. 1000-Series 2, No. 26. Washington, D. C.: U. S. Government Printing Office.

———. 1977. Model state health statistics act: A model state law for the collection, sharing, and confidentiality of health statistics. Hyattsville, Md.: Department of Health, Education, and Welfare. Public Health Services, NCHS.

National Central Bureau of Statistics. 1974. *Confidentiality in statistical tables.* Stockholm: SCB.

———. 1975. On probability based disclosures in frequency tables. Research Report. Stockholm: SCB.

———. 1976. Destruction, de-identification, and encryption: Integrity protection measures in statistics production. Investigation Report No. 1976-03-08. Stockholm: SCB.

———. 1977. *The National Central Bureau of Statistics and the general public: Findings of an interview survey taken in Sweden during the spring of 1976.* Stockholm: SCB.

National Research Council, 1976. *Annual Report of the Assembly of Life Sciences: Medical Follow-up Agency.* Washington, D.C.: NRC.

Nejelski, P., and Finsterbusch, K. 1973. The prosecutor and the researcher: Present and prospective variations of the Supreme Court's Branzburg decision. *Social Problems* 21: 3.

Nejelski, P., and Lerman, N. M. 1971. A researcher-subject testimonial privilege: What to do before the subpoena arrives. *Wisconsin Law Review* 1971: 1085–148.

Nejelski, P., and Peyser, H. 1975. Appendix B. A researcher's shield statute: Guarding against the compulsory disclosure of research data. In *Protecting individual privacy in evaluation research,* ed. A. M. Rivlin, pp. B-1–B-36. Washington, D.C.: National Academy of Sciences.

Nesselroade, J. R., and Baltes, P. D. 1974. Adolescent personality development and historical change: 1970–1972. *Monographs of the Society for Research in Child Development,* 39(1).

Nettler, G. 1959. Test burning in Texas. *American Psychologist* 14: 682–83.

Newman, D. 1975. Techniques for ensuring the confidentiality of census information in Great Britain. Paper presented at the 40th Session of the International Statistical Institute, Warsaw, 1–9 September.

Note. 1970. Social research and privileged data. *Valparaiso Law Review* 4: 368–99.

Nowlis, H. 1969. Statement of Dr. Helen Nowlis. In U.S. Senate Committee on Labor and Public Welfare, *Hearings on S.2608, S.1816, and Related Bills.* 91-1. Washington, D.C.: U.S. Government Printing Office.

Nycum, S. H. 1976. Criminal sanctions under the Privacy Act of 1974.

Research Report/Project No. 5068, Stanford Research Institute, Menlo Park, Cal.

O'Brien, D. M., and Cochran, R. S. 1977. The comprehension factor in randomized response. *Proceedings of the American Statistical Association: Social Statistics Section,* Part 1, pp. 270–72. Washington, D.C.: ASA.

O'Brien, D. M.; Cochran, R. S.; Marquardt, R. S.; and Makens, J. C. 1976. Randomized response vs direct question in a mail vs personal interview consumer opinion survey. Research Paper No. 85, College of Commerce and Industry, University of Wyoming, Laramie, Wyo.

Okner, B. 1974. Data matching and merging: An overview. *Annals of Economic and Social Measurement* 3: 347–52.

Olsen, W. C. 1936. The waiver of signature in personal data reports. *Journal of Applied Psychology* 20: 442–50.

Olsson, L. 1975. Protection of output and stored data in statistical data bases. ADB—information 1975:4. Stockholm: National Central Bureau of Statistics.

Orcutt, G. H.; Watts, H. W.; and Edwards, J. B. 1968. Data aggregation and information loss. *American Economic Review* 58: 773–87.

Orr, L. L.; Hollister, R. G.; Lefcowitz, M. J.; and Hester, K., eds. 1971. *Income maintenance: Interdisciplinary approaches.* Chicago: Markham.

Oyen, O. 1965. Encounter with the image of sociology. *Sociologiske Meddeleser* 10: 47–60.

———. 1966. Social class, conservatism, and submission to longitudinal research: The reaction to Project Metropolitan in Norway. Paper presented at the Sixth World Congress of Sociology, Evian, France.

———. 1976. Social research and the protection of privacy: A review of the Norwegian development. Unpublished report. Bergen, Norway: University of Bergen, Department of Sociology.

Parnes, H. S. 1975. The National Longitudinal Surveys: New vistas for labor market research. *Journal of the American Economic Association* 65: 244–49.

Parsons, C. W., Ed. 1972. *America's uncounted people: Report of the Advisory Committee on Problems of Census Enumeration.* Washington, D.C.: National Academy of Sciences.

Pearlin, L. I. 1961. The appeals of anonymity in questionnaire response. *Public Opinion Quarterly* 25: 640–47.

Perrine, M. W. 1971. Methodological considerations in conducting and evaluating roadside research surveys. Final Report. Contract No. FH-11-7543. Washington, D.C.: U.S. Department of Transportation, NHTSA.

Pollock, K. H., and Bek, Y. 1976. A comparison of three randomized response models for quantitative data. *Journal of the American Statistical Association* 71: 884–86.

Poole, W. K. 1974. Estimation of the distribution function of a continuous type random variable through randomized response. *Journal of the American Statistical Association* 69: 1002–5.

President's Commission on Federal Statistics. 1971. *Federal statistics: Report of the president's commission.* Vols 1 and 2. Washington, D. C.: U.S. Government Printing Office.

Privacy Journal. 1977. 5(3): 3.

Privacy Protection Study Commission. 1977. *Personal privacy in an information society.* Washington, D.C.: U.S. Government Printing Office.

Raghavarao, D., and Federer, W. T. 1973. Application of BIB designs as an alternative to the randomized response method in survey sampling. Mimeograph Series. Ithaca: Biometrics Unit, Cornell University.

Ramcharan, S.; Cutler, J. L.; Feldman, R.; Siegelaub, A. B.; Campbell, B.; Friedman, G. D.; Dales, L. G.; and Collen, M. F. 1973. Multiphasic checkup evaluation study: 2. Disability and chronic disease after seven years of multiphasic health checkups. *Preventive Medicine* 2: 207–20.

Rapaport, E., and Sundgren, B. 1975. Output protection in statistical data bases. Paper presented at the 40th Session of the International Statistical Institute, Warsaw, 1–9. September.

Reaser, J. M.; Hartsock, S.; and Hoehn, A. J. 1975. A test of the forced alternative random response questionnaire technique. HUMRO Technical Report 75-9. Arlington, Va.: Human Resources Research Organization.

Reaser, J. M.; Richards, J. A.; and Hartstock, S. L. 1975. The prevalence of drug abuse in the army: A comparison of urinalysis and survey rates. HUMRO Technical Report 75-17. Arlington, Va.: Human Resources Research Organization.

Reeder, L.; Sudman, S.; Cannell, C. F.; Greenberg, B. G.; and Horvitz, D. G., eds. 1976. *Advances in health survey research: Proceedings of a national invitational conference.* Rockville, Md.: National Center for Health Services Research and National Center for Health Statistics.

Regan, O. G. 1973. Statistical reforms accelerated by sixth census errors. *Journal of the American Statistical Association* 68: 540–46.

Riecken, H. W.; Boruch, R. F.; Campbell, D. T.; Caplan, N.; Glennan, T. K.; Pratt, J.; Rees, A.; and Williams, W. W. 1974. *Social experimentation: A method for planning and evaluating social programs.* New York: Seminar Press.

Rivlin, A. M. and Timpane, D. M., eds. 1975. *Ethical and legal issues of social experimentation.* Washington, D.C.: Brookings Institution.

Robertson, L. S.; Kelley, A. B.; O'Neill, B.; Wixom, C. W.; Eiswirth, R. S.; and Haddon, W. 1972. *A controlled study of the effect of television messages on safety belt use.* Washington, D.C.: Insurance Institute for Highway Safety.

Robins, L. N. The reluctant respondent. 1963. *Public Opinion Quarterly* 17: 276–86.

Robinson, J. P.; Rush, J. G.; and Head, K. B. 1974. Criteria for an attitude scale. In *Scaling: A sourcebook for behavioral scientists,* ed. G. M. Maranell, pp. 244–57. Chicago: Aldine.

Robinson, W. S. 1950. Ecological correlations and behavior of individuals. *American Sociological Review* 15: 351–57.

Roman, N. A. 1960. Anonymity and attitude measurement. *Public Opinion Quarterly* 24: 675–79.

Rosen, N. A. 1960. Anonymity and attitude measurement. *Public Opinion Quarterly* 24: 675–79.

Rossi, P. H.; Groves, W. E.; and Grafstein, D. 1971. Life styles and campus communities, Pamphlet-questionnaire. Baltimore: Johns Hopkins University, Department of Social Relations.

Rosteck, H. 1976. Rechtliche kollisionen bei empirischer forschung: ein kritischer bericht. In *Forshung im konflikt mit recht and ethik,* ed. A. Eser and K. F. Schumann, pp. 40–60. Stuttgart: Enkeverlag.

Ruebhausen, O. M., and Brim, O. G. 1965. Privacy and behavioral research. *Columbia Law Review* 65: 1184–211.

Sale, K. 1974. *SDS.* New York: Vintage.

Schaie, K. W. 1963. A general model for the study of developmental problems. *Psychological Bulletin* 64(2): 92–107.

Scheuren, F., and Colvey W. 1975. Selected bibliography on matching. In F. Scheuren et al., Exact match research using the 1973 Current Population Survey. *Studies from Interagency Data Linkages.* Report No. 4. Washington, D.C.: Office of Research and Statistics, Social Security Administration.

Schlörer, J. 1974. Schnuffeltechiken und Schutzmabnahmen bei Statistichen Datenbank-Information system mit dialogausbuertung. Materialien Nr. 29, der Abteilung fur Medizinische Statistik, Universitat Ulm.

———. 1975. Identification and retrieval of personal records from a statistical data bank. Research Report. Ulm, Germany: University of Ulm, Department of Medical Statistics, Documentation, and Data Processing. Also in *Methods of Information in Medicine* 14: 7–13.

Schwartz, R. D., and Orleans, S. 1967. On legal sanctions. *University of Chicago Law Review* 34: 274–300.

Secretary's Advisory Committee on Automated Personal Data Systems, DHEW. 1973. *Records, computers, and the rights of citizens.* DHEW Publication No. (05) 73–94. Washington, D.C.: U.S. Government Printing Office.

Sen, P. K. 1974. On unbiased estimation for randomized response models. *Journal of the American Statistical Association* 69: 997–1001.

Sewell, W. H., and Hauser, R. M., with Alwin, D. F.; Ellegaard, D. M.; Fisher, J. A.; Lutterman, K. G.; and Shah, V. P. 1975. *Education, occupation, and earnings: Achievement in the early career.* New York: Academic Press.

Sewell, W. 1972. Proposal for research: The effects of education. University of Wisconsin, Department of Sociology.

Sherrill, P. N., and Field, M. D. 1974. Are survey respondents really anonymous? Paper presented at the Annual Meeting of the American Association of Public Opinion Researchers, Itasca, Ill.

Shils, E. A. 1949. Social inquiry and the autonomy of the individual. In *The human meaning of the social sciences,* ed. Daniel Lerner, pp. 114–57. New York: Meridian Books.

Shimizu, I. M., and Bonham, G. S. 1978. Randomized response technique in a national survey. *Journal of the American Statistical Association* 73:- 31, 35–39.

Simmons, D. S. 1968. Invasion of privacy and judged benefit of personality test inquiry. *Journal of General Psychology* 79: 177–78.

Simmons, W. R. 1970. Response to randomized inquiries: A technique for reducing bias. *Administrative Applications Conference Transactions: American Society for Quality Control* 1(10): 4–13.

Singer, E. 1978a. Informed consent: Consequences for response rate and response quality in social surveys. *American Sociological Review* 43: 144–62.

————. 1978b. Informed consent procedures in surveys: Some reasons for minimal effects on response. Paper presented at the Conference on Solutions to Ethical and Legal Problems in Social Research, Washington, D.C., 27–29 February.

Smith, L.; Federer, W. T.; and Raghavarao, D. 1974. A comparison of three techniques for eliciting truthful answers to sensitive questions. *Proceedings of the American Statistical Association: Social Statistics Section*, pp. 447–52. Washington, D. C.: ASA.

Social Science Research Council, Committee on Evaluation Research. 1978. Report to the U.S. General Accounting Office. New York: SSRC.

Sofaer, A. D. 1977. Executive power and control of information: Power under the framers. *Duke Law Review* 1977: 1–57.

Spergel, I. A. 1969. Community action research as a political process. In *Community organization: Studies in social constraint,* ed. I. A. Spergel, pp. 231–63. Beverly Hills, Cal.: Sage.

Steinberg, J. 1970. Data-linkage problems and solutions. In *Data bases, computers and the social sciences,* ed. R. L. Bisco, pp. 238–51. New York: Wiley-Interscience.

Steinberg, J. and Cooper, H. C. 1967. Social security statistical data, social science research, and confidentiality. *Social Security Bulletin,* October, pp. 2–14.

Steinberg, J. and Pritzker, L. 1969. Some experiences with and reflections on data linkage in the United States. *Bulletin of the International Statistical Institute* 42 (Book 2): 786–805.

Stroud, T. W. F. 1974. Comparing regressions when measurement error variances are known. *Psychometrika* 39: 53–67.

Subcommittee on Disclosure-Avoidance Techniques, Committee on Federal Statistical Methodology. 1978. *Report on statistical disclosure and disclosure avoidance techniques.* Washington, D.C.: U.S. Department of Commerce, Federal Statistical Policy and Standards. May.

Sudman, S. 1972. *Letter and Chicago Community Study Questionnaire.* University of Illinois, Survey Research Laboratory.

Sudman, S., and Bradburn, N. M. 1974. *Response effects in surveys: A review and synthesis.* Chicago: Aldine.

Sudman, S.; Greeley, A.; and Pinto, L. 1965. The effectiveness of self-administered questionnaires. *Journal of Marketing Research* 2: 293–97.

Swensson, B. 1975. Combined independent questions: I. Confidentiality in Surveys Report No. 7, Department of Statistics, University of Stockholm, Stockholm.

————. 1976a. Combined independent questions: II. Confidentiality in Surveys Report No. 11, Department of Statistics, University of Stockholm, Stockholm.

———. 1976b. Using mixtures of techniques for estimating sensitive attributes. Confidentiality in Surveys Report No. 13, Department of Statistics, University of Stockholm, Stockholm.

Takahasi, K., and Sakasegawa, H. 1977. A randomized response technique without making use of a randomizing device. *Annals of the Institute of Statistical Mathematics* 29(a): 1–8.

Teitelbaum, L. E. Spurious, tractable, and intractable legal problems: A positivist approach to law and social science research. In *Proceedings and background papers: conference on ethical and legal problems in applied social research,* eds. R. F. Boruch, J. Ross, and J. S. Cecil. Evanston, Ill.: Northwestern University, 1979.

Thorndike, R. L.; Hagen, E.; and Kemper, R. A. 1952. Normative data obtained in the house to house administration of a psychosomatic inventory *Journal of Consulting Psychology* 16: 257–60.

Tillery, D. 1967. Seeking a balance between the right of privacy and the advancement of social research. *Journal of Educational Measurement* 4: 11–16.

Turn, R. 1973. Privacy transformations for databank systems. Research Report P4955. Santa Monica, Cal.: Rand.

Turn, R., and Shapiro, N. Z. 1972. Privacy and security in databank systems: Measures of effectiveness, cost, and protector-intruder interactions. *Proceedings, Fall Joint Computer Conference: American Federation of Information Processing Societies,* pp. 435–44. Montvale, N. J.: AFIPS Press.

Tybout, A. M., and Zaltman, G. 1974. Ethics in marketing research: Their practical relevance. *Journal of Marketing Research* 11: 357–68.

U.S. Bureau of the Census. 1969. *Census confidentiality: How it grew.* U.S. Department of Commerce Pamphlet. Washington, D.C.: U.S. Government Printing Office.

U.S. Bureau of the Census. 1974. *Indexes to survey methodology literature.* Technical Paper No. 34. Washington, D.C.: U.S. Government Printing Office.

———. 1975. Some preliminary results from the 1973 CPS-IRS-SSA exact match study: Invited papers on the reconciliation of survey and administrative income distribution statistics through data linkage. Reproduced report. Washington, D.C.: U.S. Department of Commerce, Bureau of the Census, 30 September.

U. S. Department of Commerce. 1975. Opinions about the 1974 Census of Agriculture. Undated report. Washington, D.C.: Census Bureau.

U. S. Department of Commerce, National Bureau of Standards. 1974. *Guidelines for automatic data processing physical security and risk management.* Washington, D. C.: U. S. Government Printing Office.

U.S. General Accounting Office. 1974. *Report of the Controller General: Difficulties in assessing results of Law Enforcement Assistance Administration projects to reduce crime.* Washington, D.C.: GAO.

———. 1976. *Proceedings of the conference on social experimentation.* Washington, D.C.: GAO.

———. 1977. The Experimental Housing Allowance Program: A status report. Report to the Congress by the Comptroller General of the United States. Washington, D.C.: GAO.

U.S. House of Representatives, Committee on Post Office and Civil Service, Subcommittee on Census and Population. 1975a. *Regulations for use and transfer of population census records to National Archives: Hearings on I.T.R. 10686.* (94-1). Washington, D.C., U.S. Government Printing Office.

———. 1975b. *Availability of Census records.* Report No. 94-971 (94-1). Washington, D.C.: U.S. Government Printing Office.

U.S. Senate Committee on the Judiciary, Subcommittee on Constitutional Rights. 1974. *Drug abuse data banks: Case studies in the protection of privacy/Staff Report* (93-2), Washington, D.C.: U.S. Government Printing Office.

U.S. Senate Committee on Labor and Public Welfare. 1969. *Hearings on the Comprehensive Narcotic Addiction and Drug Abuse Care and Control Act of 1969.* (91-1). Washington, D.C.: U.S. Government Printing Office.

———. 1970. *Hearings on the Comprehensive Narcotic Addiction and Drug Abuse Care and Control Act of 1969.* (91-2, Part 2). Washington, D.C.: U.S. Government Printing Office.

Vinge, P. G. 1973. *Företagen inför datalagen* (Swedish Data Act). Stockholm: Federation of Swedish Industries.

Wall, W. D., and Williams, H. L. 1970. *Longitudinal studies and the social sciences.* London: Heineman.

Walsh, J. 1969a. ACE Study of campus unrest: Questions for behavioral scientists. *Science* 165: 158–60.

———. 1969b. Antipoverty R & D: Chicago debacle suggests pitfalls facing OEO. *Science* 165: 1243–45.

Walsh, J. A.; Layton, W. L.; and Klieger, D. M. 1966. Relationships between social desirability scale values, probability of endorsement; and invasion of privacy ratings of objective personality items. *Psychological Reports* 18: 671–75.

Warner, S. L. 1965. Randomized response: A survey technique for eliminating evasive answer bias. *Journal of the American Statistical Association* 60: 63–69.

———. 1971. Linear randomized response model. *Journal of the American Statistical Association* 66: 884–88.

Weissman, C. 1967. Programming protection: How much do you want to pay? *SDC Magazine* 10: 30–31.

Wender, P. H.; Rosenthal, D.; Kety, S. S.; Schulsinger, F.; and Welner, J. 1974. Cross-fostering: A research strategy for clarifying the role of genetic and experiential factors in the etiology of schizophrenia. *Archives of General Psychiatry* 30: 121–28.

Westin, A. F., and Baker, M., with others. 1972. *Databanks in a free society.* New York: Quadrangle.

Wigmore, J. H. 1972. *Evidence,* vol. 8 (McNaughton Revision). Boston: Little, Brown.

Wilson, T. R. and Rosen, T. H. 1975. Self-disclosure on army surveys: Survey procedures and respondent beliefs related to candidness. HUMRO Technical Report 75-2. Arlington, Va.: Human Resources Research Organization.

Wohlwill, J. F. 1969. Methodology and research strategy in the study of developmental change. ETS Research Memorandum RM-69-24. Princeton: Educational Testing Service.

————. 1970. The age variable in psychological research. *Psychological Bulletin* 77: 49–64.

Wortman, P. M. and St. Pierre, R. 1975. Reanalysis of the evaluation of the Voucher Demonstration project. Research memo. Psychology Department, Northwestern University, Evanston, Ill.

Yates, P. B. 1975. Implications of the Freedom of Information and Privacy Acts for voluntary labor statistics programs. *Proceedings of the American Statistical Association: Social Statistics Section,* pp. 217–20. Washington, D.C.: ASA.

Yinger, M.; Ikeda, K.; and Laycock, F. 1977. *Middlestart: Supportive interventions for higher education among students of disadvantaged backgrounds.* Cambridge University Press.

Young, A. F.; Selove, J. M.; and Koons, D. A. 1966. Measuring quality of housing. *Proceedings of the American Statistical Association: Social Statistics Section,* pp. 33–42. Washington, D.C.: ASA.

Zdep, S. M., and Rhodes, I. N. 1977. Making the randomized response technique work. *Public Opinion Quarterly* 41: 531–37.

Index

Author Index

Subject Index